CW01215173

Acculturation

Acculturation

Advances in Theory, Measurement, and Applied Research

Edited by
Kevin M. Chun,
Pamela Balls Organista,
and Gerardo Marín

DECADE of BEHAVIOR 2000–2010

American Psychological Association
Washington, DC

Copyright © 2003 by the American Psychological Association. All rights reserved. Except as permitted under the United States Copyright Act of 1976, no part of this publication may be reproduced or distributed in any form or by any means, or stored in a database or retrieval system, without the prior written permission of the publisher.

Published by
American Psychological Association
750 First Street, NE
Washington, DC 20002
www.apa.org

To order
APA Order Department
P.O. Box 92984
Washington, DC 20090-2984

Tel: (800) 374-2721; Direct: (202) 336-5510
Fax: (202) 336-5502; TDD/TTY: (202) 336-6123
Online: www.apa.org/books/
Email: order@apa.org

In the U.K., Europe, Africa, and the Middle East, copies may be ordered from
American Psychological Association
3 Henrietta Street
Covent Garden, London
WC2E 8LU England

Typeset in Century Schoolbook by EPS Group Inc., Easton, MD

Printer: United Book Press, Inc., Baltimore, MD
Cover Designer: NiDesign, Baltimore, MD
Technical/Production Editor: Kristen R. Sullivan

The opinions and statements published are the responsibility of the authors, and such opinions and statements do not necessarily represent the policies of the American Psychological Association.

Library of Congress Cataloging-in-Publication Data
Acculturation : advances in theory, measurement, and applied research / edited by Kevin Chun, Pamela Balls Organista, and Gerardo Marín.
    p. cm.—(Decade of behavior)
  Includes bibliographical references and index.
  ISBN 1-55798-920-6 (alk. paper)
    1. Acculturation—Research. 2. Ethnicity. 3. Ethnopsychology.
 I. Chun, Kevin M. II. Organista, Pamela Balls. III. Marín, Gerardo.
IV. Series.

GN366 .A27 2002
303.48′2—dc21

2002018508

British Library Cataloguing-in-Publication Data
A CIP record is available from the British Library.

Printed in the United States of America
First Edition

To my parents Wilfred and Cynthia, my sister Annett, my brother-in-law Shaun, and my nephews Harrison and Garrett for your unconditional love and for being ever-present reminders of life's many gifts. Also, to my family of friends in San Francisco, who continue to fill my life with much joy and bliss.

—Kevin M. Chun

To my daughters Zena Laura and Zara Luz and my husband Kurt. My beloved ones, you answer the "Why?" of this book. You sustain me.

—Pamela Balls Organista

To my daughter Melisa and my son Andrés.

—Gerardo Marín

APA Science Volumes

Attribution and Social Interaction: The Legacy of Edward E. Jones

Best Methods for the Analysis of Change: Recent Advances, Unanswered Questions, Future Directions

Cardiovascular Reactivity to Psychological Stress and Disease

The Challenge in Mathematics and Science Education: Psychology's Response

Changing Employment Relations: Behavioral and Social Perspectives

Children Exposed to Marital Violence: Theory, Research, and Applied Issues

Cognition: Conceptual and Methodological Issues

Cognitive Bases of Musical Communication

Cognitive Dissonance: Progress on a Pivotal Theory in Social Psychology

Conceptualization and Measurement of Organism–Environment Interaction

Converging Operations in the Study of Visual Selective Attention

Creative Thought: An Investigation of Conceptual Structures and Processes

Developmental Psychoacoustics

Diversity in Work Teams: Research Paradigms for a Changing Workplace

Emotion and Culture: Empirical Studies of Mutual Influence

Emotion, Disclosure, and Health

Evolving Explanations of Development: Ecological Approaches to Organism–Environment Systems

Examining Lives in Context: Perspectives on the Ecology of Human Development

Global Prospects for Education: Development, Culture, and Schooling

Hostility, Coping, and Health

Measuring Patient Changes in Mood, Anxiety, and Personality Disorders: Toward a Core Battery

Occasion Setting: Associative Learning and Cognition in Animals

Organ Donation and Transplantation: Psychological and Behavioral Factors

Origins and Development of Schizophrenia: Advances in Experimental Psychopathology

The Perception of Structure

Perspectives on Socially Shared Cognition

Psychological Testing of Hispanics

Psychology of Women's Health: Progress and Challenges in Research and Application

Researching Community Psychology: Issues of Theory and Methods

The Rising Curve: Long-Term Gains in IQ and Related Measures

Sexism and Stereotypes in Modern Society: The Gender Science of Janet Taylor Spence

Sleep and Cognition

Sleep Onset: Normal and Abnormal Processes

Stereotype Accuracy: Toward Appreciating Group Differences

Stereotyped Movements: Brain and Behavior Relationships

Studying Lives Through Time: Personality and Development

The Suggestibility of Children's Recollections: Implications for Eyewitness Testimony

Taste, Experience, and Feeding: Development and Learning

Temperament: Individual Differences at the Interface of Biology and Behavior

Through the Looking Glass: Issues of Psychological Well-Being in Captive Nonhuman Primates

Uniting Psychology and Biology: Integrative Perspectives on Human Development

Viewing Psychology as a Whole: The Integrative Science of William N. Dember

APA Decade of Behavior Volumes

Acculturation: Advances in Theory, Measurement, and Applied Research

Animal Research and Human Health: Advancing Human Welfare Through Behavioral Science

Computational Modeling of Behavior in Organizations: The Third Scientific Discipline

Family Psychology: Science-Based Interventions

Memory Consolidation: Essays in Honor of James L. McGaugh

The Nature of Remembering: Essays in Honor of Robert G. Crowder

New Methods for the Analysis of Change

Personality Psychology in the Workplace

Psychosocial Interventions for Cancer

Unraveling the Complexities of Social Life: A Festschrift in Honor of Robert B. Zajonc

Contents

Contributors xiii

Decade of Behavior Foreword xv

Foreword.. xvii
Stanley Sue

Preface.. xxiii

Introduction: Social Change and Acculturation 3
Joseph E. Trimble

Part I: Advances in Theory and Measurement..................... 15

    1. Conceptual Approaches to Acculturation................... 17
       John W. Berry

    2. Major Approaches to the Measurement of Acculturation
       Among Ethnic Minority Populations: A Content Analysis
       and an Alternative Empirical Strategy 39
       Nolan Zane and Winnie Mak

Part II: Understanding Individual and Family Processes 61

    3. Ethnic Identity and Acculturation......................... 63
       Jean S. Phinney

    4. Acculturation and Changes in Cultural Values 83
       Gerardo Marín and Raymond J. Gamba

    5. Acculturation Among Ethnic Minority Families............ 95
       Kevin M. Chun and Phillip D. Akutsu

    6. The Influence of Acculturation Processes
       on the Family 121
       Daniel A. Santisteban and Victoria B. Mitrani

**Part III: Acculturation, Psychosocial Adjustment,
and Health**.. 137

    7. The Relationship Between Acculturation and Ethnic
       Minority Mental Health 139
       *Pamela Balls Organista, Kurt C. Organista, and
       Karen Kurasaki*

    8. Acculturation and Physical Health in Racial and Ethnic
       Minorities... 163
       Hector F. Myers and Norma Rodriguez

Part IV: Advances in Applied Research **187**

9. Acculturation, Psychological Distress, and Alcohol Use: Investigating the Effects of Ethnic Identity and Religiosity 189
   *Fang Gong, David T. Takeuchi,
   Pauline Agbayani-Siewert, and Leo Tacata*

10. Idioms of Distress, Acculturation, and Depression: The Puerto Rican Experience 207
    Dharma E. Cortés

11. Acculturation, Alcohol Consumption, Smoking, and Drug Use Among Hispanics............................. 223
    Raul Caetano and Catherine L. Clark

Author Index... 241

Subject Index 251

About the Editors 259

Contributors

Pauline Agbayani-Siewert, School of Public Policy and Social Research, University of California, Los Angeles
Phillip D. Akutsu, Department of Psychology, University of Michigan, Ann Arbor
Pamela Balls Organista, Department of Psychology, University of San Francisco, San Francisco, CA
John W. Berry, Department of Psychology, Queen's University, Kingston, Ontario, Canada
Raul Caetano, University of Texas School of Public Health, Dallas Regional Campus
Kevin M. Chun, Department of Psychology, University of San Francisco, San Francisco, CA
Catherine L. Clark, Sun Microsystems, San Jose, CA
Dharma E. Cortés, Harvard Medical School, Boston, MA
Raymond J. Gamba, Department of Psychology, City College of San Francisco, CA
Fang Gong, Department of Sociology, Indiana University, Bloomington
Karen Kurasaki, Department of Psychology, University of California, Davis
Winnie Mak, Department of Psychology, The Chinese University of Hong Kong
Gerardo Marín, Department of Psychology, College of Arts and Sciences, University of San Francisco, San Francisco, CA
Victoria B. Mitrani, Department of Psychiatry and Behavioral Sciences, University of Miami School of Medicine, Miami, FL
Hector F. Myers, Department of Psychology, University of California, Los Angeles
Kurt C. Organista, School of Social Welfare, University of California, Berkeley
Jean S. Phinney, Department of Psychology, California State University, Los Angeles
Norma Rodriguez, Department of Psychology, Pitzer College, Claremont, CA
Daniel A. Santisteban, Department of Psychiatry and Behavioral Sciences, University of Miami School of Medicine, Miami, FL
Stanley Sue, Department of Psychology, University of California, Davis
Leo Tacata, Asian American Recovery Services, Inc., San Francisco, CA
David T. Takeuchi, Department of Sociology, Indiana University, Bloomington
Joseph E. Trimble, Department of Psychology, Western Washington University, Bellingham
Nolan Zane, Department of Psychology, University of California, Davis

Decade of Behavior Foreword

In early 1988, the American Psychological Association (APA) Science Directorate began its sponsorship of what would become an exceptionally successful activity in support of psychological science—the APA Scientific Conferences program. This program has showcased some of the most important topics in psychological science and has provided a forum for collaboration among many leading figures in the field.

The program has inspired a series of books that have presented cutting edge work in all areas of psychology. At the turn of the millennium, the series was renamed the Decade of Behavior series to help advance the goals of this important initiative. The Decade of Behavior is a major interdisciplinary campaign designed to promote the contributions of the behavioral and social sciences to our most important societal challenges in the decade leading up to 2010. Although a key goal has been to inform the public about these scientific contributions, other activities have been designed to encourage and further collaboration among scientists. Hence, the series that was the "APA Science Series" has continued as the "Decade of Behavior Series." This represents one element in APA's efforts to promote the Decade of Behavior initiative as one of its endorsing organizations. For additional information about the Decade of Behavior, please visit http://www.decadeofbehavior.org

Over the course of the past years, the Science Conference and Decade of Behavior Series has allowed psychological scientists to share and explore cutting-edge findings in psychology. The APA Science Directorate looks forward to continuing this successful program and to sponsoring other conferences and books in the years ahead. This series has been so successful that we have chosen to extend it to include books that, although they do not arise from conferences, report with the same high quality of scholarship on the latest research.

We are pleased that this important contribution to the literature was supported in part by the Decade of Behavior program. Congratulations to the editors and contributors of this volume on their sterling effort.

Kurt Salzinger, PhD
Executive Director for Science

Virginia E. Holt
Assistant Executive Director for Science

Foreword

Stanley Sue

This book represents a landmark effort to assemble the top scholars in the field to reflect on the history of acculturation research and forge new, exciting paths for future investigations. The reader will find a wealth of information and ideas in these pages that truly illuminate the complexities and challenges in this burgeoning area of research. Moreover, the chapters provide compelling insights into the prevailing questions of our time, including those pertaining to assimilation vs. pluralism in the United States: Should we advocate Americanization as soon as possible, or should we allow ethnic customs, traditions, and cultures to flourish? Is it wise for immigrants to acculturate as soon as possible to enhance functioning, well-being, and mental health?

In the past, it was assumed that acculturation and Americanization were conducive to mental health. For example, it was assumed that immigrants needed to learn English to function in society. More recently, numerous individuals have advocated pluralism, which refers to the coexistence of distinct cultural groups in society. Those who encourage pluralism believe cultural differences should be maintained and appreciated and that different groups with different cultural orientations can peacefully coexist.

In the mental health arena, this controversy involves the relationship between acculturation and mental health. Is acculturation mentally healthy? The question has obvious implications for policy, program, and theory. If acculturation enhances mental health, then we must quickly help others to acculturate. The reasons acculturation relates to mental health must also be studied.

The importance of acculturation to mental health is, of course, an empirical issue. Previous researchers have come to very different conclusions about the correlation between these two variables. Some have found that extremes (very high or very low levels) in acculturation are associated with poorer mental health. The difficulties in finding a consistent relationship between acculturation and mental health are many. This book comprehensively addresses four particular conditions that have hindered acculturation research.

1. Measures of acculturation are often proxy variables (e.g., language use, generation, self-reported ethnic identity). It is often difficult to capture the construct of acculturation with these variables. Furthermore, these variables are sometimes unrelated. For example, in one study (Sue, Zane, & Ito, 1979), we measured acculturation of Asian Americans using variables such as socialization (i.e., the extent to which one socializes with Whites rather than members

of one's ethnic minority group), ability to speak the ethnic language, and generation of self. These indicators of acculturation have been used in previous research. Our findings revealed that not all of the measures were significantly related. In a correlation matrix, significant and expected relationships existed between socialization and speaking the ethnic language and between speaking the ethnic language and generation. However, socializing and generation failed to have a significant association.
2. Acculturation may be a multidimensional construct, so measures used to determine level of acculturation on a single dimension may be inappropriate. Previous measures have been primarily unidimensional. Nevertheless, if acculturation is multidimensional, how many dimensions exist, and which ones are more important? These are questions that remain unanswered.
3. Investigators have used different measures of acculturation, which makes it very difficult to compare findings from one study with findings from another.
4. Finally, there is a potential conceptual problem. Acculturation may shape the way individuals experience distress. Therefore, the relationship between acculturation and mental health is not straightforward, and the two variables may interact.

It is not meaningful to seek a simple answer to the question of whether acculturation promotes mental health. Too many qualifiers and interaction variables are involved. Several considerations should be addressed.

One of the most obvious facts of life is that people live in various settings and environments. How they match or fit the environment is a critical factor in acculturation and mental health. For example, Kelly (1979; Kelly, Azelton, Burzette, & Mock, 1994) has argued that the same settings and environments may be associated with positive or negative outcomes, depending on the person. His classic studies examined adjustment in high schools. He investigated two types of high school environments, which he labeled as either *stable* or *fluid*. In comparison with fluid high schools, stable high schools had more limited means of achieving school status, longer lasting social relationships because student turnover was low, greater emphasis on interpersonal relationships, greater homogeneity in students' clothing and appearance, and less noise. Adjustment of students depended on the person–environment match. That is, student characteristics that were effective and successful in a stable school could be maladaptive in a fluid school.

Given the importance of the person–environment match, why do we persist in studying acculturation and mental health without considering the effects of the environment? This persistence is apparent when researchers administer acculturation and mental health questionnaires and then examine the relationship between the two. This research strategy ignores the nature of an individual's living environment. For example, an unacculturated Chinese person may function and be relatively well adjusted in San Francisco's Chinatown but experience adjustment problems in Iowa City. Interestingly, although the importance of match, or fit, has been recognized, it is surprising that researchers tend to ignore it.

Regarding the issue of measuring acculturation, four additional considerations are echoed throughout this book:

1. As mentioned previously, problems often occur if individuals have the behavioral repertoire from one culture (Culture A) but live in a very different culture (Culture B). The situation is even more complex because people in the United States tend to live in multicultural environments. For example, an immigrant may come from a traditional Chinese family and community but be employed in a business with non-Chinese coworkers. How is that person going to adjust and adapt? Obviously, the person must be, to some extent, bicultural, with skills to function in different cultures. Researchers can measure degree of knowledge or preference for Culture A and Culture B. If a person scores high on both cultural measures, the individual is assumed to be bicultural. However, given a behavioral repertoire with elements of Culture A and Culture B, which behaviors should be used? Measures of acculturation need to assess not only the presence of skills or knowledge of different cultures but also the strategies employed in using the skills. Otherwise, the relationship between acculturation and mental health cannot be adequately determined.
2. Cost of acculturation is another factor to consider. We are aware of the existence of culture conflict—value clashes that develop when a person is socialized by different cultures. Acculturation to the mainstream culture may be achieved but at great cost to the individual, especially to one who is rooted in a minority culture. Acculturation may yield positive gains in some areas of life but have a negative impact on other areas.
3. Measures of acculturation may not identify factors that are important or unimportant in acculturation. Hsu (1971) posited that human beings behave according to rules and roles and an affective need for intimacy. Acculturation and behavioral assimilation in roles are most likely to occur first. The ethnic language is often lost in one generation. Asian immigrants, for instance, can learn relatively easily and quickly how to behave as teachers, students, or store clerks. Affective aspects such as kinship bonds are more enduring and less likely to be extinguished by exposure to American society. Researchers tend to measure what is easy (e.g., generation, language, food preferences) rather than tackle the important but difficult-to-measure phenomena such as affective and intimate relationships and values.
4. In the analysis of acculturation, investigators often overlook the role of majority–minority group relations when examining cultural differences between groups. However, minority group status is also pertinent to the discussion of acculturation (Sue, Kurasaki,

& Srinivasan, 1999). The term *minority* has historically been associated with notions of inferiority and deficits. Furthermore, the concept of minority implies that a majority exists, but one could argue that the United States has no real ethnic majority group (because Whites can be classified as a mix of many different ethnic groups) and Whites are not the majority in the world. The concept of minority status is important because the situation of American Indians, African Americans, Asian Americans, and Latinos is not solely a function of their own cultures or of value discrepancies with mainstream Americans. Rather, members of these minority groups have also experienced historical and contemporary forms of prejudice and discrimination. For example, alcohol abuse among American Indians cannot be fully understood by references to cultural differences. Patterns of exploitation have also accompanied their history. Thus, both culture and minority group status must be analyzed. Steele's research (1997), in which he found that stereotyping situations (e.g., involving African Americans) could promote a self-fulfilling prophecy, illustrates the importance of ethnic relations. The stereotypes are formed by majority–minority relationships rather than by cultural differences between majority and minority groups. Minority status distinguishes cross-cultural research, which involves examination of different cultural groups, from ethnic minority research, which involves cultural differences *and* ethnic relations.

Obviously, the effects of culture and minority status can be easily confounded. Over time, cultural values of a group may change as a result of ethnic relations. Minority status is likewise confounded with acculturation. If one is a member of a minority group that is considered *disadvantaged*, racial self-hatred may accompany acculturation; a member of a minority group that is not disadvantaged may develop feelings of competence with acculturation. Again, the main point is that the effects of culture and minority status are pertinent to the understanding of ethnic minority groups.

Toward Solutions

In our attempts to investigate the relationship between acculturation and mental health, how can we address some of these issues? First, attempts should be made to focus on mini theories rather than broad and inclusive theories. Broad generalizations, such as the notion that acculturation is related to mental health, must be replaced with mini theories that examine the conditions and principles that govern the relationship. Second, the characteristics used to define acculturation must be carefully examined. Researchers routinely use proxy variables such as language, generation, and time spent in the United States to define acculturation. We need to understand how proxy variables vary in relationship to each other and study the conditions under which some behaviors are extinguished and others are maintained according to various measures of acculturation. Finally, researchers must investigate the relationship between people and their environments. Which aspects of acculturation are important in which kinds of environmental contexts with which kinds of people? Which strategies do people use to negotiate in a multicultural environment? How can we devise measures that have greater meaning—that more adequately capture our sense of acculturation? These fundamental questions along with the many others presented throughout this remarkable book highlight the new challenges that face researchers. It is my hope that the reader not only gains an appreciation of these issues but also becomes intellectually engaged and stimulated to seek the many possible future scientific discoveries.

References

Hsu, F. L. K. (1971). *Americans and Chinese*. New York: Doubleday.

Kelly, J. G. (1979). *Adolescent boys in high school: A study of coping and adaptation*. Hillsdale, NJ: Erlbaum.

Kelly, J. G., Azelton, L. S., Burzette, R. G., & Mock, L. O. (1994). Creating social settings for diversity: An ecological thesis. In E. J. Trickett, R. J. Watts, & D. Birman (Eds.), *Human diversity: Perspectives on people in context* (pp. 424–451). San Francisco: Jossey-Bass.

Steele, C. M. (1997). A threat in the air: How stereotypes shape intellectual identity and performance. *American Psychologist, 52*, 613–629.

Sue, S., Kurasaki, K. S., & Srinivasan, S. (1999). Ethnicity, gender, and cross-cultural issues in clinical research. In P. C. Kendall, J. N. Butcher, & G. N. Holmbeck (Eds.), *Handbook of research methods in clinical psychology* (pp. 54–71). New York: John Wiley & Sons.

Sue, S., Zane, N., & Ito, J. (1979). Alcohol drinking patterns among Asians and Caucasian Americans. *Journal of Cross-Cultural Psychology, 10*, 41–56.

Preface

Acculturation is undoubtedly a core construct in contemporary social and behavioral research with ethnic groups. Indeed, Berry (1997) has argued that an understanding of the process and implications of acculturation is one of the main contributions of cross-cultural psychology. Practitioners and researchers alike have underscored the need to consider the effects of acculturation on various individual behaviors and conditions, such as mental health status, substance abuse, socioeconomic standing, and culture maintenance and diffusion. Although uncertainty about the nature and processes of acculturation still exists, the study of this particular construct compels us to consider the behaviors and beliefs of different ethnic groups in multicultural societies.

A fairly consistent belief seems to be that acculturation is important in considering the behavior and beliefs of members of ethnic groups in any multicultural society. Furthermore, a broad consensus among researchers, which is reflected in this book, is that individuals who are exposed to a different cultural context exhibit a "complex pattern of continuity and change in how [they] go about their lives . . ." (Berry, 1997, p. 6).

As a construct in the social and behavioral sciences, acculturation has an early history of benign neglect. The last 3 decades have nevertheless been characterized by a resurgence of interest in defining, measuring, and reconceptualizing acculturation to understand its role in shaping people's attitudes, norms, values, and actions. Early interest in acculturation primarily began in the anthropological community, which set out to describe the nature and effects of contact among distinct cultural groups. Many anthropologists focused on defining and properly understanding the dynamic processes that occur when cultures interact.

Redfield, Linton, and Herskovits (1936) established one of the first classical definitions of acculturation—encompassing changes in original cultural patterns that occur as a result of ongoing contact among groups of individuals with different cultures. In 1954 the Social Science Research Council proposed an expanded definition by stating that acculturation is the merger of two or more independent cultural systems, leading to dynamic processes that include the adaptation of value systems and transformation within relationships and personality traits. This definition suggests assimilation is not necessarily the only outcome possible when cultures interact, and acculturation is a selective process that may cause changes in one area of human behavior but not in another. Despite their long history, these initial conceptualizations of acculturation continue to influence our current thinking in the field.

Recently, researchers have been trying to develop more sophisticated acculturation measures and assess the impact or relationship of acculturation with a panoply of behaviors, beliefs, attitudes, and perceptions. Our understanding of acculturation in the psychological literature has increased significantly with the development of conceptual frameworks (e.g.,

Berry, 1990; Padilla, 1980), analyses of methodological constraints (e.g., Berry, Trimble, & Olmedo, 1986; Olmedo, 1979), and appearance of critical reviews of the literature (e.g., Berry & Sam, 1996; Ward, 1996).

As is true with significant portions of research with ethnic groups, many seminal publications dealing with theoretical and empirical issues on acculturation appeared in difficult-to-find sources or ephemeral outlets. These circumstances produced a situation in which advances in the field sometimes went unrecognized and the significance of the construct was obscured. Reviews of the literature (e.g., Berry & Sam, 1996; Ward, 1996) have helped to alleviate this problem, but few researchers have tried to compile diverse perspectives into a singular source. This situation essentially contributed to the genesis of this book.

An international conference held at the University of San Francisco in December 1998 was an additional impetus for this publication. The conference brought together leading scholars in the field of acculturation to explore recent findings and identify the needs for future theory development, measurement, and basic and applied research. A central goal of the conference was to analyze the significance of the construct of acculturation for research with African Americans, American Indians, Asian Americans, and Hispanics/Latinos.

This book begins with methodological considerations about theory and measurement and concludes with current examples of empirical investigations of acculturation. Some chapters are literature reviews and empirical overviews, whereas others are single studies that illustrate methodology or applied research that can advance the field. In the introduction, Trimble constructs a historical context for the study of acculturation and describes the social relevance of this topic. The first part of the book further identifies the conceptual and methodological foundations of acculturation. In chapter 1, Berry provides an overview of his classic acculturation theory, including a discussion of strategies of acculturation, ethnographic approaches, and construct and scale development. Zane and Mak (see chapter 2) describe the various conceptual models guiding acculturation methodologies and analyze the content of several of the most common measures used in acculturation research. In addition, they present an innovative alternative methodology, the single psychological element approach, for studying specific aspects of acculturation.

The second part of the book focuses on the influence of acculturation on individual and family processes. Phinney (see chapter 3) presents a comprehensive review of the relationship between ethnic identity and personal transformations that occur during the process of acculturation. In chapter 4, Marín and Gamba review research findings on changes in cultural values and beliefs that can be anticipated as a result of the process of acculturation. Chapter 5, by Chun and Akutsu, and chapter 6, by Santisteban and Mitrani, address acculturation within a family context. Chun and Akutsu provide a comprehensive review and critique of empirical and qualitative studies of ethnic minority families. They offer several recommendations for conducting family research on acculturation. Santisteban and Mitrani make an in-depth assessment of some of the empirically established core family processes, values, beliefs, and behaviors that may result from immigration and acculturation processes in families. They describe the reason these issues can often be the focal point of families who enter treatment.

The final two parts of the book focus on the relationship between acculturation and adjustment. Balls Organista and her colleagues (see chapter 7) provide an overview and analysis of research that centers on the relationship between acculturation and mental health among the four major ethnic minority groups in the United States. In chapter 8, Myers and Rodriguez review the role of acculturation and acculturative stressors as sociocultural factors implicated in the persistent ethnic group differences in physical health status. In addition, they offer a conceptual model for investigating such relationships.

The last three chapters describe the applied research of concepts discussed in previous chapters. Gong and her colleagues (see chapter 9) and Cortés (see chapter 10) examine the relationship between symptoms of psychological distress and acculturation. Gong et al. take a quantitative approach to studying this relationship with Filipinos, whereas Cortés utilizes qualitative methodology to examine specific idioms of distress in Puerto Ricans. In chapter 11, Caetano and Clark conduct a more comprehensive empirical analysis of acculturation and alcohol use, smoking, and drug use among Hispanics.

Some caveats to this book are worth noting. Showing the pains of birth and adolescent development of the field, the label *acculturation* is used by some authors to denote patterns of adaptation that imply only one outcome is possible—assimilation (Vasquez, 1984). Despite our efforts to resolve this problem, at times the reader will find the assumption is made in the literature that assimilation is tantamount to acculturation. In this sense, many researchers and practitioners assume that certain components of one's culture of origin are lost when a new repertoire of skills and behaviors are learned from another distinct culture. This unidimensional notion of acculturation continues to plague the field despite numerous suggestions by researchers to think of this process as a multifaceted phenomenon. Another difficulty is that most research has solely focused on *psychological acculturation* (Berry, 1997) involving changes in individual beliefs, attitudes, and emotions while ignoring macrosocial levels of cultural change influenced by social institutions. However, the significance of one's environmental context in adaptation cannot be overstated. Finally, we allowed authors to use their preferred labels for given ethnic groups (e.g., Hispanics, Latinos, Chicanos) primarily because ethnic psychologists (as well as other social scientists) continue to search for appropriate ethnic descriptors. Unfortunately, this diversity in referent labels sometimes adds unnecessary confusion in the evaluation of research findings.

Acknowledgments

We are confident that readers will appreciate the richness in the following pages and hope that this book will be the spark that motivates and directs researchers toward greater achievements in the field. We would like to thank some of the many individuals who made the publication of this book possible. First, we acknowledge Stanley D. Nel, dean of the College of Arts and Sciences at the University of San Francisco, who supported our idea (in words and deeds) and continually fosters an atmosphere of cultural respect and scholarly advancement at the university. Sharon Li, administrative assistant to Gerardo Marín, went many extra miles during the preparation of the manuscript but never lost her temper and always provided ideas born of her experience. We also thank the students at the University of San Francisco, whose questions and comments contribute to our professional growth. Finally, we thank the various chapter authors, who graciously labored under tight deadlines to produce a very important book.

Collaborating on this book was a tremendously rewarding experience. This publication represents our continued sharing of experiences, a process that characterized the production of our first joint book (Balls Organista, Chun, & Marín, 1998). In our joint scholarly activities, we have shared our diverse cultures and learned from our various fields of expertise while enjoying our love for good food and fine wines.

Like most scholarly pursuits, this book is the product of varied influences on the lives of the editors, influences that should be recognized. Gerardo Marín acknowledges the role played by the many individuals who at different times acted as professional mentors, particularly Robert E. Brewer, Amado M. Padilla, and Harry C. Triandis. Pamela Balls Organista is grateful for the wisdom and support provided by special individuals in her life—scholars who love to teach almost as much as they love to learn. She gives special gratitude to Gerardo Marín, Ricardo Muñoz, and her partner in intellectual and other passionate pursuits, Kurt C. Organista. Kevin Chun is indebted to his many mentors, particularly Stanley Sue, Gerardo Marín, and Francis Abueg, who continue to serve as sources of personal inspiration and professional guides.

References

Balls Organista, P., Chun, K., & Marín, G. (Eds.). (1998). *Readings in ethnic psychology.* New York: Routledge.

Berry, J. W. (1990). Psychology of acculturation. In J. Berman (Ed.), *Nebraska Symposium on Motivation: Cross-cultural perspectives, 1989* (pp. 201–234). Lincoln: University of Nebraska Press.

Berry, J. W. (1997). Immigration, acculturation, and adaptation. *Applied Psychology: An International Review, 46,* 5–34.

Berry, J. W., & Sam, D. (1996). Acculturation and adaptation. In J. W. Berry, M. H. Segall, & C. Kagitcibasi (Eds.), *Handbook of cross-cultural psychology, Vol. 3, Social behavior and applications* (2nd ed., pp. 291–326). Boston: Allyn & Bacon.

Berry, J. W., Trimble, J., & Olmedo, E. (1986). The assessment of acculturation. In W. J. Lonner & J. W. Berry (Eds.), *Field methods in cross-cultural research* (pp. 291–324). Newbury Park, CA: Sage.

Olmedo, E. L. (1979). Acculturation: A psychometric perspective. *American Psychologist, 34,* 1061–1070.

Padilla, A. M. (1980). The role of cultural awareness and ethnic loyalty in acculturation. In A. M. Padilla (Ed.), *Acculturation: Theory, models and some new findings* (pp. 47–84). Boulder, CO: Westview Press.

Redfield, R., Linton, R., & Herskovits, M. (1936). Memorandum on the study of acculturation. *American Anthropologist, 38,* 149–152.

Social Science Research Council. (1954). Acculturation: An exploratory formulation. *American Anthropologist, 56,* 973–1002.

Vasquez, A. (1984). Les implications ideologiques du concept d'acculturation [Ideological implications of the concept of acculturation]. *Cahiers de Sociologie Economique et Culturelle, 1,* 83–121.

Ward, C. (1996). Acculturation. In D. Landis & R. Bhagat (Eds.), *Handbook of intercultural training* (2nd ed., pp. 124–147). Newbury Park, CA: Sage.

Acculturation

Introduction: Social Change and Acculturation

Joseph E. Trimble

Within the past 200 years, seemingly all nations of the world have been experiencing extraordinary, almost explosive changes. Almost every known element of society has been affected to the point that in some societies, change is being challenged. At an environmental level, for example, we are witnessing the ravages of deforestation, the erosion of once-abundant fertile land, the degradation of air quality, the depletion of natural food sources, and the consequences of mismanaged and poorly planned urban development. At a sociocultural level, transnational immigration has created significant economic, health, and social–psychological problems in societies and nations where problems of any significance have rarely occurred. Changes are also occurring rapidly in the social structure and organization of many of the world's countries. For most indigenous aboriginal populations, changes have been imposed or produced invariably through legislation, colonization, war, disease, and industrialization. Moreover, immigrant masses have left their communities of origin in search of change as they look for accepting political climates, improved economic conditions, and the protection of their beliefs and values. These changes, in addition to the proverbial "shrinking" of the world prompted by improved communication and travel channels and the globalization of economic and legal and social systems, have produced more intense culture and ethnic contact then ever before in the history of humankind. Sociocultural change is therefore the progenitor of acculturation.

Change and Acculturation

Change is an undeniable, enduring fact of human life, if not of all living forms. Some change is preprogrammed and determined by evolutionary

---

I extend my deepest gratitude to the administration and research staff at the Radcliffe Institute for Advanced Study at Harvard University for providing me with the time, resources, and support that allowed me to conduct research for the preparation and writing of this section. Additionally, I extend my warm appreciation to my Radcliffe Research Junior Partners—Harvard College seniors Peggy Ting Lim and Maiga Miranda—who conducted research and provided me with wonderful, thought-provoking commentary and advice for many topics covered here.

and sociobiological forces. The remaining portion is acquired through a multitude of circumstantial and sociocultural influences. The study of acquired and imposed change forms the bulk of research initiatives in the social and behavioral sciences. At one level of inquiry, research is centered on social change, or the "modification or alteration in the social structure of a society" (Fisher, 1982, p. 488). However, limiting the interest to just the change of some structural or functional social force is hardly inclusive. Because of a slight nudging of the genes, humans are constantly conforming, changing, and striving for a new stability—new ways of thinking, perceiving, and understanding. They seek out alternatives for an improved quality of life and new forms of technology that can improve outmoded tools. Another view of social change spreads the forces among more discrete elements. Katz (1974), for example, categorized social change into four types: (a) individual change, including variations in personality; (b) incremental change, which is represented by gradual modifications in the structure of society; (c) radical change, which involves the reorganization and restructuring of a social system; and (d) cultural change, in which attitudes, beliefs, and behavior changes are the major focus of interest. Katz's conceptual scheme, therefore, proceeds from the individual to the structure of society to the psychosocial characteristics of group members. The four elements roughly follow the general level of inquiry in sociology, anthropology, and psychology.

Social change creates an apparent paradox for the theoretician and the practical-minded researcher. At any given time, life has the contrasting qualities of being static and changing. Eitzen (1974) emphasized that two forces provide the basis for social change in contemporary society. The first force involves the general desire for technological change—actually, for any form of change. The second force places restrictions on one's freedom to promote and achieve new and improved ways to meet and achieve needs and goals. In many sociocultural systems, rituals, taboos, religious convictions, and similar forms of social control govern and regulate individual and group change efforts. Consequently, the two processes, in addition to various social control mechanisms, constitute the dialectic of society—that is, weighing and reconciling contradictory arguments for the purpose of understanding society's forces and dynamics. "As contrary tendencies, they generate tension [and] change" (Eitzen, 1974, p. 12).

As a concept and a theoretical construct, social change has been examined and explored under a number of aliases. In anthropology the concepts of enculturation, acculturation, and assimilation include, wittingly or unwittingly, the concept of change brought about by societal influences. In sociology, presumably the origin of the social change construct, social change topics such as social movements and collective behavior form the major source of information for change enthusiasts. Moreover, in psychology, change, especially at the individual level of analysis, is explored through studies on learning, clinical intervention, individuation, socialization, conformity, modernization, and to a lesser extent, acculturative stress and identity development and formation.

Acculturation is a salient form of social change. Certainly, acculturation may well be synonymous with sociocultural change. Originally identified and conceptualized by anthropologists, the concept now is included in the research agenda of psychologists, psychiatrists, sociologists, social workers, and educators. Because of the increased interest in the topic, acculturation's meaning and application is changing. Similarly, techniques and procedures for measuring the concept are changing, too, to the point that some critics argue that researchers are measuring an elusive construct whose meaning is undergoing change. Escobar and Vega (2000), for example, forcefully challenge the meaning and measurement of acculturation on the grounds that it has become a catchall for anything that has to do with social and individual change of people from different ethnocultural groups. Many researchers tend to attribute the results of social and individual change solely to the acculturative process. Moreover, social change has been offered as an explanation for producing different acculturative changes in members of given cultures. Unfortunately, some are now blaming negative adaptation and adjustment to acculturation as though acculturation has a direct effect on adaptive outcomes. Such attributions, however well intended, have confounded the research process and muddled the field of inquiry. Yet, there is no doubt that when two or more intact cultural groups come into direct contact and experience change, conflict is one predictable outcome. How individuals and groups deal with the contact and the possible cultural conflict continues to be an important and significant research question.

Acculturation

The concept of acculturation has a long history in the social and behavioral sciences particularly among anthropologists and sociologists. Acculturation has been used to better understand the modernization processes that various cultures and communities were undergoing during the 19th and early 20th centuries. More recently, acculturation became an important concept in the explanation of the varied experiences of ethnic and cultural minorities as international migration, economic globalization, and political conflicts supported the creation of multicultural societies. As a construct, acculturation includes changes not only at the individual or psychological level but also at the sociocultural level. Indeed, analyses of the construct cannot ignore the influences of social and environmental changes on an individual's values, beliefs, behaviors, and affect. Regardless of the approach used to study acculturation and the acculturative process, individual and social change must be factored in the process.

History

Early in the 20th century, anthropologists were the first social scientists to recognize the significance and importance of cultural contact between disparate groups. To account for and draw attention to this dynamic and important phenomenon, Redfield, Linton, and Herskovits (1936) proposed the term *acculturation* and defined it as "phenomena which results when groups of individuals having different cultures come into continuous first-hand contact with subsequent changes in the original culture patterns of either or both groups" (p. 149). The essential phrase in this definition is "continuous first-hand contact," with *continuous* being the key word. Acculturation was therefore perceived to be the result of long-term contact among individuals from different cultures (excluding other short-term interactions produced by travel, war, commercial or missionary activities, or even temporary expatriate employment). Another important distinction is that the cultural groups possess a unique and identifiable "eidos" and "ethos" (i.e., "lifeways" and "thoughtways"). In the course of the interaction between the groups, much cultural diffusion, borrowing, and conflict typically occur, often leading to immutable changes in an individual's "lifeways" and "thoughtways." Also important in this initial definition is the emphasis on change in all cultures involved in the interaction, not just on the acculturating group that is accommodating or becoming assimilated into the dominant, or *host*, culture.

In 1954, the Social Science Research Council (SSRC) revised the concept of acculturation and defined it as follows:

> ... culture change that is initiated by the conjunction of two or more autonomous cultural systems. Its dynamics can be seen as the selective adaptation of value systems, the processes of integration and differentiation, the generation of developmental sequences, and the operation of role determinants and personality factors. (p. 974)

The essential concepts in the SSRC definition are *change* and *adaptation*. Subsequent research and exploration of the two processes generated different views of the acculturation construct.

The more traditional definition implies that a cultural group progresses from a native or tradition-oriented state through a transitional stage to an elite acculturated stage (Spindler & Spindler, 1967). According to this notion, cultural changes proceed away from one's own lifeway in a linear manner and culminate in the full and complete internalization of another culture's lifeways. More contemporary social researchers voice their difficulty with the traditional view, claiming that acculturation is neither a linear process nor an achievable end, especially if the process occurs during the initial contact and change period.

If the elements of a *dominant or contributing* culture have not been fully and thoroughly internalized, then full acculturation (or assimilation, in the words of Gordon, 1964) cannot occur. Indeed, assimilation, if it does take place, may take several generations for the process to become complete—if it does become complete. Many acculturation theories assume that the terms *assimilation* and *acculturation* are used interchangeably. Suarez-Orozco (2001) pointed out that assimilation and acculturation themes predict that change is "directional, unilinear, nonreversible, and continuous" (p. 8); however, this is not what occurs with immigrant populations. Ethnic, or cultural, groups select portions of a *dominant or contributing* culture that fit their original worldview and, at the same time, strive to retain vestiges of their traditional culture. Some of the limited research on the acculturative process shows that acculturation promotes and brings about positive change. Yet, another by-product of acculturation can be negative, disruptive, and stressful circumstances. Such change is often referred to as *acculturative disorganization* (Chance, 1965). Building on this notion, Berry (1980) developed a definition of acculturation that involves intergroup contact, conflict, and adaptation. He maintained that "acculturation may be treated as a two-level phenomenon involving the group and the individual" (p. 11). Berry's emphasis on individual adaptation led him to conceptualize the interaction as *psychological acculturation*.

According to Berry (1980), psychological acculturation produces four types of adaptation: assimilation, integration, separation, and marginalization. Berry and Annis (1974) elaborated on this definition and developed an ecological–cultural–behavioral model. The model attempts to show how behavior varies as a function of ecocultural settings. The primary interest involves the shift in behavior, which existed prior to and during contact and stress, or disruptive behaviors that emerge as a result of the influences and contributions of the *dominant or contributing* culture. In this context, acculturation is considered a multidimensional process generating several definitive outcomes.

Dimensionality

The acculturative process was once thought to be a unidirectional course of cultural change eventually resulting in full assimilation (cf. Berry, Trimble, & Olmedo, 1986; Suarez-Orozco, 2001). Nevertheless, a more recent understanding of the construct suggests acculturation is multifaceted and that true assimilation may never occur. Indeed, adaptation and change are essential components of the definition; however, moderating variables, preferences, and the desire for ethnic affiliation must be considered. In a related article, Richman, Gaviria, Flaherty, Birz, and Wintrob (1987) pointed out yet another component—the possibility that the dominant, or *donor*, culture may undergo a change process influenced by aspects of the *newcomer* culture or acculturating group. This assumption, of course, had been inherent in some of the initial definitions of acculturation.

Researchers promoting and advancing acculturation research are adopting bidimensional and multidimensional perspectives. Following pioneering work by Berry (1980) and others, researchers (many of whom are contributors to this book) currently acknowledge the fact that acculturation is a process in which elements of the *newcomer* and *dominant and contributing* cultures are retained and internalized (e.g., Mendoza, 1984; Sodowsky, Lai, & Plake, 1991). Instead of attempting to isolate individuals using an index that approaches full assimilation, one must consider the possibility that many options are available to individuals interacting with a new culture. Furthermore, as argued by Trimble (1989), the response to culture contact may depend on a person's situation. This phenomenon can be called *situational acculturation*; the person and situation form a coterminous interaction. This interaction is an intricate recursive process that determines cognitive and perceptual appraisals; in turn, these appraisals influence behavioral outcomes. Mendoza (1984) suggested that an acculturating individual may reject religious practices, assimilate dress customs, and integrate food preferences and celebration of certain holidays. One's acculturative status, therefore, is best understood from a composite of indexes rather than from an aggregated summative index.

Racial, Ethnic, or Cultural Identification and Acculturation

The argument has been made that acculturation is intimately related to ethnic, racial, or cultural identity and that one can be measured from the other. Furthermore, some researchers expect changes in identification as a result of changes in acculturation. The extent of the relationship between these two constructs is further explored by Phinney in chapter 3. Nevertheless, it is important to explore how the social change process that produces acculturative stress may also produce changes in an individual's self-identification.

Just as acculturation has several definitions, a construct such as ethnic identity generates many viewpoints. To understand the complications, one must consider the meanings of race and ethnicity. Feagin (1978) defined a racial group as one in which "persons inside or outside the group have decided what is important to single out as inferior or superior, typically on the basis of real or alleged physical characteristics subjectively selected" (p. 7). An ethnic group (Feagin, 1978) is one "which is socially distinguished or set apart, by others and/or by itself, primarily on the basis of cultural or nationality characteristics" (p. 9). Thompson (1989) elaborated on the term *ethnic group* and chose to view it as a culturally distinct population that can be set apart from other groups. Such groups, Thompson argued, engage in behaviors "based on cultural or physical criteria in a social context in which these criteria are relevant" (p. 11). Instead of *ethnic group*, Berry (see chapter 1) prefers the term *ethnocultural group*.

Although the terms *ethnic* and *race* often are used interchangeably, Helms (1990) maintained that "'racial identity' actually refers to a sense of group or collective identity based on one's *perception* that he or she shares a common racial heritage with a particular racial group" (p. 3; see also Burlew, Bellow, & Lovett, 2000). The three terms (cultural, ethnic, racial) may share a common meaning but only in that people congregate according to common core characteristics. The source of the core characteristics can be criteria established and deeply held by the in-group, but out-groups can also set their own criteria for designating and differentiating one group from another. Thompson (1989) is highly critical of the labeling process and draws attention to theoretical and practical matters of "those who have had the fortune or, in most cases, the misfortune of being labeled 'ethnics' in the modern world" (p. 42; see also Trimble, 2001).

Helms (1990) concurred, to an extent, as she found it rather confusing "since one's racial-group designation does not necessarily define one's racial, cultural, or ethnic characteristics" (p. 7).

To distinguish one group or individual from another using race, ethnicity, or culture is an attempt to be culturally distinctive. Labeling a group as a distinct cultural (i.e., racial or ethnic) unit, however, tends to promote stereotypy and lead to overgeneralizations, further compounding the complexity of the problem. It is not uncommon for outsiders to believe that identifiable members of a racial group act as a single unitary whole —"a group mind"—and are more homogeneous than heterogeneous (Trimble, 1991, 2001).

Whether one chooses to investigate and explore acculturation from an individual or group level of analysis, change and identity must be included in the investigation. In this volume, several significant and compelling studies and reviews of acculturation correlates are presented to explain, as Berry states (see chapter 1), "how people go about their acculturation."

Understanding Acculturation and Social Change

As mentioned, there is an emerging need to better understand the relationship between acculturation and identity and the collinear effects of social change. Chapter 3 (Phinney) advances the field in this respect. Regardless, a better understanding of acculturation and social change requires the cooperative efforts of future researchers, who must move beyond previous research questions toward the answers of the issues raised in this book. For example, researchers need to better understand the relationship between acculturation and identity and explore the fact that acculturating individuals often experience racism and discrimination. These experiences are not uncommon in societies undergoing social change, and they are expected to have profound effects on individuals' levels of acculturation, their concurrent acculturative stress, and the level of personal identification with the culture of origin and the dominating or contributing culture.

As researchers increase their understanding of acculturation as a social change process, better measures are needed. Although this argument is made very strongly in a chapter in this book (see chapter 2, Zane & Mak), it is worth mentioning here. Acculturation measures are in desperate need of intense psychometric evaluation and scrutiny. Most acculturation measures assume measurement equivalence between and within study groups. Few if any acculturation measurement studies adequately explore the various components of measurement equivalence (e.g., construct, functional, metric). These measurement approaches provide researchers with the unique opportunity to isolate scale and item properties that go well beyond use of standard correlation procedures.

Research on the association between personality variables and acculturating individuals is another area ripe for exploration because little information is available on the subject. We may find that certain personality styles are more resilient to the negative effects of acculturation than others, and the effects may vary within and among ethnocultural groups. The possibility of personality changes produced by social change and acculturation is an area that deserves attention if we are to better understand the results of a process that seems even more powerful during this century than it has been in the previous 2 centuries.

In a related domain, research and measurement must include studies of situational acculturation—the way situations shape and determine behavior, cognition, and affect of acculturating individuals. It makes intuitive sense that one's acculturative status varies from situation to situation. When at home and with the family, people's behavior may be more similar to the prescriptions of their culture of origin than when they are at work or in an educational institution. In short, the situation and the corresponding demands of the *dominant or contributing* culture may contribute considerably more to people's choice of behavioral repertoires than the general acculturating expectations that they have learned. Therefore, it also makes sense for researchers to actively explore the role that emotion plays in the acculturation process and the influences various emotions have on determining appropriate behavioral choices.

Inherent in many of the models for acculturation described is the notion that biculturalism is possible and common among individuals exposed to two or more cultures. Indeed, numerous recent studies have shown that biculturalism is not only common but also quite beneficial to individuals (Johnson et al., 1997; LaFromboise, Coleman, & Gerton, 1993; Root, 2001). Unfortunately, acculturation and social change research seldom includes bicultural influences. There is another aspect of biculturalism that is of interest among ethnic minority groups in the United States and in other multicultural societies. Specifically, this is the learning and experiencing of two cultures by an individual who is the child of parents who have a mixed cultural background (e.g., an Asian American father and a non-Hispanic White mother). Little research is currently found on these individuals, often labeled biracial or of mixed race, although in the last few years more attention has been given to analyzing their situation (Root, 1992, 1996, 2001; Zack, 1995).

Conclusion

Much work obviously remains for social and behavioral scientists to sufficiently understand the process of acculturation and its relationship to social and sociocultural change. The challenges are significant, but so are the opportunities. A proper understanding of the acculturative change produced by social change will help advance the field, but more important, the expected increase in knowledge should help alleviate the personal and societal costs associated with unchecked and misunderstood social change.

Before any additional research is undertaken however, the overlap between and the nature of the two constructs must be clearly delineated, operationalized, and measured in culturally appropriate ways with the principles of measurement equivalence serving as guides. The following example may help clarify the source of many of the problems associated with the use and meaning of the constructs. In 1928, the renowned anthropologist Margaret Mead traveled to the Admiralty Islands off the Northeastern coast of New Guinea to study the thought patterns of "primitive" children on the island of Manus. From 1928 to 1929, Mead described the Manus as a rather carefree, peaceful, and simple people who were extremely competitive, tense, apprehensive, demanding, high tempered, imperious, intolerant of delays, and persistent. Daily activities were primarily fishing and trading. Their society was held together by an entrenched belief that the "ghosts of the recently dead" influenced lives at all levels (Mead, 1956, p. 21; Mead, 1977).

Mead returned to the Admiralty Islands and the Manus in 1953 to find that major changes had occurred among the people, changes fostered and influenced by a multitude of circumstances, including missionaries, trading, World War II, and technology. In general, Manus adults were more friendly and relaxed and less competitive than in 1928. Instead of living in stilted huts above the shallow lagoons, most lived in tightly clustered tents and shelters constructed by the military during their occupation in the early 1940s. The schedules of daily activities, which were traditionally tied to chance and the "rhythm of human lives," were replaced by the Christian calendar. Women seemed to have gained new freedoms. Mead noted that "the removal of old taboos, the disappearance of then old name avoidances, the prohibition of child betrothals, the permission for women to consent to their own seductions, the prohibition against fathers or brothers becoming angered by the behavior of daughters and brothers" dramatically thrust Manus women into a nominally equitable status with men—a status they had not experienced for centuries, if ever (Mead, 1956, p. 402). Moreover, Mead discovered that many or most Manus had completely abandoned traditional ways by integrating their lifestyles with those of the modern world.

Although considerably more can be written about the changes experienced by the Manus and the changes they are experiencing now, the brief discussion raises a few profound questions. Which change-related constructs do we use to describe and understand the nature of the changes? Did the Manus experience acculturation? Psychological acculturation? Acculturation stress? Sociocultural change? Social change? Modernization brought on by social contact and "cultural borrowing and fusion"? Surely, individual, social, and cultural changes occurred among the Manus. However, which construct would thoroughly explain and clarify the change process and its consequences? In light of the contents of this chapter and others in this book, relying solely on acculturation and social change constructs would be insufficient and shortsighted.

References

Berry, J. W. (1980). Acculturation as varieties of adaptation. In A. Padilla (Ed.), *Acculturation: Theory, models and some new findings* (pp. 9–25). Boulder, CO: Westview.

Berry, J. W., & Annis, R. C. (1974). Acculturative stress: The role of ecology, culture and differentiation. *Journal of Cross-Cultural Psychology, 5,* 382–405.

Berry, J. W., Trimble, J. E., & Olmedo, E. L. (1986). Assessment of acculturation. In W. J. Lonner & J. W. Berry (Eds.), *Field methods in cross-cultural research* (pp. 291–324). Beverly Hills, CA: Sage.

Burlew, A. K., Bellow, S., & Lovett, M. (2000). Racial identity measures: A review and classification system. In R. Dana (Ed.), *Handbook of cross-cultural and multicultural assessment* (pp. 173–196). Mahweh, NJ: Lawrence Erlbaum.

Chance, N. A. (1965). Acculturation, self-identification and personality adjustment. *American Anthropologist, 67,* 372–393.

Eitzen, D. (1974). *Social structure and social problems in America.* Boston: Allyn & Bacon.

Escobar, J., & Vega, W. (2000). Mental health and immigration's AAAs: Where are we and where do we go from here? *The Journal of Nervous and Mental Disorders, 188,* 736–740.

Feagin, J. R. (1978). *Racial and ethnic relations.* Englewood Cliffs, NJ: Prentice-Hall.

Fisher, R. (1982). *Social psychology: An applied approach.* New York: St. Martin's Press.

Gordon, M. (1964). *Assimilation in American life.* London: Oxford University Press.

Helms, J. E. (1990). Introduction: Review of racial identity terminology. In J. E. Helms (Ed.), *Black and White racial identity: Theory, research, and practice* (pp. 3–8). Westport, CT: Greenwood Press.

Johnson, T., Jobe, J., O'Rourke, D., Sudman, S., Warnecke, R., Chavez, N., et al. (1997). Dimensions of self-identification among multiracial and multiethnic respondents in survey interviews. *Evaluation Review, 21,* 671–687.

Katz, D. (1974). Factors affecting social change: A socio-psychological interpretation. *Journal of Social Issues, 30*(3), 159–180.

LaFromboise, T., Coleman, H. L. K., & Gerton, J. (1993). Psychological impact of biculturalism: Evidence and theory. *Psychological Bulletin, 114,* 395–412.

Mead, M. (1956). *New lives for old.* New York: Morrow.

Mead, M. (1977). *Letters from the field, 1925–1975.* New York: Harper & Row.

Mendoza, R. (1984). Acculturation and sociocultural variability. In J. L. Martinez & R. Mendoza (Eds.), *Chicano psychology* (2nd ed., pp. 61–75). Orlando: Academic Press.

Redfield, R., Linton, R., & Herskovits, M. (1936). Memorandum for the study of acculturation. *American Anthropologist, 38,* 149–152.

Richman, J., Gaviria, M., Flaherty, J., Birz, S., & Wintrob, R. (1987). The process of acculturation: Theoretical perspectives and an empirical investigation in Peru. *Social Science Medicine, 25,* 839–847.

Root, M. (Ed.). (1992). *Racially mixed people in America.* Thousand Oaks, CA: Sage.

Root, M. (Ed.). (1996). *The multiracial experience: Racial borders as the new frontier.* Thousand Oaks, CA: Sage.

Root, M. (2001). *Love's revolution: Interracial marriage.* Philadelphia: Temple University Press.

Social Science Research Council. (1954). Acculturation: An exploratory formulation. *American Anthropologist, 56,* 973–1002.

Sodowsky, G., Lai, E., & Plake, B. (1991). Moderating effects of sociocultural variables on acculturation attitudes of Hispanics and Asian Americans. *Journal of Counseling Development, 70,* 194–204.

Spindler, L., & Spindler, G. (1967). Male and female adaptations in culture change: Menomini. In R. Hunt (Ed.), *Personalities and cultures* (pp. 56–78). New York: Natural History Press.

Suarez-Orozco, M. (2001). Everything you ever wanted to know about assimilation but were afraid to ask. In R. Shweder, M. Minow, & H. Markus (Eds.), *The free exercise of culture* (pp. 1–30). New York: Russell Sage Foundation.

Thompson, R. H. (1989). *Theories of ethnicity: A critical appraisal.* New York: Greenwood.

Trimble, J. E. (1989). Multilinearity of acculturation: Person–situation interactions. In D. M. Keats, D. Munro, & L. Mann (Eds.), *Heterogeneity in cross-cultural psychology* (pp. 173–186). Amsterdam: Swets & Zeitlinger.

Trimble, J. E. (1991). Ethnic specification, validation prospects and the future of drug abuse research. *International Journal of the Addictions, 25*, 149–169.

Trimble, J. E. (2001). Social psychological perspectives on changing self-identification among American Indians and Alaska Natives. In R. Dana (Ed.), *Handbook of cross-cultural and multicultural assessment* (pp. 197–222). Mahweh, NJ: Lawrence Erlbaum.

Zack, N. (1995). *American mixed race: The culture of microdiversity.* Lanham, MD: Rowman & Littlefield.

Part I

Advances in Theory and Measurement

1

Conceptual Approaches to Acculturation

John W. Berry

Initial interest in acculturation grew out of a concern for the effects of European domination of colonial and indigenous peoples (Hallowell, 1945). Later, people focused on how immigrants (voluntary and involuntary) changed after their entry and settlement into receiving societies (Beiser, 2000). More recently, much of the work has been involved with how ethnocultural groups relate to each other and change as a result of their attempts to live together in culturally plural societies (Padilla, 1980a). Today, all three foci are important as globalization results in ever-larger trading and political relations. Indigenous national populations experience neocolonization; new waves of immigrants, sojourners, and refugees flow from these economic and political changes; and large ethnocultural populations become established in most countries.

In psychology, acculturation has been examined for two reasons (Berry, Trimble, & Olmedo, 1986): first, to control for experiences of social and cultural change (such as schooling, telecommunications, and industrialization) that could interfere with comparative studies of psychological phenomena (such as values or cognitive abilities). Second, acculturation is studied for its own sake, as a set of psychological phenomena of interest that arise at the intersection of two cultures. Acculturation has become an integral and important part of the field of cross-cultural psychology. Its inclusion in the editorial policy of many journals, in textbooks (e.g., Berry, Poortinga, Segall, & Dasen, 2002; Segall, Dasen, Berry, & Poortinga, 1999), and in handbooks (e.g., Berry & Sam, 1997; Liebkind, 2000; Ward, 1996) attests to the centrality of the process of acculturation. My treatment of the topic in this chapter is a personal one, based largely on my own views; those of others are frequently referenced, but the focus remains on my own understanding of the issues.

Acculturation

Although there is wide consensus that acculturation is an important part of cross-cultural psychology, there is disagreement about how to conceptualize and measure it. In my view, most researchers and policymakers have an implicit view about the process, and this colors every aspect of acculturation—how to define it, how to measure it, and what its consequences and policy implications are. At the heart of these implicit views are two core issues: (a) whether acculturation affects all groups in contact (dominant and nondominant) and hence is a mutual process and (b) whether acculturation is essentially unidimensional (and unidirectional) or whether it is multidimensional (with complex variations taking place). These issues constitute the underlying themes of this chapter.

This chapter has three purposes: First, it is an attempt to review the issues and some of the findings related to acculturation and to try to establish some common ground on which researchers can advance the field. Second, the chapter emphasizes one key aspect: individual differences in how people go about their acculturation (mainly using the concept of acculturation strategies). Third, the chapter outlines what is currently known about the consequences of choosing the various acculturation strategies.

Cultural Level

Early views about the nature of acculturation are a useful foundation for contemporary discussion. Two formulations in particular have been widely quoted. The first is as follows:

> Acculturation comprehends those phenomena which result when groups of individuals having different cultures come into continuous first-hand contact, with subsequent changes in the original culture patterns of either or both groups ... under this definition, acculturation is to be distinguished from culture change, of which it is but one aspect, and assimilation, which is at times a phase of acculturation. (Redfield, Linton, & Herskovits, 1936, pp. 149–152)

In another formulation, acculturation was defined as follows:

> Culture change that is initiated by the conjunction of two or more autonomous cultural systems. Acculturative change may be the consequence of direct cultural transmission; it may be derived from noncultural causes, such as ecological or demographic modification induced by an impinging culture; it may be delayed, as with internal adjustments following upon the acceptance of alien traits or patterns; or it may be a reactive adaptation of traditional modes of life. (Social Science Research Council, 1954, p. 974)

In the first formulation, acculturation is seen as one aspect of the broader concept of culture change (an aspect that results from intercultural contact), is considered to generate change in "either or both groups," and is distinguished from assimilation (of which acculturation may at times be a phase). These are important distinctions for psychological work and are pursued later in the chapter. In the second definition, a few extra features are added: Acculturation can include change that is indirect (not cultural, but "ecological"), can be delayed (because internal adjustments, presumably of a cultural and psychological character, take time), and can be reactive (i.e., rejecting the cultural influence and changing toward a more traditional way of life rather than inevitably toward greater similarity with the dominant culture).

Although the term *acculturation* can mean anything one wants, I believe that these formulations are a sound basis for contemporary psychological work on the topic. By making these original meanings explicit, researchers can at least see where the ideas have come from, even though some may want to move away from them.

Psychological Level

As for all types of cross-cultural psychology, it is imperative that researchers root their work on acculturation in its cultural context. In a sense, rooting the conception of psychological acculturation in the original anthropological meanings of the process (as outlined previously) is one example of this practice. More broadly, the discipline requires practitioners to understand, in ethnographic terms, both cultures that are in contact if they are to understand the individuals. Thus, a linkage is sought between the acculturation of an individual's group and the psychological acculturation of that individual. For Graves (1967), *psychological acculturation refers to changes in an individual who is a participant in a culture-contact situation—a person who is being influenced directly by the external culture and by the changing culture of which the individual is a member.* There are two reasons for keeping these two levels distinct. The first is that the field insists that individual human behavior interacts with the cultural context within which it occurs; hence, separate conceptions and measurements are required at the two levels. The second reason is that not every individual enters into, participates in, or changes in the same way; vast individual differences exist in psychological acculturation, even among individuals who live in the same acculturative arena.

General Framework

A framework that outlines and links cultural and psychological acculturation and identifies the two (or more) groups in contact is presented in Figure 1.1. This framework serves as a map of the phenomena that I believe need to be conceptualized and measured during acculturation research. At the cultural level (*left*), practitioners need to understand key features of the two original cultural groups (A and B) prior to their major contact, the nature of their contact relationships, and the resulting cultural changes in both groups and in the emerging ethnocultural groups during the process of acculturation. The gathering of this information requires extensive ethnographic, community-level work. These changes can

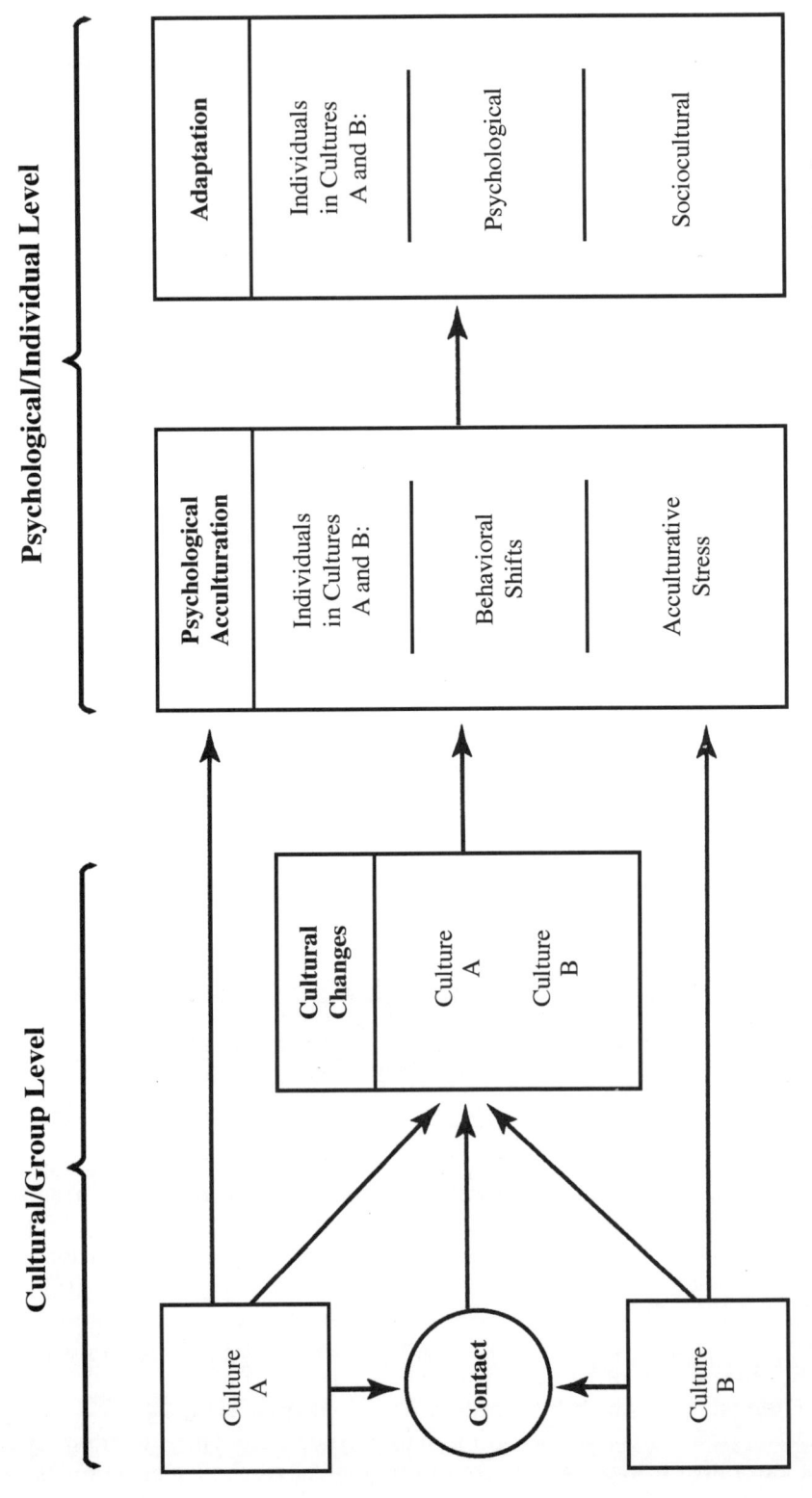

Figure 1.1. A preliminary framework for understanding acculturation: cultural and psychological levels.

be minor or substantial and range from being easily accomplished to being a source of major cultural disruption.

At the individual level (*right*), one must consider the psychological changes that individuals in both groups undergo and the effects of eventual adaptation to their new situations. Identifying these changes requires sampling a population and studying individuals who are variably involved in the process of acculturation. These changes can be a set of rather easily accomplished behavioral changes (e.g., in ways of speaking, dressing, or eating; in cultural identity), or they can be more problematic, producing *acculturative stress* as manifested by uncertainty, anxiety, and depression (Berry, 1976). Adaptations can be primarily internal, or *psychological* (i.e., adaptations that affect the sense of well-being or self-esteem), or *sociocultural* (i.e., adaptations that link the individual to others in the new society as manifested, e.g., in competence in the activities of daily intercultural living; Searle & Ward, 1990). General overviews of this process and these specific features can be found in the literature (e.g., Berry, 1980, 1990, 1997; Berry & Sam, 1997; Birman, 1994; Ward, 1996).

The remainder of this chapter is related primarily to the concept of *acculturation strategies*, which is relevant to all components of the general framework. It is clear that groups and individuals engage in the process of acculturation in different ways. Which strategies are used depends on a variety of antecedent factors (cultural and psychological), and there are variable consequences of these different strategies (again, cultural and psychological). These strategies consist of two components that are usually related: *attitudes* and *behaviors* (i.e., the preferences and actual outcomes) that are exhibited in day-to-day intercultural encounters. Earlier, the strategies were termed *modes of acculturation* (Berry, 1974) or *varieties of acculturation* (Berry, 1980), the attitude component was called *relational attitudes* (Berry, 1970) and later *acculturation attitudes* (Berry, 1984a), and behavioral indicators throughout have been used to validate the attitudinal preferences (Berry, Kim, Power, Young, & Bujaki, 1989). Of course, there is rarely a one-to-one match between what an individual prefers and seeks (attitudes) and what one is actually able to do (behavior). This discrepancy is widely studied in social psychology (see discussion of work by Camilleri that follows) and is usually explained as being the result of social constraints on behaviors (e.g., norms, opportunities, discrimination). Nevertheless, there is often a significant positive correlation between acculturation attitudes and behaviors, permitting the use of an overall assessment of individual acculturation strategies.

The centrality of the concept of acculturation strategies can be illustrated by the components of Figure 1.1. At the cultural level, the two groups in contact (whether dominant or nondominant) usually have some notion about what they are attempting to do (e.g., colonial policies, motivations for migration) or what is being done to them. Similarly, the kinds of changes that are likely to occur are influenced by their strategies. At the individual level, both the behavioral changes and acculturative stress phenomena are now known to be a function, at least to some extent, of what people try to do during their acculturation, and the longer term outcomes (both psychological and sociocultural adaptations) often correspond to the strategic goals set by the groups of which they are members.

Conceptualization

Dimensionality. Perhaps the key issue in conceptualizing the process of cultural and psychological acculturation generally (and more specifically acculturation strategies) has been its dimensionality. Does acculturation take place along a single dimension (which is the *unidimensional,* or *unilinear,* view), with groups and individuals only moving over time from one pole (i.e., from their traditional way of living) toward another (e.g., Western, modern, acculturated)? If so, then the measurement of acculturation can be rendered as a single score on such a single dimension and can be properly referred to as the *level,* or *degree,* of acculturation. Alternatively, is acculturation a *multidimensional* or *multilinear* process in which people change on more than one dimension? If so, then measurements must take these other dimensions into account. Of course, if one is referring to acculturation only in the sense of how much contact people have had (i.e., how long people have lived together or the intensity of their relationships), it is possible to use *degree* or *level* to describe it. But, if one is referring to the cultural and psychological processes and consequences of this contact, I maintain that it is not appropriate to use these terms, which in essence are rooted in the unilinear conception of acculturation.

The dimensionality debate has been under way in psychology for 30 years but goes back to the original formulation in anthropology. In the 1936 statement by Redfield et al., it was noted that assimilation is not the only form of acculturation; there are other ways of going about it. Taking this assertion as a starting point, Berry (1970; Sommerlad & Berry, 1970) first distinguished between *assimilation* and *integration* and later between *separation* and *marginalization* as various ways in which acculturation (both of groups and individuals) could take place. Since then, many others in psychology have developed multidimensional models (e.g., Garcia & Lega, 1979; Padilla, 1980b; Ryder, Alden, & Paulhus, 2000; Sanchez & Fernandez, 1993; Szapocznik, Kurtines, & Fernandez, 1980; Zak, 1973). Similarly in anthropology, Clark, Kaufman, and Pierce (1976) and Teske and Nelson (1974) have described group-level acculturation as more than a unilinear process of assimilation. Despite the current prevalence of multidimensional conceptualizations, in psychology, some researchers still conceptualize and measure individual acculturation in a unilinear way (e.g., Cuellar, Arnold, & Maldonado, 1995; Ghuman, 1991; Landrine & Klonoff, 1994).

What are these multilinear alternatives? In my view, it is essential to make the distinction between orientations toward one's own group and toward other groups (Berry, 1970, 1974, 1980). This distinction is rendered as a relative preference for maintaining one's heritage culture and identity and a relative preference for having contact with and participating in the larger society along with other ethnocultural groups (see Figure 1.2).

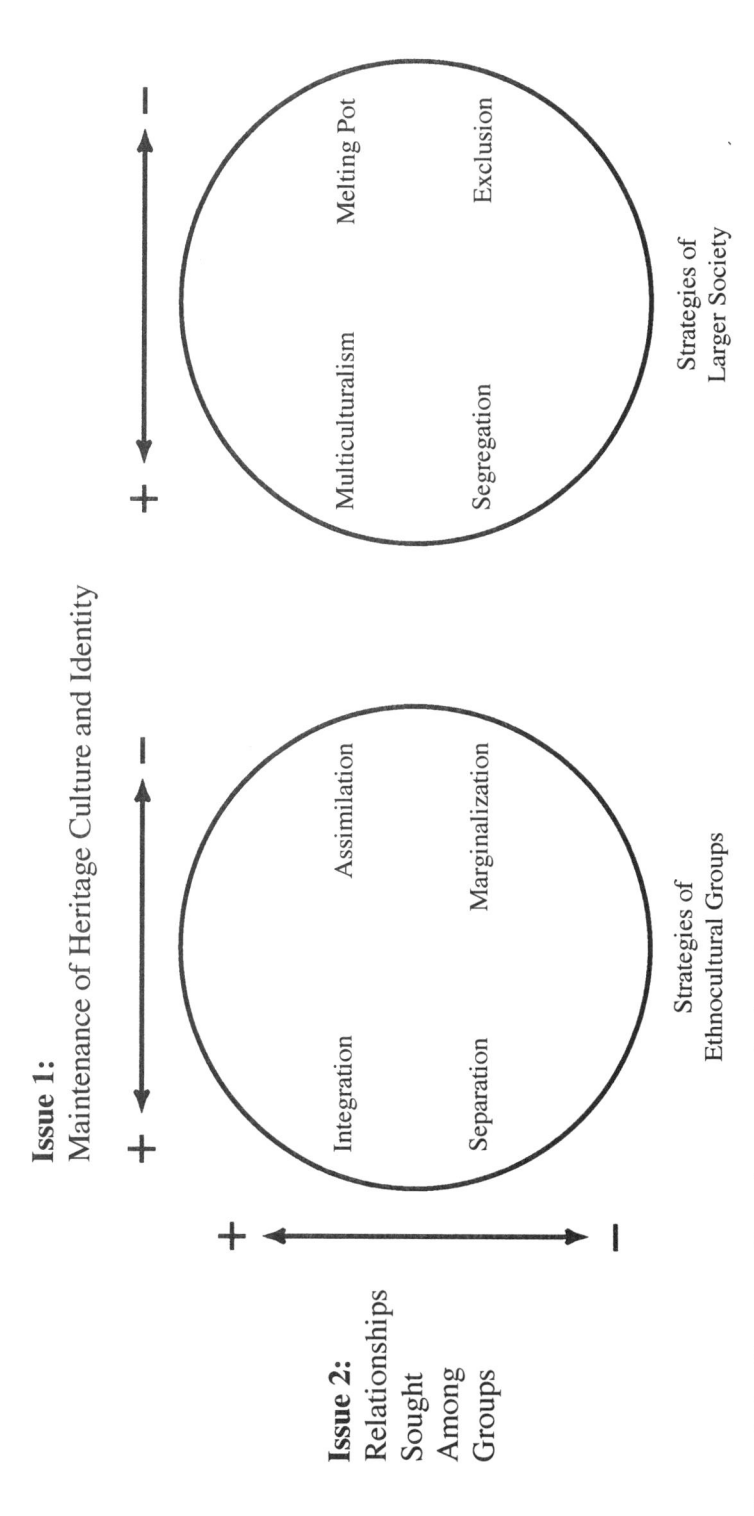

Issue 1:
Maintenance of Heritage Culture and Identity

Issue 2:
Relationships Sought Among Groups

Strategies of Ethnocultural Groups:
- Integration
- Assimilation
- Separation
- Marginalization

Strategies of Larger Society:
- Multiculturalism
- Melting Pot
- Segregation
- Exclusion

Figure 1.2. Four acculturation strategies based on two issues—views of ethnocultural groups (*left*) and of larger society (*right*).

These two issues can be addressed using attitudinal dimensions represented by bipolar arrows. For purposes of presentation, generally positive or negative (*yes* or *no* responses) to these issues intersect to define four acculturation strategies. These strategies have different names depending on which ethnocultural group (dominant or nondominant) is being considered. From the point of view of the nondominant groups (*left*), when individuals do not wish to maintain their cultural identity and seek daily interactions with other cultures, they are using the *assimilation* strategy. In contrast, when individuals place a value on holding on to their original culture and at the same time wish to avoid interacting with others, they are using the *separation* alternative. When people have an interest in maintaining their original culture during daily interactions with other groups, they use the *integration* strategy. In this case, there is some degree of cultural *integrity,* and at the same time they seek, as a member of an ethnocultural group, to participate as an *integral* part of the larger social network. Finally the *marginalization* strategy is used when there is little possibility of or interest in cultural maintenance and little interest in having relationships with others. Although marginalization can be a strategy that people choose as a way of dealing with their acculturative situation, it can also result from failed attempts at assimilation (involving cultural loss) combined with failed attempts at participating in the larger society. Such cases may be due in part to discriminatory attitudes and practices of the dominant group.

This portrayal of acculturation strategies was based on the assumption that nondominant groups and their individual members have the freedom to choose how they want to acculturate. This, of course, is not always the case (Berry, 1974). When the dominant group enforces certain forms of acculturation or constrains the choices of nondominant groups or individuals, then other terms need to be used. Integration can only be freely chosen and successfully pursued by nondominant groups when the dominant society has an open and inclusive orientation toward cultural diversity (Berry, 1991). Thus, a mutual accommodation is required for integration to be attained, involving the acceptance by both groups of the right of all groups to live as culturally different peoples within the civic framework of the larger society. This strategy requires nondominant groups to *adopt* the basic values of the larger society, and at the same time the dominant group must be prepared to *adapt* its national institutions (e.g., education, health, labor) to better meet the needs of all groups now living together in the plural society. Obviously, the integration strategy can be pursued only in societies that are explicitly multicultural and in which certain psychological preconditions are established (Berry & Kalin, 1995): (a) the widespread acceptance by a society of the value of cultural diversity (i.e., the presence of a positive "multicultural ideology"), (b) relatively low levels of prejudice (i.e., minimal ethnocentrism, racism, and discrimination), (c) positive mutual attitudes among ethnocultural groups (i.e., no specific intergroup hatreds), and (d) a sense of attachment to or identification with the larger society by all individuals and groups (Kalin & Berry, 1995).

Just as obvious, integration (and separation) can be pursued only when other members of one's ethnocultural group share in the wish to maintain the group's cultural heritage. In this sense, these two strategies are *collectivistic,* whereas assimilation is more *individualistic* (Lalonde & Cameron, 1993; Moghaddam, 1988). Other constraints on one's choice of acculturation strategy have also been noted. For example, those whose physical features set them apart from the society of settlement (e.g., Koreans in Canada, Turks in Germany) may experience prejudice and discrimination and thus be reluctant to pursue assimilation to avoid being rejected.

These two basic issues were initially approached from the point of view of the nondominant ethnocultural groups only. However, the original anthropological definition clearly established that *both* groups in contact would become acculturated. Hence, in 1974 a third dimension was added: *acculturation expectations* and the powerful role played by the dominant group in influencing the way in which mutual acculturation would take place (Berry, 1974, 1980, 2001). The addition of this third dimension produces a corresponding set of views in the larger society (*right side,* Figure 1.2). In the 1974 version, when assimilation was sought by the nondominant acculturating group, the process was termed the *melting pot,* but when assimilation was demanded by the dominant group, it was called the *pressure cooker.* When separation is forced by the dominant group, it is called *segregation*, and when marginalization is imposed by the dominant group, it is called *ethnocide* (or *exclusion,* according to Bourhis, Moise, Perreault, & Sénécal, 1997). Finally, when diversity is an accepted feature of the larger society as a whole, the process of integration is termed *multiculturalism* (Berry, 1980). Although most contemporary societies are now culturally plural, I prefer to use the term *multicultural* for those societies in which all ethnocultural groups (dominant and nondominant) like it that way rather than attempting to reduce or eliminate their pluralism.

Locus. A classification of the locus of views about acculturation is presented in Table 1.1. This shows six places in which acculturation orientations can be located, using two dimensions. In the right column are the views held by the dominant or larger, society; in the left column are those held by the various ethnocultural groups (who usually are nondominant in the intercultural relationship). There are three levels: The most encompassing category (the national or ethnocultural groups) is at the top and is followed by the least encompassing (the individual). At the bottom of

Table 1.1. Use of Acculturation Strategies in Ethnocultural Groups and the Larger Society

Levels	Nondominant ethnocultural groups	Dominant larger society
National	Group goals	National policies
Individual	Acculturation strategies	Multicultural ideology
Institutional	Diversity and equity	Uniform or plural

the scheme are various social groupings called *institutions,* which can be governmental agencies, educational or health systems, or workplaces. The first level includes national policies and the stated goals of particular ethnocultural groups within the plural society. For example, the Canadian policy of multiculturalism corresponds to the integration strategy (Berry, 1984b) by which both heritage cultural maintenance and full participation in the larger society are promoted. In contrast, the United States has been more assimilationist[1] (Taylor & Lambert, 1996).

At the individual level, one can measure the general multicultural ideology in the overall population or the attitudes that individuals have toward these four strategies. At the institutional level, competing visions rooted in these alternative intercultural strategies confront and even conflict with each other daily. Most frequently, nondominant ethnocultural groups seek the joint goals of diversity and equity. This involves (a) the recognition of the group's cultural uniqueness and specific needs and (b) having their group receive the same level of understanding, acceptance, and support as those of the dominant groups. The dominant society, however, may often prefer more uniform programs and standards (based on their own cultural views) in such core institutions as education, health, justice, and defense. The goals of diversity and equity correspond closely to the integration strategy (combining cultural maintenance with inclusive participation), whereas the push for uniformity resembles the assimilation approach (see Berry, 1996).

With the use of this framework, comparisons can be made between individuals and their groups and between nondominant peoples and the larger society within which they are acculturating. The ideologies and policies of the dominant group constitute an important element of ethnic relations research (Berry, Kalin, & Taylor, 1977; Bourhis et al., 1997; Montreuil & Bourhis, 2001), whereas preferences of nondominant peoples are a core feature in understanding the process of acculturation in nondominant groups (Berry et al., 1989). Inconsistencies and conflicts among these various acculturation preferences are some sources of difficulty for acculturating individuals. Generally, when acculturation experiences cause problems for acculturating individuals, it results in the phenomenon of *acculturative stress.*

Views held by dominant groups were first studied in 1974 by Berry, Kalin, and Taylor (1977). In a national survey in Canada, the attitudes of the general population were sought about how they thought nondominant groups should acculturate. In that study, integration views were loaded positively on a scale called *multicultural ideology,* whereas assimilation and segregation items were loaded negatively. In another study concerned with the acculturation of aboriginal peoples (Berry, 1975), views about how they should acculturate (i.e., *acculturation expectations*) were assessed us-

---

[1]As a reminder: "The whole continent of North America appears to be destined by Divine Providence to be peopled by one nation, speaking one language, professing one general system of religious and political principles, and accustomed to one general tenor of social usages and customs" (Quincy Adams in 1811). Of course, my own advocacy of Integration may well be due to my living and working in an explicitly multicultural society.

ing the four alternatives. This interest in the views of the dominant society has recently come to the fore and may well become a major theme in acculturation research (e.g., Berry & Kalin, 1995; Bourhis et al., 1997; Piontkowski, Florack, & Hoelker, 2000).

Focus. In much acculturation research using the two dimensions, the attitude objects analyzed are (a) the maintenance of one's own culture and (b) seeking contact and participation with other cultural groups (see Figure 1.2). This basic in-group/out-group distinction can be formulated in many ways. For example, attitudes dealing with participation in the larger society can be rephrased with respect to a preference for *adopting* the culture rather than in terms of *participating* in the culture of the larger society. For example, Dona and Berry (1994) used two scales to assess Latin American refugees in Toronto; the scales included items expressing preference for one's heritage culture and items expressing preference for Canadian national culture. Similarly, Berry and Sabatier (1996) have used two cultural preference scales among Greek, Haitian, Italian, and Vietnamese adolescents in Montreal. There is probably a strong empirical similarity between these two ways of seeking out-group attitudes; however, their relationship has not been tested empirically in a common study.

Many other researchers have proposed two or more dimensions of acculturation, some theoretically based and some empirically derived. Perhaps the best known is that of Padilla (1980b), who used the two dimensions of cultural awareness and ethnic loyalty. The first dimension involves knowledge about one's heritage culture and the dominant culture (e.g., values, language, ways of living), whereas the second refers to a relative preference for the heritage or that of the dominant culture. In essence the first seems to be primarily cognitive in nature, whereas the second is more affective. Although this is clearly a bidimensional model, it is just as clear that the two dimensions are not the same as those in my own two-dimensional framework.

A parallel focus has been on the concept of cultural or ethnic identity. Instead of seeking attitudes toward aspects of the two groups, there is a tradition of seeking to discover how one self-categorizes or how strongly one feels attached to either or both groups (e.g., Phinney, 1990). Whether in national surveys (e.g., Kalin & Berry, 1995) or with specific cultural groups (e.g., Berry, 1999), people's cultural orientations have been measured through their identity preferences. *Parallel* refers to the similar use of bidimensional conceptualizations; that is, one can identify with one, the other, both, or neither of the groups in contact.

An example of a two-dimensional identity model is that of Camilleri (1990, 1991). He distinguished two aspects of identity: the *ontological function* (i.e., the constructing of our ideal, or desired, self) and the *pragmatic function* (i.e., the instrumental or utilitarian reality of who a person can actually be). During acculturation in intercultural contact settings (particularly of North Africans in France, where he has done most of his work), individuals attempt to achieve a coherent sense of who they are by balancing the ideal with the realistic constraints of living in a society that is substantially prejudiced against them. In a series of studies (reviewed by Camilleri & Malewska-Peyre, 1997), evidence is presented to support the existence of these two dimensions and of the *identity strategies* used to achieve coherence. Once again, these two dimensions resemble but are not identical to those proposed by Berry (1980) and Padilla (1980b).

Assessment. My basic conceptualization of acculturation strategies is that there are two dimensions, which are indicated by the two bidirectional arrows in Figure 1.2. Crossing the two dimensions creates an "attitude space" (the circles in Figure 1.2) in which individual preferences can be located. How to locate a person in this space is a measurement issue and involves two choices among measurement alternatives: (a) to assess the two underlying issues or dimensions themselves (using a single-item scale or multiple-item scales for "own group" and "other group" preference) or (b) to assess the four sectors in this space (using single or multiple items for each attitude: assimilation, integration, separation, and marginalization).

Before discussing each method, it is important to establish two points: first, is the question of where the two issues came from. In keeping with usual practice in cross-cultural research (e.g., Munroe & Munroe, 1997), ethnographic work is carried out prior to psychometric work. In this case, preliminary qualitative work in each cultural community has almost always uncovered the two issues (dealing with orientations toward cultural maintenance, and intercultural contact) that underlie the acculturation strategies framework. The finding of these two issues resulted from emic views of their acculturative situation among Australian Aborigines (Sommerlad & Berry, 1970) and has consistently emerged in research with aboriginal peoples in Canada (Berry, 1976, 1999), as well as in studies in India (Mishra, Sinha, & Berry, 1996) and Africa (Berry et al., 1986). These two issues have also appeared over and over again among immigrant, refugee, sojourner, and ethnocultural populations in many parts of the world (Berry & Sam, 1997). During the course of this research, these two issues have moved from being an emic for only one group to being an emic for other groups and eventually to being a derived etic (perhaps a universal concept) for many groups during their intercultural contact.

Second, the conceptualization of these strategies was not intended to categorize individuals. Rather, the goal was to discover where individuals are located in acculturation space—either on the two underlying dimensions or with respect to their relative preferences for the four strategies. Although many psychologists (usually clinicians or educators) do categorize individuals, I believe this practice loses valuable information about the complexity of an individual's acculturation situation and pigeonholes a person in a stereotypical way.

The initial operationalization of this conceptualization used four scales, with multiple items for each scale. As outlined in a previous review paper (Berry et al., 1989), the items were constructed to reflect concerns in various acculturation "domains" (e.g., what to eat, what to wear, with whom to interact, where to live) that were identified by informants during the initial ethnographic phase. Typically, items in the pool were generated by informants who were experiencing the process of acculturation. Then other informants, who had been introduced to the four strategies framework, were asked to sort the items according to which strategy they judged the item was measuring (a form of face validation). The four scales were then used with samples of individuals, and scores were calculated (usually following item selection and factor analytic procedures) on each scale for each individual. Means for their particular group were then calculated.

An alternative to crossing the two dimensions to yield four measurable attitudes is to assess preferences along the two dimensions themselves: (a) preference for maintenance of one's own culture and (b) preference for contact and participation with other groups in the larger society (e.g., Berry & Sabatier, 1996; Dona & Berry, 1994). Items are constructed in much the same way, using key informants to identify domains of concern and to suggest item phrasing. Scores on the two dimension scales can also be used in various cross-tabulations: Those high on both dimensions are considered to favor *integration,* those high on one but low on the other to favor either *assimilation* or *separation,* and those low on both to favor *marginalization*. The four scores calculated in this way are less useful in multivariate analyses but are fine for answering questions about differences, such as whether those favoring one strategy over another have lower stress or better adaptation. Whichever method is used, there is limited possibility of creating a "standard" acculturation measure that can be used with every acculturating group. This is because there are many unique features to each acculturation situation, including the varied cultures of the groups in contact and the differing nature of the domains that are issues between them.

When scales are constructed to assess the two dimensions rather than the four strategies, correlational analyses can speak directly to the basic issue raised at the outset: Is acculturation to be conceptualized as unidimensional or as bidimensional? If the two scores were highly negatively correlated, then this would indicate that they could be collapsed into one dimension (ranging from *more traditional* to *more acculturated*). If, on the other hand, interscale correlations were positive or varied across studies, this would indicate that the two dimensions are necessary to allow individuals to be positive on both or some other pattern. The empirical evidence is clear: As proposed in the framework in Figure 1.2 and as expected from the frequent finding of a preference for integration, positive interscale correlations are the most common pattern (e.g., Ryder et al., 2000). Although negative correlations have been found, Nguyen, Messé, and Stollak (1999) noted that they usually account for only a small portion of the variance rather than most of it, which is required for support of the unidimensional concept.

Outcomes

Although integration is typically the most frequently chosen strategy, differences in how people go about their acculturation are evident. Not everyone has the same goals or follows the same path. For example, the analysis by Ho (1995) revealed seven distinct patterns among Hong Kong immigrants to New Zealand (e.g., a path of *"separation* changing to *integration"*). The general framework (see Figure 1.1) includes the possibility for cultural group and individual factors to influence the choice of people's acculturation strategies and thereby the course of their acculturation outcomes.

Arguments and evidence have been presented in the literature about the importance of some group factors. For example, people in voluntary contact are more likely to seek greater participation (i.e., assimilation or integration) than those who are not in voluntary contact, such as refugees (Williams & Berry, 1991). Those whose appearance makes them distinct from the dominant population may be less attracted by assimilation or be kept away by racism and discrimination (Kim & Berry, 1986). Another factor is social ecology and vitality (i.e., sheer numbers of people in the group), which may increase the possibility of (and perhaps preference for) cultural maintenance, leading to integration or even separation strategies. Finally (see Table 1.1), national policies in the larger society may provide encouragement for one or the other strategy, whereas the positive or negative multicultural ideology encountered in daily interactions with members of the dominant society may reinforce certain preferences.

Many of these group-level factors have been examined in a comprehensive way by Moise and Bourhis (1997). They found that features of the contact situation (especially the attitudes encountered) and the "vitality" of one's cultural group were important predictors of which acculturation strategy was adopted. For example, the vitality of one's group combined with minimal discrimination against one's group predicted stronger attitudes toward integration. Conversely, a weak sense of collective efficacy for one's own group and a weak in-group network predicted a stronger preference for assimilation. What is emerging from all these studies is that acculturation strategies are not adopted at random. The various preferences are part of a network of relationships with measurable features of one's group and the group's situation in relation to other groups. It is thus possible to claim that the acculturation strategies are an outcome of contextual factors rather than just a correlate because individuals have little influence over many of these group-level factors.

Individual (psychological) factors are also clearly linked to one's acculturation strategies. Most evident are other indicators of how one is oriented to the two cultures in contact (such as one's cultural identity and perceived similarity) and intercultural experiences (such as actual contact and discrimination). With respect to cultural identity (Berry & Sabatier, 1996; Moise & Bourhis, 1997; Piontkowski et al., 2000), the expected pattern of relationships holds. That is, an *ethnic and cultural* identity is related to a preference for separation, a *national* identity predicts assimilation, a combination of both identities (e.g., as in a hyphenated identity such as Greek-Canadian) predicts integration, and no clear identity predicts marginalization.

In the vast literature on acculturation, there has been a central concern with two psychological acculturation outcomes that begin early in the process (behavioral changes and acculturative stress) and with two specific forms of longer term adaptation (psychological and sociocultural). With respect to the early consequences (see Figure 1.1), when acculturation experiences are judged to pose no problems for an individual, the changes are likely to be rather easy, and the behavioral changes follow smoothly. This process encompasses three subprocesses: *culture shedding, culture learning,* and *culture conflict* (Berry, 1992). The first two processes involve the selective, accidental, or deliberate loss of behaviors and their replacement by behaviors that allow the individual a better fit with the society of settlement. This process is usually called *adjustment* (Ward & Kennedy, 1993a), because virtually all the adaptive changes take place in the acculturating individual, with few changes occurring among members of the larger society. Most of these adjustments are typically made with minimal difficulty, in keeping with the appraisal of the acculturation experiences as nonproblematic. However, some degree of conflict may occur, which is usually resolved by the acculturating person yielding to the behavioral norms of the dominant group. In this latter case, assimilation is the most likely outcome.

When greater levels of conflict develop and the experiences are judged to be problematic but controllable and surmountable, then the acculturative stress paradigm is the appropriate conceptualization (Berry, Kim, Minde, & Mok, 1987). In this case, individuals understand that they are facing problems resulting from intercultural contact that cannot be dealt with easily or quickly by simply adjusting or assimilating to them. Drawing on the broader stress and adaptation paradigms (e.g., Lazarus & Folkman, 1984), this approach advocates studying the process of how individuals deal with acculturative problems when they first encounter them and over time. In this sense, acculturative stress is a stress reaction to challenging life events that are rooted in the experience of acculturation.

Relating these two concepts to acculturation strategies, some consistent empirical findings allow for the following generalizations (Berry, 1997; Berry & Sam, 1997). For behavioral changes, the fewest changes result from the separation strategy, and most result from the assimilation strategy. Integration involves the selective adoption of new behaviors from the larger society and retention of valued features of one's heritage culture. Marginalization is often associated with major heritage culture loss and the appearance of many dysfunctional and deviant behaviors (e.g., delinquency and substance and familial abuse). For acculturative stress, there is a clear picture that the pursuit of integration is the least stressful (at least when integration is accommodated by the larger society), whereas marginalization is the most stressful. Between these two extremes are the assimilation and separation strategies, with sometimes one and sometimes the other being the less stressful. This pattern of findings holds for various indicators of mental health (Berry & Kim, 1988; Schmitz, 1992) and self-esteem (Phinney, Chavira, & Williamson, 1992).

Individuals engage in the appraisal of these experiences and behavioral changes. When they are appraised as challenging, some basic coping mechanisms are activated. Lazarus and Folkman (1984) identified two major coping functions: problem-focused coping (attempting to change or solve the problem) and emotion-focused coping (attempting to regulate the emotions associated with the problem). More recently, Endler and Parker (1990) identified a third coping strategy: avoidance-oriented coping. It is not yet clear how the first two coping strategies relate to acculturation strategies because both forms of coping are likely to be involved in assimilation and integration. However, the third (avoidance) closely resembles the separation strategy and possibly the marginalization strategy.

One key distinction, made by Diaz-Guerrero (1979), is between active and passive coping. Active copers seek to alter the situation and hence may be similar to problem-focused copers. They may have only limited success if the problem originates in the dominant society, especially if the dominant group has little interest in accommodating the needs of acculturating groups or individuals. Passive coping reflects patience and self-modification and resembles the assimilation acculturation strategy. These strategies are likely to be successful only if the dominant society has positive attitudes toward and is willing to accept members of the acculturating groups. If attitudes are hostile, the passive coping strategy may well lead to unacceptable levels of exclusion or domination.

As a result of attempts to cope with these acculturation changes, some long-term adaptations may be achieved (*right side,* Figure 1.1). As mentioned previously, *adaptations* are the relatively stable changes that take place as an individual or group responds to external demands. Moreover, adaptation may or may not improve the fit between individuals and their environments, thus, it is not a term that necessarily implies that individuals or groups change to become more like their environments (i.e., adjustment by way of assimilation). Adaptation may involve resistance and attempts to change the environment or to move away from it altogether (i.e., by separation). In this context, adaptation is an outcome that may or may not be positive in valence (i.e., meaning only well adapted). This bipolar sense of the concept of adaptation is used in the framework in Figure 1.1, in which long-term adaptation to acculturation is highly variable, ranging from well to poorly adapted and varying from a situation in which individuals can manage their new lives well to a situation in which they are unable to function in their new society.

Adaptation is also multifaceted. The initial distinction between psychological and sociocultural adaptation was proposed and validated by Ward and colleagues (Searle & Ward, 1990; Ward, 1996; Ward & Kennedy, 1993a). *Psychological* adaptation largely involves one's psychological and physical well-being (Schmitz, 1992), whereas *sociocultural* adaptation refers to how well an acculturating individual is able to manage daily life in the new cultural context. Although conceptually distinct, the two types of adaptation are empirically related to some extent. (Correlations between the two measures are typically in the +.4 to +.5 range.) However, they are also empirically distinct in the sense that they usually have different time courses and different experiential predictors. Psychological problems often increase soon after contact and are followed by a general (but variable) decrease over time. Sociocultural adaptation, however, typically has a linear improvement with time. Analyses of the factors affecting adaptation reveal a generally consistent pattern. Good psychological adaptation is predicted by personality variables, life change events, and social support, whereas good sociocultural adaptation is predicted by cultural knowledge, degree of contact, and positive intergroup attitudes (Ward, 1996). Both aspects of adaptation are usually predicted by the successful pursuit of the integration acculturation strategy and minimal cultural distance (Ward & Kennedy, 1993b; Ward, 1996). A third aspect of adaptation has been suggested: economic adaptation (Aycan & Berry, 1996). The authors showed that psychological and sociocultural adaptation was predicted by a similar set of variables as those in Ward's studies, whereas economic adaptation was predicted by migration motivation, perception of relative deprivation, and status loss on first entry into the work world.

Research relating adaptation to acculturation strategies allows for some additional generalizations (Berry, 1997; Ward, 1996). For all three forms of adaptation, those who pursue and accomplish integration appear to be better adapted, whereas those who are marginalized are the least well adapted. Again, the assimilation and separation strategies are associated with intermediate adaptation outcomes. Although there are occasional variations on this pattern, it is remarkably consistent and parallels the generalization regarding acculturative stress presented previously.

Conclusion

Before turning to some more positive conclusions, it is important to review some dangers that have been either explicit or implicit in this overview. First, there is the danger that researchers who view acculturation solely in terms of broad social categories (e.g., "minorities," "Asians") could overlook the specific realities of particular ethnocultural groups and the large variations across groups and across individuals within them. Second, ethnographic research at the level of the groups in contact is essential for understanding the contexts in which people operate. Without this research, there is the danger that researchers may simply name a group and assume that everyone knows all its important cultural and contextual features, thereby inviting our stereotypes to come into play. Third, research at the level of the individual is also essential. Although this is the type of research psychologists usually do best, in my view it is often done poorly when working with individuals who are experiencing acculturation.

The last issue—research on the individual—has two aspects. First, there is widespread evidence that most people who have experienced acculturation actually do survive! They are not destroyed or substantially diminished by it; rather, they find opportunities and achieve their goals, sometimes goals that are beyond what they initially imagined (e.g., Beiser, 2000). The tendency to "pathologize" the acculturation process and outcomes may be partly due to the history of acculturation's study in psychiatry and in clinical psychology. Second, researchers often presume to know what acculturating individuals want and to impose their own ideologies rather than learn about culturally rooted individual preferences and differences. One key concept (but certainly not the only one) involved in understanding this variability was emphasized in this chapter: acculturation strategies. Why this danger (i.e., presuming people's desires and imposing one's own ideologies) exists may be due to the usual problem of ethnocentrism. However, it is easy to suspect that it may be rooted in a more fundamental issue, on in which researchers simply adopt the dominant ideology of their national society. Indeed, an important question is whether the prevalence of unidimensional and assimilationist orientations to research on acculturation is rooted in long-standing assumptions about the basic nature of the history and destiny of a country.

As mentioned previously, the concept of acculturation strategies can be used in many ways, specifically when one attempts to understand national, institutional, and individual orientations in dominant and nondominant cultural groups (see Table 1.1). The generalizations that have been made in this chapter on the basis of a wide range of empirical findings allow researchers to propose that public policies and programs seeking to improve intercultural relationships should emphasize the integration approach to acculturation. This is equally true for national policies, institutional arrangements, and the goals of ethnocultural groups, and it is also true for individuals in the larger society as well as members of nondominant acculturating groups.

In Canada, the integrationist perspective has become legislated in a multiculturalism policy that encourages and supports the maintenance of valued features of all cultures for those who would like to retain them, and at the same time supports full participation of all ethnocultural groups in the evolving institutions of the larger society[2] (Berry, 1984b; Berry & Kalin, 1995). There is widespread public support for this vision of how to live together in a plural society (Berry & Kalin, 1995), and there appear to be no serious contradictions between ethnic (particular) and civic (national) identities (Kalin & Berry, 1995). Whether or not this pattern exists in all plural societies is a matter of local conceptualizing and empirical research in the respective societies. What seems certain is that diversity and the resultant acculturation are here to stay. Finding a way to accommodate each other poses a challenge to and an opportunity for social and cross-cultural psychologists everywhere (Berry & Kalin, 1999). Diversity is a fact of contemporary life; whether it is the "spice of life" or a source of irritation is probably the central question that confronts everyone, citizens and scientists alike.

References

Aycan, Z., & Berry, J. W. (1996). Impact of employment related experiences on immigrants' adaptation to Canada. *Canadian Journal of Behavioural Science, 28,* 240–251.

---

[2]It is important to note that multicultural policies actually permit any preference on the two dimensions of Figure 1.2. There is no one prescribed way to live in a multicultural society. In contrast, all other policy options demand a "yes" or "no" orientation to either or both issues.

Beiser, M. (2000). *Strangers at the gate.* Toronto: University of Toronto Press.
Berry, J. W. (1970). Marginality, stress, and ethnic identification in an acculturated Aboriginal community. *Journal of Cross-Cultural Psychology, 1,* 239–252.
Berry, J. W. (1974). Psychological aspects of cultural pluralism: Unity and identity reconsidered. *Topics in Culture Learning, 2,* 17–22.
Berry, J. W. (1975). Amerindian attitudes toward acculturation: Multicultural policy and reality in Canada. *Journal of Institute of Social Research, 1,* 47–58.
Berry, J. W. (1976). *Human ecology and cognitive style: Comparative studies in cultural and psychological adaptation.* New York: Sage/Halsted.
Berry, J. W. (1980). Acculturation as varieties of adaptation. In A. Padilla (Ed.), *Acculturation: Theory, models, and findings* (pp. 9–25). Boulder, CO: Westview.
Berry, J. W. (1984a). Cultural relations in plural societies. In M. Brewer & N. Miller (Eds.), *Groups in contact* (pp. 11–27). New York: Academic Press.
Berry, J. W. (1984b). Multicultural policy in Canada: A social psychological analysis. *Canadian Journal of Behavioural Science, 16,* 353–370.
Berry, J. W. (1990). Psychology of acculturation. In J. Berman (Ed.), *Cross-cultural perspectives: Nebraska symposium on motivation* (pp. 201–234). Lincoln: University of Nebraska Press.
Berry, J. W. (1991). Understanding and managing multiculturalism. *Journal of Psychology and Developing Societies, 3,* 17–49.
Berry, J. W. (1992). Acculturation and adaptation in a new society. *International Migration, 30,* 69–85.
Berry, J. W. (1996). Individual and group relations in plural societies. In C. Granrose & S. Oskamp (Eds.), *Cross-cultural workgroups* (pp. 17–35). Thousand Oaks, CA: Sage.
Berry, J. W. (1997). Immigration, acculturation, and adaptation. *Applied Psychology, 46,* 5–68.
Berry, J. W. (1999). Aboriginal cultural identity. *Canadian Journal of Native Studies, 19,* 1–36.
Berry, J. W. (2001). A psychology of immigration. *Journal of Social Issues, 57,* 615–631.
Berry, J. W., & Kalin, R. (1995). Multicultural and ethnic attitudes in Canada. *Canadian Journal of Behavioural Science, 27,* 310–320.
Berry, J. W., & Kalin, R. (1999). Multicultural policy and social psychology: The Canadian experience. In S. Renshon & J. Duckitt (Eds.), *Political psychology in cross-cultural perspective* (pp. 263–284). New York: Macmillan.
Berry, J. W., Kalin, R., & Taylor, D. (1977). *Multiculturalism and ethnic attitudes in Canada.* Ottawa: Supply & Services.
Berry, J. W., & Kim, U. (1988). Acculturation and mental health. In P. Dasen, J. W. Berry, & N. Sartorius (Eds.), *Health and cross-cultural psychology* (pp. 207–236). Newbury Park, CA: Sage.
Berry, J. W., Kim, U., Minde, T., & Mok. D. (1987). Comparative studies of acculturative stress. *International Migration Review, 21,* 491–511.
Berry, J. W., Kim, U., Power, S., Young, M., & Bujaki, M. (1989). Acculturation attitudes in plural societies. *Applied Psychology, 38,* 185–206.
Berry, J. W., Poortinga, Y. H., Segall, M. H., & Dasen, P. R. (2002). *Cross-cultural psychology: Research and applications* (2nd ed.). New York: Cambridge University Press.
Berry, J. W., & Sabatier, C. (1996, July). *Comparative study of acculturation of four groups of second generation youth in Montreal.* Paper presented at the biennial meeting of the International Association for Cross-Cultural Psychology Congress, Montreal.
Berry, J. W., & Sam, D. (1997). Acculturation and adaptation. In J. W. Berry, M. H. Segall, & C. Kagitcibasi (Eds.), *Handbook of cross-cultural psychology: Vol. 3. Social behavior and applications* (pp. 291–326). Boston: Allyn & Bacon.
Berry, J. W., Trimble, J., & Olmedo, E. (1986). The assessment of acculturation. In W. J. Lonner & J. W. Berry (Eds.), *Field methods in cross-cultural research* (pp. 291–324). Newbury Park, CA: Sage.
Birman, D. (1994). Acculturation and human diversity in a multicultural society. In E. Trickett, R. Watts, & D. Birman (Eds.), *Human diversity* (pp. 261–284). San Francisco, CA: Jossey-Bass.
Bourhis, R., Moise, C., Perreault, S., & Sénécal, S. (1997). Towards an interactive accultur-

ation model: A social psychological approach. *International Journal of Psychology, 32,* 369-386.

Camilleri, C. (1990). Identité et gestion de la disparité culturelle: Essai d'une typologie [Identity and management of cultural difference: Towards a typology]. In C. Camilleri, H. Malewska-Peyre, & A. Vasquez (Eds.), *Stratégies identitaires* (pp. 85-110). Paris: Presses Universitaires de France.

Camilleri, C. (1991). La construction identitaire: Essai d'une vision d'ensemble [Identity and construction: Towards a vision of living together]. *Les Cahiers Internationaux de Psychologie Sociale, 9-10,* 91-104.

Camilleri, C., & Malewska-Peyre, H. (1997). Socialization and identity strategies. In J. W. Berry, P. R. Dasen, & T. R. Saraswathi (Eds.), *Handbook of cross-cultural psychology: Vol. 2. Basic processes and human development* (pp. 41-67). Boston: Allyn & Bacon.

Clark, M., Kaufman, S., & Pierce, R. (1976). Explorations of acculturation. *Human Organization, 35,* 231-238.

Cuellar, I., Arnold, B., & Maldonado, R. (1995). Acculturation rating scale for Mexican Americans—II: A revision of the original ARSMA scale. *Hispanic Journal of Behavioral Sciences, 17,* 275-304.

Diaz-Guerrero, R. (1979). The development of coping style. *Human Development, 22,* 320-331.

Dona, G., & Berry, J. W. (1994). Acculturation attitudes and acculturative stress of Central American refugees in Canada. *International Journal of Psychology, 29,* 57-70.

Endler, N., & Parker, J. (1990). Multidimensional assessment of coping. *Journal of Personality and Social Psychology, 58,* 844-854.

Garcia, M., & Lega, L. (1979). Development of a Cuban ethnic identity questionnaire. *Hispanic Journal of Behavioral Sciences, 1,* 247-261.

Ghuman, P. A. S. (1991). Best or worst of two worlds? A study of Asian adolescents. *Educational Review, 33,* 121-132.

Graves, T. (1967). Psychological acculturation in a tri-ethnic community. *South-Western Journal of Anthropology, 23,* 337-350.

Hallowell, A. I. (1945). Sociopsychological aspects of acculturation. In R. Linton (Ed.), *The science of man in the world crisis* (pp. 310-332). New York: Columbia University Press.

Ho, E. (1995). Chinese or New Zealander? Differential paths of adaptation of Chinese Adolescent immigrants in New Zealand. *New Zealand Population Review, 21,* 27-49.

Kalin, R., & Berry, J. W. (1995). Ethnic and civic self-identity in Canada. *Canadian Ethnic Studies, 27,* 1-15.

Kim, U., & Berry, J. W. (1986). Predictors of acculturative stress among Korean immigrants in Toronto. In L. Ekstrand (Ed.), *Ethnic minorities and immigrants* (pp. 159-170). Lisse, The Netherlands: Swets & Zeitlinger.

Lalonde, R., & Cameron, J. (1993). An intergroup perspective on immigrant acculturation with a focus on collective strategies. *International Journal of Psychology, 28,* 57-74.

Landrine, H., & Klonoff, E. (1994). The African-American acculturation scale. *Journal of Black Psychology, 20,* 104-127.

Lazarus, R. S., & Folkman, S. (1984). *Stress, appraisal, and coping.* New York: Springer.

Liebkind, K. (2000). Acculturation. In R. Brown & S. Gaertner (Eds.), *Blackwell handbook of social psychology: Vol 4. Intergroup processes* (pp. 386-404). Oxford, England: Blackwell.

Mishra, R. C., Sinha, D., & Berry, J. W. (1996). *Ecology, acculturation, and psychological adaptation.* New Delhi: Sage.

Moghaddam, F. M. (1988). Individualistic and collective integration strategies among immigrants. In J. W. Berry & R. C. Annis (Eds.), *Ethnic psychology* (pp. 69-79). Amsterdam: Swets & Zeitlinger.

Moise, C., & Bourhis, R. (1997, November). *Correlates of acculturation orientations of Haitian and West Indian Immigrants in Montreal.* Paper presented at the conference of the Canadian Ethnic Studies Association, Montreal.

Montreuil, A., & Bourhis, R. (2001). Majority acculturation orientations toward "valued" and "devalued" immigrants. *Journal of Cross-Cultural Psychology, 32,* 698-719.

Munroe, R. L., & Munroe, R. H. (1997). A comparative anthropological perspective. In J. W.

Berry, Y. Poortinga, & J. Pandey (Eds.), *Handbook of cross-cultural psychology: Vol. 1. Theory and method* (pp. 171–214). Boston: Allyn & Bacon.

Nguyen, H. H., Messé, L., & Stollak, G. (1999). Toward a more complex understanding of acculturation and adjustment. *Journal of Cross-Cultural Psychology*, 30, 5–31.

Padilla, A. (Ed.). (1980a). *Acculturation: Theory, models, and some new findings*. Boulder, CO: Westview.

Padilla, A. (1980b). The role of cultural awareness and ethnic loyalty in acculturation. In A. Padilla (Ed.), *Acculturation* (pp. 47–84). Boulder, CO: Westview.

Phinney, J. (1990). Ethnic identity in adolescents and adults: A review of research. *Psychological Bulletin*, 108, 499–514.

Phinney, J., Chavira, V., & Williamson, L. (1992). Acculturation attitudes and self-esteem among school and college students. *Youth and Society*, 23, 299–312.

Piontkowski, U., Florack, A., & Hoelker, P. (2000). Predicting acculturation attitudes of dominant and non-dominant groups. *International Journal of Intercultural Relations*, 24, 1–26.

Redfield, R., Linton, R., & Herskovits, M. (1936). Memorandum on the study of acculturation. *American Anthropologist*, 38, 149–152.

Ryder, A., Alden, L., & Paulhus, D. (2000). Is acculturation unidimensional or bidimensional? *Journal of Personality and Social Psychology*, 79, 49–65.

Sanchez, J., & Fernandez, D. (1993). Acculturative stress among Hispanics: A bidimensional model of ethnic identification. *Journal of Applied Social Psychology*, 23, 654–668.

Schmitz, P. (1992). Acculturation styles and health. In S. Iwawaki, Y. Kashima, & K. Leung (Eds.), *Innovations in cross-cultural psychology* (pp. 360–370). Amsterdam: Swets & Zeitlinger.

Searle, W., & Ward, C. (1990). The prediction of psychological and sociocultural adjustment during cross-cultural transitions. *International Journal of Intercultural Relations*, 14, 449–464.

Segall, M. H., Dasen, P. R., Berry, J. W., & Poortinga, Y. H. (1999). *Human behavior in global perspective* (2nd ed.). Boston: Allyn & Bacon.

Social Science Research Council. (1954). Acculturation: An exploratory formulation. *American Anthropologist*, 56, 973–1002.

Sommerlad, E., & Berry, J. W. (1970). The role of ethnic identification in distinguishing between attitudes towards assimilation and integration. *Human Relations*, 23, 23–29.

Szapocznik, J., Kurtines, W., & Fernandez, T. (1980). Bicultural involvement and adjustment in Hispanic American youths. *International Journal of Intercultural Relations*, 4, 353–365.

Taylor, D. M., & Lambert, W. E. (1996). The meaning of multiculturalism in a culturally diverse urban American area. *Journal of Psychology*, 136, 727–740.

Teske, R., & Nelson, B. (1974). Acculturation and assimilation: A clarification. *American Ethnologist*, 1, 351–368.

Ward, C. (1996). Acculturation. In D. Landis & R. Bhagat (Eds.), *Handbook of intercultural training* (2nd ed., pp. 124–147). Newbury Park, CA: Sage.

Ward, C., & Kennedy, A. (1993a). Psychological and sociocultural adjustment during cross-cultural transitions: A comparison of secondary students overseas and at home. *International Journal of Psychology*, 28, 129–147.

Ward, C., & Kennedy, A. (1993b). Where's the "culture" in cross-cultural transition? Comparative studies of sojourner adjustment. *Journal of Cross-Cultural Psychology*, 24, 221–249.

Williams, C., & Berry, J. W. (1991). Primary prevention of acculturative stress among refugees. *American Psychologist*, 46, 632–641.

Zak, I. (1973). Dimensions of Jewish-American identity. *Psychological Reports*, 33, 891–900.

2

Major Approaches to the Measurement of Acculturation Among Ethnic Minority Populations: A Content Analysis and an Alternative Empirical Strategy

Nolan Zane and Winnie Mak

Acculturation constitutes one of the most important individual difference variables in the study of ethnic minority populations. Acculturation involves the changes that result from sustained contact between two distinct cultures (Berry, Trimble, & Olmedo, 1986). Psychologically, acculturation reflects the extent to which individuals learn the values, behaviors, lifestyles, and language of the host culture. Ethnic minorities have great social, economic, and political pressure to adjust to the traditions and lifestyle norms of White American culture. Consequently, it is not surprising that acculturation is often involved in the mental health issues of ethnic minorities. Important individual differences in acculturation have been associated with the willingness to use counseling or see a counselor (Atkinson & Gim, 1989; Gim, Atkinson, & Whiteley, 1990), personality variables (Sue & Kirk, 1972), educational achievement (Padilla, 1980), attitudes toward mental health (Atkinson & Gim, 1989), and the credibility of a counselor (Atkinson & Matsushita, 1991; Gim, Atkinson, & Kim, 1991).

Given the importance of acculturation to the psychological study of ethnic minority issues, extensive efforts have been made to operationalize and assess the acculturation level among ethnic minority individuals. Ethnic minority–based research has developed numerous measures to assess individual differences with respect to acculturation to White American culture. Primarily self-report in nature, these measures have assessed behaviors as well as attitudes related to acculturation. The behavioral and attitudinal domains have included language use, preference, and proficiency; social affiliation; daily living habits; cultural traditions and cus-

---

This study was supported in part by the National Research Center on Asian American Mental Health (National Institute of Mental Health Grant MH 59616).

toms; communication styles; perceived prejudice and discrimination; family socialization; cultural knowledge and beliefs; cultural values; and cultural identification, pride, and acceptance. However, these measures also reflect the wide range of methods that investigators have used to assess acculturation. Notwithstanding the widespread use that some of these measures have enjoyed, it has often been unclear to what extent these measures have content validity—namely, the extent to which a measure adequately samples the behavior of interest. Some of this variation can be attributed to the lack of consensus in the field about which behavioral and attitudinal domains are directly associated with acculturative change. Needless to say, this would not be a problem if the domains were concordant such that individual variation in one domain directly covaried with change in other domains. However, Berry (1980) noted that the acculturative process and its effects on various aspects of behaviors and attitudes can vary greatly among different people.

In the past 2 decades, acculturation has become recognized as a major explanatory variable in the study of the psychological issues of ethnic minorities. Thus, it seems wise to more closely examine the content validity of the major measures that have been used to operationalize this important construct. This analysis should be informative in several ways. First, by studying the variation in domains assessed by different measures, an assessment can be made of the extent to which studies can converge in terms of investigating the same construct. Second, a content analysis of these measures may clarify the pattern of findings among studies of acculturation. Finally, the assessment of content validity can identify measures that may be more suited to assessing certain types of acculturation.

This analysis examines the various approaches to conceptualizing and operationalizing acculturation, particularly with respect to the study of immigrant ethnic minority populations. First, the various conceptual models that often guide the development of acculturation measures are presented. Second, content analyses are conducted on the most commonly used acculturation measures to determine which specific aspects of acculturation are being operationalized in various studies. Finally, an alternative approach to the study of acculturation is proposed based on assessing single psychological elements such as culturally based values. A case example of research that focuses on one such value orientation, loss of face, is presented to demonstrate the potential utility of this approach for studying acculturation among Asian Americans.

Approaches to the Assessment of Acculturation

Approaches to the assessment of acculturation among ethnic minorities have differed in numerous ways. First, investigators have varied in their sampling of the domains of psychosocial functioning that change with acculturation (e.g., language use, social affiliations). Depending on the investigator, one particular area of functioning may be emphasized. Second, approaches can vary in the assumptions made about change parameters that specify how ethnic minority group members can relate to their culture of origin and host culture. Some measurement approaches have assumed more of a bipolar type of adaptation. It is assumed that as people become more acculturated to the host White American society, the attachment to their culture of origin (i.e., the culture of their own ethnic group) simultaneously weakens. In contrast, other measures have allowed for the possibility that acculturation (to White American culture) and retention of one's ethnic minority culture can vary independently. Finally, the populations for which the measures have been developed tend to vary with respect to their psychosocial characteristics. A closer examination of each type of variation can help explain the differences in acculturation instrumentation.

Domains of Psychosocial Functioning

Acculturation measures vary in the types of domains that are assessed for cultural change. The most frequently assessed domain seems to be the use of language, either a person's ethnic language, English, or both. However, within this domain are great differences in how language use is assessed. This variation is apparent even when the analysis is confined to one particular ethnic minority group, such as Hispanic Americans. With respect to this group, some measures primarily assess language use (e.g., the Hispanic Background Scale; Martinez, Norman, & Delaney, 1984), others primarily assess language preference (e.g., the Bicultural Involvement Questionnaire; Szapocznik, Kurtines, & Fernandez, 1980), and other measures primarily assess language proficiency (e.g., the Bidimensional Acculturation Scale; Marín & Gamba, 1996). Moreover, variation exists within these modes of language sampling. For example, even when language use or preference is sampled, measures may differ on the specificity of the context in which language is used (or preferred). Some instruments sample language use in general or across situations, whereas others assess use in specific social contexts such as with family members, at work, or with friends.

Another frequently sampled domain involves the people with whom an individual chooses to socialize and affiliate. Moreover, measures that sample social affiliation tendencies can vary in whether they assess only actual affiliation practices (e.g., the Biculturalism/Multiculturalism Experience Inventory; Ramirez, 1983) or affiliation practices and social preferences (e.g., the Cultural Life Styles Inventory; Mendoza, 1989). Daily living habits such as the types of foods eaten or the type of music to which one listens are another frequently sampled area of functioning (the Behavioral Acculturation Scale; Szapocznik, Scopetta, Kurtines, & de los Angeles Aranalde, 1978). In this domain, measures again can vary depending on whether preferences in daily living habits (e.g., the Bicultural Involvement Questionnaire; Szapocznik et al., 1980) or actual practices (e.g., the

African American Acculturation Scale; Landrine & Klonoff, 1994) are assessed.

Another domain that is often assessed involves a person's identification with a particular culture, either one's own ethnic culture or the White American culture. In this domain, measures can differ in whether they assess actual identification (e.g., the Suinn–Lew Asian Self-Identity Acculturation Scale; Suinn, Rickard-Figueroa, Lew, & Vigil, 1987), cultural pride (e.g., the Cultural Life Styles Inventory; Mendoza, 1989), or perceived acceptance by a certain cultural group (the Acculturation Rating Scale for Mexican Americans–Revised; Cuellar, Arnold, & Maldonado, 1995). Other areas less frequently sampled include cultural traditions; communication style; perceived discrimination or prejudice; generational status; family socialization; and cultural knowledge, beliefs, or values.

Change Parameters on the Pattern of Acculturation

Measures often differ in assumptions about how a person can acculturate. The majority of measures assume a bipolar adaptation in which individuals' ties and psychological involvement with their culture of origin weaken as they acculturate to the majority culture. On the other hand, Berry (1980) developed a two-dimensional model of acculturation that recognized the possibility that acculturation to the majority culture did not preclude retention of one's ethnic group culture. However, few of the acculturation scales have adapted this multidimensional orthogonal framework by measuring two or more cultures independently along various dimensions (e.g., Cuellar et al., 1995; Marín & Gamba, 1996; Szapocznik et al., 1978; Ramirez, 1983).

The bipolar model of adaptation becomes even more problematic when one considers the environmental and social ecology of U. S.-born members of ethnic minority groups, which makes the whole acculturation model of adaptation questionable. In other words, it is unclear whether U.S.-born ethnic minority individuals such as third- or fourth-generation Asian Americans actually experience acculturation in the sense of having to learn and adapt to a new culture. First-generation immigrants have been socialized to their own culture of origin and after immigration must adapt by learning the culture of the host society. In contrast to this discrete and sequential process of socialization, U.S.-born ethnic minorities are situated in a multicultural context beginning from birth that comprises ethnic minority and primarily Western European cultures. In these cases, it is unclear whether acculturation measures, particularly bipolar-based measures, are sensitive to cultural variations among these individuals.

Tsai (1998) conducted a study on U.S.-born Chinese and immigrant Chinese and measured the extent to which they were living according to "being Chinese" or "being American." For immigrants, she found a bipolar relationship between these two acculturation attitudes ($r = .26$ for early immigrants—in the United States for more than 6 years; $r = -.33$ for recent immigrants—in the United States for 6 years or less), whereas for their U.S.-born counterparts, she found no correlation between the Chinese and American acculturation attitudes. These findings tend to indicate that the bipolar pattern of adaptation only holds for certain subgroups of ethnic minorities, and the low correlations suggest that even this pattern is a weak one. A related study (Huh-Kim & Zane, 1998) provided more empirical support for the orthogonal model of adaptation than for the bipolar model. Ethnic identity measures based on the orthogonal model of adaptation were more strongly related to other personality measures than a measure based on the bipolar model of adaptation.

Differences Among the Ethnic Populations for Which Measures Were Developed

The psychosocial characteristics of an ethnic minority population largely determine which domains of psychosocial functioning are assessed and which models of cultural adaptation are emphasized. Consequently, the types of domains that are assessed by a measure and the underlying adaptation model point to salient behaviors, attitudes, and values that are primarily involved in the acculturation process for that group.

Challenges arise when particular subgroups of that ethnic minority population experience major ecological and social changes. As indicated previously, one of the most striking examples involves assessing U.S.-born and immigrant subgroups within an ethnic group such as Asian Americans. In this case, significant differences in the salience of certain adaptation issues as well as patterns of adaptation may exist between the two groups. In fact, growing empirical evidence shows that adaptation for U.S.-born ethnic minorities is qualitatively different than for immigrants, which suggests that the former may be a great source of error variance when assessed by acculturation measures (e.g., Atkinson & Matsushita, 1991; Tsai, 1998).

It is clear from the previous analysis that a large array of psychosocial domains has been addressed by different measures of acculturation. It also seems that substantial variation exists among the measures in how one particular domain is assessed. To better examine this variation in domains among and within measures, a content analysis study was conducted on the most frequently cited acculturation measures that have been used with ethnic minority groups in the United States.

Content Analysis Study

The content analysis study examined the most frequently cited acculturation measures that have been used to assess acculturation variation among three major ethnic minority groups in the United States, namely, Asian, Hispanic, and African American.

Measures Evaluated

The contents of the following 21 measures were examined.

Behavioral Acculturation Scale. The Behavioral Acculturation Scale (BAS; Szapocznik et al., 1978) assesses the extent to which respondents adopt overt and observable aspects of the host American culture relative to the Spanish/Cuban culture. It consists of 24 items measuring the relative frequency with which the respondent engages in each behavior on a 5-point Likert scale. Although the wording of the anchors differ among the four sets of items (language use and preference, daily cultural activities, adherence to cultural tradition, and personal preferences), they generally follow the bipolar format from 1 (*Spanish/Cuban all of the time*) to 3 (*both cultures equally*) to 5 (*American all of the time*). The BAS had high internal consistency (Cronbach's alpha = .97) and a 4-week test–retest reliability of .96. The measure was positively related to years living in the United States for both males ($r = .49$) and females ($r = .59, p < .001$) and negatively related to age, with early adolescents (ages 13–17) having the highest mean acculturation score. After controlling for age, males also had higher acculturation scores than their female counterparts (Szapocznik et al., 1978).

Value Acculturation Scale. The Value Acculturation Scale (VAS; Szapocznik et al., 1978) measure was developed concurrently with the BAS to assess acculturation with respect to cultural values and behavioral practices among Cuban Americans. The measure consists of 6 problem situations in which the respondents choose what they consider to be the best alternative and the worst alternative among the three options provided for each situation. The VAS's internal consistency was .77, and its 4-week test–retest reliability was .86; it was related to years living in the United States for men ($r = .31$) and women ($r = .38, p < .005$). VAS was related to psychosocial stage, with respondents in their early adulthood (ages 23–30) being the most acculturated in value orientations in comparison with older and younger respondents (Szapocznik et al., 1978).

Bicultural Involvement Questionnaire. The Bicultural Involvement Questionnaire (BIQ; Szapocznik et al., 1980), which is based on the BAS, consists of (a) 24 items that independently measure the respondent's level of enculturation to Hispanic culture and acculturation to the majority American culture and (b) 9 bipolar items that assess the respondent's cultural preferences. For the first two sets of items (items 1–10), the respondent indicates the level of comfort in speaking either Spanish or English in different situational contexts (e.g., at home, at work, with friends) using a 5-point Likert scale ranging from 1 (*not at all comfortable*) to 5 (*very comfortable*). The third and fourth sets of items (items 11–24) measure the extent to which the respondent enjoys participating in either Hispanic or American activities (e.g., music, dances, television programs) using a 5-point Likert scale ranging from 1 (*not at all*) to 5 (*very much*). The final set of items (items 25–33) assesses the respondent's lifestyle preferences (e.g., food, language, music) in a bipolar format using a 5-point Likert scale ranging from 1 (*completely Hispanic*) to 3 (*both Hispanic and American*) to 5 (*completely American*). "Americanism" scores are obtained by summing all items related to involvement in the American culture (items 6–10, 18–24, and 25–33). "Hispanicism" scores are obtained by summing all items related to involvement in the Hispanic culture (items 1–5, 11–17, and the reversed scores of 25–33). Based on these two scores, the BIQ measures biculturalism (the difference between the Hispanicism and Americanism scores) and cultural involvement (the sum of two scores). Its internal consistency was .93 and .89 for the Hispanicism and Americanism scales, respectively; .94 for the biculturalism scale; and .79 for the cultural involvement scale. The 6-week test–retest reliabilities for the Cubanism, Americanism, biculturalism, and cultural involvement scales were .50, .54, .79, and .14, respectively. Biculturalism ($r = .42$, $p < .001$) and cultural involvement ($r = .22$, $p < .05$) were positively related to the teacher's impression of the student's level of biculturation (Szapocznik et al., 1980).

Acculturation Rating Scale for Mexican Americans. The Acculturation Rating Scale for Mexican Americans (ARSMA; Cuellar, Harris, & Jasso, 1980) is the most widely used instrument in the assessment of acculturation among Mexican Americans. Moreover, other acculturation measures either have been modeled after the ARSMA (e.g., the Suinn–Lew Asian Self-Identity Acculturation Scale) or have extensively adapted items from this measure. The ARSMA consists of 20 items that evaluate a respondent's extent of acculturation to the White American culture in the areas of language use and preference, ethnic identification, social affiliation, and daily practices on a 5-point Likert scale ranging from 1 (*Mexican/Spanish*) to 3 (*bicultural/bilingual*) to 5 (*Anglo/English*). In the original validation study, the ARSMA had an internal reliability coefficient of .88 for nonhospitalized respondents and .81 for the hospitalized respondents, and its 5-week test–retest reliability was .80 and .72 for the respective samples (Cuellar et al., 1980). Its high internal consistency (Cronbach's alpha = .92) was replicated in another validation study with a college sample (Montgomery & Orozco, 1984). The measure was positively related to hospital staff ratings of Mexican American patients' level of acculturation (Spearman $r = .75$, $p < .01$). The ARSMA also was significantly related to age and socioeconomic status (Montgomery & Orozco, 1984). The measure was able to differentiate three different ethnocultural groups: Mexicans ($M = 1.67$), Mexican Americans ($M = 2.88$), and Anglos ($M = 4.39$). It was positively related to generation status in two separate studies: (a) Kendall's Tau B = .55, $p < .01$ (Cuellar et al., 1980) and (b) $r = .62$, $p < .001$ (Montgomery & Orozco, 1984). Cuellar et al. (1980) found support for the measure's concurrent validity in that the ARSMA was positively related to the BAS and to the Biculturalism/Multiculturalism Experience Inventory (Ramirez, 1983): Spearman $rs = .76$ and $.81$, $p < .001$, respectively.

Biculturalism/Multiculturalism Experience Inventory. The Biculturalism/Multiculturalism Experience Inventory (B/MEI; Ramirez, 1983) is a

69-item questionnaire that is divided into three sections: demographic–linguistic information, personal history, and multicultural participation. Part 1 uses mostly open-ended questions in the assessment of generation status and language use and close-ended questions in the assessment of length of residence, ethnic identification, and social affiliation. It also assesses demographic information including gender, age, marital status, educational level, and occupation. Part 2 assesses the ethnicity of the respondent's social affiliations (e.g., friends, coworkers, church members) on a 6-point Likert scale ranging from 1 (*all Mexican Americans and/or Latinos*), to 3 (*Mexican Americans and/or Latinos about evenly*), to 5 (*all Anglos*) to 6 (*other*). Part 3 measures the respondent's level of involvement in various interpersonal activities and social contact with both majority American culture and the Latino culture on a 5-point Likert scale ranging from 1 (*extensively*) to 5 (*never;* Ramirez, 1983). Split-half reliability coefficients for Parts 2 and 3 of the measure were .79 and .68, respectively. To assess the measure's concurrent validity, a respondent's cultural identification was categorized based on life history interviews as well as from scores on the B/MEI. Almost all of the respondents (97%) were similarly classified as either bicultural, traditional, or atraditional by the two methods (Ramirez, 1984).

Children's Acculturation Scale. The Children's Acculturation Scale (CAS; Franco, 1983) consists of 10 items assessing language usage, language preference and proficiency, cultural identification, and social affiliation on a 5-point scale ranging from 1 (*Spanish only*) to 3 (*both Spanish and English*) to 5 (*English only*). The CAS had an internal consistency of .77 and a 5-week test–retest reliability of .97 among a sample of first-grade children. The mean CAS scores increased significantly with education and age in a comparison of first, third, and sixth graders, and the measure clearly differentiated Mexican American students from their Anglo counterparts. The CAS also was significantly correlated with the ARSMA: $r = .76, p < .01$ (Franco, 1983).

Children's Hispanic Background Scale. The Children's Hispanic Background Scale (CHBS; Martinez et al., 1984) is a 30-item inventory that measures the respondent's exposure to the Hispanic culture by assessing language use with family members (23 items), language preferences in using the media (5 items), and food preferences (2 items) on a 4-point Likert scale ranging from 1 (*almost always*) to 4 (*almost never*). The CHBS had a test–retest reliability of .92, $p < .001$. The measure was related to the parents' ratings of the child on a bilingual classification scale used by schools: $r = .50, p < .001$. It was also positively related to generational status and significantly differentiated between Chicano and Anglo students (Martinez et al., 1984).

Media-Based Acculturation Scale for Mexican Americans. The Media-Based Acculturation Scale for Mexican Americans (MAS; Ramirez, Cousins, Santos, & Supik, 1986) is a 4-item measure of acculturation that focuses on language use, media preferences, and language proficiency. The items have dichotomous alternatives involving 0 (*all/some or Spanish only*) or 1 (*rarely/never or English only*). The MAS was significantly and positively related to place of birth, years living in the community, education, and income as well as negatively related to age (Ramirez et al., 1986).

Short Acculturation Scale for Hispanics. The Short Acculturation Scale for Hispanics (SAS; Marín, Sabogal, VanOss Marín, Otero-Sabogal, & Pérez-Stable, 1987) is a 12-item measure that evaluates the extent to which the respondent engages in behaviors related to the culture of origin (Hispanic) or the host American culture on a 5-point Likert scale ranging from 1 (*only Spanish/all Latinos*) to 3 (*both equally/about half and half*) to 5 (*only English/all Americans*). The SAS emphasizes language use but has 4 items assessing social affiliation. The measure had an internal consistency of .92. It was significantly related to generational status ($r = .65$), length of residence in the United States ($r = .70$), self-evaluation of one's acculturation ($r = .76$), and age of arrival in the U.S. ($r = -.69$, $p < .001$). The SAS also accurately discriminated Hispanic respondents from their non-Hispanic counterparts (Marín et al., 1987).

Suinn–Lew Asian Self-Identity Acculturation Scale. The Suinn–Lew Asian Self-Identity Acculturation Scale (SL–ASIA; Suinn, Rickard-Figueroa, Lew, & Vigil, 1987) is the most widely used instrument in assessing acculturation variation among Asian Americans. It is a 21-item instrument consisting of multiple-choice questions, many of which were modeled after items on the ARSMA. The respondents provide information about resident experiences in the United States such as the number of years they have been living there. This information is used to determine their generational status. The SL–ASIA also assesses language use, ethnic identity, personal preferences, and friendships. Responses are elicited using a 5-point Likert scale, with higher scores reflecting greater acculturation to the American society. The measure demonstrated high internal consistency reliability across different Asian American samples (Cronbach's alphas ranging from .88 to .91; Atkinson & Gim, 1989; Suinn et al., 1987; Suinn, Ahuna, & Khoo, 1992). In terms of concurrent validity, the SL–ASIA was correlated with the following demographics: total years going to school in the United States ($r = .61$), age entering school in the United States ($r = -.60$), years living in the United States ($r = .56$), age entering the United States ($r = -.49$), and years living in a non-Asian neighborhood ($r = .41$), $ps < .001$ (Suinn et al., 1992).

Cultural Life Styles Inventory. The Cultural Life Styles Inventory (CLSI; Mendoza, 1989) assesses the extent to which the respondent can be classified into one of the four types of acculturation (cultural resistance, cultural shift, cultural incorporation, and cultural transmutation) as proposed by Mendoza and Martinez (1981). The CLSI is a 29-item measure that assesses culture-related practices and personal preferences in five areas: intrafamily language use, extrafamily language use, social affiliation, cultural familiarity, and cultural identification. The items are rated on a 5-point Likert scale from 1 (*Spanish*) to 3 (*both Spanish and English*) to 5 (*English*) for the first two sections on language use and from 1 (*Hispanic*) to 3 (*both Hispanic and American*) to 5 (*American*) for the last three sections on social affiliation, cultural familiarity, and cultural identification. The internal reliability coefficients for the five acculturation dimensions were .87, .91, .89, .84, and .89, respectively. Two-week test–retest reliabilities ranged from .88 to .95, $p < .001$, for groups that completed the measure in either English or Spanish. In the evaluation of its construct validity, cultural resistance scores decreased, whereas cultural shift scores increased with generation level. Unexpectedly, cultural incorporation scores were not related to generation level because bicultural adaptation seemed to be prevalent across generations. Exposure to mainstream culture was positively correlated with cultural shift ($r = .66$, $p < .001$) and negatively correlated with cultural resistance and incorporation ($r = -.60$, $p < .001$ and $r = -.25$, $p < .01$, respectively). Moreover, concordant patterns were found; the respondent's CLSI score was significantly related to the CLSI rating made by an immediate family member (father, mother, or sibling; $r = .71$, $p < .001$; Mendoza, 1989).

Acculturation Scale for Southeast Asians. The Acculturation Scale for Southeast Asians (AS–SEA; Anderson et al., 1993) is a 13-item self-report measure of acculturation that was specifically developed for adult Southeast Asian (Cambodian, Laotian, and Vietnamese) immigrants and refugees. It assesses language proficiency in both English and the respondent's language of origin on a 4-point Likert scale from 1 (*very well*) to 4 (*not at all*), language usage on a 5-point scale ranging from 1 (*only origin*) to 3 (*origin and English equally*) to 5 (*only English*), social affiliation on a 3-point scale ranging from 1 (*mostly origin*) to 3 (*mostly American*), and food preference on a 5-point scale ranging from 1 (*only origin*) to 3 (*origin and English equally*) to 5 (*only English*). Factor analysis of the measure yielded three factors: English proficiency; proficiency in the language of origin; and language, social, and food preferences. The internal consistency reliability coefficients of the three factors for Cambodians, Laotians, and Vietnamese ranged from .77 to .99. For all three Southeast Asian groups, the AS–SEA was significantly and negatively related to age on entering the United States and positively related to length of residence and percentage of lifetime in the United States, with the Vietnamese respondents having somewhat lower validity coefficients than their Cambodian and Laotian counterparts (Anderson et al., 1993).

Na Mea Hawai'i Scale. The Na Mea Hawai'i Scale (NMHS; Rezentes, 1993) is a rationally derived measure and a 21-item questionnaire used to assess the respondent's knowledge of Hawaiian vocabulary, customs, history, and participation in cultural activities. The respondent answers the items according to a *yes, no,* or *don't know* or provides information to open-ended items that ask for a definition of a Hawaiian phrase (e.g. "*Aloha wau ia 'oe*") or cultural term (e.g., *kahuna, maika'i, ali'i*). The NMHS significantly differentiated Hawaiian respondents from Japanese and Caucasian respondents (Rezentes, 1993; Streltzer, Rezentes, & Arakaki, 1996).

African American Acculturation Scale. The African American Acculturation Scale (AAAS; Landrine & Klonoff, 1994) consists of 74 items that assess the extent to which the respondent engages in African American behaviors and is knowledgeable about African American culture. Responses are elicited using a 7-point Likert scale ranging from 1 (*I totally disagree, this is not at all true of me*) to 7 (*I totally agree, this is absolutely true of me*), with higher scores indicating a more African American cultural orientation. The measure can be organized into eight subscales that involve family socialization, adherence to cultural traditions, language, daily cultural activities, social affiliation, perceived discrimination, spirituality, and cultural beliefs. Internal consistency for the subscales ranged from .71 to .90, and the entire measure had a split-half reliability of .93. The AAAS was not significantly related to gender, socioeconomic status, or education, and similar mean levels of acculturation were found for college and community samples (Landrine & Klonoff, 1995). A short form (33 items) was derived from the original measure (Landrine & Klonoff, 1995).

ARSMA–Revised. The ARSMA–Revised (ARSMA–II; Cuellar et al., 1995) is a two-part questionnaire that attempts to capture four typologies of acculturation adaptation (assimilation, integration, separation, and marginalization; Berry, 1980) by using an orthogonal approach of assessing attitudes and behaviors toward the culture of origin (Hispanic culture) and the host culture (American culture). Part 1 consists of 30 items that measure the respondent's extent of involvement in the Mexican culture (17 items) and Anglo culture (13 items) by assessing a person's cultural practices, language proficiency and preferences, social affiliation, and ethnic identification. Respondents indicate the relative frequency with which they engage in certain behaviors using a 5-point Likert scale, ranging from 1 (*not at all*) to 5 (*extremely often or almost always*). Items related to involvement in the Mexican culture are summed to form the Mexican Orientation Subscale (MOS), and items related to involvement with the Anglo culture are summed to form the Anglo Orientation Subscale (AOS). Part 2 consists of 18 items that measure the respondent's acceptance of attitudes and behaviors in the Mexican culture (6 items), the Mexican American culture (6 items), and the Anglo culture (6 items). Three marginality subscales to the Mexican (MEXMAR), Mexican American (MAMARG), and Anglo (ANGMAR) cultures were developed based on the responses to the cultural acceptance items. The internal consistency of the various subscales ranged from .68 to .91, and their 1-week test–retest reliability ranged from .72 to .96. The difference score (MOS–AOS) of the ARSMA–II was significantly related to the original ARSMA ($r = .89$). In relation to generational status, the MOS scores decreased, whereas the AOS scores increased with each generation. Although no gender differences were found on the ARSMA–II, the measure was positively correlated with socioeconomic status ($r = .22$, $p < .001$; Cuellar et al., 1995).

Bidimensional Acculturation Scale. The Bidimensional Acculturation Scale (BiAS; Marín & Gamba, 1996) consists of 24 items that assess the respondent's adherence to Hispanic and American (English-based) cultures on three domains: language use (6 items), linguistic proficiency (12 items), and preferences for electronic media (6 items). Responses are elicited using a 4-point Likert scale ranging from 1 (*not at all*) to 4 (*almost always/very well*). The internal reliability coefficients of the six subscales ranged from .81 for the English electronic media subscale to .97 for the English linguistic proficiency subscale. The reliabilities for the combined scores of the three subscales were .90 for the Hispanic domain and .96 for the American domain. For the American domain, the language use, linguistic proficiency, and the electronic media subscales were significantly related to generational status (rs = .52, .61, .40, respectively), length of residence in the United States (rs = .44, .55, .23, respectively), age at arrival in the United States (rs = −.65, −.75, −.55, respectively), proportion of life in the United States (rs = .43, .54, .22, respectively), and ethnic self-identification (rs = .46, .50, .40, respectively) for both Mexican American and Central American samples (Marín & Gamba, 1996).

Brief Acculturation Scale. The Brief Acculturation Scale (BrAS; Norris, Ford, & Bova, 1996) is a 10-item measure of acculturation that was derived from the language use subscale of the SAS (Marín et al., 1987). Language use is assessed by four items on a 5-point Likert scale ranging from 1 (*only Spanish*) to 3 (*both equally*) to 5 (*only English*). One item assesses the respondent's generational status. Five items assess the respondent's perceived closeness to African Americans, White Americans, and Hispanic Americans in different cultural contexts (e.g., Mexico, Puerto Rico, and other countries) on a 4-point Likert scale ranging from 1 (*very close*) to 4 (*not close at all*). The measure had an internal consistency of .90. For both Mexican American and Puerto Rican respondents, the BrAS was positively related to generational status (r = .74 and r = .40, respectively), length of time in the United States (r = .59 and r = .46, respectively), and perceived closeness to U.S. Whites (r = .25 and r = .19, respectively) and African Americans (r = .30 and r = .14, respectively) and negatively related to perceived closeness to their country of origin (r = −.43 and r = −.18, respectively; Norris et al., 1996).

General Ethnicity Questionnaire. The General Ethnicity Questionnaire (GEQ; Levenson, 1994) is a 47-item scale that measures the degree of acculturation into European American culture on a 5-point Likert scale from 1 (*exclusively*) to 5 (*not at all*). Its items were derived from the CLSI (Mendoza, 1989), BAS (Szapocznik et al., 1978), and ARSMA (Cuellar et al., 1980). The first half of the GEQ assesses the respondents' experience with European American culture and their attitudes toward that culture. The second half measures the respondents' preference for English and its usage in different social contexts. The GEQ can be adopted for use with any ethnic group.

Asian Values Scale. The Asian Values Scale (AVS; Kim, Atkinson, & Yang, 1999) consists of 36 items that examine the degree to which a respondent endorses specific value orientations that have been associated with East Asian societies. The measure samples a wide range of psychosocial domains including attitude toward educational achievement, family/relational orientation, expression of emotions, and communication style. Respondents indicate the extent of agreement with each value statement on a 7-point Likert scale ranging from 1 (*strongly disagree*) to 4 (*neither agree or disagree*) to 7 (*strongly agree*); 18 items are reverse coded. The overall AVS had an internal consistency of .82 and a 2-week test–retest reliability of .83. Based on exploratory factor analysis, six latent factors were derived with the following alpha coefficients: .69 for conformity to norms, .62 for family recognition through achievement, .47 for emotional self-control, .54 for collectivism, .57 for humility, and .38 for filial piety (Kim et al., 1999). In a confirmatory factor analytic study, the AVS demonstrated concurrent validity with the value-oriented collectivism subscales (vertical and horizontal collectivism) of the Individualism and Collectivism Scale (INDCOL; Triandis, 1995) and discriminant validity with behavioral acculturation as indicated by the various subscales of the SL–ASIA (Kim et al., 1999).

African American Acculturation Scale. The African American Acculturation Scale (AfAAS; Snowden & Hines, 1999) consists of 10 items that assess the extent to which respondents engage in behaviors and attitudes concerning (a) media preferences, (b) social interactions, and (c) race relations. Respondents rate their endorsement of African American cultural involvement for each item on a 4-point Likert scale ranging from 0 (*most or all / strongly agree*) to 3 (*few / rarely / strongly disagree*). Consequently, scores range from 0 to 30, with higher scores indicating greater acculturation to mainstream American culture. Factor analysis of the measure yielded a unidimensional structure for the scale. The measure had an internal consistency of .75. For African American men, acculturation was positively related to age, income, employment, likelihood of marriage, urban residence and negatively related to the belief in the importance of religion. For African American women, acculturation was positively related to divorce or separation, income, education, urban residence, and religious affiliation.

Stephenson Multigroup Acculturation Scale. The Stephenson Multigroup Acculturation Scale (SMAS; Stephenson, 2000) consists of two independent dimensions that measure the degree of ethnic society immersion (ESI; 17 items) and dominant society immersion (DSI; 15 items), and the measure can be used with different ethnic groups. Respondents rate their endorsement of attitudes and behaviors related to language, social interaction, food, and the media on a 4-point Likert scale ranging from 1 (*false*) to 4 (*true*). Alpha reliability coefficients were .86 for the entire scale, .97 for ESI, and .90 for DSI. In terms of construct validity, DSI was found to increase successively from first-generation to third-generation individuals, whereas there were decrements in ethnic society immersion with each successive generation. Both subscales also correlated significantly with ethnic group affiliation. Finally, the ESI and the DSI were significantly correlated with the ethnic retention/attachment and acculturation subscales, respectively, of the ARSMA–II (Cuellar et al., 1995) and the BiAS (Marín & Gamba, 1996).

Content Analysis

The content analysis of each acculturation measure was conducted in the following manner: First, the second investigator categorized each item of a particular measure into one of the domains described previously. Second, the first investigator independently categorized the items, and any disagreements were reconciled. The percentage of disagreements across all the measures was 8.9%. Finally, a percentage of the total items of a particular measure that were classified as belonging to each domain was calculated and tabled.

Results and Discussion

Most scales examined the acculturation process among Hispanic Americans, with few measuring the acculturation of Asian/Pacific Islanders and African Americans. Because acculturation is related to mental and physical health and various life experiences and the U.S. population is becoming increasingly diverse, it is important to increase efforts to assess this variable for other major ethnic minority groups. As seen in Table 2.1, the content analysis showed substantial variation in the areas that the acculturation scales measure. Some measures have some content overlap, but others have little or no overlap in content. It is questionable whether the measures are assessing the same acculturation phenomena across different ethnic groups. As indicated earlier, the possibility exists that the measures are assessing acculturation in the domains most salient to a particular ethnic minority group. However, it is important to note that there is a lack of content overlap even among measures that were designed to assess the same ethnic minority group such as Hispanics or Asian Americans. Another marked pattern shown in the table is that very few measures sample more than two or three domains extensively. This raises a content validity issue because it is unclear whether any of these measures have adequately sampled the various behavioral and attitudinal domains in which acculturative change would be expected to occur.

Among all the categories represented, language was heavily used as an indicator of acculturation. Although language retention and acquisition may be an important component in the acculturation process, they do not wholly represent the acculturation process. Other important dimensions, such as attitudes, behaviors, beliefs, and values are believed to be important in the acculturation process. For example, as can be seen from Table 2.1, all but three instruments measure language; however, only 5 of the 21 scales assessed cultural value orientations. Numerous researchers have

MEASUREMENT OF ACCULTURATION   53

Table 2.1. Percentage of Items From Each Acculturation Measure in a Particular Content Category

Acculturation scales	Language use/ preference	Social affiliation	Daily living habits	Cultural traditions	Communication style	Cultural identity/ pride	Perceived prejudice/ discrimination	Generational status	Family socialization	Cultural values
BAS (B)[a]	38		41	13	8					
VAS (B)					14					86
BIQ Part 1 (I)[b]	42		58							
BIQ Part 2 (B)	11		67	22						
ARSMA (B)	25	20	20			25		10		
B/MEI (I)	17	68				4		11		
CAS (B)	30	10	10			10		10		
CHBS (B)	80		20							
MAS (B)	100									
SAS (B)	67	33								
SL–ASIA (B)	24	20	16	12		20		8		
CLSI (B)	45	21	10	10		14				
AS–SEA (B)	77	15	8							
NMHS (B)	14	5	10	32	10	5	5		5	14
AAAS (B)	1	11	30	5	1	1	11		10	30
ARSMA–II (I)	14	22	18			43		2		
BiAS (I)	75		25							
BrAS (B)	40					50		10		
GEQ (I)	39	10	20	8	2	12			6	2
AVS (I)					14					86
AfAAS (B)		70	30							
SMAS (I)	47	16	25	6		3	3			

Note. [a](B) = Bipolar measurement of cultures. [b](I) = Independent measurement of cultures. BAS = Behavioral Acculturation Scale; VAS = Value Acculturation Scale; BIQ = Bicultural Involvement Questionnaire; ARSMA = Acculturation Rating Scale for Mexican Americans; B/MEI = Biculturalism/Multiculturalism Experience Inventory; CAS = Children's Acculturation Scale; CHBS = Children's Hispanic Background Scale; MAS = Media-Based Acculturation Scale for Mexican Americans; SAS = Short Acculturation Scale for Hispanics; SL–ASIA = Suinn–Lew Asian Self-Identity Acculturation Scale; CLSI = Cultural Life Styles Inventory; AS–SEA = Acculturation Scale for Southeast Asians; NMHS = Na Mea Hawai'i Scale; AAAS = African American Acculturation Scale; ARSMA–II = Acculturation Rating Scale for Mexican Americans–Revised; BiAS = Bidimensional Acculturation Scale; BrAS = Brief Acculturation Scale; GEQ = General Ethnicity Questionnaire; AVS = Asian Values Scale; AfAAS = African American Acculturation Scale; SMAS = Stephenson Multigroup Acculturation Scale.

suggested that the acculturation process is multidimensional and differential. In other words, acculturation occurs along various dimensions and at different paces depending on the dimension. Thus, the preponderance of language and the underrepresentation of other dimensions in the measurement scales may result in a skewed assessment of an individual's acculturation.

In addition to their uneven representation of content areas, the large majority of the measures were bipolar. Specifically, 14 of the 21 measures were bipolar in nature. The findings support the initial general impression that most acculturation measures assume a bipolar adaptation pattern of cultural change. They measured acculturation along a continuum representing the culture of origin at one extreme and the host culture at the other extreme. This linear model precludes the possibility that individuals may retain various elements of their culture of origin while simultaneously learning about another culture.

The results of the content analysis strongly suggest that acculturation researchers who focus on ethnic minority issues face a number of challenges in their efforts to assess this construct. First, there does not appear to be a measure that adequately samples the major behavioral and attitudinal domains related to acculturative change. Second, the possibility exists that the salience of these domains may differ depending on the ethnic minority group being studied. If this is the case, no guiding framework articulates which domains may be more salient for a particular ethnic minority group. Finally, it seems that cultural values—a key domain associated with acculturative changes—have received relatively little coverage by the measures currently in use.

Indeed, cultural changes related to acculturation can be so complex and varied that efforts to comprehensively assess them may not be practical or useful. On the other hand, assessment research on acculturation has been very effective in identifying the psychosocial domains of functioning that are often associated with cultural change. Building on this work, it is proposed that an alternative approach to the study of acculturation effects is to focus assessment efforts on capturing specific psychological elements from a particular domain such as cultural values (Betancourt & Lopez, 1993). This approach has several advantages. First, by examining a finite number of psychological elements that are related to acculturation, researchers can actually determine the extent to which individuals have or have not become acculturated on those dimensions. In this way the assessment of acculturation becomes more idiographic in that investigators can locate an individual on a number of acculturation dimensions. Second, the assessment of a specific psychological dimension such as a particular value orientation provides stronger explanatory models by allowing investigators to test what *specifically* about acculturation accounts for a certain effect. Third, the deconstruction of acculturation into specific psychological elements provides opportunities to examine the interactive effects of different aspects of acculturation. Recently, a number of studies have used this specific element approach to study acculturation effects involved with Asian American clients' response to psychotherapy.

Specific Element Approach: Case Study of Research on Loss of Face

Research on the psychological treatment of Asian Americans has consistently found that less acculturated Asians are less likely to seek mental health services, tend to stay in therapy for shorter periods of time, and experience poorer treatment outcomes compared with more acculturated Asian clients (Sue, Zane, & Young, 1994). However, it is unclear which aspect of acculturation affects treatment utilization and outcomes. One hypothesis is that the strong, confessional nature of psychotherapy in which clients must disclose very personal issues to a stranger can lead to great *face loss*. Loss of face has been identified as a key interpersonal dynamic in East Asian cultures (Ho, 1976). Given that change in therapy is mediated through the client–therapist relationship, it is important to examine certain interpersonal constructs that may be relatively more culturally salient for different ethnic groups. Based on various accounts of face in both East Asian and Western psychology, it seems that face has certain conceptual parameters. First, "face" is not simply prestige or social reputation obtained through success and personal achievements. According to Hu (1944), face represents people's moral reputation or social integrity, integrity that is gained and maintained by the performance of specific social roles that are well recognized by others. Goffman (1955) noted, "face is an image of self delineated in terms of approved social attributes." Thus, *face* can be defined as people's social integrity; the integrity is tied to the fact that people perceive themselves to be integral members of a group with certain prescribed roles that imply the responsibility of being perceived as representatives of that group. The fact that face has esteem implications extending beyond the individual to the individual's reference groups is probably the main reason it has such psychological power in certain shame-based societies such as East Asian cultures. Less acculturated Asian clients would be expected to be more concerned with face issues. Consequently, the face-threatening nature of psychotherapy may cause less acculturated Asian clients to respond less favorably to treatment than their more acculturated counterparts.

Studies on Loss of Face

Validation study. Using the rational approach to item development and selection, Zane and Yeh (2002) constructed a 21-item, 7-point Likert scale measure of loss of face. The selected items reflected concern about violating social norms or expectations as well as concerns about not causing any loss of face for others (e.g., not embarrassing others, not confronting others about their mistakes). The loss of face (LOF) measure was internally consistent with an alpha of .83. The measure also demonstrated concurrent and discriminant validity. As predicted, loss of face correlated positively with other-directedness, private self-consciousness, public self-consciousness, and social anxiety, and loss of face correlated negatively with extraversion and "acting," or the desire to perform before others. In addition, loss of face was not correlated with psychological maladjustment. Finally, loss of face was significantly correlated with a measure of acculturation (SL–ASIA): $r = -.37, p < .001$. Asians ($M = 91.8, SD = 16.9$) scored significantly higher on loss of face than Whites ($M = 80.4, SD = 16.3$), even after controlling for the effects of cultural identity, social anxiety, extraversion, acting, and other-directedness: $F(1, 153) = 12.07, p < .01$. These results provide support for the reliability and construct validity of the loss of face measure and indicate that the measure is sensitive to ethnic differences and acculturation variation.

Loss of face and self-disclosure in treatment. Another study examined how loss of face may be related to a key process in psychotherapy—self-disclosure (Zane, Umemoto, & Park, 1998). In a treatment analog study, 128 Asian American students were randomly assigned to conditions in a 2 (ethnic match/nonmatch) × 2 (gender match/nonmatch) experimental design. Participants completed a demographic questionnaire and the LOF measure and then listened to an audiotape of a counselor who introduced himself or herself and described counseling to the participant. The effects of loss of face, ethnic match, and gender match were examined on three types of self-disclosure: (a) aspects of one's personality, (b) negative experiences or aspects of self, and (c) aspects of one's intimate relationships. The findings point to the importance of the face loss issues in treatment. Face loss was negatively associated with all three types of self-disclosure: aspects about one's personality ($r = -.21, p < .05$), negative aspects about self ($r = -.22, p < .05$), and aspects about one's intimate relationships ($r = -.31, p < .01$). Moreover, consistent with the face loss model, the greatest effect of loss of face was associated with a specific type of self-disclosure that the face model predicted would incur the greatest face loss, namely, disclosing one's problems to significant others. Such disclosure risks the greatest face loss because of the likelihood of causing face loss for someone else, especially someone in an individual's most personal network (Goffman, 1955).

Loss of face and preference for directive treatment. The last study examined the role of face in Asian American preferences for directive counseling (Park, 1998). A number of studies have found that Asian Americans tend to prefer the more directive counseling approach (e.g., Atkinson, Maruyama, & Matsui, 1978), but it was unclear which cultural factors associated with less acculturated Asians accounted for this effect. One possibility is that Asian Americans have different expectations when entering counseling or treatment (Zane, Enomoto, & Chun, 1994). In this case, the greater credibility for the directive approach among Asians may be simply a result of the fact that this approach tends to be aligned with the type of help they expect in treatment. However, another possibility is that directive approaches reduce ambiguity between client and therapist in the therapeutic situation, thereby minimizing threats to face. Hwang (1987) hypothesized that in situations in which roles are ambiguous, face loss issues are very salient simply because it is unclear which social behaviors are

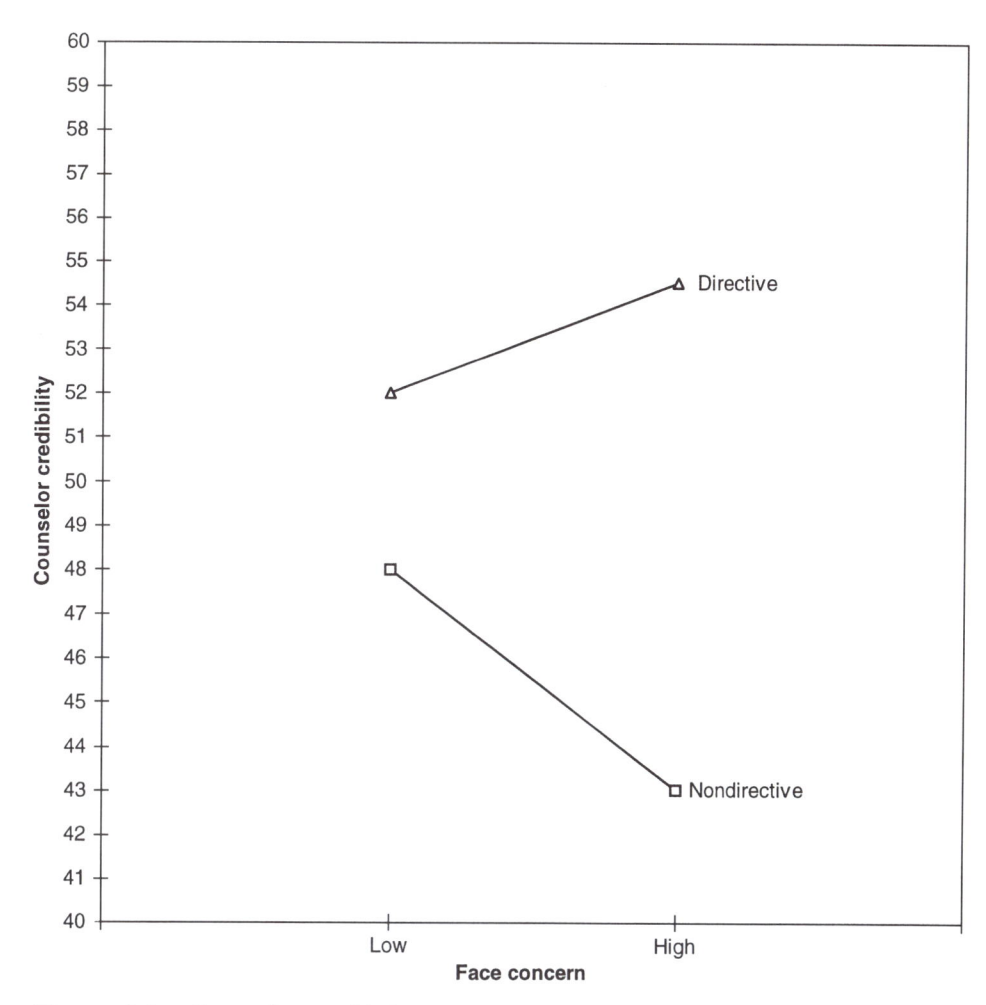

Figure 2.1. Counselor credibility ratings of counselor style (directive vs. nondirective) as a function of face concern.

proper or needed. A directive counseling approach would reduce this ambiguity and consequently, threats involving face loss. Students with an interest in counseling services were randomly assigned to either a directive counseling condition or a nondirective counseling condition. To enable a test of these two explanatory models, the LOF measure and a measure of treatment expectations that had been developed for Asian American clients were administered. In replicating findings from the earlier studies, Asian Americans and White Americans preferred more directive counseling styles. Moreover, a significant interaction between face concerns and counseling approach was found, but the interaction effect involving treatment expectations and counseling approach was not significant. As Figure 2.1 shows, when people have less face loss concerns, they have little difference in credibility between the two approaches. It is only when a person has high face loss concerns that significant differences in credibility occur, resulting in the directive approach being rated as significantly more credible than the nondirective approach.

The last two studies tend to provide evidence that for Asian American clients, face issues are quite salient in treatment. More importantly, the research has provided compelling evidence that at least some of the specific effects of acculturation in the psychological treatment of Asian American clients are mediated through effects of the cultural value dimension of face loss concerns. In other words, for Asian Americans, acculturation is associated with varying levels of face loss concerns, which in turn seem to affect important processes in psychotherapy.

Acculturation is one of the most significant psychological processes of psychosocial adaptation for many ethnic minority individuals, particularly those from immigrant backgrounds. In mental health research, it is clear that more efforts are needed to deconstruct acculturation into specific psychological elements that are proximal to psychopathology, seeking help, response to treatment, and other mental health issues. Moreover, this type of research can systematically build on previous efforts to measure acculturation. Many of the psychosocial domains sampled by these measures, such as value orientations, language use, and social affiliation, seem to be prime candidates for development using the single-element approach. For example, with respect to social affiliation, few studies have examined how social support networks change with acculturation and how such changes may affect psychological adjustment and attitudes toward treatment or mental health services. In the area of language use and preference, some research has documented that languages vary in the extent to which they use context outside of the verbal word to convey meaning (Lynch & Hanson, 1998). The differential use of context among different cultures raises the possibility that a person's communication style may change with acculturation. This change in communication style may in turn affect important interpersonal processes such as the working alliance between the client and therapist in psychotherapy (Horvath & Luborsky, 1993; Lambert, 1989). The study of acculturation continues to be one of the most important areas of research for ethnic minority populations. The research that has been presented demonstrates that the single-element approach, although not supplanting general measures of acculturation, can help provide more definitive information about which aspects of acculturation can affect particular behaviors or attitudes.

References

Anderson, J., Moeschberger, M., Chen, M. S., Jr., Kunn, P., Wewers, M. E., & Guthrie, R. (1993). An acculturation scale for Southeast Asians. *Social Psychiatry and Psychiatric Epidemiology, 28,* 134–141.

Atkinson, D. R., & Gim, R. (1989). Asian-American cultural identity and attitudes toward mental health services. *Journal of Counseling Psychology, 36,* 209–212.

Atkinson, D. R., Maruyama, M., & Matsui, S. (1978). Effects of counselor race and counseling approach on Asian Americans' perceptions of counselor credibility and utility. *Journal of Counseling Psychology, 25,* 76–85.

Atkinson, D. R., & Matsushita, Y. (1991). Japanese-American acculturation, counseling style, counselor ethnicity, and perceived counselor credibility. *Journal of Counseling Psychology, 38,* 473–478.

Berry, J. W. (1980). Acculturation as varieties of adaptation. In A. M. Padilla (Ed.), *Acculturation: Theory, models and some new findings* (pp. 9–25). Boulder, CO: Westview.

Berry, J. W., Trimble, J. E., & Olmedo, E. L. (1986). Assessment of acculturation. In W. J. Lonner & J. W. Berry (Eds.), *Field methods in cross-cultural research* (pp. 291–345). Beverly Hills, CA: Sage.

Betancourt, H., & Lopez, S. R. (1993). The study of culture, ethnicity, race, in American psychology. *American Psychologist, 48,* 629–637.

Cuellar, I., Arnold, B., & Maldonado, R. (1995). Acculturation Rating Scale for Mexican Americans—II: A revision of the original ARSMA scale. *Hispanic Journal of Behavioral Sciences, 17,* 275–304.

Cuellar, I., Harris, L. C., & Jasso, R. (1980). An acculturation scale for Mexican American normal and clinical populations. *Hispanic Journal of Behavioral Sciences, 2,* 199–217.

Franco, J. N. (1983). An acculturation scale for Mexican-American children. *Journal of General Psychology, 108,* 175–181.

Gim, R. H., Atkinson, D. R., & Kim, S. J. (1991). Asian-American acculturation, counselor ethnicity and cultural sensitivity, and ratings of counselors. *Journal of Counseling Psychology, 38,* 57–62.

Gim, R. H., Atkinson, D. R., & Whiteley, S. (1990). Asian-American acculturation, severity of concerns, and willingness to see a counselor. *Journal of Counseling Psychology, 37,* 281–285.

Goffman, E. (1955). On face-work: An analysis of ritual elements in social interaction. *Psychiatry, 18,* 213–232.

Ho, D. Y. (1976). On the concept of face. *American Journal of Sociology, 81,* 867–884.

Horvath, A. O., & Luborsky, L. (1993). The role of the therapeutic alliance in psychotherapy. *Journal of Consulting and Clinical Psychology, 61,* 561–573.

Hu, H. C. (1944). The Chinese concepts of "face." *American Anthropologist, 46,* 45–64.

Huh-Kim, J., & Zane, N. (1998). *The bipolar versus orthogonal model of cultural identification: An empirical test.* Manuscript in preparation.

Hwang, K. K. (1987). Face and favor: The Chinese power game. *American Journal of Sociology, 92,* 944–974.

Kim, B. S. K., Atkinson, D. R., & Yang, P. H. (1999). The Asian values scale (AVS): Development, factor analysis, validation, and reliability. *Journal of Counseling Psychology, 46,* 342–352.

Lambert, M. J. (1989). The individual therapist's contribution to psychotherapy process and outcome. *Clinical Psychology Review, 9,* 469–485.

Landrine, H., & Klonoff, E. A. (1994). The African American Acculturation Scale: Development, reliability, and validity. *Journal of Black Psychology, 20,* 104–127.

Landrine, H., & Klonoff, E. A. (1995). The African American Acculturation Scale II: Cross-validation and short form. *Journal of Black Psychology, 21,* 124–152.

Levenson, R. W. (1994). *General ethnicity questionnaire.* Berkeley: University of California, Department of Psychology.

Lynch, E. W., & Hanson, M. J. (Eds.). (1998). *Developing cross-cultural competence* (2nd ed.). Baltimore: Paul H. Brooks.

Marín, G., & Gamba, R. J. (1996). A new measurement of acculturation for Hispanics: The Bidimensional Acculturation Scale for Hispanics (BAS). *Hispanic Journal of Behavioral Sciences, 18,* 297–316.

Marín, G., Sabogal, F., VanOss Marín, B., Otero-Sabogal, R., & Pérez-Stable, E. J. (1987). Development of a short acculturation scale for Hispanics. *Hispanic Journal of Behavioral Sciences, 9,* 183–205.

Martinez, R., Norman, R. D., & Delaney, H. D. (1984). A children's Hispanic background scale. *Hispanic Journal of Behavioral Sciences, 6,* 103–112.

Mendoza, R. H. (1989). An empirical scale to measure type and degree of acculturation in Mexican-American adolescents and adults. *Journal of Cross-Cultural Psychology, 20,* 372–385.

Mendoza, R. H., & Martinez, J. L., Jr. (1981). The measurement of acculturation. In A. Baron Jr. (Ed.), *Exploration in Chicano psychology* (pp. 71–82). New York: Praeger.

Montgomery, G. T., & Orozco, S. (1984). Validation of a measure of acculturation for Mexican Americans. *Hispanic Journal of Behavioral Sciences, 6,* 53–63.

Norris, A. E., Ford, K., & Bova, C. A. (1996). Psychometrics of a brief acculturation scale for Hispanics in a probability sample of urban Hispanic adolescents and young adults. *Hispanic Journal of Behavioral Sciences, 18,* 29–38.

Padilla, A. M. (1980). *Acculturation: Theory, models, and some new findings.* Boulder, CO: Westview.

Park, S. (1998). *A test of explanatory models of Asian American and White students' preferences for a directive counseling style.* Unpublished doctoral dissertation, University of California, Santa Barbara.

Ramirez, A. G., Cousins, J. H., Santos, Y., & Supik, J. D. (1986). A media-based acculturation scale for Mexican-Americans: Application to public health education programs. *Family and Community Health, 9*(3), 63–71.

Ramirez, M., III (1983). *Psychology of the Americas: Mestizo perspectives on personality and mental health.* New York: Pergamon.

Ramirez, M., III (1984). Assessing and understanding biculturalism–multiculturalism in Mexican-American adults. In J. L. Martinez Jr. & R. H. Mendoza (Eds.), *Chicano Psychology* (2nd ed., pp. 77–94). Orlando, FL: Academic Press.

Rezentes, W. C., III (1993). Na Mea Hawai'i: A Hawaiian acculturation scale. *Psychological Reports, 73,* 383–393.

Snowden, L. R., & Hines, A. M. (1999). A scale to assess African American acculturation. *Journal of Black Psychology, 25,* 36–47.

Stephenson, M. (2000). Development and validation of the Stephenson Multigroup Acculturation Scale (SMAS). *Psychological Assessment, 12*(1), 77–88.

Streltzer, J., Rezentes, W. C., III, & Arakaki, M. (1996). Does acculturation influence psychosocial adaptation and well-being in Native Hawaiians? *International Journal of Social Psychiatry, 42*(1), 28–37.

Sue, D. W., & Kirk, B. (1972). Psychological characteristics of Chinese American students. *Journal of Counseling Psychology, 19,* 471–478.

Sue, S., Zane, N., & Young, K. (1994). Research on psychotherapy with culturally diverse populations. In A. Bergin & S. Garfield (Eds.), *Handbook of psychotherapy and behavior change* (4th ed., pp. 783–817). New York: Wiley.

Suinn, R. M., Ahuna, C., & Khoo, G. (1992). The Suinn–Lew Asian Self-identity Acculturation Scale: Concurrent and factorial validation. *Educational and Psychological Measurement, 52,* 1041–1046.

Suinn, R. M., Rickard-Figueroa, K., Lew, S., & Vigil, P. (1987). The Suinn–Lew Asian Self-Identity Acculturation Scale: An initial report. *Educational and Psychological Measurement, 47,* 401–407.

Szapocznik, J., Kurtines, W. M., & Fernandez, T. (1980). Bicultural involvement and adjustment in Hispanic-American youths. *International Journal of Intercultural Relations, 4,* 353–365.

Szapocznik, J., Scopetta, M. A., Kurtines, W., & de los Angeles Aranalde, M. (1978). Theory and measurement of acculturation. *Inter-American Journal of Psychology, 12,* 113–130.

Triandis, H. C. (1995). *Individualism and collectivism.* Boulder, CO: Westview.

Tsai, J. (1998, November). *The meaning of "being Chinese" and of "being American": Variation among Chinese American young adults.* Paper presented at the conference on the Conceptual, Methodological, and Practice Issues in the Mental Health Assessment of Asian Americans, University of California, Davis.

Zane, N., Enomoto, K., & Chun, C. (1994). Treatment outcomes of Asian and White American clients in outpatient therapy. *Journal of Community Psychology, 22,* 177–191.

Zane, N., Umemoto, D., & Park, S. (1998). *The effects of ethnic and gender match and face concerns on self-disclosure in counseling for Asian American clients.* Manuscript in preparation.

Zane, N., & Yeh, M. (2002). Use of culturally-based variables in assessment: Studies on loss of face. In K. Kurasaki, S. Okazaki, & S. Sue (Eds.), *Asian American mental health: Assessment theories and methods* (pp. 123–138). Dordrecht, Netherlands: Kluwer Academic.

Part II

Understanding Individual and Family Processes

3

Ethnic Identity and Acculturation

Jean S. Phinney

Ethnic identity is a dynamic, multidimensional construct that refers to one's identity or sense of self as a member of an ethnic group. *Ethnic groups* are subgroups within a larger context that claim a common ancestry and share one or more of the following elements: culture, phenotype, religion, language, kinship, or place of origin. Ethnic identity is not a fixed categorization but rather is a fluid and dynamic understanding of self and ethnic background. Ethnic identity is constructed and modified as individuals become aware of differences among ethnic groups and attempt to understand the meaning of their ethnicity within the larger setting.

As the previous definition emphasizes, ethnic identity is not a static category; rather it is subject to change along various dimensions: over time or across generations in a new culture, in different contexts, and with age or development. Of these changes, those that occur over time in a new culture can be thought of as changes related to acculturation. The question addressed in this chapter is the extent to which changes in ethnic identity are related to changes that occur in the process of acculturation. The chapter attempts to address this question with evidence from empirical research rather than from theoretical conceptualizations. The focus is on ethnic groups in the United States with limited reference to important research from other English-speaking countries. The chapter does not attempt to address the complex questions of ethnic change in other parts of the world, where ethnic identity has widely differing implications based on particular historical and contextual factors.

Change is central to an understanding of both ethnic identity and acculturation. However, the study of change is a complex undertaking, and studying changes in ethnic identity in relation to acculturation presents a number of challenges. First, changes in acculturation and ethnic identity can best be conceptualized in terms of at least two dimensions: (a) retention of or identification with the ethnic, or original, culture and (b) adaptation to or identification with a dominant, host, or "new" culture (Berry & Sam, 1997; Laroche, Kim, Hui, & Joy, 1996; Leong & Chou, 1994; Phinney, 1990). Additional dimensions are possible and increasingly likely, including identification with a third culture (Oetting & Beauvais, 1991; Oetting, Swaim, & Chiarella, 1998) or multiple cultures (Root, 1996). Although this multidimensional conceptualization is increasingly accepted in writings about acculturation, it is still ignored in much research and discourse on acculturative change. People continue to refer to individuals or groups as being "more" or "less" acculturated, implying a linear change in the direction of becoming assimilated into the larger society. This terminology ignores other possible dimensions of ethnic change such as becoming bicultural.

Although the conceptualization of change along two or more dimensions is important in understanding ethnic identity, it has not been widely used in research. Changes in ethnic identity over time are accompanied by changes in identity relative to the dominant or host culture (e.g., the "American" identity in the case of the United States). A bicultural identity is not simply a midpoint between an ethnic and American identity; it is rather the result of identification with two cultures. Simple linear models of change are just as inappropriate for ethnic identity as they are for acculturation. Even two-dimensional models are limited in their ability to provide an understanding of identity in multiethnic individuals.

A second challenge to understanding the relationship of ethnic identity and acculturation is that two types of change over time need to be considered. On the one hand, changes occur among generations, as indicated by the differences that can be observed between immigrants and their children and grandchildren. The majority of acculturation research has assessed acculturation by comparing different generations of immigrants. On the other hand, changes occur during the lifetimes of immigrants and their descendants as they adapt to new situations and balance the demands and expectations of an old and a new culture. In this case, age at time of immigration and length of time in the new culture are important markers of acculturation. It is therefore important to keep in mind whether the changes under consideration occur at the individual level, during a lifetime, or at the group level (over generations). In addition, although change is the key concept, virtually all research has been cross-sectional, so that reported effects are typically differences among cohorts and generations or correlations with age, not change within individuals.

A third issue is that to examine the relationship between ethnic identity and acculturation, it is essential to define the particular aspects of each construct being compared. Because both constructs are complex and multidimensional (Berry, Poortinga, Segall, & Dasen, 1992; Keefe & Padilla, 1987; Phinney, 1990), there is little value in simply making global comparisons between them. Rather, the relationship between specific components and processes of change needs to be specified.

The most frequently used marker of acculturation is generation. Describing differences in ethnic identity by generation can be a useful starting point in examining the relationship between the two constructs. However, generational status is a poor measure of acculturation, and other factors are better indicators of acculturative change (Phinney & Flores, 2002). Generational status reveals little about how specific changes, such as language acquisition and loss, changing social networks, and evolving cultural values, may relate to ethnic identity. Acculturative changes over time in a new culture are uneven and can occur at differing rates for different aspects of acculturation and ethnic identity. A clear understanding of the relationship between the two requires examination of which aspects of acculturation are related to which components of ethnic identity.

Nevertheless, identifying and studying the relationship among aspects of acculturation and ethnic identity is not a straightforward process because of the differing views on exactly what constitutes each construct. Existing measures of the two reveal the confounding of the constructs, because the same items are often included in measures of each. Ethnic self-identification is a central aspect of ethnic identity (Phinney, 1990), but one's self-identification is often included in acculturation scales. For example, the Suinn–Lew Asian Self-Identity Acculturation Scale (SL–ASIA; Suinn, Ahuna, & Khoo, 1992) includes the item "How do you identify yourself?" (e.g., Asian, Asian American, or American); the Acculturation Rating Scale for Mexican Americans–Revised (ARSMA–II; Cuellar, Arnold, & Maldonado, 1995) asks for ratings of items such as "I like to identify myself as . . . [an Anglo American, a Mexican American, a Mexican]." On the other hand, behavioral markers of acculturation such as language and behavioral preferences are often included in measures of ethnic identity (e.g., Felix-Ortiz, 1994; Rogler, Cooney, & Ortiz, 1980). This overlap of items complicates the attempt to make clear empirical distinctions between the two constructs and thus to examine their interrelationship. Progress in empirical research in the field requires that the two constructs be clearly distinguished.

Components of Ethnic Identity

The definition and measurement of acculturation are addressed in a previous chapter in the volume (see chapter 2, Zane & Mak). Ethnic identity can be thought of as one aspect of the acculturation process that can be distinguished from other aspects by virtue of its focus on subjective feelings about one's ethnicity. By focusing on the subjective aspects and the theoretical bases for the construct, the specific aspects of ethnic identity that are amenable to precise measurement can be identified (Phinney, 1990, 1992). The aspects include (a) the ethnic self-identification, or self-label, that people use to identify themselves ethnically; (b) the subjective sense that people have of belonging to an ethnic group and their feelings about their group membership (i.e., the strength and valence of their ethnic identity); and (c) their level of ethnic identity development (i.e., the extent to which their feelings and understandings about their group have been consciously examined and issues surrounding ethnicity have been resolved, leading to an achieved ethnic identity). Changes associated with acculturation may be different for each of these components. The following sections explore research dealing with acculturative changes in each of these aspects of ethnic identity.

Acculturative Changes in Self-Identification or Self-Label

Ethnic self-identification, the most obvious and straightforward aspect of ethnic identity, is the group name or label that one chooses for oneself. The self-label carries meanings with it (Buriel, 1987; Larkey, Hecht, & Martin, 1993), but it is categorical. People either do or do not endorse a particular label as part of their self-identification. The label should not be confused conceptually with the aspects of the construct that reflect variation in strength, valence, or understanding of one's ethnicity.

Ethnic self-identification is most often measured through an open-ended question eliciting the name used for one's ethnic group or with checklists from which respondents select the appropriate label. Self-labels can include the country of origin (e.g., *Mexican, Chinese*), compound terms (e.g., *Mexican American, Chinese American*), or simply the new country (e.g., *American*). In addition, *panethnic* labels (Rumbaut, 1994), such as *Hispanic* and *Asian American*, are a reflection of a "denationalized identification with racial–ethnic minority groups in the country of destination" (p. 763), and multiethnic labels, such as *Black Japanese*, include more than one group (Phinney & Alipuria, 1996).

Changes in ethnic self-identification involve issues similar to the issues used to identify acculturation attitudes (Berry & Sam, 1997), such as whether or not to adopt the host country label and whether or not to retain the ethnic label. On arrival, immigrants are identified by their country of origin—that is, as a foreign national (e.g., *Mexican, Russian*). This identification is unlikely to be abandoned during their lifetime. The central question for immigrants is whether they identify themselves as American as well (i.e., by using a compound label such as *Mexican American*). In contrast, their U.S.-born children and grandchildren are citizens of the United States and are likely to include *American* in their self-labels. The question for them is whether to continue to identify themselves as ethnic by using a compound label, for example, *Mexican American* or identify themselves as simply *American*.

Research has generally shown that the use of an ethnic or national label dominates in the first generation, and the use of a compound or bicultural label becomes more common in the second generation. Data on changes in self-label by generation are available from a large study (Rumbaut, 1994) of more than 5,000 U.S. adolescents in Southern California and Florida, both first generation (foreign-born) and second generation (U.S. born), from Latin American and Asian immigrant families. An open-ended question was used to elicit self-identification. Responses were then coded into one of four categories, and the percentages in each category reported by generation. The first category, a national origin label such as *Chinese* or *Mexican*, was used by 43% of the first generation and 11% of the second generation. The use of a compound self-label such as *Chinese American* increased from 32% in the first generation to 49% in the second. Finally, a single label such as *American* increased from 3% to 20% across the two generations. Interestingly, the fourth category—a panethnic label such as *Asian American* or *Hispanic*—was used by about the same percentage, 20% to 22%, in each group. These panethnic labels represent new groupings that have appeared as a result of the structuring of ethnicity in the United States on the basis of broad ethnic categories. Presumably, immigrants do not arrive in the United States using self-labels such as *Hispanic* or *Asian American*; they learn over time that this is the way they are identified in the United States and then adopt the labels.

Previous research by Rogler and colleagues (1980) gave similar results; they showed that children of Puerto Rican immigrants were less likely than their parents to consider themselves as exclusively Puerto Rican and more likely to consider themselves as partly American (i.e., Puerto Rican American). Research in Britain (Hutnik, 1986) showed that some members of the second generation dropped the ethnic label altogether. Among second-generation Asian Indian adolescent girls in Britain, 36% considered themselves only British and not Indian, 26% considered themselves Indian only, whereas the remainder saw themselves to be both (or, in a few cases, neither). On the other hand, Phinney and Devich-Navarro (1997) found that no second-generation Mexican American adolescents labeled themselves just *American*.

In one of the few studies that have examined self-labels used by immigrants for three generations, Buriel and Cardoza (1993) found a substantial change from the first to the second generation but little change thereafter. Among first-generation seventh graders of Mexican descent, 62% called themselves *Mexican*, 23% called themselves *Mexican American*, and the remainder used other labels such as *Hispanic, Chicano,* or *Latino*. In both second- and third-generation students, 10% to 18% continued to call themselves *Mexican*, whereas about 60% used the label *Mexican American*.

The reason for the persistence of ethnic labels beyond the third generation may be unrelated to acculturation. European Americans of later generations are unlikely to label themselves as ethnic unless explicitly probed for ethnicity (Waters, 1990). In contrast, members of immigrant groups who are visually identifiable are likely to be ethnically labeled by others if not by themselves, regardless of their degree of acculturation. The most obvious example is African Americans, who after many generations have little choice about their label. Fourth- and fifth-generation Japanese Americans report being thought of as recent immigrants, in spite of their flawless English (Uba, 1994). Other markers of ethnicity, such as a Spanish surname, can also result is being labeled by others and hence labeling oneself (e.g., as *Hispanic* or *Latino*). Thus, at least to some extent, permanent characteristics determine labels for later generations.

A number of other factors influence ethnic labels. The way questions are asked and the options available on lists provide preselected categories that may influence the labels used (Phinney & Alipuria, 1996). The 2000 census in the United States, which allowed individuals to select labels from more than one category, provided a stimulus for people of mixed ethnicity to think more about the implications of their self-labels. Labels become politically sensitive in situations in which numbers are used as the basis for distribution of resources or determining voting districts. Ethnic groups may pressure individuals to use a certain label depending on group interests. Current attention to issues of multiculturalism has raised the salience of ethnicity for all groups. For these reasons the use of ethnic labels seems unlikely to decline during future generations in the United States.

Although categorical self-labels are important indicators of identification and have implications for attitudes and behaviors (Buriel, 1987), they do not encompass the full range of the psychological meaning of ethnic identity. To get a more complete understanding of its relationship to acculturation, other aspects of ethnic identity need to be considered.

Acculturative Changes in the Strength and Valence of Ethnic Identity

Perhaps the most fundamental aspect of ethnic identity is its strength and valence, or how strongly and positively individuals feel about their group membership. Conceptualization of ethnic identity in terms of strength and valence derives from the social identity theory of Tajfel and his colleagues (e.g., Tajfel & Turner, 1986), who defined *social identity* in terms of one's sense of belonging to a group and the attitudes and feelings that accompany a sense of group membership. Social identity theory posits that group identity is an important part of the self-concept; people generally attribute value to the groups to which they belong and derive self-esteem from their sense of belonging. Ethnic identity is one type of group identity that is central to the self-concept of members of ethnic minority groups. On the basis of social identity theory, ethnic identity is assumed to include the strength of one's sense of belonging to an ethnic group and valence, or the degree to which attitudes toward one's group membership are positive.

Changes in the strength and valence of ethnic identity that are related to acculturation have been studied in a variety of ways. Early conceptualizations focused on qualitatively different types of ethnic identity. Sue and Sue (1973) described three distinct types of ethnic identity for Asian Americans: (a) the traditionalists, who have strongly internalized cultural values; (b) the marginal people, who are between the two cultures and deny their own culture while striving for assimilation; and (c) the Asian Americans, who emphasize group pride and group esteem. Keefe and Padilla (1987) distinguished five types, ranging from a type similar to Sue and Sue's traditionalist to highly Anglicized, or assimilated, individuals. These types are generally assumed to represent different degrees of acculturation, but it is unclear whether these types differ over generations or whether they might change within a lifetime.

Research examining changes in ethnic identity strength have used a variety of measures to assess the construct. Because of differences in how the concept is operationalized, studies are difficult to compare (Phinney, 1990). Generally, however, when generation is used as the marker of acculturation, research with non-European ethnic minorities fairly consistently shows a decline in the strength and valence of ethnic identity from the first to the second generation, followed by a leveling off or much slower decline in later generations. On the other hand, measures assessing cultural knowledge, cultural practices, or ethnic behaviors, such as language proficiency rather than strength of identification typically show a substantial and continuing decline across generations.

Keefe and Padilla (1987) used the term *ethnic loyalty* to refer to a desire for cultural preservation, a preference for association with people of the same ethnic group, and perceptions of ethnic discrimination. Their study of several generations of Mexican-origin individuals and a follow-up of the study with a similar population (Arbona, Flores, & Novy, 1995) both showed that ethnic loyalty declined initially from the first to the second generations and then leveled off and remained largely constant. Cultural awareness, involving familiarity with Mexican culture, continued to decline from one generation to the next.

Rosenthal and Feldman (1992) examined changes in ethnic identity in first- and second-generation Chinese adolescents in Australia and the United States. Ethnic identity, defined as the rated importance and evaluation of Chinese origins, did not differ between first- and second-generation adolescents in Australia or the United States. On the other hand, behaviors and language ability (e.g., Chinese customs, fluency in Chinese) showed significant generational differences.

The previously mentioned research focused on the ethnic dimension of identity change. However, as noted, changes in identity must be considered in terms of two dimensions: (a) strength of identification with the ethnic group and (b) identification with the larger society. Far more research attention has been directed toward the former, but a few studies have included both dimensions.

Cameron and Lalonde (1994), in a study of first- and second-generation Italian Canadians, determined strength of identity by having participants rate their similarity to various reference groups, including *ethnic* and *Canadian*. Multidimensional scaling showed clear differences between the generations, with the second generation appearing more bicultural (i.e., retaining their ethnic identity but also feeling Canadian). A study of Chinese American college students by Ting-Toomey (1981) included Chinese American students from first- (immigrant) through fourth-generation (all grandparents born in the United States) immigrant families and assessed independently attitudes, values, and feelings toward each culture (Chinese and American) and toward both cultures (bicultural). On the basis of scores on these measures, students were classified as Chinese, American, or bicultural. As expected, most first-generation students strongly identified with the Chinese culture, and most second-generation students were bicultural. The bicultural identification continued into later generations, with more than three fourths of the third generation and two thirds of the fourth generation maintaining a bicultural identity. An exclusively American identity was found in only 5.6% of the third generation but was found in 33% of the fourth generation.

Virtually all the research discussed so far has used generational status as the marker of acculturation. However, although generational status is the most widely used marker of acculturation, it is simply what Bronfenbrenner and Crouter (1983) called a *social address*. Identification of generation indicates only where individuals and their ancestors were born, not which processes associated with acculturation may be operating in their lives. The exclusive use of generation does not allow examination of behavioral or attitude changes that may provide the underlying explanation of changes in ethnic identity (Phinney & Flores, 2002). Studies that have examined ethnic identity in relation to specific aspects of acculturation rather than simply to generation can help clarify the relationship between acculturation and ethnic identity.

Cuellar, Nyberg, Maldonado, and Roberts (1997) studied the relationship between ethnic identity and acculturation in a sample of university students of predominantly Mexican origin representing three generations.[1] Acculturation was measured with the ARSMA–II (Cuellar et al., 1995). This scale assesses acculturation on two dimensions—Mexican orientation and Anglo orientation. The scale measures primarily behavioral aspects of each type of orientation (e.g., language, friends) but also includes ratings of self-identification in four categories (Anglo American, Mexican American, Mexican, and American). Ethnic identity was assessed with the Multigroup Ethnic Identity Measure (MEIM; Phinney, 1992), which assesses three components of ethnic identity: ethnic affirmation and sense of belonging, ethnic identity achievement, and ethnic behaviors. The affirmation and belonging subscale is the component most closely represented by social identity theory (i.e., the strength and valence of ethnic identity; Tajfel & Turner, 1986). Cuellar and colleagues (1997) found no differences by generation in the total ethnic identity score or in any of the subscales. Using continuous generation scores, they found low negative correlations between generation and the total MEIM score and its subscales. Thus, generation does not appear to be a powerful predictor of ethnic identity. On the other hand, acculturation as measured by the Mexican orientation scale showed a strong relationship with the MEIM and its subscales. Specifically, the Mexican orientation score was highly correlated with total ethnic identity and with ethnic affirmation and belonging. In contrast, the Anglo orientation subscale had a very weak correlation to total ethnic identity and ethnic affirmation.

These results show that generation alone does not strongly predict ethnic identity change. When generation and acculturation are considered in relation to ethnic identity, acculturation, as assessed by process variables such as language and friendship, is a more powerful predictor of ethnic identity than generation. With generation controlled, ethnic identity change is strongly related to retention of ethnic cultural involvement and largely independent of orientation toward the dominant or Anglo culture. Furthermore, those with a high orientation toward both cultures had eth-

---

[1]In the article, Cuellar et al. (1997) referred to five generation levels: those in the first generation are all born outside the United States, whereas those in the fifth generation are born in the United States, as are all their grandparents. These five levels include what are generally considered the first, second, and third generations.

nic identity scores as high as or higher than those oriented only toward the Mexican culture. These results demonstrate that ethnic identity does not necessarily diminish with greater orientation toward the host culture; ethnic identity can remain strong without interfering with participation in the larger society.

Although these data allow for separate examination of the role of generation and of ethnic and American orientations, they nevertheless combine in single measures a number of different aspects of acculturation. Data from a recent study that we carried out in Los Angeles included assessment of ethnic identity and American identity and the acculturation process variables of language and social interaction. This study further clarifies the specific aspects of acculturation that are related to changes in identity. The study[2] included 474 adolescents (mean age = 14.6 years) from Armenian, Vietnamese, and Mexican backgrounds who were either U.S.-born children of immigrants or who were foreign born and arrived in the United States before age 7. Ethnic identity was assessed with seven items based on the MEIM (Phinney, 1992) that tapped ethnic affirmation and belonging. American identity was measured with three items assessing how strongly American the respondents felt. Reliabilities for these scales, using Cronbach's alpha, were .80 and .85, respectively. Ethnic identity did not differ by birth cohort, but American identity was significantly higher among the U.S.-born individuals. These results suggest that ethnic identity remains strong, whereas American identity increases between the foreign- and U.S.-born cohorts of adolescents in immigrant families.

In addition to identity measures, participants completed measures to assess directly characteristics that are considered to be indicators of acculturation. Language and social interaction have been generally considered to be central to acculturation and are widely used to measure it (Bankston & Zhou, 1995; Cuellar et al., 1995; Laroche, Kim, Hui, & Tomiuk, 1998; Marín & Marín, 1991; Suinn, et al., 1992). Ethnic language and peer social networks predict ethnic identity across diverse ethnic groups (Phinney, Romero, Nava, & Huang, 2001). In the current case, measures included the extent of peer interactions with their own and other ethnic groups and proficiency in the ethnic language and English. Preliminary analyses of variance for each ethnic group separately showed that these variables differed by place of birth. Specifically, social interaction with own-group peers was higher for the foreign-born adolescents than for the U.S. born, whereas social interaction with peers from other groups was higher for the U.S.-born adolescents. Similarly, ethnic language proficiency was higher among the foreign-born adolescents, whereas English proficiency was higher among the U.S. born. Similar changes in language over

---

[2] This study was carried out by Jean Phinney as part of the project "International Comparative Studies of Ethnocultural Youth," which is being carried out in fourteen countries that receive immigrants. Current members of the project group are J. Berry & K. Kwak (Canada), G. Horenczyk (Israel), K. Liebkind (Finland), F. Neto (Portugal), J. Phinney (United States), C. Sabatier (France), David L. Sam (Norway), D. Sang (Australia), P. Schmitz (Germany), P. Vedder (Netherlands), E. Virta (Sweden), F. van de Vijver (Netherlands), C. Westin (Sweden), and C. Ward (New Zealand).

time have been shown in other research studies (Portes & Schauffler, 1994). Thus, these variables seem to be useful as indicators of the acculturation process (i.e., changes that occur over time in a new culture).

To explore the relationship of ethnic identity to language and social interaction, multiple regression analyses were conducted with ethnic language proficiency, in-group peer interactions, and generation (U.S. born or foreign born) as predictors of ethnic identity. In-group peer interactions and ethnic language proficiency were significant predictors of ethnic identity, but generation was not. These results support the findings of Cuellar et al. (1997), which showed that generation alone is not strongly related to ethnic identity. To explore differences in the relationship of these acculturation process variables to identity that is independent of generation, separate analyses were carried out for each birth cohort (U.S. born and foreign born) for ethnic and American identities. In-group peer interaction and ethnic language were used as predictors of ethnic identity, and out-group interactions and English proficiency were used as predictors of American identity. The results, summarized in Table 3.1, demonstrate the influence of the process variables of language and social interaction on group identity. For both the U.S.-born and the foreign-born adolescents, more in-group peer interactions were associated with stronger ethnic identity, and more out-group peer interaction was associated with stronger American identity. In-group and out-group socialization patterns are important aspects of acculturation that change over time; these data suggest that as they change, one's sense of identity is likewise altered.

Language was also related to identity, but the results differed by birth cohort. For the foreign-born adolescents, greater English language proficiency predicted a stronger American identity, but ethnic language was unrelated to their ethnic identity. These adolescents are more likely to retain proficiency in their ethnic language; for them, English is more important in defining their identity than is the ethnic language. In contrast, for the U.S.-born adolescents, greater ethnic language proficiency predicted stronger ethnic identity, but English was not related to American

Table 3.1. Regression Analyses Predicting Ethnic and American Identity for Foreign-Born and U.S.-Born Adolescents From Immigrant Families

	Ethnic identity		American identity	
	Foreign born	U.S. born	Foreign born	U.S. born
Peer social interaction				
Same ethnic group	.15*	.33**		
Other ethnic groups			.25**	.38**
Language proficiency				
Ethnic language	.09	.21**		
English			.24**	.05
R^2	.07	.26	.16	.16
F	6.19**	24.03**	14.75**	12.19**

*$p < .05$. **$p < .001$.

identity. These youth typically are native English speakers, and their ethnic language has a stronger influence on their identity. However, in each case, as language proficiency changes over time during the acculturation process, the sense of group identity is likely to change.

Language was also examined in relation to ethnic identity by Laroche et al. (1998). With diverse ethnic samples in Canada (French, English, Italian, and Greek), they assessed French and English language usage and strength of ethnic identification. The latter was measured with a single item that indicated how strongly participants considered themselves to be group members (Francophone, Anglophone, Italian Canadian, Greek Canadian). The results suggest that increasing usage of the dominant language is associated with a decline in ethnic identity. However, the relationship was not linear. Generation was not included in the study, and the authors suggest that the relationship between the variables may change over generations.

Although language acculturation is important in the first and second generations, ethnic identity can remain strong in later generations, even when the ethnic language is not retained and social interaction with ethnic peers declines (Keefe & Padilla, 1987; Ting-Toomey, 1981). Other factors besides language and social interactions are important (Arbona et al., 1995). In particular, developmental changes and contextual factors need to be considered.

Developmental Changes in Ethnic Identity

In addition to changes directly associated with acculturation, ethnic identity varies developmentally over the life span. Developmental changes have implications for the relationship of ethnic identity to acculturation because differences that seem to be associated with acculturation may in fact be accounted for by development (Schonpflug, 1997). These effects are difficult to untangle because developmental and acculturative changes occur simultaneously. Nevertheless, they should be taken into account in attempting to understand acculturative changes, at least when dealing with children and adolescents.

The understanding of changes in identity with development is based on the developmental theory of Erikson (1968). According to Erikson, identity formation takes place through a process of exploration and commitment that typically occurs during adolescence and leads eventually to a commitment or decision in important identity domains, termed *identity achievement*. Many researchers have developed models of ethnic or racial identity development that parallel Erikson's, including those of Phinney (1989, 1993), Cross (1991; Cross & Fhagen-Smith, 2001), Helms (1990), and Atkinson, Morten, and Sue (1993). Each of these models posits a developmental progression leading to an achieved or internalized ethnic (or racial) identity (Phinney, 1990).

In a study using interviews to examine ethnic identity development in high school students, Phinney (1989, 1993) identified three stages of ethnic identity. An initial stage, termed the *unexamined* stage, is characterized by the lack of awareness or understanding of one's ethnicity. This initial stage ends when adolescents, as part of the identity formation process, engage in a period of exploration, similar to the moratorium described by Erikson (1968), to learn more about their group and themselves as group members. Ideally, this second phase leads to an achieved ethnic identity characterized by a commitment to one's ethnicity that is based on a clear understanding of its implications and a secure, confident sense of one's group membership. This developmental view suggests that ethnic identity varies with age, and individuals become increasingly clear about and committed to their ethnicity as they grow older.

Several models of racial identity development suggest similar changes over time. Cross and Fhagen-Smith (2001), focusing on African Americans, describe changes in Black identity over the life span. Black identity formation is considered a complex, interactive process that is highly influenced by the context, with individuals showing different patterns of change across the age range. Nevertheless the process involves a sequence similar to the ethnic identity stages described previously: the preencounter (unexamined) stage, the encounter experience that initiates exploration, immersion/emersion (moratorium), and internalization (achieved identity). Models of identity development have been proposed for other ethnic groups, including Asian Americans (Kim, 2001) and Latinos (Ferdman & Gallegos, 2001).

A conceptual model linking ethnic identity development and acculturation has been proposed by Leong and Chou (1994). They suggested that the earliest stage (unexamined, or pre-encounter) is equivalent to assimilation in that individuals at this stage would like to and perhaps try to be part of the larger society and may deny or downplay their own ethnicity. During the second stage (moratorium, or immersion/emersion), individuals become deeply involved in exploring and understanding their own culture and thus may seem separated from the larger society. Finally, with ethnic identity achievement (or internalization), individuals accept and value their own group and the larger society, and so they seem to be integrated.

However, Leong and Chou (1994) provided no data to support the model, and available evidence suggests that an achieved ethnic identity alone does not imply being integrated. Group identity among immigrants can best be thought of in terms of two distinct dimensions: (a) ethnic identity and (b) identity as a member of the larger society (i.e., national identity; Phinney, Horenczyk, Liebkind, & Vedder, 2001), similar to the two dimensions of acculturation (e.g., Berry & Sam, 1997). Having a strong ethnic identity and a strong national identity defines a bicultural identity, which implies integration into the larger society. A bicultural identity can take many different forms, such as blended, alternating, or multicultural (LaFromboise, Coleman, & Gerton, 1993; Phinney & Devich-Navarro, 1997). Most evidence suggests that a bicultural identity is the most adaptive identity for immigrants (Phinney et al., 2001), and the development of bicultural competence is an essential task for individuals dealing with two cultures (LaFromboise et al., 1993).

Few studies have attempted to examine empirically the changing relation of acculturation and ethnic identity with age. Developmental changes are best studied through longitudinal research, but little research has used this approach. As an alternative, Gurung and Mehta (1998) used a retrospective method to study developmental changes in ethnic self-labels. They asked Asian Indian young adults to describe their current self-labels and those they used in childhood, adolescence, and young adulthood. A clear pattern emerged; the use of a bicultural label (i.e., Indian American) increased from 29% in childhood to 48% in adolescence and 65% during college. In the period from childhood to young adulthood, there was a decline in labeling oneself as only *Indian* (from 43% to 27%) and in labeling oneself as only *American* (from 23% to 5%). These patterns are in accord with developmental theory. Young children have difficulty keeping in mind two aspects of a single stimulus, such as having two identities. With increasing age, children are better able to integrate various aspects of the self (Hart & Damon, 1986); as they enter adolescence, they are better able to understand the possibility of being bicultural, both ethnic and American. Interestingly, individuals used the label *American* less as they grew older, perhaps reflecting a move away from the early assimilationist attitudes suggested by Cross (1991). There was also a decline in separatist attitudes as a bicultural identity emerged.

Another method of studying ethnic identity development is through questionnaires. The previously mentioned MEIM (Phinney, 1992) contains an ethnic identity achievement sub-scale that assesses exploration of and commitment to one's ethnicity. This scale provides a continuous score ranging from *low* (lacking exploration or commitment to ethnicity) to *high* (having explored and made a commitment to an ethnicity); it does not, however, permit assignment of individuals to discrete stages of ethnic identity achievement. Using this scale, Tonks (1998) examined the relationship of ethnic identity achievement to acculturation attitudes among college students in Canada. Canadian acculturation attitudes were assessed with a measure developed for the study on the basis of work by Berry and colleagues (Berry, Kim, Power, Young, & Bujaki, 1989). Ethnic identity achievement was positively correlated with integration and separation attitudes and negatively correlated with assimilation and deculturation.[3] The results indicate that those with an achieved ethnic identity (i.e., those who have thought about and resolved issues related to their ethnicity) have attitudes that support cultural retention (either separation of integration). The results suggest a direct link between acculturation attitudes and developmental changes in ethnic identity.

Furthermore, as young people develop an increasingly secure ethnic identity, they become more accepting of other groups (Phinney, Ferguson, & Tate, 1997). These attitudes may contribute to a more bicultural or integrated position with regard to acculturation. However, the extent to

---

[3]Tonks (1998) used the term *deculturation* to refer to the absence of concern with ethnicity and culture per se, distinguishing it from the more negative connotations of marginalization as alienation and loss of identity.

which individuals become integrated is likely to depend to a considerable degree on contextual factors as well.

Contextual Factors in Ethnic Identity Retention

In addition to changes in ethnic identity over time, the community and larger setting in which ethnic group members live and work have an important impact on ethnic identity (Phinney & Rosenthal, 1992; Rosenthal & Hrynevich, 1985). The vitality of the ethnic community is clearly central to ethnic identity. The opportunity to engage in ethnic festivals, enjoy ethnic dance groups, obtain ethnic foods in markets and restaurants, and meet and marry coethnic individuals can be factors that enhance feelings of ethnic belonging and positive ethnic attitudes. The presence (or absence) of an ethnic community may be more powerful than generation as a factor in an individual's ethnic identity. However, the context generally and the community in particular are not necessarily directly linked to acculturation. The vitality of ethnic communities may wax and wane over time in reaction to forces unrelated to acculturation. For example, ethnic communities may be deliberately revitalized (Roosens, 1989). For groups with continuing immigration, the cultural context is renewed by newcomers from the culture of origin (Suarez-Orozco & Suarez-Orozco, 1995). Community and broader contextual effects thus are likely to interact in complex ways with both acculturation and ethnic identity.

One particular aspect of the context that has been studied in relation to ethnic identity is the experience of discrimination. Social identity theory (Tajfel & Turner, 1986) suggests that in the face of discrimination or prejudice, members of minority groups may assert their group identity as a way of dealing with the threats to their sense of self. Research findings indeed suggest a link between discrimination and ethnic identity (Felix-Ortiz, 1994; Romero & Roberts, 1998). Rumbaut (1994) found that adolescents who reported more discrimination were less likely to identify themselves as American. Discrimination is generally greater for members of the first generation as a result of their more evident differences from the larger society (e.g., an accent, different customs and clothing, other related characteristics; Gordon, 1964). It is possible therefore, that ethnic identity might be stronger in the first generation in response to such discrimination. In this case, as the discrimination declines over generations, ethnic identity might also decrease.

Although differences in language and customs diminish over generations, phenotypical (racial) differences do not. Visibility, or identifiability, is clearly a factor in discrimination, as well as in the maintenance of ethnic identity (Lalonde, Taylor, & Moghaddam, 1992). Members of ethnic groups that are racially identifiable have experienced continuing discrimination for many generations. For them, a strong ethnic identity may be thought of, at least in part, as a reaction to negative interactions with the larger society (Gaines & Reed, 1995; Hurtado, Gurin, & Peng, 1994; Keefe, 1992;

Matute-Bianchi, 1986). Insofar as the reception one experiences from the larger society is negative, ethnic identity would be expected to increase with time in the United States and remain strong over many generations. Among a group of African foreign students at universities in the United States, ethnic identity was significantly correlated with the number of years in the United States; the longer their stay, the higher their ethnic identity (Phinney & Onwughalu, 1996). Similarly, in a study of Asian American college students in a Midwestern university in the United States, Juang and Nguyen (1998) found that ethnic identity was significantly stronger in the second generation than in the first. In particular the second generation engaged in more ethnic exploration. The authors speculated that because the first generation grew up in Asia, they would already have a secure sense of being Asian and have no need to explore. In contrast, because those belonging to the second generation were growing up among a predominantly Caucasian population, they would be more likely to question and explore their Asian background.

In the United States the groups with the longest history of discrimination, which has continued for many generations, are American Indians and African Americans (Hacker, 1992; Pettigrew, 1988; Trimble, 1988). A consistent finding in research on ethnic identity is that African Americans typically have the highest ethnic identity scores among a variety of American ethnic groups (e.g., Phinney, 1992). Research with American Indians also documents a strong and continuing ethnic identity (Attneave, 1982). For these groups, as for members of any identifiably distinct group, the experience of discrimination may be inextricably linked to ethnic identity. In fact, several measures of ethnic identity include discrimination as a component (e.g., Felix-Ortiz, 1994).

Because of continuing discrimination, exploration of one's ethnicity may be necessary for each generation of visible minorities, as part of the ethnic identity formation process. During the period of exploration (Phinney, 1989) or immersion/emersion (Cross, 1991), young people typically learn the history of their group and become more aware of discrimination, a process that may lead to a deeper commitment to their ethnicity. On the other hand, additional experiences with discrimination as their social world widens in school or at work may motivate a deeper exploration of their ethnicity. Our own data from a study of immigrant adolescents show that the more perceived discrimination that is reported, the greater the ethnic exploration, although the relationship is not very strong. A similar relationship between perceived discrimination and ethnic exploration was reported by Romero and Roberts (1998). The outcome of this developmental process, a secure or achieved ethnic identity, is generally seen as leading to greater acceptance of other groups and the recognition of the value of working together across ethnic lines to eliminate discrimination (Atkinson et al., 1993; Phinney & Kohatsu, 1997; Tatum, 1992). However, the intergroup climate and attitudes within the community can be assumed to set the limits for the degree of integration that is possible.

Conclusion

The relationship of ethnic identity to acculturation is complex and difficult to study because the two constructs have been defined and measured using a variety of often overlapping indicators. It seems clear nevertheless that the two constructs are closely linked. Accompanying the acculturative changes that occur over time in a new culture are related changes in identity. Currently in the United States, members of non-European immigrant groups generally develop bicultural identities—that is, they become American but also retain their ethnic identity over time. Generational status has been the most widely used criterion of acculturation in research, but generation alone is not a good predictor of identity. Rather, changes in attitudes, behaviors, and values that occur with acculturation are better predictors of modifications in an individual's ethnic identity.

The important indicators of identity change are somewhat different for each succeeding generation. For members of the first generation, identity as a member of their culture of origin is secure and unlikely to change substantially. They may or may not develop an "American" identity; the extent to which they begin to feel American seems to be associated, in part, with learning English, developing social networks beyond their group, and becoming culturally competent in the new context (LaFromboise et al., 1993). For members of the second generation, an "American" identity is generally secure, in part because citizenship is granted with birth, and ethnic identity is likely to be associated with retention of ethnic language and social networks. For the third and later generations, the issues become more complex. Various contextual, historical, and political factors unrelated to acculturation influence the extent to which ethnic identity is retained. For non-European ethnic groups, racism and discrimination play a role in the preservation of ethnic identity, perhaps because a strong ethnic identity can provide a sense of group solidarity in the face of discrimination. Until immigrants and their descendants from non-European groups are accepted and treated as equals in the United States, as have been later generations of European immigrants (Waters, 1990), ethnic identity will remain important in their lives regardless of their level of acculturation.

References

Arbona, C., Flores, C., & Novy, D. (1995). Cultural awareness and ethnic loyalty: Dimensions of cultural variability among Mexican American college students. *Journal of Counseling and Development, 73*, 610–614.

Atkinson, D., Morten, G., & Sue, D. (1993). *Counseling American minorities* (4th ed.). Dubuque, IA: Brown & Benchmark.

Attneave, C. (1982). American Indians and Alaska Native families: Emigrants in their own homeland. In M. McGoldrick, J. Pearce, & J. Giordano (Eds.), *Ethnicity and family therapy* (pp. 55–83). New York: Guilford Press.

Bankston, C., & Zhou, M. (1995). Effects of minority language literacy on the academic achievement of Vietnamese youths in New Orleans. *Sociology of Education, 68*, 1–17.

Berry, J., Kim, U., Power, S., Young, M., & Bujaki, M. (1989). Acculturation attitudes in plural societies. *Applied Psychology, 38,* 185–206.

Berry, J., Poortinga, Y., Segall, M., & Dasen, P. (1992). *Cross-cultural psychology: Research and applications.* New York: Cambridge University Press.

Berry, J., & Sam, D. (1997). Acculturation and adaptation. In J. Berry, M. Segall, & C. Kagitcibasi (Eds.), *Handbook of cross-cultural psychology: Vol 3. Social behavior and applications* (pp. 291–326). Boston: Allyn & Bacon.

Bronfenbrenner, U., & Crouter, A. (1983). The evolution of environmental models in developmental research. In W. Kessen (Ed.), *Handbook of child psychology: History, theories, and methods* (Vol. 1, pp. 357–414). New York: Wiley.

Buriel, R. (1987). Ethnic labeling and identity among Mexican Americans. In J. P. &. M. Rotheram (Eds.), *Children's ethnic socialization: Pluralism and development* (pp. 134–152). Newbury Park, CA: Sage.

Buriel, R., & Cardoza, D. (1993). Mexican American ethnic labeling: An intrafamilial and intergenerational analysis. In M. Bernal & G. Knight (Eds.), *Ethnic identity: Formation and transmission among Hispanics and other minorities* (pp. 197–210). Albany: State University of New York Press.

Cameron, J., & Lalonde, R. (1994). Self, ethnicity, and social group memberships in two generations of Italian Canadians. *Personality and Social Psychology Bulletin, 20,* 514–520.

Cross, W. (1991). *Shades of Black: Diversity in African-American identity.* Philadelphia: Temple University Press.

Cross, W., & Fhagen-Smith, P. (2001). Patterns of African American identity development: A life span perspective. In C. Wijeyesinghe & B. Jackson III (Eds.), *New perspectives on racial identity development: A theoretical and practical anthology* (pp. 243–270). New York: New York University Press.

Cuellar, I., Arnold, B., & Maldonado, R. (1995). Acculturation rating scale for Mexican Americans–II: A revision of the original ARSMA scale. *Hispanic Journal of Behavioral Sciences, 17,* 275–304.

Cuellar, I., Nyberg, B., Maldonado, R., & Roberts, R. (1997). Ethnic identity and acculturation in a young adult Mexican-origin population. *Journal of Community Psychology, 25,* 535–549.

Erikson, E. (1968). *Identity: Youth and crisis.* New York: Norton.

Felix-Ortiz, M. (1994). A multidimensional measure of cultural identity for Latino and Latina adolescents. *Hispanic Journal of Behavioral Sciences, 16,* 99–116.

Ferdman, B., & Gallegos, P. (2001). Racial identity development and Latinos in the United States. In C. Wijeyesinghe & B. I. Jackson (Eds.), New perspectives on racial identity development: A theoretical and practical anthology (pp. 32–66). New York: New York University Press.

Gaines, S., Jr., & Reed, E. (1995). Prejudice from Allport to DuBois. *American Psychologist, 50,* 96–103.

Gordon, M. (1964). *Assimilation in American life: The role of race, religion, and national origin.* New York: Oxford University Press.

Gurung, R., & Mehta, V. (1998, August). *Minority health care providers: Relating identity, acculturation and beliefs.* Paper presented at the meeting of the American Psychological Association, San Francisco.

Hacker, A. (1992). *Two nations: Black and White, separate, hostile, unequal.* New York: Scribner's.

Hart, D., & Damon, W. (1986). Developmental trends in self understanding. *Social Cognition, 4,* 388–407.

Helms, J. (1990). *Black and White racial identity: Theory, research, and practice.* New York: Greenwood.

Hurtado, A., Gurin, P., & Peng, T. (1994). Social identities: A framework for studying the adaptations of the Mexican-descent population. *Social Problems, 41,* 129–151.

Hutnik, N. (1986). Patterns of ethnic minority identification and modes of social adaptation. *Ethnic and Racial Studies, 9,* 150–167.

Juang, L., & Nguyen, H. (1998, February). *Ethnic identity, other-group attitudes, genera-*

tional status, and adjustment in Asian American late adolescents. Paper presented at the meeting of the Society for Research on Adolescence, San Diego.

Keefe, S. (1992). Ethnic identity: The domain of perceptions of and attachment to ethnic groups and cultures. *Human Organizations, 51*(1), 35–43.

Keefe, S., & Padilla, A. M. (1987). *Chicano ethnicity.* Albuquerque: University of New Mexico Press.

Kim, J. (2001). Asian American identity development theory. In C. Wijeyesinghe & B. Jackson, III (Eds.), *New perspectives on racial identity development: A theoretical and practical anthology* (pp. 67–90). New York: New York University Press.

LaFromboise, T., Coleman, H., & Gerton, J. (1993). Psychological impact of biculturalism: Evidence and theory. *Psychological Bulletin, 114,* 395–412.

Lalonde, R., Taylor, D., & Moghaddam, F. (1992). The process of social identification for visible immigrant women in a multicultural context. *Journal of Cross-Cultural Psychology, 23,* 25–39.

Larkey, L., Hecht, M., & Martin, J. (1993). What's in a name? African American ethnic identity terms and self-determination. *Journal of Language and Social Psychology, 12,* 302–317.

Laroche, M., Kim, C., Hui, M., & Joy, A. (1996). An empirical study of multidimensional ethnic change: The case of the French Canadians in Quebec. *Journal of Cross-Cultural Psychology, 27,* 114–131.

Laroche, M., Kim, C., Hui, M., & Tomiuk, M. (1998). Test of a nonlinear relationship between linguistic acculturation and ethnic identification. *Journal of Cross-Cultural Psychology, 29,* 418–433.

Leong, F., & Chou, E. (1994). The role of ethnic identity and acculturation in the vocational behavior of Asian Americans: An integrative review. *Journal of Vocational Behavior, 44,* 155–172.

Marín, G., & Marín, B. (1991). *Research with Hispanic populations.* Newbury Park: Sage.

Matute-Bianchi, M. (1986). Ethnic identities and patterns of school success and failure among Mexican-descent and Japanese-American students in a California high school. *American Journal of Education, 95,* 233–255.

Oetting, E., & Beauvais, F. (1991). Orthogonal cultural identification theory: The cultural identification of minority adolescents. *International Journal of the Addictions, 25,* 655–685.

Oetting, E., Swaim, R., & Chiarella, M. (1998). Factor structure and invariance of the orthogonal cultural identification scale among American Indian and Mexican American youth. *Hispanic Journal of Behavioral Sciences, 20,* 131–154.

Pettigrew, T. (1988). Integration and pluralism. In P. Katz & D. Taylor (Eds.), *Eliminating racism: Profiles in controversy* (pp. 19–30). New York: Plenum Press.

Phinney, J. (1989). Stages of ethnic identity development in minority group adolescents. *Journal of Early Adolescence, 9,* 34–49.

Phinney, J. (1990). Ethnic identity in adolescents and adults: A review of research. *Psychological Bulletin, 108,* 499–514.

Phinney, J. (1992). The multigroup ethnic identity measure: A new scale for use with diverse groups. *Journal of Adolescent Research, 7,* 156–176.

Phinney, J. (1993). A three-stage model of ethnic identity development. In M. Bernal & G. Knight (Eds.), *Ethnic identity: Formation and transmission among Hispanics and other minorities* (pp. 61–79). Albany: State University of New York Press.

Phinney, J., & Alipuria, L. (1996). At the interface of culture: Multiethnic/multiracial high school and college students. *Journal of Social Psychology, 136,* 139–158.

Phinney, J., & Devich-Navarro, M. (1997). Variations in bicultural identification among African American and Mexican American adolescents. *Journal of Research on Adolescence, 7,* 3–32.

Phinney, J., Ferguson, D., & Tate, J. (1997). Intergroup attitudes among ethnic minority adolescents: A causal model. *Child Development, 68,* 955–969.

Phinney, J., & Flores, J. (2002). "Unpackaging" acculturation: Components of acculturation as predictors of traditional sex role attitudes. *Journal of Cross-Cultural Psychology, 33,* 319–330.

Phinney, J., Horenczyk, G., Liebkind, K., & Vedder, P. (2001). Ethnic identity, immigration, and well-being: An interaction perspective. *Journal of Social Issues, 57*, 493–510.

Phinney, J., & Kohatsu, E. (1997). Ethnic and racial identity development and mental health. In J. Schulenberg, J. Maggs, & K. Hurrelman (Eds.), *Health risks and developmental transitions in adolescence* (pp. 420–443). New York: Cambridge University Press.

Phinney, J., & Onwughalu, M. (1996). Racial identity and perceptions of American ideals among African American and African students in the United States. *International Journal of Intercultural Relations, 20*, 127–140.

Phinney, J., Romero, I., Nava, M., & Huang, D. (2001). The role of language, parents, and peers in ethnic identity among adolescents in immigrant families. *Journal of Youth and Adolescence, 30*, 135–153.

Phinney, J., & Rosenthal, D. (1992). Ethnic identity formation in adolescence: Process, context, and outcome. In G. Adams, T. Gulotta, & R. Montemayor (Eds.), *Identity formation during adolescence* (pp. 145–172). Newbury Park, CA: Sage.

Portes, A., & Schauffler, R. (1994). Language and the second generation: Bilingualism yesterday and today. *International Migration Review, 28*, 640–661.

Rogler, L., Cooney, R., & Ortiz, V. (1980). Intergenerational change in ethnic identity in the Puerto Rican family. *International Migration Review, 14*, 193–214.

Romero, A., & Roberts, R. (1998). Perception of discrimination and ethnocultural variables in a diverse group of adolescents. *Journal of Adolescence, 21*, 641–656.

Roosens, E. (1989). *Creating ethnicity: The process of ethnogenesis*. Thousand Oaks, CA: Sage.

Root, M. (1996). *The multiracial experience*. Thousand Oaks, CA: Sage.

Rosenthal, D., & Feldman, S. (1992). The nature and stability of ethnic identity in Chinese youth. *Journal of Cross-Cultural Psychology, 23*, 214–227.

Rosenthal, D., & Hrynevich, C. (1985). Ethnicity and ethnic identity: A comparative study of Greek-, Italian-, and Anglo-Australian adolescents. *International Journal of Psychology, 20*, 723–742.

Rumbaut, R. (1994). The crucible within: Ethnic identity, self-esteem, and segmented assimilation among children of immigrants. *International Migration Review, 28*, 748–794.

Schonpflug, U. (1997). Acculturation: Adaptation or development? *Applied Psychology: An International Review, 46*, 52–55.

Suarez-Orozco, C., & Suarez-Orozco, M. (1995). *Transformations: Immigration, family life, and achievement motivation among Latino adolescents*. Stanford, CA: Stanford University Press.

Sue, S., & Sue, D. (1973). Chinese American personality and mental health. In S. Sue & N. Wagner (Eds.), *Asian Americans: Psychological perspectives* (pp. 111–124). Palo Alto, CA: Science & Behavior Books.

Suinn, R., Ahuna, C., & Khoo, G. (1992). The Suinn–Lew Asian self-identity acculturation scale: Concurrent and factorial validation. *Educational and Psychological Measurement, 52*, 1041–1046.

Tajfel, H., & Turner, J. (1986). The social identity theory of intergroup behavior. In S. Worchel & W. Austin (Eds.), *Psychology of intergroup relations* (pp. 7–24). Chicago: Nelson-Hall.

Tatum, B. (1992). Talking about race, learning about racism: The application of racial identity development theory in the classroom. *Harvard Educational Review, 62*, 1–24.

Ting-Toomey, S. (1981). Ethnic identity and close friendship in Chinese-American college students. *International Journal of Intercultural Relations, 5*, 383–406.

Tonks, R. (1998). *Towards a hermeneutical understanding of identity and ethnicity in Canada*. Dissertation, Simon Fraser University, Burnaby, BC, Canada.

Trimble, J. (1988). Stereotypical images, American Indians, and prejudice. In P. Katz & D. Taylor (Eds.), *Eliminating racism: Profiles in controversy* (pp. 181–202). New York: Plenum Press.

Uba, L. (1994). *Asian Americans: Personality patterns, identity, and mental health*. New York: Guilford Press.

Waters, M. (1990). *Ethnic options: Choosing identities in America*. Berkeley: University of California Press.

4

Acculturation and Changes in Cultural Values

Gerardo Marín and Raymond J. Gamba

The role of acculturation in changing or modifying the central values of a group is a question that has received limited attention in the literature despite its significance in understanding the process of culture learning by individuals and the development of multicultural societies. This interest by researchers in identifying the power of the acculturative process in changing basic, cultural values or beliefs stems from a number of reasons. First, cultural values or beliefs are often used to identify specific ethnic or cultural groups or differentiate among them (e.g., Hofstede, 1980; Kluckhohn & Strodbeck, 1961). The possible power of acculturation to produce significant changes in these values has important implications for their continued existence, for defining the characteristics of these groups, and for characterizing the nature of multicultural societies. Also supporting the need for studying the role of acculturation in changing cultural values is the assumption made by researchers that these values *do* shape people's actions (e.g., Marín, Marín, Pérez-Stable, Otero-Sabogal, & Sabogal, 1989; Marín, Posner, & Kinyon, 1993; Marks et al., 1987). Again, a change in values caused by the acculturative process can dictate a change in the behaviors that would be expected from the members of an ethnic or cultural group undergoing acculturation. Another factor that supports the need to identify the role of acculturation in changing a group's values is the fact that these values are often considered important components in the design of culturally appropriate interventions to change people's behavior (Cuellar, Arnold, & Gonzalez, 1995; Marín, 1993a). Indeed, a significant modification introduced by acculturation into a group's values would demand the need to consider the acculturation level of the targeted individuals while designing a culturally appropriate intervention to change the behavior of an individual or the members of a group.

As mentioned, despite the importance of identifying how acculturation modifies the cultural values and beliefs of a group, the literature is fairly limited in describing the possible relationship and related changes. This chapter briefly summarizes some of the findings available in the literature

---

Preparation of this chapter was partially funded by Grants 6PT-6001 and 6RT-0407 from the Tobacco-Related Disease Research Program in California.

on the changes in values and beliefs that can be expected as the result of the process of acculturation. The object of analysis is the values and beliefs that are used to characterize a culture or an ethnic group, not the personal values (e.g., religious, ethical) that an individual may have. Although cultural and personal values both influence behavior and may indeed be modified by acculturation, the emphasis in this chapter is placed solely on cultural values and beliefs (i.e., macrosocial values such as familialism or power distance). This distinction is made because of the lack of relevant research on the effects of acculturation on personal values. In addition, cultural values are perceived by researchers as directly relevant to the description and identification of cultural and ethnic groups and the design of massive behavior change interventions (Marín, 1992, 1993a).

Significance of Cultural Values and Beliefs

Defining and identifying a group's cultural values and beliefs is an area of research that has received significant attention from social scientists interested in cultural issues. Indeed, Kluckhohn (1951) made values a central component of his definition of *culture:*

> Culture consists in patterned ways of thinking, feeling and reacting, acquired and transmitted by symbols, constituting the distinctive achievements of human groups, including their embodiments in artifacts; the essential core of culture consists of traditional (i.e., historically derived and selected) ideas and especially their attached values. (p. 86)

The significance of values in defining a cultural group also can be observed in more recent definitions of culture. For example, Matsumoto (1996) expanded on Barnouw's (1973) definition of culture by suggesting that culture is a set of attitudes, values, beliefs, and behaviors that is shared by a group of people and communicated from one generation to the next through language or other means of communication. This last definition of culture is of particular significance because it suggests that culture is maintained and possibly changed as individuals interact and communicate. Acculturation, as a process of culture learning, could therefore be expected to indeed change the nature of a group's culture and the defining characteristics of nations and societies (Redfield, Linton, & Herskovits, 1936).

Empirical Evidence on the Relationship Between Acculturation and Values

As mentioned, few studies have tried to document the changes in cultural values and beliefs produced by the process of acculturation. In most instances, these studies have been part of the process of scale development, and in almost all cases the populations studied have been of Hispanic origin. Further complicating the analysis of the data is that in many studies, acculturation has been perceived as a unidirectional process by which characteristics of the culture of origin are shed in favor of acquiring those of the host culture. Nevertheless, an overview of the findings in the literature serves as a heuristic device for defining future research needs. To simplify the presentation, the literature is reviewed in the following sections according to the specific cultural values studied. This selective listing of research findings shows the ample concerns of researchers and at the same time identifies gaps in knowledge.

Worldviews and Problem-Solving Strategies

One of the first attempts to identify changes in cultural values and beliefs was carried out by a team of researchers in Miami, Florida, while studying the acculturation process among Cuban Americans (Szapocznik, Scopetta, Kurtines, & Aranalde, 1978). In the study the authors included a section containing questions about language, daily customs and habits, and idealized lifestyles, whereas another section of the survey contained problem situations centered on relational style, the person–nature relationship, beliefs about human nature, time orientation, and activity orientation. The data showed a change in the type of preferred values underlying problem-solving strategies as a function of length of residence in the United States. In that study, Cuban Americans with longer residence in the United States tended to respond similarly to non-Hispanic, White respondents. Respondents were found, therefore, to change from a more Hispanic orientation as acculturation was assumed to proceed. Subsequent research with Cuban adolescents and their parents in Dade County, Florida (Szapocznik & Kurtines, 1980), showed that large intergenerational gaps on acculturation scores were associated with drug abuse, and drug abuse was significantly correlated with changes in value orientation but not with behavioral changes. These patterns of generational differences and conflict have also been found recently among Russian immigrants to the United States (Birman & Trickett, 2001), although in this case, adolescents tended to identify more with Russian culture than their parents.

More recently, Cuellar et al. (1995) examined the relationship between a behavioral measure of acculturation (Cuellar, Arnold, & Maldonado, 1995) and five scales that measured cultural cognitive constructs (i.e., machismo, familialism, folk beliefs, fatalism, and personalismo). The sample consisted of college students in Texas. Items related to the machismo construct attempted to measure positive and negative aspects of the assumed Hispanic male role (e.g., womanizer, brave, courageous). Familialism items examined the size, relationships, and emotional support of the family, whereas folk beliefs were measured by identifying the acceptance of folk illnesses and supernatural influences on health and treatment of health problems. Fatalism items measured the extent to which respondents believed that their behavior and future were beyond their control, and personalismo items measured the cultural construct of a warm and personal way of relating to an individual. Results showed that with the exception of the personalismo construct, acculturation decreased the personal significance of the four remaining cultural constructs so that as individuals became more assimilated, they tended to report lower personal significance of the cultural values (i.e., familialism, fatalism, machismo, and folk beliefs). The authors concluded that although past research has demonstrated a relationship between acculturation and behavioral changes, their research has shown that the acculturation process also influenced cognitive aspects.

Familialism

The relationship between acculturation and the cultural value of familialism has probably received the greatest amount of attention in the literature. Familialism has been suggested to be one of the most important cultural values of Latinos (e.g., Alvirez & Bean, 1976; Moore, 1970) and is often mentioned as important among other ethnic groups in the United States including Asian Americans, African Americans (Landrine & Klonoff, 1996), and American Indians (Mindel & Habenstein, 1981). Familialism is usually described as a cultural value that is related to a strong identification and attachment with nuclear and extended families as well as feelings of loyalty, reciprocity, and solidarity (Triandis, Marín, Betancourt, Lisansky, & Chang, 1982). Indeed, studies have found that Hispanics value familialism more than do non-Hispanic Whites (e.g., Marín, 1993b).

Studies on the relationship between familialism and acculturation have looked at the behavioral as well as the attitudinal aspects of this value primarily among Latino populations. Keefe (1980) for example, examined the hypothesis that acculturation is related to changes in family organization. More specifically, she expected to find that as individuals from a migrating culture came into contact with the host culture, they would adopt a nuclear family structure as opposed to an extended family structure. This longitudinal study, part of Padilla's (1980) study of cultural awareness and ethnic loyalty, included Mexican Americans and non-Hispanic Whites from three Southern California cities (Santa Paula, Santa Barbara, and Oxnard). Keefe's research indicated that the extended family pattern remained as an important part of the Mexican-American experience, and in fact the extended family was strengthened and became larger as contact with the host culture increased. Correlational analyses revealed that the extended family did not decline as cultural awareness and ethnic loyalty decreased. On the contrary, interaction with primary and secondary kin increased with declining cultural awareness and ethnic loyalty. Keefe suggested the following:

> Respondents who are more "Mexican" in ethnicity have few nearby primary or secondary kin with whom they visit or exchange aid. Respondents who are more "American" in ethnicity, on the other hand, have

primary and secondary kin nearby with whom they frequently visit and exchange aid. (p. 93)

The pattern of findings first identified by Keefe (1980) was also found by Rueschenberg and Buriel (1989) among Mexican Americans in the San Fernando and San Gabriel areas of Los Angeles County. Using a systems perspective, the researchers examined changes in internal (e.g., closeness, expressiveness, conflict, organizing, and control mechanisms) and external (independence, achievement orientation, intellectual/cultural orientation, and active/recreational orientation) aspects of family functioning. Families were classified as unacculturated, moderately acculturated, or acculturated depending on the number of years spent in the United States and the primary language spoken at home. Basic internal family systems (cohesion, expressiveness conflict, organization, and control) remained the same among the three acculturation groups, but the external family systems were found to change as acculturation was perceived to increase. A different study using a variety of dimensions (mostly internal) related to family functioning (e.g., respect for authority figures, child-rearing practices, gender role differentiation) showed no effect of acculturation on the strength of the attitudes measured (Negy, 1993).

A study with Latinos from San Francisco and Miami (Sabogal, Marín, Otero-Sabogal, VanOss Marín, & Pérez-Stable, 1987) investigated the relationship between acculturation and certain attitudinal components of the Hispanic value of familialism. The study attempted to clarify the conflicting findings in the literature: that acculturation either (a) breaks down the structure of the extended family (Edgerton & Karno, 1971) or (b) is related to strengthening and integrating the extended family (Griffith & Villavicencio, 1985; Keefe, 1980). Acculturation was measured using a short unidimensional scale (Marín, Sabogal, VanOss Marín, Otero-Sabogal, & Pérez-Stable, 1987) that included behavioral acculturation items measuring proficiency and preference for speaking a language in a number of settings (e.g., as a child, at home, while thinking, with a friend, at school or work). Three components of attitudinal familialism were measured: (a) familial obligations, (b) perceived support from the family, and (c) family as referents. The family obligations component is related to the perceived need to provide material and emotional support to members of the extended family. Perceived support from the family is related to the perception of family members as reliable providers of help and support to solve problems. Finally, the role of the family as referents scale asked about the influence of relatives on the individual's behavior and attitude formation. Results showed that some aspects of the cultural value of familialism (e.g., perceived support from the family) were not influenced by acculturation pressures. Perceived support from the family remained strong and personally important regardless of having acculturated to the host culture of the United States. At the same time, other components or aspects of the cultural value of familialism (i.e., familial obligations and the power of family members as referents) did diminish in importance as acculturation progressed. These latter findings supported previous research and theorizing suggesting that acculturation modified only certain aspects of family relationships among Hispanics (e.g., Edgerton & Karno, 1971; Grebler, Moore, & Guzman, 1970; Landy, 1959; Mindel, 1980).

Familialism is also considered of particular significance among other ethnic groups. Landrine and Klonoff (1996) included items measuring familialism in their African American Acculturation Scale and found that agreement with those items tended to correlate with behavioral health indicators (e.g., use of tobacco).

Gender Roles

A few studies have found changes in perceived gender roles. A study of 204 Vietnamese adolescents living in Australia showed that the belief of traditional family and gender values decreased with time spent in the host country (Rosenthal, Rainieri, & Klimdis, 1996). In a recent study of 106 Chinese university students in Toronto, men were more traditional than women in their expectations regarding family hierarchy and the social roles of men and women (Tang & Dion, 1999). Most interesting was the fact that women valued these traditions less than did men. Both studies conclude that greater conflict and dissatisfaction exists among women with regard to gender roles during exposure to a new culture. Another study of 50 Mexican American married mothers and 33 Mexican American married fathers showed that as these parents acculturated, they tended to adopt gender-egalitarian attitudes (Leaper & Valin, 1996). The implication of these studies seems to be that gender roles change fairly rapidly as individuals pass through the acculturative process, which usually reflects a modification of traditional values and an approach toward those of the host culture.

Need for Achievement

Despite the significant amount of attention that the need for achievement construct received in the literature in the past, it seems that only one study has analyzed how acculturation may influence this cultural value (Lew, Allen, Papouchis, & Ritzler, 1998). The sample consisted of Asian American students from California and New York. The Asian Anglo Acculturation Scale (Kohatsu, 1992) was used to measure acculturation by evaluating the extent to which an individual had cognitively, affectively, and behaviorally incorporated American mainstream and Asian cultural values. The results showed that identification with Asian cultures (labeled Asian acculturation) was related to endorsement of social-oriented achievement, whereas bicultural individuals were more likely to endorse individual-oriented achievement. The authors concluded that an individual with a bicultural identity tends to adopt a multifaceted achievement style that does not necessarily discourage individual independence and achievement as long as individual successes reflect positively on the family.

Collectivism and Individualism

Cross-cultural studies have analyzed how a collectivistic or individualistic orientation is affected by acculturative experiences. Rosenthal, Bell, Demetriou, and Efklides (1989) examined whether acculturation among Greek immigrants in Australia was related to changes in individualistic and collective values. Overall, the results of the study suggested that the collectivist values were still prominent among Greek immigrant parents and that they contrasted with the individualistic values of their Anglo-Australian counterparts.

In another cross-cultural study, Feldman, Mont-Reynaud, and Rosenthal (1992) examined how acculturation was related to eight value domains among seven samples: first- and second-generation Chinese youth in the United States and Australia, adolescents from Hong Kong, and Anglo adolescents in the United States and Australia. Acculturation was measured by the proxy measure of generational status of the respondents (i.e., place of birth). In general, results showed that the values of the respondents were influenced by acculturation to Western values. This was most clearly shown in the first-generation individuals. First-generation Chinese youths living in the West compared with their Hong Kong counterparts placed less value on "traditional values" (i.e., the importance of rites and rituals, noncompetitiveness, cultural superiority, tradition, disinterest and purity, and repaying favors) and "family as residential unit" (i.e., the importance of aging parents living at home or single individuals living at home) and more value on "outward success" (i.e., the importance of wealth, power, a comfortable life, saving face, and social recognition). There were only modest differences in values between first- and second-generation Chinese youth. Only "family as residential unit" significantly differentiated first- from second-generation youths. Regardless of their acculturation and that they were born in the West, second-generation Chinese adolescents did differ from Western adolescents in valuing the family. Finally, and perhaps most interesting, respondents' scores on individualism did not differ across all samples.

Acculturation and Cultural Values and Beliefs

The literature reviewed in the previous sections seems to provide support for the assumption that acculturation does influence certain cultural values and beliefs of the members of a given ethnic group. These influences seem to be strong enough to be revealed even when researchers use poor sampling techniques or when the constructs are not properly measured. The consistency in the changes suggests that the results are not random and could be understood to support the notion that as acculturation proceeds, individuals modify certain aspects of the cultural values and beliefs they hold.

The literature also clearly shows that some cultural values, or at least some dimensions of a given cultural value (e.g., familialism), remain strong as an individual acculturates. In a study of familialism among Latinos (Marín, 1992; Sabogal et al., 1987), the authors suggested that the more basic aspect of familialism ("attitudinal familialism") was less likely to be influenced by acculturation than the less significant "behavioral familialism." Attitudinal aspects of familialism were perceived to include feelings of loyalty, solidarity, and reciprocity. Behavioral familialism, on the other hand, referred to aspects such as visiting patterns and other behaviors associated with familial relationships that can easily change as a function of acculturation and other external factors such as migration, marriage, and economic mobility. Indeed, Berry (1997) recently called for a differentiation between deeper and superficial changes in values that are expected to be produced by acculturation.

The need for understanding these changes has important implications, not just for the provision of culturally appropriate services but also in terms of understanding family functioning and intergenerational conflict. Based on the studies reviewed in this chapter, future studies conducted with various acculturating groups must not only examine which values change as acculturation proceeds but also distinguish among the various components of the cultural values. Identifying these patterns is essential in properly describing the relationship between acculturation and cultural values. Yet to be properly defined are the characteristics, or nature, of those components of cultural values and beliefs that resist change as acculturation proceeds. An assumption could be that the highly valued components of a cultural value or belief would be the best candidates for maintenance in the face of acculturation. In this case, the components that are most central to the cultural value or belief would remain strong despite acculturation and generational changes. At the same time, an argument could be made that the components that remain significant despite acculturation are those that define a group's own identity and value structure. Unfortunately, the data available are limited and do not strongly support an explanation.

The call for additional research is not foreign to many literature reviews in developing areas of psychological knowledge. Nevertheless, research on the relationship between acculturation and cultural values has often suffered from faulty conceptualization, poor instrumentation, and incomplete analyses that provide little confidence on the status of the field. At the same time, the available evidence seems to be potentially useful and relevant for designing better and more comprehensive studies that will enhance understanding of this relationship. The current evidence tends to support the notion that indeed an important relationship exists, the nature and strength of which needs to be studied.

It is clear from the research reviewed that there is a need to continue developing research projects that clarify the relationship between acculturation and the process of change in core values across a variety of cultures. Most work in this area has been hindered by many methodological shortcomings, including the fact that the vast majority of studies are either one-time, retrospective, or cross-sectional by design. To truly assess how acculturation influences core values, more serious attempts at creating longitudinal designs are necessary. Given the evidence from familialism, it is plausible that other core values may be multidimensional; therefore, certain aspects of the core value may be subject to change while other aspects remain stable.

Understanding core values and how they change or remain stable as a result of the acculturation process has various implications in service delivery and in basic and applied research. Culturally appropriate services, whether in the physical or mental health areas, must reflect the relevant significance of a cultural value in the target population. An appropriate understanding of societal forces must include an analysis of family functioning and generational conflict (e.g., Birman & Trickett, 2001) that takes into consideration the acculturation level of the individuals involved and the effects of acculturation on the group's values. These outcomes can only be achieved after a more thorough understanding of the role of acculturation on changes of core cultural values has been obtained. These needs can only be met with more and better multidisciplinary research.

References

Alvirez, D., & Bean, F. D. (1976). The Mexican American family. In C. H. Mindel & R. N. Haberstein (Eds.), *Ethnic families in America* (pp. 271–291). New York: Elsevier.

Barnouw, V. (1973). *Culture and personality*. Homewood, IL: Dorsey Press.

Berry, J. W. (1997). Immigration, acculturation, and adaptation. *Applied Psychology: An International Review, 46,* 5–34.

Birman, D., & Trickett, E. J. (2001). Cultural transitions in first-generation immigrants: Acculturation of Soviet Jewish refugee adolescents and parents. *Journal of Cross-Cultural Psychology, 32,* 456–477.

Cuellar, I., Arnold. B., & Gonzalez, G. (1995). Cognitive referents of acculturation: Assessment of cultural constructs in Mexican Americans. *Journal of Community Psychology, 23,* 339–356.

Cuellar, I., Arnold, B., & Maldonado, R. (1995). Acculturation rating scale for Mexican Americans–II: A revision of the original ARSMA scale. *Hispanic Journal of Behavioral Sciences, 17,* 275–304.

Edgerton, R. B., & Karno, M. (1971). Mexican-American bilingualism and the perception of mental illness. *Archives of General Psychiatry, 24,* 286–290.

Feldman, S. S., Mont-Reynaud, R., & Rosenthal, D. A. (1992). When East moves West: The acculturation of values of Chinese adolescents in the U.S. and Australia. *Journal of Research on Adolescence, 2,* 147–173.

Grebler, L., Moore, J. W., & Guzman, R. C. (1970). *The Mexican American people.* New York: Free Press.

Griffith, J., & Villavicencio, S. (1985). Relationships among acculturation, sociodemographic characteristics, and social support in Mexican American adults. *Hispanic Journal of Behavioral Sciences, 7,* 75–92.

Hofstede, G. (1980). *Culture's consequences: International differences in work-related values.* Beverly Hills, CA: Sage.

Keefe, S. M. (1980). Acculturation and the extended family among urban Mexican Americans. In A. M. Padilla (Ed.), *Acculturation: Theory, models, and some new findings* (pp. 85–110). Boulder, CO: Westview.

Kluckhohn, C. (1951). The study of culture. In D. Lerner & H. D. Lasswell (Eds.), *The policy sciences* (pp. 86–101). Stanford, CA: Stanford University Press.

Kluckhohn, F. R., & Strodbeck, F. L. (1961). *Variations in value orientations.* Westport, CT: Greenwood Press.

Kohatsu, E. L. (1992). The effects of racial identity and acculturation on anxiety, assertiveness, and ascribed identity among Asian American college students. (Doctoral dissertation, University of Maryland, 1992.) *Dissertation Abstracts International, 54*(2), 1102-B.

Landrine, H., & Klonoff, E. A. (1996). *African American acculturation: Deconstructing race and reviving culture.* Thousand Oaks, CA: Sage.

Landy, D. (1959). *Tropical childhood: Cultural transmission and learning in a rural Puerto Rico village.* Chapel Hill: University of North Carolina Press.

Leaper, C., & Valin, D. (1996). Predictors of Mexican American mothers' and fathers' attitudes toward gender equity. *Hispanic Journal of Behavioral Sciences, 18*, 343–355.

Lew, A. S., Allen, R., Papouchis, N., & Ritzler, B. (1998). Achievement orientation and fear of success in Asian American college students. *Journal of Clinical Psychology, 54*, 97–108.

Marín, B. V., Marín, G., Pérez-Stable, E. J., Otero-Sabogal, R., & Sabogal, F. (1989). Cultural differences in attitudes toward smoking: Developing messages using the theory of reasoned action. *Journal of Applied Social Psychology, 20*, 478–493.

Marín, G. (1992). Issues in the measurement of acculturation among Hispanics. In K. F. Geisinger (Ed.), *Psychological testing of Hispanics* (pp. 235–252). Washington, DC: American Psychological Association.

Marín, G. (1993a). Defining culturally appropriate community interventions: Hispanics as a case study. *Journal of Community Psychology, 21*, 149–161.

Marín, G. (1993b). Influence of acculturation on familialism and self-identification among Hispanics. In M. E. Bernal & G. P. Knight (Eds.), *Ethnic identity: Formation and transmission among Hispanics and other minorities* (pp. 181–196). New York: University of New York Press.

Marín, G., Posner, S., & Kinyon, J. (1993). Alcohol expectancies among Hispanics and non-Hispanic whites: Role of drinking and acculturation. *Hispanic Journal of Behavioral Sciences, 15*, 373–381.

Marín, G., Sabogal, F., VanOss Marín, B., Otero-Sabogal, R., & Pérez-Stable, E. (1987). Development of short acculturation scale for Hispanics. *Hispanic Journal of Behavioral Sciences, 9*, 183–205.

Marks, G., Solis, J., Richardson, J. L., Collins, L. M., Birba, L., & Hisserich, J. C. (1987). Health behavior of elderly Hispanic women: Does cultural assimilation make a difference? *American Journal of Public Health, 77*, 1315–1319.

Matsumoto, D. (1996). *Culture and psychology.* Pacific Grove, CA: Brooks/Cole.

Mindel, C. H. (1980). Extended familialism among urban Mexican Americans, Anglos, and Blacks. *Hispanic Journal of Behavioral Sciences, 2*, 21–34.

Mindel, C. H., & Habenstein, R. W. (1981). *Ethnic families in America: Patterns and variations.* New York: Elsevier.

Moore, J. W. (1970). *Mexican Americans.* Englewood Cliffs, NJ: Prentice-Hall.

Negy, C. (1993). Anglo- and Hispanic-Americans' performance on the family attitude scale and its implications for improving measurements of acculturation. *Psychological Reports, 73*, 1211–1217.

Padilla, A. M. (1980). The role of cultural awareness and ethnic loyalty in acculturation. In A. M. Padilla (Ed.), *Acculturation: Theory, models, and some new findings* (pp. 47–84). Boulder, CO: Westview Press.

Redfield, R., Linton, R., & Herskovits, M. J. (1936). Memorandum on the study of acculturation. *American Anthropologist, 38*, 149–152.

Rosenthal, D. A., Bell, R., Demetriou, A., & Efklides, A. (1989). From collectivism to individualism? The acculturation of Greek immigrants to Australia. *International Journal of Psychology, 24*, 57–71.

Rosenthal, D., Rainieri, N., & Klimdis, S. (1996). Vietnamese adolescents in Australia: Relationships between perceptions of self and parental values, intergenerational conflict, and gender dissatisfaction. *International Journal of Psychology, 31*, 81–91.

Rueschenberg, E., & Buriel, R. (1989). Mexican American family functioning and acculturation: A family systems approach. *Hispanic Journal of Behavioral Sciences, 11*, 232–244.

Sabogal, F., Marín, G., Otero-Sabogal, R., VanOss Marín, B., & Pérez-Stable, E. J. (1987).

Hispanic familialism and acculturation: What changes and what doesn't? *Hispanic Journal of Behavioral Sciences, 9,* 397–412.

Szapocznik, J., & Kurtines, W. (1980). Acculturation, biculturalism, and adjustment among Cuban Americans. In A. M. Padilla (Ed.), *Acculturation: Theory, models and some new findings* (pp. 139–159). Boulder, CO: Westview Press.

Szapocznik, J., Scopetta, M. A., Kurtines, W., & Aranalde, M. (1978). Theory and measurement of acculturation. *Interamerican Journal of Psychology, 12,* 113–130.

Tang, T., & Dion, K. (1999). Gender and acculturation in relation to traditionalism: Perceptions of self and parents among Chinese students. *Sex Roles, 41,* 17–29.

Triandis, H. C., Marín, G., Betancourt, H., Lisansky, J., & Chang, B. (1982). *Dimensions of familialism among Hispanic and mainstream Navy recruits.* Unpublished report, Department of Psychology, University of Illinois, Champaign–Urbana.

5

Acculturation Among Ethnic Minority Families

Kevin M. Chun and Phillip D. Akutsu

Examining acculturation within a family context brings forth rich opportunities to understand the dynamic and multidimensional nature of this construct. This is particularly evident when considering how acculturation affects not only the entire family system but also marital and parent–child subsystems and individual family members. Furthermore, the varying developmental abilities and tasks of family members, the ecological context of family development, and the presence of continuing or new life stressors and events add to the complexity of this research area. Compared with the other chapter topics in this book, there exists a paucity of studies that systematically examine acculturation within families. Furthermore, the scope of research topics in this area varies depending on the ethnicity of the population under investigation. Nonetheless, recent attention to multiculturalism and pluralism in psychology has spawned a relatively new body of acculturation research, especially research conducted with newer Asian and Latino immigrant and refugee families.

A primary goal of this chapter is to provide one of the first reviews and critiques of acculturation research involving African American, Asian American, Latino, and American Indian families. This includes a discussion of past findings from empirical and qualitative journal articles and chapters primarily from the past decade. This body of scholarship points to four broad areas of inquiry. One area involves the study of modified or new family socialization practices during acculturation. For example, researchers have investigated alterations or adaptations in child-rearing techniques, parental disciplining methods, and parental expectations for their children's behavior in new cultural environments. Another area includes studies on the effects of acculturation on family functioning and family environments. Many of these studies also assess individual psychological problems and risk behaviors that are associated with disrupted family environments during acculturation. An additional area of research centers on parent–child relations, with particular attention to parent–child discord caused by conflicts in cultural values and shifts in family responsibilities. Finally, researchers have investigated the influence of acculturation on marital relations, including changes in gender attitudes and roles among immigrant couples.

The following literature review is thus organized according to four general categories that reflect these primary research areas: family socialization and parenting practices, family functioning, parent–child relations, and marital relations. These four categories are not absolute representations of the family acculturation literature but instead help organize the majority of topics for analysis and discussion. In addition, these categories are more comprehensively addressed for Asian American and Latino families because most of the acculturation research has focused on these two ethnic groups. Such inequities in ethnic representation deserve further consideration and are briefly discussed in the Critique and Recommendations section at the end of this chapter.

Review of the Literature

African Americans

The acculturation experiences of African Americans and their families have received little attention, primarily because of two misperceptions of African Americans in the field of psychology: (a) African Americans are essentially without a distinct culture because it was destroyed during slavery, and (b) African Americans are a race, not an ethnic or a cultural group (Landrine & Klonoff, 1996). Such assumptions have been refuted by recent scholarly works that highlight the complex value systems found in many families of African origin (e.g., Black, 1996). The complex systems include family values that center on collective kinship bonds and a strong spiritual and religious orientation (Hines & Boyd-Franklin, 1996). Theoretical frameworks have been developed to demonstrate how these values and beliefs may transform and evolve during acculturation. One such framework has been outlined by Landrine and Klonoff (1996), who believe that acculturation among African Americans is best represented by a dynamic and circuitous process that follows "the principle of return." According to this principle, individuals return to the values and customs of their culture of origin by the end of their lives regardless of their initial acculturation level. Furthermore, these researchers asserted that this acculturation process is influenced by fractionization and allopatricity. *Fractionization* refers to the idea that acculturation occurs when fractions of individuals are separated from "parent groups" who reside in African American enclaves and act as guardians of traditional culture. *Allopatricity* refers to the notion that individuals who are either psychologically or geographically displaced from their traditional cultural group are the most prepared for acculturation. Finally, Landrine and Klonoff proposed that acculturation is further influenced by the quality of contact with the dominant group and the messages imparted about dominant groups during socialization.

These concepts have broad implications for acculturation in African American families. Based on the principle of return, a family's ability to adapt to challenging social conditions may be enhanced as members strengthen their ties with their culture of origin over time, which includes upholding cultural values and beliefs that may facilitate coping with racist and discriminatory environments. Fractionization and allopatricity highlight the fact that differential rates of acculturation may occur in African American families, especially when contact with other African Americans and dominant culture varies for individual members. Still, these concepts require additional study and empirical support.

Family acculturation experiences for African Americans have not been entirely overlooked, even though most studies do not directly measure acculturation. In this case, some empirical inquiries indirectly evaluate family acculturation by examining various indexes of marginalization. As presented in chapter 1, this mode of acculturation occurs when an ethnic group faces a loss of cultural identity in conjunction with a problematic or absent relationship with the dominant group. Marginalization is likewise supported by social stratification in which minority groups are afforded limited access to society's wealth and resources (Marger, 1997). The deleterious effects of marginalization and economic hardship on African American family functioning cannot be understated. Past research demonstrates that it has profound negative effects on child and adolescent development by disrupting and diminishing supportive, stable, and involved parenting (McLoyd, 1990). Parenting deficits may in turn contribute to behavioral problems among children. For instance, among poor, urban African American families, punitive and less nurturing parenting is associated with externalizing behavior problems for boys (Florsheim, Tolan, & Gorman-Smith, 1996). Past research also indicates that economic hardship limits parents' ability to play an active role in their child's education. This was demonstrated in a study of African American middle school girls (Connell, Halpern-Felsher, Clifford, Crichlow, & Usinger, 1995). Results from this study showed that socioeconomic status is inversely related to parental support of education, resulting in poorer self-perceptions of academic competence, fewer positive relationships with teachers and classmates, and eventual loss of engagement in school.

Economic pressures may also lead to early "parentification" of young family members, requiring them to fulfill household duties and responsibilities when their parents maintain extended work hours (Hines & Boyd-Franklin, 1996). This is supported by past findings showing that on average, African American urban school children care for family members more often than their European American peers (Kilmer, Cowen, Wyman, Work, & Magnus, 1998). The authors of this study state that the presence of more children in African American families may contribute to this finding, in addition to pressing child care demands imposed by poverty.

Such poverty-related stressors are especially relevant to African American families with single women as the head of the household. Approximately 40% of these families have incomes that are less than the federal poverty line, which is 2 times higher than the percentage of impoverished households headed by single European American women (U.S. Bureau of the Census, 1999). For these African American women and their families, economic survival and social marginalization may dominate their acculturation experience.

Discrimination and prejudice are additional indexes of marginalization that may influence family socialization and parenting practices. In discriminatory environments, African American parents may actively engage in racial socialization of their children by providing them with information that helps them understand the nature of race and how it affects their lives (Thompson, 1994). In addition to conveying specific messages regarding race, racial socialization involves modeling behaviors and exposure of children to different cultural contexts and environments (Thornton, Chatters, Taylor, & Allen, 1990). Racial socialization can thus be regarded as an important feature of acculturation for some African American families; it entails transmitting adaptive behaviors and strategies across generations to deal with a potentially threatening social environment. Finally, African American parents may be less willing to grant their children independence and autonomy so that they can protect their children's welfare in a racist environment. This tendency is reflected in past findings that African American parents exert more direct control over their adolescents' behavior inside and outside of the home compared with European American parents (Bulcroft, Carmody, & Bulcroft, 1996).

American Indians

Few empirical studies have identified how acculturation affects the family functioning of American Indians. This is not entirely surprising given the lack of empirical data on family processes and functioning for ethnic minorities in general. Nevertheless, researchers have proposed conceptual schemes to highlight varying patterns of family acculturation for this diverse ethnic group. For example, LaFromboise, Trimble, and Mohatt (1990) stated that American Indian families could be grouped into four categories—traditional, transitional, bicultural, or assimilated—that reflect different levels of cultural commitment. According to these researchers, traditional families adhere to traditional customs, values, and practices and tend to speak in their native language. In contrast, assimilated families attempt to adopt the dominant society's traits and lifestyle and are generally accepted into the dominant society. The families who tend to maintain the cultural traits of their own ethnic group and the dominant group but do not fully identify with either group are considered transitional. Finally, bicultural families are accepted by the dominant society and have established ties with the American Indian and dominant cultures.

Although this model illustrates the diverse experiences of American Indian families, its reliance on discrete categorizations fails to address the complex and dynamic process of changing cultural commitments. In this case, family members may conceivably exhibit an amalgam of cultural commitment patterns to meet different social demands. Varying abilities (e.g., intellectual, cognitive, interpersonal) and personal characteristics (e.g., age, stage of ethnic identity formation, level of motivation) may further contribute to multiple commitment patterns within a single family. Still, this model is an important first step in conceptualizing how American Indian families may maintain or modify their cultural identities during acculturation. Furthermore, it lays the groundwork for future acculturation research that may determine whether different cultural commitment patterns lead to differential exposure to acculturation stressors and subsequent variations in adaptation difficulties.

Analysis of acculturation among American Indian families must also account for the lengthy history of government-sponsored oppression against this ethnic group. Beginning in the early 19th century, federally backed programs promoted Christian proselytism, forced matriculation of Indian youths into boarding schools, and removed Indian nations from their tribal lands (Harjo, 1993; LaDue, 1994). Such governmental actions may be regarded as acts of cultural genocide because they attempted to systematically destroy American Indian culture and family networks. Furthermore, they provide the sociocultural context for understanding past findings on substance abuse, domestic violence, and adolescent suicide. Studies have shown that American Indian youths tend to abuse drugs at a younger age than European American youths (Oetting, Edwards, & Beauvais, 1989). Such instances of substance abuse tend to co-occur with a constellation of related family and individual problems. Cherokee families, for example, report higher rates of parental substance abuse, family violence, poverty, and crime than European American families (Costello, Farmer, Angold, Burns, & Erkanli, 1997). Navajo women who face economic hardship are also at risk for being targets of domestic violence (Fairchild, Fairchild, & Stoner, 1998). Additionally, suicide attempts among Navajo youths have been linked to the use of hard liquor and feelings of alienation from family and the community (Grossman, Milligan, & Deyo, 1991). Again, most of these studies implicitly link these problems with stressful social conditions associated with continued acts of oppression and discrimination by the dominant group. Marginalization is thus a predominant feature of acculturation for many American Indian families. However, the relationship of this acculturation mode to family adjustment remains somewhat speculative because of the lack of acculturation measures in the majority of investigations.

Specific family processes such as family support, involvement, and enculturation may guard against the potentially disruptive effects of marginalization. In this case, high familial support is related to lower self-reported alcohol use and intoxification for American Indian high school students (Dick, Manson, & Beals, 1993). In addition, American Indian youths are more likely to affiliate with peers who do not abuse drugs (and thus are less likely to abuse drugs) if their families establish explicit sanctions against substance abuse (Swaim, Oetting, Thurman, Beauvais, & Edwards, 1993). Finally, risk for drug abuse among American Indian youths decreases when their self-esteem improves and their cultural identity is strengthened through enculturation (Zimmerman, Ramirez-Valles, Washienko, Walter, & Dyer, 1996). Again, additional studies with American Indian families are needed to uncover the true nature and course of acculturation and the causal links of acculturative stress to family and individual dysfunction.

Asian Americans

Navigating through the growing body of acculturation literature on Asian American families presents multiple challenges. For instance, conducting comparative analyses and interpreting data across studies are complicated by the use of varying or unrelated acculturation measures. Also, Asian Americans are frequently considered to be a monolithic population. Important sociocultural differences between and within different Asian groups are consequently neglected despite their potential influence on acculturation processes. Similarly, Asian American family relations are often viewed stereotypically, which is most evident when researchers unquestioningly assume that Asian immigrant parents are the most static family members and are highly resistant to cultural change. In such instances, culture conflicts between immigrant parents and their American-born children often become the focal point of investigation. Although this family dynamic exists for many Asian Americans, the capacity of immigrant parents to develop bicultural competencies and adaptive skills is frequently overlooked. These and other inherent complexities and dilemmas associated with Asian American family research are discussed in the following literature review.

Family socialization and parenting practices. Certain acculturation patterns in family socialization and parenting practices have received considerable attention in the literature. For instance, researchers have noted that Asian immigrant parents may maintain "traditional" collectivistic family values in new cultural environments (Shon & Ja, 1982; Uba, 1994), a practice that includes reinforcing the importance of filial obligations over individual needs, obedience to parental authority, deference to elders, and conformity to a hierarchical, patrilineal family structure. In addition, researchers have identified ensuing intergenerational differences or conflicts that develop when Asian American youths adopt a more individualistic social orientation than their parents. For example, Vietnamese American parents may strongly believe in absolute parental authority, deference to elders, and filial obligation, whereas their adolescents may be more inclined to reject these values (Nguyen & Williams, 1989).

Past findings suggest that immigrant parents are authoritarian as indicated by high involvement in their children's lives and strict regulation of their children's behaviors. For instance, Taiwanese-national and first-generation Taiwanese American parents exert more parental control than European American parents (Lin & Fu, 1990). Similar reports have been made about immigrant Cantonese parents, who may monitor their children well into their junior high school years (Sung, 1985). Among South Asian Indians, immigrant parents may attempt to control the everyday activities and life decisions of their children because they fear that their children may experience "cultural contamination" by the dominant culture (Segal, 1991). Parental control, however, may become attenuated during acculturation as indicated by Taiwanese American mothers who reported less authoritarian and controlling child-rearing attitudes than mothers who reside in Taiwan (Chiu, 1987).

Still, these widely recognized acculturation patterns are not entirely applicable for many Asian American families. For instance, in respect to family socialization, Asian immigrant parents do not uniformly favor collectivistic values over individualistic ones. In addition, adoption of individualistic values in a new culture does not preclude the maintenance of collectivistic values. In one study, Taiwanese-national and first-generation Taiwanese Americans encouraged their children to be independent but exerted more parental control than European American parents (Lin & Fu, 1990). Similarly, first- and second-generation Chinese American adolescents have shown both a collectivistic concern for harmonious family relationships and an individualistic orientation in their reasoning and justifications for hypothetical family conflicts (Yau & Smetana, 1993). Bicultural family values have also been reported for elderly Asian American immigrants despite their being stereotyped as the most traditional family members. For example, one study found that elderly, first-generation Korean American immigrants who lived in their own separate households expressed an appreciation for independence and individual freedom within the family (Kauh, 1997).

Asian national and immigrant parents are not exclusively authoritarian. In fact, past findings revealed that Taiwanese-national and first-generation Taiwanese American mothers may exhibit more democratic attitudes than European American mothers as measured by encouragement of verbal expression, endorsement of egalitarianism in the parent–child relationship, and development of comradeship and sharing with their children (Chiu, 1987). Additionally, Asian American parents do not necessarily become less involved in their children's lives during acculturation. Instead, greater acculturation may alter gender roles and thus increase parental involvement. This phenomenon was seen among highly acculturated South Asian Indian fathers who were more likely to teach, discipline, play with, and care for their children than their less acculturated peers (Jain & Belsky, 1997).

Finally, Asian American mothers and fathers may not exhibit uniform parenting practices during the acculturation process. For example, among first-generation South Asian Indian parents, mothers may encourage North American cultural characteristics in their children, whereas fathers may promote Indian values (especially in girls) related to deference to authority and attention to manners and politeness (Patel, Power, & Bhavnagri, 1996).

Family functioning. Past studies have also focused on the relationship of acculturation to family problems and disrupted family environments, including examining heightened conflict between family members and behavioral problems among children during acculturation. Such issues are particularly relevant to Southeast Asian refugees who have experienced premigration and migration stressors and traumas, which may compound the effects of acculturative stress. Vietnamese and Cambodian refugees in particular report a broad array of family problems ranging from parent–child communication difficulties to antisocial behavior among children (Boehnlein et al., 1995). Significant ethnic differences also exist between these two refugee groups. A higher percentage of Vietnamese parents report more family problems (especially involving disrespectful children) and poorer health resulting from their children's behavioral problems (Boehnlein et al., 1995). In any case, refugee families may report multiple family problems that have variable courses. For instance, Vietnamese families have reported "family hassles" (e.g., conflicts with siblings, disagreements with parents regarding educational goals or potential spouse) that increase over time and "acculturation-related hassles" (e.g., self-reported instances of prejudice and discrimination) that decrease over time (Lay & Nguyen, 1998). Interestingly, research shows that social support networks do not always buffer families from these problems and may actually become a significant source of stress. For example, Vietnamese and Cambodian families who have active social networks report less family cohesion and more family conflict, which may stem from added social obligations and strained family resources (Rousseau, Drapeau, & Corin, 1997).

Although acculturation may place considerable stress on the family environment, global deficits in family functioning are not always experienced. For example, significant ethnic or generational differences in family cohesion and family conflict were not found in a study of first- and second-generation Chinese Americans, Hong Kong Chinese, and European Americans (Rosenthal & Feldman, 1989). Likewise, acculturation was not related to family cohesion, conflict, or satisfaction for a Filipino college sample (Heras & Revilla, 1994). These nonsignificant relationships between acculturation and family environment are difficult to explain. They may partly stem from the study measures, which inadequately assessed the multifaceted nature of family acculturation experiences. Additionally, family members may have possessed certain adaptive characteristics or skills that acted as protective factors against acculturative stress. For instance, bicultural competence seems to protect families from acculturative stress and potential disruption. Past findings show that bicultural Vietnamese American adolescents (i.e., those equally involved in Vietnamese and American cultures) report more positive family relationships compared with adolescents with less bicultural involvement (Nguyen, Messé, & Stollak, 1999). In such instances, family members who skillfully adapt to different cultural environments may be especially adroit in preventing conflicts related to acculturation.

Parent–child relations. The influence of acculturation on parent–child relations is another important topic in the literature. Acculturative stress combined with the demands of normative developmental milestones (e.g., the development of autonomy among adolescents) place considerable strain on parent–child relations. For instance, shifts in power or role reversals may occur if children are more proficient in English or more familiar with American society and customs than their parents. In these situations, children may be required to shoulder parental responsibilities and concerns (e.g., paying bills, responding to mail, acting as an intermediary in business dealings), which complicates their ability to meet their developmental goals.

The potential for parent–child conflict in Asian American families seems to vary by age and generational status; the likelihood of parent–child conflict seems to be greater for older adolescents (Yau & Smetana, 1993). In addition, second-generation Chinese American teenagers may be more likely to experience conflict with their parents than their first-generation peers because they face more parental regulation, monitoring, and decision-making (Rosenthal & Feldman, 1989). Still, parental control does not always lead to parent–child conflict. In fact, parents who feel competent and sufficiently in control of their children may report fewer problems. For instance, immigrant Chinese American parents who perceive themselves as effective, responsible, and influential caretakers report more positive relationships with their children (Ying, 1999). Newer immigrant children may also view parental control favorably. In this case, parental control is positively related to perceived parental warmth and negatively related to perceived parental neglect among Korean adolescents (Rohner & Pettengill, 1985).

Marital relations. Researchers have also investigated the relationship of acculturation to psychosocial adjustment in the marital dyad, including the significance of changing gender roles. Immigrant women who enter the job market to support their families often acquire greater family responsibilities and newfound independence, whereas their husbands experience a loss of status and lowered self-esteem. Researchers have commented that such changes increase the risk for domestic violence against immigrant women, especially when their husbands have patriarchal ideas of marriage (Ho, 1990; Kim & Grant, 1997; Lovell, Tran, & Nguyen, 1987). The risk for spousal abuse further increases when men abuse substances to cope with acculturative stress (Rhee, 1997). The stress resulting from changing gender roles and marital dynamics may explain why married Asian immigrant couples tend to report less life satisfaction than their unmarried peers (Ying, 1996).

Latinos

It is difficult to discern any definitive conclusions regarding Latino family acculturation because most study results are inconsistent and incomplete. In addition, the experiences of Mexican Americans, Puerto Ricans, and Cuban Americans have received greater attention at the expense of other groups such as Central and South Americans. As such, there continues to be much conjecture about the influence of acculturation on family values and roles, socialization, child rearing, and parenting styles for Latino families.

As mentioned previously, it is important to reiterate that the term *Latino* is used in this section to describe many different ethnic groups. This ethnic label unfortunately fails to describe the rich and diverse sociocultural and immigrant experiences of each group; therefore, certain individuals choose not to use this term to describe their ethnic membership.

Family socialization and parenting practices. The concept of *familism*, or *familialism,* is one of the most distinct and important culture-specific values of Latinos as a whole (Marín, 1993; Vega, 1995). Social scientists have identified this cultural phenomenon in various Latino subgroups including Mexican Americans (Alvirez & Bean, 1976; Mindel, 1980), Puerto Ricans (Cortés, 1995; Glazer & Moynihan, 1963), Cuban Americans (Sabogal, Marín, Otero-Sabogal, Marín, & Pérez-Stable, 1987; Szapocznik & Kurtines, 1980), and South Americans (Cohen, 1979). Specifically, *familism* is described as a cultural commitment to Latino family life and consists of strong identification with and attachment to members of the nuclear and extended family as well as strong feelings of loyalty, reciprocity, and solidarity toward members of the family (Marín, 1993; Triandis, Marín, Betancourt, Lisansky, & Chang, 1982; Vega, 1995).

Several studies have attempted to determine which aspects of familism are significantly affected by acculturation. For example, among Mexican Americans, higher levels of acculturation are associated with less family involvement (Brooks, Stuewig, & Lecroy, 1998), less family support (Barrett, Joe, & Simpson, 1991), and increased family conflict (Samaniego & Gonzales, 1999). As Cortés (1995) has suggested, it is likely that beliefs in certain aspects of familism become less salient as acculturation occurs in various Latino families. Past findings have shown that increased acculturation is related to lower levels of familial obligations (e.g., to provide material and emotional support to family) and considering family members to be referents, or role models, among Mexican, Cuban, and Central Americans (Sabogal et al., 1987) and Puerto Ricans (Rogler & Cooney, 1991). Increased acculturation is also reported to have a critical effect on the way Latino families seek help or assistance for troubled family members (Chun & Akutsu, 1999). For instance, among Mexican Americans, higher levels of acculturation are related to increased help-seeking from extended family members (Keefe, Padilla, & Carlos, 1979; Rogler & Cooney, 1991) and mental health professionals (Edgerton & Karno, 1971; Karno & Edgerton, 1969)—in other words, seeking help above and beyond the nuclear family.

In contrast, several studies found that increased acculturation stimulated greater familism or family cohesion. For example, more acculturated Mexican Americans report increased contact with social network members in general (e.g., nuclear family members, extended family members, friends and neighbors), more "reciprocal helping" relationships, and increased dependence on nuclear family members for social support than less acculturated Mexican Americans (Griffith & Villavicencio, 1985). Other studies with Mexican Americans also reported that familism and social support increases with acculturation (Keefe & Padilla, 1987; Luna et al., 1996; Ramirez & Arce, 1981). Similarly, acculturation is positively related to family obligations and support from relatives among Puerto Ricans (Rodriguez & Kosloski, 1998). For a largely Salvadoran sample, greater acculturation is linked to higher family competence (Birman, 1998). However, most of the individuals in this latter study lived in Spanish-speaking, Latino-oriented homes, and the author suggests this finding should be interpreted within this limited context.

Other studies have found that acculturation does not have a detectable effect on familism. No significant changes in levels of family support or cohesion across successive generations were reported for Mexican Americans (Fuligni, 1998; Rueschenberg & Buriel, 1989; Sabogal et al., 1987) and Cuban and Central Americans (Sabogal et al., 1987). Considering these mixed results as a whole, it is possible that researchers have not fully captured the complexity of acculturation effects on familism across various Latino groups. For example, in one study with Mexican, Cuban, and Central Americans, the importance of familial obligations and family as referents decreased as acculturation increased, although perceived support from the family was unaffected by acculturation level, generational status, place of birth, and place where the individuals were raised (Sabogal et al., 1987). Marín (1993) suggested that a possible reason for these inconsistencies in the literature may be caused by the failure to distinguish between attitudinal and behavioral components of familism for Latino families. That is, internal attitudes about familism may remain strong, but behavioral correlates of familism may change over time. Recent research by Cortés (1995) on beliefs about familism among Puerto Ricans suggested that acculturative processes affecting attitudinal familism, including familial obligations and support from relatives, may be different across generations. The complexity of this relationship between acculturation and family processes is further illustrated by the results of a recent study on Puerto Rican adolescent mothers (Contreras, Lopez, Rivera-Mosquera, Raymond-Smith, & Rothstein, 1999). Specifically, increased grandmother involvement contributed to less parenting stress for Puerto Rican adolescent mothers when acculturation was low but more parenting stress when acculturation was high.

Some study findings suggest that socialization to Latino cultural norms may be reinforced between mothers and their children. For instance, mothers who score high in "Mexicanism" have children who possess more correct ethnic self-labels, correctly sort more pictures of Mexican American and non-Mexican American children, use more ethnic behaviors, and have more ethnic knowledge and preferences (Knight, Bernal, Garza, Cota, & Ocampo, 1993). A recent study also found that lower levels of parental acculturation were associated with increased ethnic behaviors for Mexican American elementary school children (Quintana & Vera, 1999). Some evidence even suggests that acculturation may promote more competitive behavior in Latino children, behavior that is contrary to the traditional Latino values emphasizing cooperative interactions. For example, greater acculturation (as inferred by nationality) is associated with less cooperative and more competitive game playing for preschool- and elementary-school-age Mexican immigrant and Mexican American children (Kagan & Madsen, 1971). Knight and Kagan (1977) reported similar findings, suggesting that second- and third-generation Mexican American children lose cooperative values through successive generations. However, several researchers caution that social class may provide a better explanation for this phenomenon (Ramirez & Castaneda, 1974).

In terms of parenting practices, several researchers have asserted that less acculturated Latino parents may be more authoritarian in their parenting style as reflected in stricter discipline strategies and less permission for child autonomy (Zapata & Jaramillo, 1982). Likewise, high acculturation may contribute to inconsistent discipline practices for mainly Spanish-speaking, low socioeconomic status, Mexican immigrant and Mexican American women (Dumka, Roosa, & Jackson, 1997). Researchers have also noted that acculturation may promote greater acceptance or adoption of Western discipline practices, such as using time-out techniques instead of corporal punishment strategies. For example, after controlling for the impact of socioeconomic differences, foreign-born Mexican American mothers were more likely to use spanking to discipline their children than their U.S.-born Mexican American counterparts (Buriel, Mercado, Rodriguez, & Chavez, 1991). However, for both Mexican American groups, the removal of special privileges (e.g., no television or playing with a friend) was used more often than spanking for disciplining. Some researchers (Samaniego & Gonzales, 1999; Sommers, Fagan, & Baskin, 1993) have suggested the traditional parenting style of Latinos should not be viewed solely in negative terms because these stringent parenting practices—in the context of a stable and caring Latino family—may buffer Latino youths from possible negative influences and delinquent behaviors. This may be particularly true for recent immigrant Hispanic youths, who report greater parental monitoring than their more acculturated peers (Fridrich & Flannery, 1995). Although findings are inconclusive, parental monitoring can be an important factor in deterring delinquency for early adolescents (Patterson & Stouthamer-Loeber, 1984). In support of this notion, past findings indicate that unsupervised socialization with friends leads to greater delinquency among Mexican American adolescents (Yin, Katims, & Zapata, 1999). Whatever the case may be, parental disciplining practices must be viewed in their cultural context to accurately assess how they are perceived by Latino youths of varying acculturation levels.

Several studies have suggested that acculturation may influence maternal teaching and reinforcement strategies. For example, Mexican American mothers who have fewer traditional Latino values use more directive strategies in teaching their children certain lessons (Cousins, Power, & Olvera-Ezzell, 1993). In contrast, for Puerto Rican and Dominican mothers, acculturation is positively related to the use of inquiry (mother asks the child a question) and praise (mother expresses approval of child's action) but negatively related to modeling (mother works on task as child watches; Planos, Zayas, & Busch-Rossnagel, 1995).

In regards to reinforcement strategies, one study found differences between immigrant and U.S.-born Mexican American mothers. Under conditions of high effort and failure by their children, U.S.-born Mexican American mothers offer more reinforcement to their children compared with immigrant Mexican American mothers. However, under conditions of low effort and success, immigrant Mexican American mothers give more reinforcement than U.S.-born Mexican American mothers (Chavez & Buriel, 1986). Based on these limited findings, few conclusions can be drawn about the impact of acculturation on maternal teaching methods. More important, Planos et al. (1995) questioned whether such attempts to generalize about how Latina mothers teach their children are fruitful endeavors given the mothers' culturally heterogeneous characteristics.

Family functioning. Greater acculturation has been related to increased family conflict and problem behaviors in various Latino families (Szapocznik & Kurtines, 1980; Szapocznik et al., 1986). For example, highly acculturated Mexican American families (and non-Hispanic White families) are more likely than less acculturated families to have high stress and less satisfaction with family life during child-rearing years (Vega et al., 1986). Similarly, Mexican American youths perceive less family support when they speak more English and less Spanish than their parents (Barrett, Joe, & Simpson, 1991). Increased acculturation is also strongly associated with lower levels of family cohesion for Cuban and Nicaraguan American adolescents (Gil & Vega, 1996). Other studies have indicated that acculturation is positively related to increased family dysfunction, higher levels of personal disorganization, and in particular, a higher risk for adolescent pregnancy, deviant behavior, and drug use (Amaro, Whitaker, Coffman, & Heeren, 1990; Brook, Whiteman, Balka, Win, & Gursen, 1997; Gil, Vega, & Dimas, 1994; Vega & Amaro, 1994).

Researchers also warn that acculturation may undermine the protective influence of parental power and authority. For example, among first-generation Mexican American immigrants, more acculturated adolescents are more susceptible to peer influence to perform antisocial acts, although this characteristic decreases with age (Wall, Power, & Arbona, 1993). For Mexican American male adolescents, high acculturation is related to less family involvement and less positive peer affiliation (Brooks et al., 1998). Still, some researchers have found that acculturation provides positive experiences for Latino youths. Past reports have shown that acculturated Mexican American adolescents are more likely than their less acculturated counterparts to be involved with positive social networks and programs outside of the family (Rueschenberg & Buriel, 1989). Other studies reported that highly acculturated Puerto Rican adolescents are more likely to exhibit positive peer involvement than those who are less acculturated (Sommers et al., 1993). Finally, higher levels of acculturation to the American culture (Americanism) are linked to positive perceptions of social acceptance by non-Latino peers and family competence (Birman, 1998).

Although these contradictory findings are difficult to resolve, it is plausible that the home environment ultimately differentiates these acculturation effects on peer affiliation and influence. Latino youths who have stable and nurturing home environments may be more likely to receive mentorship and support from their parents. Such youths may be more socially skillful and inclined to select positive peer groups and develop positive social support networks during acculturation.

Parent–child relations. Most of the research on parent–child dyads points to heightened conflict during acculturation across Latino and Mexican American groups. For instance, acculturation (as measured by birth in the United States) is positively associated with increased parent–child difficulties for Puerto Rican adolescents (Brook et al., 1997). Among Cuban and Nicaraguan American adolescents, increased acculturation again is strongly related to increased parent–child acculturation conflicts (Gil & Vega, 1996). Higher levels of acculturation are also related to increased willingness to defy authority and tolerance of deviance among Mexican American adolescents (Wall et al., 1993). Several researchers believe this problem is mitigated by differential rates of acculturation between Latino children and youths and their parents. For instance, parent–child conflicts are exacerbated in Cuban American families when acculturation levels significantly differ between adolescents and their parents (Szapocznik et al., 1986). Szapocznik and Hernandez (1988) found that the rate of acculturation is more rapid for Cuban American children and youths than for their parents. In a similar vein, more acculturated Mexican American adolescents (determined by generational status) are more willing to openly disagree with their parents and report earlier expectations for autonomy (Fuligni, 1998).

Still, some investigations did not find a relationship between acculturation and quality of parent–child relationships. For instance, acculturation did not significantly affect maternal behavior or infant attachment among Puerto Rican and Dominican mother–infant dyads (Fracasso, Busch-Rossnagel, & Fisher, 1994). However, the authors cautioned that their acculturation measure may have been limited in scope because it was solely based on Spanish language use and maintenance of Latino values and behaviors. Furthermore, they noted that their sample might have been too homogenous to reveal significant differences. In a separate study, perceived maternal acceptance was not related to level of acculturation for Mexican American adolescents (Samaniego & Gonzales, 1999). These findings are consistent with other findings showing that emotional closeness or warmth in the family does not differ by acculturation level for Mexican Americans (Rueschenberg & Buriel, 1989; Sabogal et al., 1987) and Cuban and Central Americans (Sabogal et al., 1987).

Marital relations. Marital relationships among Latinos are often characterized by strict gender roles in which a dominant role is imparted to the husband and the wife assumes a secondary or more passive role (Montenegro, 1973; Montiel, 1973; Senour, 1977). These roles are supported by the concept of *machismo,* which refers to the idea that Latino men often maintain dominance in the marriage by assuming the responsibilities of primary provider and protector of the family (Grebler, Moore, & Guzman, 1973). Several researchers caution, however, that such observations only promote gender role stereotypes that are no longer representative of contemporary marital relationships (Amaro, Russo, & Johnson, 1987).

Many acculturation studies have highlighted how Hispanic women have moved beyond traditional gender roles and attained more egalitarian roles in their daily relationships. For example, acculturation is positively related to more liberal views about women and negatively related to more feminine role-type behavior for Mexican American women (Kranau, Green, & Valencia-Weber, 1982). Similarly, second-generation Puerto Rican women are less likely to endorse stereotyped gender roles and are known to report more assertive behavior than first-generation Puerto Rican women (Soto, 1983; Soto & Shaver, 1982). However, these researchers noted that level of education is a stronger predictor of these changes than generational status. Similar findings concerning changing gender roles and attitudes toward Latino women are reported by other researchers (Espin, 1987; Leaper & Valin, 1996; O'Guinn, Imperia, & MacAdams, 1987; Rosario, 1982; Soto & Shaver, 1982; Torres-Matrullo, 1980; Valentine & Mosley, 2000). Unfortunately, little attention has focused on changing views of marital relationships and gender roles among Latino men. Nevertheless, findings from a few studies suggest that Puerto Rican men are moving toward less traditional gender-role expectations (De Leon, 1990; Del Valle, 1990; Ginorio, 1979; Ramos-McKay, 1977).

Although such changes have occurred, inequities between the sexes still exist. For example, Mexican American immigrant women report more nonreciprocity and support from their husbands than their more acculturated Mexican American female peers (Vega, Kolody, & Valle, 1988). Similarly, Mexican American men tend to be more supportive of traditional roles for women in the workplace and at home than Mexican American women (Gowan & Trevino, 1998). Interestingly, acculturation did not significantly affect the latter findings, a fact that parallels past results showing that acculturation (as measured by education level) does not necessarily lead to equal sharing of child-care responsibilities between Puerto Rican wives and husbands (Roopnarine & Ahmeduzzaman, 1993). Specifically, the men in the latter study only averaged spending one third of the time that mothers spent on child care. Finally, Negy and Snyder (1997) found that greater acculturation might actually increase marital distress for Mexican American wives but not for Mexican American husbands.

The literature has also suggested that acculturation may be related to spousal abuse and violence, although past findings are inconsistent. For example, lower levels of acculturation are tied to greater risk for wife abuse among Mexican Americans (Champion, 1996). However, a recent study of Puerto Ricans, Mexican immigrants, Mexican Americans, and Cuban Americans reported that increased acculturation is associated with higher rates of husbands engaging in minor assaults (e.g., throwing, pushing, grabbing, slapping) but not in severe violent acts (Jasinski, 1998).

Critique and Recommendations

Formulating general conclusions and research recommendations from the corpus of family acculturation research is complicated by numerous issues. The sheer range of investigative topics, the varied sociocultural characteristics across study samples, and inadequate or inappropriate acculturation measures underscore this point. As previously noted, such circumstances have in part contributed to inconsistent or seemingly contradictory findings. Nonetheless, several important conceptual and methodological issues can be raised. These issues, as outlined in the following paragraphs, warrant further attention to advance the state of acculturation research with ethnic minority families.

1. Acculturation Has Been Primarily Viewed as a Unidimensional and Static Construct

Although similar assertions have been made in other chapters in this book, the fundamental weaknesses of this conceptual scheme are particularly apparent when considering acculturation processes within a family. As previously discussed, acculturation levels may be highly variable for individual members. Such differences may be partially attributed to each member's unique and evolving developmental tasks and abilities, which potentially shape adaptation experiences in new cultural milieus. For instance, adolescents who are struggling with autonomy issues may display different modes of acculturation than younger children who face different developmental tasks. Likewise, members may exhibit varying degrees of bicultural competence, which further diversifies acculturation experiences in a given family. In this respect, those who can successfully alter their behaviors to fit different cultural settings may conceivably experience less acculturative stress. From a social learning perspective, such biculturally competent individuals may also contribute to overall family adjustment by modeling adaptive behavior for other members. More sophisticated conceptual schemes must therefore be developed to account for the multifaceted and possibly interdependent nature of acculturation in ethnic minority families

2. Measurement Strategies Are Insufficient and Inconsistent

Past descriptions of family acculturation experiences are often incomplete or, at their worst, inaccurate because of restricted or insufficient measurement strategies. This weakness mainly stems from a lack of coherent theories and models of acculturation. Comprehensive measurement of acculturation is especially important for family research because various acculturation indexes may have different effects on the dependent variables under investigation. For example, Jain and Belsky (1997) found that the number of years in the United States (a widely used index of acculturation) did not predict the fathers' involvement in their children's lives, whereas other indexes (e.g., cultural attitudes and feelings, behaviors, home artifacts) were significant predictors.

The construct–validation approach (Cronbach & Meehl, 1955) may help resolve such measurement issues. This approach entails using multiple measures and observations to test the underlying nomological network of assumptions and propositions that comprise acculturation. This approach is particularly helpful given that acculturation can only be evaluated indirectly in the absence of definitive criterion measures and specific operations. Data gathered from this approach may lead to revisions and modifications to the causal network of variables that are implicated in acculturation processes. Consequently, it promotes more refined and accurate operational definitions and conceptualizations of acculturation. Additionally, the emphasis on multiple measures allows for greater flexibility and creativity in assessment strategies. For instance, researchers who adopt this approach would be encouraged to supplement their quantitative measures with other data-gathering methods. This may include gathering qualitative data from ethnographic interviews with families. Open-ended questions that ask immigrant families to describe changes in their family, work, and social settings may offer rich sources of information that may enhance quantitative data. Ethnographic interviews can then be analyzed or coded for specific themes or variables that may inform the selection of additional measures. Ultimately, this may contribute to a more comprehensive portrait of a family's acculturation experiences.

Last, family acculturation research should include longitudinal study designs. The preponderance of studies overlook the dynamic *process* associated with acculturation by measuring this phenomenon exclusively on one occasion. Future investigations should therefore evaluate families across time to better understand how their adaptive behaviors, strategies, and goals evolve along with changing intrafamilial and extrafamilial environments.

3. *Most Acculturation Research Ignores Macrolevel Influences on Family Acculturation*

Past research demonstrates that a family's ecological context plays a vital role in shaping family functioning and child development (Bronfenbrenner, 1986). Still, little information exists on the relationship of social settings and institutions to acculturation experiences for ethnic minority families; this includes examining the effects of social stratification and institutional racism on family acculturation patterns. Such issues deserve consideration given that historical instances of discrimination and racism (e.g., slavery among African Americans, forced matriculation into boarding schools for American Indian youths, exclusionary immigration laws aimed at Asian Americans and Latinos) have rendered acculturation a form of oppression rather than a voluntary process of adaptation.

4. *Acculturation Is Primarily Viewed as a Postmigration Phenomenon*

Unlike earlier waves of immigrants coming to this country, many immigrants who have recently arrived were increasingly exposed to the U.S. culture in their countries of origin because of heightened globalization in communications and commerce. Future studies should therefore account for acculturation that occurs before migration and may include investigating the relationship of postmigration adjustment to prior knowledge of American customs and behaviors acquired in one's country of origin.

5. *Acculturation Experiences of Generational Cohorts Are Perceived to Be Monolithic and Uniform*

Researchers should recognize that significant sociocultural differences exist among generational cohorts from different time periods. Such differences may be attributed to an ongoing stream of domestic and worldwide events, fluctuating attitudes and opinions toward American culture, and changing international relations. This may consequently lead to varied acculturation patterns for families representing the same generational cohort. For instance, the sociocultural realities of the Japanese American Issei (first-generation) community in the 1940s vastly differ from those of more recently arrived Issei. Consequently, family acculturation patterns may differ for individuals who share the same generational designation but come from different historical periods.

6. *Ethnic Minority Families Are Viewed as Passive Respondents to Their Environments*

As mentioned in the previous chapters, acculturation is a process of adaptation to a set of varied and complex challenges. Thus, families should not be viewed as passive entities who simply react to their environments but as agents of change who may shape the environments and institutions that they encounter. Future studies might therefore examine how immigrant families alter social institutions and policies of a host society.

Individual and family goals for adaptation also deserve further exploration. For example, many immigrant families might have multiple goals beyond economic success, such as attainment of greater individual liberties, reunion with other family members, or simply escape from political persecution. Future studies might examine the nature, evolution, and significance of such goals and might include examining the implications for family adjustment when goals are not mutually shared or conflict across members.

7. *Transnational Experiences and Identities Are Frequently Overlooked*

Few studies recognize that acculturation may represent an ongoing dialectical exchange between cultures. This shortcoming seems to rest on the assumption that immigrants invariably surrender or decrease their ties with their countries of origin on resettlement in the United States. However, many individuals actively maintain transnational identities and residences as evidenced in diasporic communities. How might this affect family acculturation experiences? Such questions are particularly relevant to immigrant youths (e.g., "parachute kids") who are transplanted in the United States for educational purposes while their parents maintain a permanent residence in another country.

8. *Research Topics Must Be Expanded Across Ethnic Minority Groups*

As noted previously, most of the family acculturation research pertains to Asian American and Latino immigrants and refugees. However, theoretical frameworks developed for African American (e.g., Landrine & Klonoff, 1996) and American Indian (e.g., LaFromboise et al., 1990) families deserve further empirical exploration. In addition, research questions for ethnic minority groups should be expanded. To date, research on substance abuse and delinquency primarily focuses on African Americans and Latinos, whereas the study of educational achievement centers on Asian Americans. Although these research trends reflect important acculturation issues in each ethnic community, researchers should reconsider this seemingly narrow scope of topics. Why do substance abuse and delinquency issues among Asian American youths receive less attention? Why have fewer studies been conducted on predictors of academic success for African Americans and Latinos? Are researchers unknowingly perpetuating racial stereotypes in their selection of investigative topics?

References

Alvirez, D., & Bean, F. D. (1976). The Mexican American family. In C. H. Mindel & R. N. Habenstein (Eds.), *Ethnic families in America* (pp. 271–279). New York: Elsevier.

Amaro, H., Russo, N., & Johnson, J. (1987). Family and work predictors of psychological well being among Hispanic women professionals. Hispanic women and mental health [Special issue]. *Psychology of Women Quarterly, 11,* 505–521.

Amaro, H., Whitaker, R., Coffman, G., & Heeren, T. (1990). Acculturation and marijuana and cocaine use: Findings from the HHANES 1982–1984. *American Journal of Public Health, 80*(Suppl.), 54–60.

Barrett, M. E., Joe, G. W., & Simpson, D. D. (1991). Acculturation influences on inhalant use. *Hispanic Journal of Behavioral Sciences, 13,* 276–296.

Birman, D. (1998). Biculturalism and perceived competence of Latino immigrant adolescents. *American Journal of Community Psychology, 26,* 335–354.

Black, L. (1996). Families of African origin: An overview. In M. McGoldrick, J. Giordano, & J. K. Pearce (Eds.), *Ethnicity and family therapy* (2nd ed., pp. 57–65). New York: Guilford Press.

Boehnlein, J., Tran, H., Riley, C., Vu, K. C., Tan, S., & Leung, P. (1995). A comparative study of family functioning among Vietnamese and Cambodian refugees. *Journal of Nervous and Mental Disease, 183,* 768–773.

Bronfenbrenner, U. (1986). Ecology of the family as a context for human development: Research perspectives. *Developmental Psychology, 22,* 723–742.

Brook, J. S., Whiteman, M., Balka, E. B., Win, P. E., & Gursen, M. D. (1997). African-American and Puerto Rican drug use: A longitudinal study. *Journal of the American Academy of Child Adolescent Psychiatry, 36,* 1260–1268.

Brooks, A. J., Stuewig, J., & Lecroy, C. W. (1998). A family based model of Hispanic adolescent substance use. *Journal of Drug Education, 28,* 65–86.

Bulcroft, R., Carmody, D., & Bulcroft, K. (1996). Patterns of parental independence giving to adolescents: Variations by race, age, and gender of child. *Journal of Marriage and the Family, 58,* 866–883.

Buriel, R., Mercado, R., Rodriguez, R., & Chavez, J. M. (1991). Mexican-American disciplinary practices and attitudes toward child maltreatment: A comparison of foreign- and native-born mothers. *Hispanic Journal of Behavioral Sciences, 13,* 78–94.

Champion, J. D. (1996). Woman abuse, assimilation, and self-concept in a rural Mexican American community. *Hispanic Journal of Behavioral Sciences, 18,* 508–521.

Chavez, J. M., & Buriel, R. (1986). Reinforcing children's effort: A comparison of immigrant, native-born Mexican American and Euro-American mothers. *Hispanic Journal of Behavioral Sciences, 8,* 127–142.

Chiu, L. H. (1987). Child-rearing attitudes of Chinese, Chinese-American, and Anglo American mothers. *International Journal of Psychology, 22,* 409–419.

Chun, K. M., & Akutsu, P. D. (1999). Utilization of mental health services. In E. J. Kramer, S. L. Ivey, & Y. W. Ying (Eds.), *Immigrant women's health: Problems and solutions* (pp. 54–64). San Francisco, CA: Jossey-Bass.

Cohen, R. (1979). *Culture, disease, and stress among Latino immigrants.* Washington, DC: Smithsonian Institution.

Connell, J. P., Halpern-Felsher, B. L., Clifford, E., Crichlow, W., & Usinger, P. (1995). Hanging in there: Behavioral, psychological, and contextual factors affecting whether African American adolescents stay in high school. *Journal of Adolescent Research, 10,* 41–63.

Contreras, J. M., Lopez, I. R., Rivera-Mosquera, E. T., Raymond-Smith, L., & Rothstein, K. (1999). Social support and adjustment among Puerto Rican adolescent mothers: The moderating effect of acculturation. *Journal of Family Psychology, 13,* 228–243.

Cortés, D. E. (1995). Variations in familism in two generations of Puerto Ricans. *Hispanic Journal of Behavioral Sciences, 17,* 249–255.

Costello, E. J., Farmer, E. M., Angold, A., Burns, B. J., & Erkanli, A. (1997). Psychiatric disorders among American Indian and White youth in Appalachia: The Great Smoky Mountains study. *American Journal of Public Health, 87,* 827–832.

Cousins, J. H., Power, T. G., & Olvera-Ezzell, N. (1993). Mexican-American mothers' socialization strategies: Effects of education, acculturation, and health locus of control. *Journal of Experimental Child Psychology, 55,* 258–276.

Cronbach, L., & Meehl, P. (1955). Construct validity in psychological tests. *Psychological Bulletin, 52,* 281–302.

De Leon, B. (1990). Sex role perceptions and levels of acculturation of Puerto Ricans: A comparative study of Puerto Rican, Black, and Anglo college students. *Dissertation Abstracts International, 50,* 3521A. (UMI No. 90-01, 497)

Del Valle, M. (1990). Acculturation, sex roles, and racial definitions of Puerto Rican college students in Puerto Rico and the United States. *Dissertation Abstracts International, 50,* 3850A.

Dick, R. W., Manson, S. M., & Beals, J. (1993). Alcohol use among male and female Native American adolescents: Patterns and correlates of student drinking in a boarding school. *Journal of Studies on Alcohol, 54,* 172–177.

Dumka, L. E., Roosa, M. W., & Jackson, K. M. (1997). Risk, conflict, mothers' parenting, and children's adjustment in low-income, Mexican immigrant, and Mexican American families. *Journal of Marriage and the Family, 59,* 309–323.

Edgerton, R. & Karno, M. (1971). Mexican-American bilingualism and the perception of mental illness. *Archives of General Psychiatry, 24,* 286–290.

Espin, O. M. (1987). Psychological impact of migration on Latinas. *Psychology of Women Quarterly, 11,* 489–503.

Fairchild, D. G., Fairchild, M. W., & Stoner, S. (1998). Prevalence of adult domestic violence among women seeking routine care in a Native American health care facility. *American Journal of Public Health, 88,* 1515–1517.

Florsheim, P., Tolan, P. H., & Gorman-Smith, D. (1996). Family processes and risk for externalizing behavior problems among African American and Hispanic boys. *Journal of Consulting and Clinical Psychology, 64,* 1222–1230.

Fracasso, M. P., Busch-Rossnagel, N. A., & Fisher, C. B. (1994). The relationship of maternal behavior and acculturation to the quality of attachment in Hispanic infants living in New York City. *Hispanic Journal of Behavioral Sciences, 16,* 143–154.

Fridrich, A. H., & Flannery, D. J. (1995). The effects of ethnicity and acculturation on early adolescent delinquency. *Journal of Child and Family Studies, 4,* 69–87.

Fuligni, A. J. (1998). Authority, autonomy, and parent–adolescent conflict and cohesion: A study of adolescents from Mexican, Chinese, Filipino, and European backgrounds. *Developmental Psychology, 34,* 782–792.

Gil, A. G., & Vega, W. A. (1996). Two different worlds: Acculturation stress and adaptation among Cuban and Nicaraguan families. *Journal of Social and Personal Relationships, 13,* 435–456.

Gil, A. G., Vega, W. A., & Dimas, J. M. (1994). Acculturative stress and personal adjustment among Hispanic adolescent boys. *Journal of Community Psychology, 22,* 43–53.

Ginorio, A. B. (1979). A comparison of Puerto Ricans in New York with native Puerto Ricans and native Americans on two measures of acculturation: Gender role and racial identification. *Dissertation Abstracts International, 41,* 983B–984B. (UMI No. 78-18, 283)

Glazer, N., & Moynihan, D. P. (1963). *Beyond the melting pot.* Cambridge, MA: MIT Press.

Gowan, M., & Trevino, M. (1998). An examination of gender differences in Mexican-American attitudes toward family and career roles. *Sex Roles, 38,* 1079–1093.

Grebler, L., Moore, J. W., & Guzman, R. C. (1973). The family: Variations in time and space. In L. I. Duran & H. R. Bernard (Eds.), *Introduction to Chicano studies* (pp. 309–331). New York: MacMillan.

Griffith, J., & Villavicencio, S. (1985). Relationships among acculturation, sociodemographic characteristics, and social supports in Mexican-American adults. *Hispanic Journal of Behavioral Sciences, 7,* 75–92.

Grossman, D. C., Milligan, C., & Deyo, R. A. (1991). Risk factors for suicide attempts among Navajo adolescents. *American Journal of Public Health, 81,* 870–874.

Harjo, S. S. (1993). The American Indian experience. In H. P. McAdoo (Ed.), *Family ethnicity: Strength in diversity* (pp. 199–207). Newbury Park, CA: Sage.

Heras, P., & Revilla, L. (1994). Acculturation, generational status, and family environment of Philipino Americans: A study in cultural adaptation. *Family Therapy, 21,* 129–138.

Hines, P. M., & Boyd-Franklin, N. (1996). African American families. In M. McGoldrick, J. Giordano, & J. K. Pearce (Eds.), *Ethnicity and family therapy* (2nd ed., pp. 66–84). New York: Guilford Press.

Ho, C. (1990). An analysis of domestic violence in Asian American communities: A multicultural approach to counseling. In L. Brown & M. Root (Eds.), *Diversity and complexity in feminist therapy* (pp. 129–150). New York: Haworth Press.

Jain, A., & Belsky, J. (1997). Fathering and acculturation: Immigrant Indian families with young children. *Journal of Marriage and the Family, 59,* 873–883.

Jasinski, J. L. (1998). The role of acculturation in wife assault. *Hispanic Journal of Behavioral Sciences, 20,* 175–191.

Kagan, S., & Madsen, M. C. (1971). Cooperation and competition of Mexican, Mexican-American, and Anglo-American children of two ages under four instructional sets. *Developmental Psychology, 5,* 32–39.

Karno, M., & Edgerton, R. (1969). Perception of mental illness in a Mexican-American community. *Archives of General Psychiatry, 20,* 233–238.

Kauh, T. O. (1997). Intergenerational relations: Older Korean-Americans' experiences. *Journal of Cross-Cultural Gerontology, 12,* 245–271.

Keefe, S. E., & Padilla, A. M. (1987). *Chicano ethnicity.* Albuquerque: University of New Mexico Press.

Keefe, S. E., Padilla, A. M., & Carlos, M. L. (1979). The Mexican-American extended family as an emotional support system. *Human Organization, 38,* 144–152.

Kilmer, R. P., Cowen, E. L., Wyman, P. A., Work, W. C., & Magnus, K. B. (1998). Differences in stressors experienced by urban African American, White, and Hispanic children. *Journal of Community Psychology, 26,* 415–428.

Kim, Y., & Grant, D. (1997). Immigration patterns, social support, and adaptation among Korean immigrant women and Korean American women. *Cultural Diversity and Mental Health, 3,* 235–245.

Knight, G. P., Bernal, M. E., Garza, C. A., Cota, M. K., & Ocampo, K. A. (1993). Family socialization and the ethnic identity of Mexican-American children. *Journal of Cross-Cultural Psychology, 24,* 99–114.

Knight, G. P., & Kagan, S. (1977). Acculturation of prosocial and competitive behaviors among second and third generation Mexican American children. *Journal of Cross-Cultural Psychology, 8,* 273–285.

Kranau, E. J., Green, V., & Valencia-Weber, G. (1982). Acculturation and the Hispanic women: Attitudes towards women, sex role attribution, sex role behavior, and demographics. *Hispanic Journal of Behavioral Sciences, 4,* 21–40.

LaDue, R. A. (1994). Coyote returns: Twenty sweats does not an Indian expert make. *Women and Therapy, 15,* 93–111.

LaFromboise, T., Trimble, J., & Mohatt, G. (1990). Counseling intervention and American Indian tradition: An integrative approach. *Counseling Psychologist, 18,* 628–654.

Landrine, H., & Klonoff, E. A. (1996). *African American acculturation: Deconstructing race and reviving culture.* Thousand Oaks, CA: Sage.

Lay, C., & Nguyen, T. (1998). The role of acculturation-related and acculturation non-specific daily hassles: Vietnamese-Canadian students and psychological distress. *Canadian Journal of Behavioural Science, 30,* 172–181.

Leaper, C., & Valin, D. (1996). Predictors of Mexican American mothers' and fathers' attitudes toward gender equality. *Hispanic Journal of Behavioral Sciences, 18,* 343–355.

Lin, C. Y., & Fu, V. (1990). A comparison of child-rearing practices among Chinese, immigrant Chinese, and Caucasian-American parents. *Child Development, 61,* 429–433.

Lovell, M., Tran, T., & Nguyen, C. (1987). Refugee women: Lives in transition. *International Social Work, 30,* 317–325.

Luna, I., de Ardon, E. T., Lim, Y. M., Cromwell, S. L., Phillips, L. R., & Russell, C. K. (1996). The relevance of familism in cross-cultural studies of family caregiving. *Western Journal of Nursing Research, 18,* 267–283.

Marger, M. N. (1997). Ethnic stratification: Power and inequality. In M. N. Marger (Ed.), *Race and ethnic relations: American and global perspectives* (4th ed., pp. 37–69). Belmont, CA: Wadsworth.

Marín, G. (1993). Influence of acculturation on familialism and self-identification among Hispanics. In M. E. Bernal & G. P. Knight (Eds.), *Ethnic identity: Formation and transmission among Hispanics and other minorities* (pp. 181–196). Albany: State University of New York Press.

McLoyd, V. C. (1990). The impact of economic hardship on Black families and children: Psychological distress, parenting, and socioemotional development. *Child Development, 61,* 311–346.

Mindel, C. H. (1980). Extended familism among urban Mexican Americans, Anglos, and Blacks. *Hispanic Journal of Behavioral Sciences, 2,* 21–34.

Montenegro, R. (1973). *Educational implications of cultural values of Mexican-American women.* Unpublished doctoral dissertation, Claremont Graduate School, Claremont, CA.

Montiel, M. (1973). The Chicano family: A review of research. *Social Work, 18,* 22–27.

Negy, C., & Snyder, D. K. (1997). Ethnicity and acculturation: Assessing Mexican American couples' relationships using the Marital Satisfaction Inventory–Revised. *Psychological Assessment, 9,* 414–421.

Nguyen, H., Messé, L., & Stollak, G. (1999). Toward a more complex understanding of acculturation and adjustment: Cultural involvements and psychosocial functioning in Vietnamese youth. *Journal of Cross-Cultural Psychology, 30,* 5–31.

Nguyen, N. A., & Williams, H. L. (1989). Transition from East to West: Vietnamese adolescents and their parents. *Journal of the American Academy of Child and Adolescent Psychiatry, 28,* 505–515.

Oetting, E. R., Edwards, R. W., & Beauvais, F. (1989). Drugs and Native American youth. *Drugs and Society, 3*(1–2), 5–38.

O'Guinn, T. C., Imperia, G., & MacAdams, E. A. (1987). Acculturation and perceived family decision-making input among Mexican American wives. *Journal of Cross-Cultural Psychology, 18*(1), 78–92.

Patel, N., Power, T., & Bhavnagri, N. (1996). Socialization values and practices of Indian immigrant parents: Correlates of modernity and acculturation. *Child Development, 67,* 302–313.

Patterson, G. R., & Stouthamer-Loeber, M. (1984). The correlation of family management practices and delinquency. *Child Development, 55,* 329–335.

Planos, R., Zayas, L. H., & Busch-Rossnagel, N. A. (1995). Acculturation and teaching behaviors of Dominican and Puerto Rican mothers. *Hispanic Journal of Behavioral Sciences, 17,* 225–236.

Quintana, S. M., & Vera, E. M. (1999). Mexican American children's ethnic identity, understanding of ethnic prejudice, and parental ethnic socialization. *Hispanic Journal of Behavioral Sciences, 21,* 387–404.

Ramirez, M., & Castaneda, A. (1974). *Cultural democracy, bicognitive development, and education.* New York: Academic Press.

Ramirez, O., & Arce, C. (1981). The contemporary Chicano family: An empirically based review. In A. Barron, Jr. (Ed.), *Explorations in Chicano psychology* (pp. 3–28). New York: Praeger.

Ramos-McKay, J. M. (1977). Locus of control, social activism, and sex role among island Puerto Rican college and non-college individuals. *Dissertation Abstracts International, 38*(4B), 1957–1958.

Rhee, S. (1997). Domestic violence in the Korean immigrant family. *Journal of Sociology and Social Welfare, 24,* 63–77.

Rodriguez, J. M., & Kosloski, K. (1998). The impact of acculturation on attitudinal familism in a community of Puerto Rican Americans. *Hispanic Journal of Behavioral Sciences, 20,* 375–390.

Rogler, L. H., & Cooney, R. S. (1991). Puerto Rican families in New York City: Intergenerational processes. *Marriage and Family Review, 16,* 331–349.

Rohner, R., & Pettengill, S. (1985). Perceived parental acceptance–rejection and parental control among Korean adolescents. *Child Development, 56,* 524–528.

Roopnarine, J. L., & Ahmeduzzaman, M. (1993). Puerto Rican fathers' involvement with their preschool-age children. *Hispanic Journal of Behavioral Sciences, 15,* 96–107.

Rosario, L. (1982). The self-perception of Puerto Rican women toward their societal roles. In R. E. Zambrana (Ed.), *Work, family, and health: Latina women in transition* (pp. 95–107). New York: Hispanic Research Center.

Rosenthal, D., & Feldman, S. (1989). The acculturation of Chinese immigrants: Perceived effects on family functioning of length of residence in two cultural contexts. *Journal of Genetic Psychology, 151,* 495–514.

Rousseau, C., Drapeau, A., & Corin, E. (1997). The influence of culture and context on the pre- and post-migration experience of school-aged refugees from Central America and Southeast Asia in Canada. *Social Science Medicine, 44,* 1115–1127.

Rueschenberg, E., & Buriel, R. (1989). Mexican American family functioning and acculturation: A family systems perspective. *Hispanic Journal of Behavioral Sciences, 11*, 232–244.

Sabogal, F., Marín, G., Otero-Sabogal, R., Marín, B., & Peréz-Stable, E. J. (1987). Hispanic familism and acculturation: What changes and what doesn't? *Hispanic Journal of Behavioral Sciences, 9*, 397–412.

Samaniego, R. Y., & Gonzales, N. A. (1999). Multiple mediators of the effects of acculturation status on delinquency for Mexican American adolescents. *American Journal of Community Psychology, 27*, 189–210.

Segal, U. (1991). Cultural variables in Asian Indian families. *Families in Society, 11*, 233–241.

Senour, M. (1977). Psychology of the Chicana. In J. L. Martinez, Jr. (Ed.), *Chicano psychology* (pp. 329–340). New York: Academic Press.

Shon, S., & Ja, D. (1982). Asian families. In M. McGoldrick, J. K. Pearce, & J. Giordano (Eds.), *Ethnicity and family therapy* (pp. 208–228). New York: Guilford Press.

Sommers, I., Fagan, J., & Baskin, D. (1993). Sociocultural influences on the explanation of delinquency for Puerto Rican youths. *Hispanic Journal of Behavioral Sciences, 15*, 36–62.

Soto, E. (1983). Sex-role traditionalism and assertiveness in Puerto Rican women living in the United States. *Journal of Community Psychology, 11*, 346–354.

Soto, E., & Shaver, P. (1982). Sex role traditionalism, assertiveness, and symptoms of Puerto Rican women living in the United States. *Hispanic Journal of Behavioral Sciences, 4*, 1–19.

Sung, B. (1985). Bicultural conflicts in Chinese immigrant children. *Journal of Comparative Family Studies, 16*, 255–269.

Swaim, R. C., Oetting, E. R., Thurman, P. J., Beauvais, F., & Edwards, R. W. (1993). American Indian adolescent drug use and socialization characteristics: A cross-cultural comparison. *Journal of Cross-Cultural Psychology, 24*, 53–70.

Szapocznik, J., & Hernandez, R. (1988). The Cuban American family. In C. H. Mindel, R. W. Habenstein, & R. Wright, Jr. (Eds.), *Ethnic families in America* (pp. 160–172). New York: Elsevier.

Szapocznik, J., & Kurtines, W. (1980). Acculturation, biculturalism, and adjustment among Cuban Americans. In A. M. Padilla (Ed.), *Acculturation: Theory, models, and some new findings* (pp. 139–159). Boulder, CO: Westview Press.

Szapocznik, J., Rio, A., Perez-Vidal, A., Kurtines, W., Hervis, O., & Santisteban, D. (1986). Bicultural effectiveness training (BET): An experimental test of an intervention modality for families experiencing intergenerational/intercultural conflict. *Hispanic Journal of Behavioral Sciences, 8*, 303–330.

Thompson, V. L. S. (1994). Socialization to race and its relationship to racial identification among African-Americans. *Journal of Black Psychology, 20*, 175–188.

Thorton, M. C., Chatters, L. M., Taylor, R. J., & Allen, W. R. (1990). Sociodemographic and environmental correlates of racial socialization. *Child Development, 61*, 401–409.

Torres-Matrullo, C. M. (1980). Acculturation sex-role values and mental health among mainland Puerto Ricans. In A. M. Padilla (Ed.), *Acculturation: Theory, models, and some new findings* (pp. 111–137). Boulder, CO: Westview.

Triandis, H. C., Marín, G., Betancourt, H., Lisansky, J., & Chang, B. (1982). *Dimensions of familism among Hispanic and mainstream Navy recruits*. Department of Psychology, University of Illinois, Chicago.

Uba, L. (1994). *Asian Americans: Personality patterns, identity, and mental health*. New York: Guilford Press.

U.S. Bureau of the Census. (1999). Poverty in the United States. *1998 Current Population Reports*. Washington, DC: U.S. Department of Commerce.

Valentine, S., & Mosley, G. (2000). Acculturation and sex-role attitudes among Mexican Americans: A longitudinal analysis. *Hispanic Journal of Behavioral Sciences, 22*, 104–113.

Vega, W. A. (1995). The study of Latino families: A point of departure. In R. E. Zambrana (Ed.), *Understanding Latino families: Scholarship, policy, and practice* (pp. 3–17). Thousand Oaks, CA: Sage.

Vega, W. A., & Amaro, H. (1994). Latino outlook: Good health, uncertain prognosis. *Annual Review of Public Health, 15,* 39–67.

Vega, W. A., Kolody, B., & Valle, J. R. (1988). Marital strain, coping, and depression among Mexican American women. *Journal of Marriage and the Family, 50,* 391–403.

Vega, W. A., Patterson, T., Sallis, J., Nader, P., Atkins, C., & Abramson, I. (1986). Cohesion and adaptability in Mexican American and Anglo families. *Journal of Marriage and the Family, 48,* 857–867.

Wall, J. A., Power, T. G., & Arbona, C. (1993). Susceptibility to antisocial peer pressure and its relation to acculturation in Mexican-American adolescents. *Journal of Adolescent Research, 8,* 403–418.

Yau, J., & Smetana, J. (1993). Chinese-American adolescents' reasoning about cultural conflicts. *Journal of Adolescent Research, 8,* 419–438.

Yin, Z., Katims, D. S., & Zapata, J. T. (1999). Participation in leisure activities and involvement in delinquency by Mexican American adolescents. *Hispanic Journal of Behavioral Sciences, 21,* 170–185.

Ying, Y. W. (1996). Immigration satisfaction of Chinese Americans: An empirical examination. *Journal of Community Psychology, 24,* 3–16.

Ying, Y. W. (1999). Strengthening intergenerational/intercultural ties in migrant families: A new intervention for parents. *Journal of Community Psychology, 27,* 89–96.

Zapata, J. T., & Jaramillo, P. T. (1982). Research on the Mexican American family. *Journal of Individual Psychology, 37,* 72–85.

Zimmerman, M. A., Ramirez-Valles, J., Washienko, K. M., Walter, B., & Dyer, S. (1996). The development of a measure of enculturation for Native American youth. *American Journal of Community Psychology, 24,* 295–310.

6

The Influence of Acculturation Processes on the Family

Daniel A. Santisteban and Victoria B. Mitrani

The immigrant family is fertile ground for family research that investigates the interplay between culture-related variables, family-related risk and protective factors, and the development of various problems. The broad diversity of family relationship patterns that exist in different ethnic cultures are made even richer and more intricate as a result of acculturation processes that create new sets of values, beliefs, and behaviors (Santisteban, Muir-Malcolm, Mitrani, & Szapocznik, 2002). The work of McGoldrick (1989) sheds light on the complexity and richness of family life among ethnic populations and points out the following:

> There is burgeoning evidence that ethnic values and identifications are retained for many generations after immigration and play a significant role in family life throughout the life cycle. Second-, third-, and even fourth-generation Americans differ from the dominant culture in values, behavior, and life cycle patterns. (p. 70)

Unfortunately, the impressive gains in understanding complex processes in family functioning and family therapy (Alexander, Holtzworth-Munroe, & Jameson, 1994) have not capitalized on the richness of ethnicity and cultural factors in relation to family life. Core processes in the family functioning and family therapy domains have been effectively articulated and become the targets of rigorous research (Liddle, 1995; Patterson, Reid, & Dishion, 1992; Schmidt, Liddle, & Dakof, 1996). However, it has been difficult to empirically link this work with the substantial literature (Guarnaccia, Canino, Rubio-Stepic, & Bravo, 1993; McGoldrick & Giordano, 1996; Rivera-Arzola & Ramos-Grenier, 1997) that shows ethnicity-related differences in how symptoms develop, are expressed, and are explained and how and to whom people communicate their distress.

A critically important challenge is to integrate these two streams of research and rigorously investigate the intricate interplay among ethnic culture, family functioning, and family intervention. This integration of ethnocultural variables can accelerate the understanding of unique processes in ethnic families and helps predict patient responses to many commonly used interventions. The latter point deserves further discussion.

The movement toward Aptitude by Treatment Interaction research (Cronbach & Snow, 1977; Shoham & Rohrbaugh, 1995) involves examining the interplay between client characteristics and treatment interventions in an effort to improve the efficacy of interventions. The Aptitude by Treatment Interaction research movement is a particularly good context in which to study the interplay of cultural factors, family factors, and treatment. Our program of research at the Center for Family Studies has demonstrated the efficacy of family interventions in reducing behavior problems and improving family functioning in Hispanic children (Santisteban et al., 1997), engaging reluctant families in treatment (Santisteban, Szapocznik, Kurtines, & Perez-Vidal, 1996; Szapocznik et al., 1988), and reducing behavior problems and drug use among Hispanic adolescents (Santisteban et al., 2001; Szapocznik et al., 1988). However, effect sizes can still be improved, a goal that may be reached by tailoring interventions to the specific cultural profile of the clients. Aptitude by Treatment Interaction research seeks to show which type of clients improve with which type of interventions and under which conditions. Within this framework, researchers working with ethnically diverse families can contribute by articulating how immigration- and acculturation-related factors influence families and help determine the efficacy of commonly used interventions.

The purpose of this chapter is to present some of the empirically established core family processes; the values, beliefs, and behaviors that may change with acculturation; the intrafamilial stressors that may result from immigration and acculturation processes; and the breakdowns that are often at the core of families seeking treatment. The hope is that by presenting this framework, researchers will not only learn what is already known but also identify the gaps that exist in the literature and topics that warrant further investigation. From a therapy effectiveness perspective, the chapter includes examples of how investigation of acculturation processes and the family's values orientation may play a pivotal role in predicting patients' responses to commonly used psychotherapy interventions.

Important Role of Family in Children's and Adolescents' Lives

Our work at the Center for Family Studies focuses on the family because it is the primary context in which the child grows, develops an identity, is socialized, is hurt and healed, and struggles with powerful developmental issues. The family is a naturally occurring unit and the context in which most intense behavior-shaping experiences occur. The family can serve a protective and an insulating role or as the fertile ground in which severe problems take root. We believe, for example, that family factors can have a great impact on the extent to which behavior problems endure and become part of a delinquent lifestyle (Santisteban, Szapocznik, & Kurtines, 1994). Family factors have been linked to adolescent delinquency or disposition to delinquency among Hispanics (Sommers, Fagan, & Baskin, 1993; Vega, Gil, Warheit, Zimmerman, & Apospori, 1993) and the general population (Alexander et al., 1994). This framework does not imply that maladaptive family functioning necessarily causes the delinquency problem, but it does mean that it can maintain problem behaviors. Furthermore, adaptive family processes can serve as a protective factor so that problem adolescent behaviors do not emerge as a result of high-risk environments or as a healing force mobilized with therapy to alleviate adolescent problems that have already surfaced.

Among immigrant families that undergo the stressful processes associated with immigration and acculturation, the family's ability to protect, guide, and nurture its members may be particularly crucial to an adolescent's success. For example, Hovey and King (1996) found that adolescents in families showing low levels of family functioning demonstrated higher acculturative stress, which in turn was associated with depressive symptoms. The importance of strong family functioning is evident when one appreciates that the already complex processes of acculturation are complicated even further within a family system. As Berry has shown (1980, 1998), acculturation processes are not synonymous with the simple act of assimilation but can actually be broken up into several types of behavioral and psychological responses that an individual may manifest when making contact with a new and different culture. *Marginalization* refers to a lack of identification with any culture. *Assimilation* refers to accepting the values and beliefs of the new culture while rejecting the original culture. *Separation* refers to becoming totally embedded in the culture of origin and refusing to participate in the new culture. Finally, *integration* refers to retaining the original culture while also accepting values and beliefs of the new culture. This complexity *increases exponentially within a family* because the family brings together members who may show very different acculturation responses. When a father showing the "separation" response rejects the "American" ideas espoused by an "assimilated" daughter, it is very difficult to distinguish between his separate rejection of the culture and rejection of his daughter as a person. Consequently, family bonds are threatened because of conflicting acculturation responses.

Conflicts that are rooted in differences in acculturation responses within the family can be approached by helping the family understand these powerful processes, thus diffusing some of the negative emotions that inhibit constructive dialogue and change. For example, suppose the previously mentioned father and daughter are at odds because the father demands to meet the parents of the daughter's friend before allowing her to spend the night at the friend's home. It would be helpful to explore how the father's normal parental monitoring practices may be intensified by the fundamental traditional imperative that a father protects his daughter's chastity and reputation, making it more difficult for him to accept sleepovers at the home of adults he does not know. It would also be helpful to explore how the daughter's framework for negotiating and arguing her point of view may be incompatible with her father's expectations of a more traditional father–daughter communication style. By understanding many aspects of this conflict as culturally based, new avenues for improved learning, comprehension, and substantive communication are opened. This is not to say that reframing the conflict as culturally based would resolve the difference of opinion, but it allows the conflict to be put in a wider, less personal context and helps the daughter understand what may have seemed like a deep-seated lack of trust or an arbitrary attempt to exert control.

Not surprisingly, one of the characteristics most studied and written about in relation to families of diverse ethnic backgrounds is their emphasis on the family (nuclear, extended, and kinship networks) rather than the individual. Familialism in one form or another has been reported in many non-Anglo populations such as Hispanics (Marín & Marín, 1991), Asian Americans (Lee, 1996), and African Americans (Hines & Boyd-Franklin, 1996). For example, Rogler and Cooney (1984) and Marín and Marín (1991) have argued that the degree of closeness in an Hispanic family is typically greater than in a White American family, with Hispanics showing higher levels of interdependence, conformity, loyalty, and readiness to sacrifice for the welfare of family members. This may partly account for the finding reported by Rodriguez and Weisburd (1991); in predicting serious behavior problems among youth, family risk factors can play a relatively more important role for Hispanics than for non-Hispanics. Rodriguez and Weisburd explained that unlike the overall National Youth Survey data, which showed peer influence to far overshadow family influence, the data on the Puerto Rican population found family factors to be much more powerful and significant and peer factors to be much less influential. The view espoused by Rodriguez and Zayas (1990) is consistent with our own clinical experiences, which show that one of the important results of adherence to familialism is that children are more likely to accept family behavior control activities shown to be associated with lower antisocial behavior (e.g., monitoring, supervision, discipline). An important implication of this finding—greater family influence among some ethnic groups such as Hispanics—is that risk models underplaying family factors and emphasizing peer factors should not be overgeneralized to all ethnic groups. The importance of these differences in designing prevention and treatment interventions for youth and families of diverse ethnicity is tremendous.

Sabogal, Marín, Otero-Sabogal, VanOss Marín, and Pérez-Stable (1987) have divided the construct of familialism into three basic dimensions: (a) a perceived obligation to assist the family (e.g., "People should share their homes with uncles, aunts, or first cousins if they are in need"), (b) a belief that the family should be a source of social support (e.g., "People can count on help from their relatives to solve most of their problems"), and (c) a belief that relatives should be used as behavioral and attitudinal referents (e.g., "People should be embarrassed by the bad things done by members of their family"). By investigating the relationship between acculturation and these dimensions, the authors found that acculturation was inversely correlated with "family obligations" and "family as referents" but did not modify the extent to which individuals perceived "support from the family." That is, "perceived support from the family" remained constant, even among highly acculturated individuals, and was always significantly higher for Hispanics than for White non-Hispanics. Interestingly, even though "family as referents" tended to decrease with acculturation, even acculturated Hispanics[1] were significantly higher on this dimension than were White non-Hispanics.

Internal Family Processes and How They Are Influenced by Acculturation Processes

To make substantial progress in understanding the interplay of acculturation processes and family functioning, the focus should be on family processes and identification of the specific ways in which they are affected by ethnicity-related values and changes in these values. Some of the most important dimensions of *Structural Family Therapy* and other systemic models of family functioning, such as leadership and guidance, bonding and communication, conflict resolution, individual and system development, and emotional and physical closeness or distance, are described in this section.

Leadership and Guidance

Leadership and guidance behaviors help organize a family so that it can fulfill its roles and carry out its functions. These behaviors include advice and information that increase the competence and success of the family members. This dimension refers to the ability to teach, lead, and influence in loving but firm ways. Competent leadership and guidance require some understanding of the child's world so that the parent has credibility in the child's eyes.

Family leadership patterns may vary considerably among cultures. From a transcultural perspective, *adaptive executive systems* are defined in a similar way: cooperative, collaborative, and effective. Three aspects of family leadership are examined: the role of parental figures in family leadership, nuclear vs. extended leadership systems, and the role of family leadership in extrafamilial systems.

Parental figures in family leadership. One of the most important characteristics of parental figures that raise children successfully is that they can work together, support each other's decisions, and deliver consistent messages to their children. Given the basic adaptive family functions, many family configurations can achieve these goals. Boyd-Franklin (1989) has written about the fact that many African American two-parent families have an egalitarian pattern involved in their decision making, sharing

---

[1]Because the authors showed these data to be consistent across groups of Mexican-, Cuban-, and Central-American backgrounds supports the finding that familialism really can be considered a core Hispanic/Latino construct.

of power, and responsibilities. Role flexibility has been considered a strength in African American families and a survival mechanism for the difficult social and economic circumstances they often face. European American culture has also moved toward equality in the executive power of men and women. However, many other cultures are characterized by marked differences in the balance of power (complementary structure), although the relationship between gender and power in traditional families is more complex than it may seem on the surface. For example, in some Hispanic family structures the husband and father may be the official executive of the family but is often "spared" the details of children's misbehavior until problems reach crisis proportions. In such cases the father often loses touch with the day-to-day operations of family life. Despite such complexities and although quite different in their day-to-day operations, each of these different structures (egalitarian or complementary parental pairs) may be adaptive. Within each structure, partners can agree on leadership roles, support one another's decisions, and maintain consistent and predictable rules and family norms.

Conversely, disagreements on the basic blueprints for leadership can be quite destructive to families. In maladaptive family relationships, parental figures struggle for power and are unable to make joint decisions, resulting in rules and consequences that are unclear and unpredictable. The children become "triangulated" in the parental/executive system conflict. They may become entangled in destructive coalitions with a parent, act out in response to ineffective control, or disengage from the family to avoid distressing interactions.

Of particular interest is how acculturation-related processes might disrupt the adaptive functioning of parental figures. For example, when employment conditions are such that a woman from a traditional (i.e., a male-dominant) couple can obtain a job more easily than a man, her new role as the breadwinner may create tensions and stress in the family structure. The natural tendency for the breadwinner to take more of a decision-making role in the family results in a reconfiguration of the power structure and the redefinition of family roles.

Acculturation also plays a role in the power structure of the family. The family member with greater cultural competence in White American culture is better prepared to negotiate with powerful extrafamilial systems such as schools, courts, and social service agencies. An employed person may be more exposed to the values of the host society and therefore may acculturate faster and to a greater degree. The person may naturally begin to decrease gender-specific behavior and embrace more equality in the roles of male and female partners. This redefinition of the foundation of the couple relationship is likely to cause temporary instability that may be resolved relatively smoothly or be highly problematic. When the prestress level of family functioning is poor (e.g., little family flexibility and poor communication), the immigration- and acculturation-related stressors can result in serious and long-lasting family deterioration.

For a couple who is struggling to maintain good family functioning, the complexity of their work can be greatly exacerbated by power issues and value differences. One of the very basic ways in which this tension is manifested is in the day-to-day negotiation of family rules and norms and decisions about acceptable child behavior. It is not uncommon for parents to disagree as a result of changes in the decision-making process, disagreements that may be exacerbated by divergent world views regarding appropriate adolescent behavior or other family rules.

As children grow, the family dynamics may become even more complex because family tensions can be exacerbated when a child or adolescent takes the side of one parent (usually the most acculturated). For example, an assimilated adolescent may ridicule a traditional father who has a difficult time accepting his wife's need for more autonomy and independence. The formation of a mother–adolescent coalition against the father (an example of triangulation) places the child in a very vulnerable position and could deteriorate the father–adolescent bond.

Although the investigation of issues of egalitarian vs. complementary relationships is clearly important in understanding family functioning, it is also important from a treatment perspective in light of research findings that these characteristics may predict the efficacy of certain types of interventions (Rohrbaugh & Shoham, 2002). Findings suggest that partners in symmetrical or egalitarian relationships may benefit more from therapies emphasizing direct negotiation (Jacobson, Follette, & Pagel, 1986), whereas clients in complementary relationships (i.e., organized according to traditional gender roles) may do better with less direct and less overt interventions, such as those promoted by the strategic interventions models. Similarly, Gollan and Jacobson (2002) reported that couples whose affiliation and independence needs follow traditional gender roles (i.e., male—independent, female—affiliative) may show attenuated effects of behavioral marital therapy.

Nuclear vs. extended family leadership. Given the importance of the extended family in providing leadership among many cultures, it is important to discuss the tensions that can exist between nuclear and extended families in the leadership dimension. In the context of a mainstream cultural framework, which has a preference toward the nuclear family, considerable involvement from extended family members can be considered dysfunctional. However, in examining executive systems across cultures, especially in cultural contexts that highly value the extended family, extended family members are often very active leaders and are culturally and functionally adaptive. One marked example of family leadership that is cross-generational and highly culture specific is the pattern found in some Asian American families. The husband's mother may be highly involved in giving her daughter-in-law direction for proper behavior, both with her husband as well as with the husband's family of origin and family of procreation. From a culture-specific perspective, the expectation is that the husband's mother is helping shape her daughter-in-law's behavior because the daughter-in-law will become a member of her husband's family. Clearly, this type of arrangement can only work when all members involved are using the same "blueprint" for nuclear-extended-family relationships. If the wife espoused a different set of values, as do most mainstream therapists, she may consider the mother-in-law's behavior to be highly intrusive and inappropriate. Caught between a traditional extended family and an acculturated wife and society, the husband's loyalties and beliefs would be severely tested.

Another example of extended family members functioning in executive roles can be found when a single mother is living in her mother's home. In these cases, a functional executive system may comprise the single mother and her own mother (the child's grandmother) acting as coparents. From the perspective of a culture that values nuclear families, extensive parenting by an extended family member might be considered dysfunctional because it undermines parental authority and keeps the biological parent immature. From the perspective of a culture that values involvement of the extended family, however, coparenting by the mother and grandmother would be considered adaptive. Regardless of the culture and who comprises the parental system, the important indicators of adaptive parental functioning are whether the coparenting relationship is serving all of its members well and whether they agree on a blueprint for decision making and power configurations (i.e., egalitarian vs. complementary).

Family leadership and extrafamilial systems. Throughout the life cycle, parents must show leadership in outside systems such as medical and school systems. As their children grow and begin to interact with outside systems such as peers and the community, parents must often increase their level of extrafamilial leadership, especially if problems emerge. For children who are ethnic minorities, this is particularly important because parents must be advocates for the children in schools or neighborhoods filled with discrimination and prejudice. In working with non-English-speaking parents it has become clear that the language barrier disempowers them in these important systems and results in a substantial loss of leadership. In most immigrant families, children become fluent in English well before their parents and have less difficulty adapting to the norms of institutional structures. It is not unusual for a child who is the subject of a disciplinary meeting involving parents and school officials to serve as a translator, thus compromising the executive power of parents in the eyes of the school and within the family.

Even when language is not a barrier, there is often a sense among individuals of some cultures that it is not their place to challenge large institutions. The power–distance formulation (Hofstede, 1980) predicts that among some cultures subscribing to this pattern, individuals feel that institutions should be greatly respected and not be challenged. Parents subscribing to this belief are less likely to assert themselves to change the behavior of the school toward the children. It is important to understand the roots of the behavior even if changing the behavior is an important goal. (Helping parents to become agents of change is significant because of the importance this society places on ensuring that parents help shape a school's behavior toward their children.) Because it is not clear the extent to which this value changes as part of the acculturation processes, it is wise to assess this important dimension. It is also important to keep in mind that it is easy to mistakenly label the behaviors resulting from this level of respect and awe of large institutions as *passivity, dependence,* or *lack of motivation.*

Bonding and Communication

The level of bonding that exists among family members has been shown to be a critical family variable that influences a child's development (Brook, Nomura, & Cohen, 1987). Bonding is relevant not only to overall cohesion in the family but also to the degree to which parental influence can continue as children become adolescents. Clinical evidence has suggested that when adolescents feel rejected by or less bonded to the family, they are more susceptible to the adverse influence of delinquent peers. When the level of bonding is low, adolescents are, in a sense, ejected from the family toward their peers; the adolescents do not feel a need to reconcile the values and beliefs of the family and their peers. When the level of bonding is high, however, and the adolescents' orientation toward their peers does not necessarily equate to a rejection of the family, adolescents may attempt to find peers whose values and beliefs are similar to those of their family.

For children, bonding overlaps the process of acculturation, so many acculturation-related variables can powerfully influence the level of family bonding. For example, consider the simple factor of language. In many families with highly assimilated adolescents, children may speak only English, whereas their parents speak only the language of origin. In families in which parents and adolescents can only speak a common language with great difficulty, communication frequency is diminished and is sometimes limited only to conflicts. Language, therefore, is a concrete obstacle to the type of effective communication needed during the stormy adolescent life cycle stage. Even when there is a shared language, however, there may be little overlap between the shared experiences and interests of parents and adolescents because of acculturation differences, meaning that they have fewer opportunities to share intimate family moments and other bonding opportunities. As a consequence, when the inevitable conflicts emerge, the parents—who may be rejecting the new culture or struggling with integration—and their assimilated children may find that they live in different worlds with different values and lifestyles and have less hope for compromise.

Conflict Resolution

An issue closely related to communication is the family's ability to resolve conflicts, a family process that has been identified as important to all families (Szapocznik et al., 1991). Conflict resolution styles vary considerably across cultures, consequently it is another dimension of family functioning in which it is important to be sensitive to transcultural as well as culture-specific differences. In the White American mental health culture, for example, full conflict emergence with resolution is valued. Negativity tends to be more easily tolerated, and positive emotions are more easily expressed. In contrast, cultures that seek to keep harmony in relationships and value *respeto* ("respect") may make frequent use of conflict avoidance techniques. The extent to which parents have a markedly hierarchical view of family relations has powerful implications for the process of family therapy. When parents view good family functioning as consisting of marked levels of authority and a high level of harmony, they may perceive open disagreements between parents and adolescents as disrespectful and unacceptable. One of the critical implications of this worldview is that parents may consider therapy interventions to be incompetent or misguided, especially when the interventions openly encourage the children to speak their minds and tell their parents what they really think. The parents may think that the intervention is making the problem worse than it was originally by encouraging what is perceived to be the dysfunctional behavior (i.e., publicly challenging their parents). Considering the link between process and outcome, the impact of this phenomenon can be profound. The types of family interactions that may be hypothesized to be therapeutic (e.g., direct negotiation and problem solving between adolescents and parents) may not lead to good outcomes in families who are highly hierarchical. Successful therapy may require less direct negotiation that is built on and does not challenge the hierarchical framework.

There is a great deal of variation between and within groups in terms of expression of emotion and open discussions of disagreements or conflict. Among Hispanics of Caribbean origin, for example, emotions are typically expressed very openly and loudly. In contrast, interactions in Central American families are typically reserved. Family members who are upset with each other may have very subtle signals for expressing these emotions (signals that are easily missed by an unprepared therapist). Such families may become silent when asked to talk together during a family therapy session about a disagreement. Encouragement to voice their emotions openly may overwhelm these families and lead to premature termination of therapy.

Individual and System Development

Systems, like individuals, go through a series of developmental stages. At each new stage in the life cycle, the system must complete certain tasks. The developmental stages of a family and individuals within the family play a crucial role in family functioning. Role expectations throughout the course of the life cycle vary considerably among cultures. These differences depend to a great extent on the culture's expectations regarding separation and individuation of children from their family of origin. The rate at which children are expected to take on responsibilities in a family varies considerably, not only from family to family but also from culture to culture. Thus, assessment of developmentally appropriate roles has to be sensitive to both transcultural and cultural-specific differences. In an urban context, some Hispanic 16-year-old girls may not be allowed to date unchaperoned, whereas others may be allowed to go on a weekend trip with females *and* males. In some Asian cultures, children may be committed to each other for marriage at a young age, and they may marry as early as the onset of puberty. Clearly, these examples show the range of expectations, which are often tied to culture of origin, regarding the quality and rate of individual development within a larger family system.

Acculturation processes can create significant tension during the developmental stages. For example, an Asian child who has assimilated White American cultural values may consider it inappropriate for a child to act as the primary source of emotional support for the mother. This idea conflicts with the ideas of the child's culture of origin and of his traditional family members; sons are expected to provide long-term emotional and material support to their family.

Likewise, a child may quickly adopt other White American family values, such as the expectation that children are to be "launched" from the home during late adolescence or early adulthood. Children in families who hold such values are encouraged to be responsible and autonomous (e.g., to find employment early in life, to maintain their own home or apartment). Conversely, traditional Hispanic parents may expect their children to remain in the parental home until they marry. It is not unusual in Hispanic culture for sons or daughters to live with their parents well into their late 20s and for the children (especially the males) to do very few household chores. These differing worldviews can bring about powerful family conflicts within the family and lead to a sense of rejection and lack of understanding.

The role of older adults also varies across cultures. In Hispanic families, it is normative for infirm parents to live with their children, especially their daughters. Such a highly supportive tradition can be a great strength, but it can also be detrimental when family members are overburdened by the expectation that all care giving is the responsibility of the family. The role of older adults is also more central in many African American and Caribbean families than in White American families. In these cultures, older adults are typically highly respected for their wisdom and the sacrifices they have made. In Asian families, in which filial piety supercedes all other relationships (Szapocznik & Hernandez, 1988), it is traditional for older adults to live with adult children, particularly their sons. This arrangement can cause intergenerational tension because members of a younger generation that has adopted mainstream values may expect their healthy parents to live independently.

Poor, urban, minority families often have multiple disruptions of the life cycle. Many women have their first children during adolescence, when they are unprepared to become mothers. Hence, either their own mothers or other adult women in the family become the mother figures for the children. Other examples of the dramatic developmental upheaval confronted by these families include untimely losses resulting from violence or illness such as HIV/AIDS; dislocations related to drug use, homelessness, unemployment, or immigration; and fluidity of household composition, all of which can result in symptoms associated with posttraumatic stress and other family problems.

Emotional and Physical Closeness or Distance

The emotional and physical closeness or distance in families is another dimension in which it is important to be sensitive to the transcultural and culture-specific differences. The sensitivity, or connectedness, among family members is usually described in terms of boundaries. These boundaries can be highly rigid, creating great emotional and psychological distance among family members, and at the other extreme the boundaries can be highly permeable, leading to a high degree of emotional and psychological closeness that may be intolerable for some family members. The degree of closeness in a Hispanic family is typically greater than that found in a White American family, with Hispanics showing higher levels of interdependence, conformity, loyalty, and readiness to sacrifice for the welfare of family members (Marín & Marín, 1991). White American culture places a relatively higher value on individuality and independence, whereas Hispanic culture values collectivism and gives precedence to the needs of the family rather than to the needs of the individual.

Families that are distant characterize themselves as being individualists who value autonomy. One strength of these families is that members learn to be competent and independent. A weakness is that in difficult times, family members may not be available to support one another or may not even be aware of other members' emotional needs. Such a premium is placed on self-sufficiency that asking for help is outside of their repertoire, so an offer of help may be perceived as offensive.

Extremely close, or "enmeshed," families are very aware of each other's problems and needs and are often available for support. However, highly enmeshed families typically do not tolerate uniqueness, so members who do not fit in may be ostracized and essentially rejected. In addition, highly enmeshed families may engender dependency and delay the emotional development of some of its members. Finally, enmeshed families can experience problems caused by the tendency of family members to make assumptions (i.e., read minds) about others' thoughts and feelings and therefore not communicate about important issues.

If assimilated children in a Hispanic family are rebelling because they are not allowed to individuate, then the tendency for greater emotional and psychological closeness in the family is related to the emergence of symptomatic behavior. As such, it needs to be addressed even though it is culturally syntonic for the parents. The opposite may also be true. For example, a White American father could give more autonomy to his 17-year-old daughter than she can handle by expecting her to go away to college. Suicidal ideation and attempts are often associated with these types of incompatibility in expected autonomy.

The importance of cultural sensitivity applies equally to the culture of White Americans that at times may clash with the "culture" of therapy. Family therapy is often perceived as promoting interdependency in families. Taken to an extreme, family therapy may run counter to the values of families who place a high value on independence and self-sufficiency. Such families may reject therapeutic maneuvers that promote high levels of cooperation because they may think that the interventions are encouraging a member to become a burden to others. Similarly, the high value of privacy among some African Americans sometimes inhibits support-seeking behavior. A sense of internal control or mastery is important to people who place a high value on self-sufficiency. Therefore, therapists must always be attentive to personal and cultural values and be careful not to undermine a family's sense of internal control by pushing too hard for a level of reliance on others that is culturally dystonic. A strategy for working with such families is to recognize and harness the strengths of competence and self-sufficiency while trying to make some small changes in the willingness of family members to band together in a time of need or crisis.

Conclusion

This chapter has attempted to more precisely describe the way acculturation-related dimensions affect core aspects of family functioning. The discussions have linked specific values, beliefs, and worldviews to specific constructs that are at the core of family functioning, family therapy, and family research. Clearly, it is impossible and may be undesirable for any one study to attempt to focus on all of these acculturation-related dimensions. It is more reasonable to expect that family clinicians and researchers working with ethnically diverse groups will assess the values and beliefs that can be predicted to directly influence the family interactions or constructs of interest. Furthermore, the clinicians must be prepared to understand divergent and often well-hidden worldviews that may cause intrafamilial conflicts and help members find common ground and adaptive solutions. Only by reaching this level of specificity will understanding of the relationship between culture-related factors and family functioning blossom.

References

Alexander, J. F., Holtzworth-Munroe, A., & Jameson, P. B. (1994). Research on the process and outcome of marriage and family therapy. In A. E. Bergin & S. L. Garfield (Eds.), *Handbook of psychotherapy and behavior change* (4th ed., pp. 595–630). New York: Wiley.

Berry, J. W. (1980). Acculturation as varieties of adaptation. In A. Padilla (Ed.), *Acculturation: Theory, models and findings* (pp. 9–25). Boulder, CO: Westview.

Berry, J. W. (1998). *Conceptual approaches to understanding acculturation.* Paper presented at Acculturation: Advances in theory, measurement, and applied research. San Francisco.

Boyd-Franklin, N. (1989). *Black families in therapy*. New York: Guilford Press.

Brook, J. S., Nomura, C., & Cohen, P. (1987). A network of influences on adolescent drug involvement: Neighborhood, school, peer and family. *Genetic, Social and General Psychology Monographs, 115*, 123–145.

Cronbach, L. J., & Snow, R. E. (1977). *Aptitudes and instructional methods: A handbook for research on interactions*. New York: Irvington.

Gollan, J., & Jacobson, N. (2002). Developments in couple therapy research. In H. Liddle, D. A. Santisteban, R. F. Levant, & J. H. Bray (Eds.), *Family psychology: Science-based interventions* (pp. 105–122). Washington, DC: American Psychological Association.

Guarnaccia, P. J., Canino, G., Rubio-Stipec, M., & Bravo, M. (1993). The prevalence of ataques de nervios in the Puerto Rico Disaster Study: The role of culture in psychiatric epidemiology. *Journal of Nervous and Mental Disease, 181*, 157–165.

Hines, P. M., & Boyd-Franklin, N. (1996). African American families. In M. McGoldrick, J. Giordano, & J. Pearce (Eds.), *Ethnicity and family therapy* (pp. 66–84). New York: Guilford Press.

Hofstede, G. (1980). *Culture's consequences: International differences in work related values*. Beverly Hills, CA: Sage.

Hovey, J. D., & King, C. A. (1996). Acculturative stress, depression, and suicidal ideation among immigrant and second-generation Latino adolescents. *Journal of the American Academy on Child and Adolescent Psychiatry, 35*, 1183–1192.

Jacobson, N. S., Follette, W. C., & Pagel, M. (1986). Predicting who will benefit from behavioral marital therapy. *Journal of Consulting and Clinical Psychology, 54*, 518–522.

Lee, E. (1996). Asian American families: An overview. In M. McGoldrick, J. Giordano, & J. Pearce (Eds.), *Ethnicity and family therapy* (pp. 249–267). New York: Guilford Press.

Liddle, H. A. (1995). Conceptual and clinical dimensions of a multidimensional, multisystems engagement strategy in family-based adolescent treatment. *Psychotherapy, 32*, 39–57.

Liddle, H. A., Santisteban, D. A., Levant, R. F., & Bray, J. H. (Eds.). (2002). *Family psychology: Science-based interventions*. Washington, DC: American Psychological Association.

Marín, G., & Marín, B. V. (1991). *Research with Hispanic populations*. Newbury Park, CA: Sage.

McGoldrick, M. (1989). Ethnicity and the family life cycle. In B. Carter & M. McGoldrick (Eds.), *The changing family life cycle: A framework for family therapy* (2nd ed., pp. 69–90). Needham Heights, MA: Allyn & Bacon.

McGoldrick, M., & Giordano, T. (1996). Overview: Ethnicity and family therapy. In M. McGoldrick, J. Giordano, & J. Pearce (Eds.), *Ethnicity and family therapy* (pp. 1–27). New York: Guilford Press.

Patterson, G. R., Reid, J. B., & Dishion, T. J. (1992). *Antisocial boys*. Eugene, OR: Castalia.

Rivera-Arzola, M., & Ramos-Grenier, J. (1997). Anger, ataques de nervios, and la mujer Puertorriquena: Sociocultural considerations and treatment implications. In J. Garcia & M. Zea (Eds.), *Psychological interventions and research with Latino populations* (pp. 125–141). Needham Heights, MA: Allyn & Bacon.

Rodriguez, O., & Weisburd, D. (1991). The integrated social control model and ethnicity: The case of Puerto Rican American delinquency. *Criminal Justice and Behavior, 18*, 464–479.

Rodriguez, O., & Zayas, L. H. (1990). Hispanic adolescents and antisocial behavior: Sociocultural factors and treatment implications. In A. R. Stiffman & L. E. Davis (Eds.), *Ethnic issues in adolescent mental health* (pp. 147–171). Newbury Park, CA: Sage.

Rogler, L. H., & Cooney, R. S. (1984). *Puerto Rican families in New York City: Integrational processes*. Maplewood, NJ: Waterfront.

Rohrbaugh, M. J., & Shoham, V. (2002). Toward family-level attribute × treatment interaction research. In H. A. Liddle, D. A. Santisteban, R. F. Levant, & J. H. Bray (Eds.), *Family psychology: Science-based interventions* (pp. 215–237). Washington, DC: American Psychological Association Press.

Sabogal, F., Marín, G., Otero-Sabogal, R., VanOss Marín, B., & Pérez-Stable, E. J. (1987). Hispanic familism and acculturation: What changes and what doesn't? *Hispanic Journal of Behavioral Sciences, 9*, 397–412.

Santisteban, D. A., Coatsworth, J. D., Perez-Vidal, A., Mitrani, V., Jean-Gilles, M., & Szapocznik, J. (1997). Brief structural strategic family therapy with African American and Hispanic high risk youth: A report of outcome. *Journal of Community Psychology, 25*, 453–471.

Santisteban, D. A., Coatsworth, J. D., Szapocznik, J., Perez-Vidal, A., Kurtines, W. M., & LaPerriere, A. (2001). *The efficacy of family therapy for behavior problems and drug abuse in Hispanic adolescents.* Manuscript submitted for publication.

Santisteban, D. A., Muir-Malcolm, J. A., Mitrani, V. B., & Szapocznik, J. (2002). Integrating the study of ethnic culture and family psychology intervention science. In H. A. Liddle, D. A. Santisteban, R. F. Levant, & J. H. Bray (Eds.), *Family psychology: Science-based interventions* (pp. 331–351). Washington, DC: American Psychological Association.

Santisteban, D. A., Szapocznik, J., & Kurtines, W. M. (1994). Behavior problems among Hispanic youths: The family as moderator of adjustment. In J. Szapocznik (Ed.), *A Hispanic family approach to substance abuse prevention* (pp. 19–49). Rockville, MD: Center for Substance Abuse Prevention.

Santisteban, D. A., Szapocznik, J., Kurtines, W., & Perez-Vidal, A. (1996). Efficacy of interventions for engaging youth/families into treatment and some factors that may contribute to differential effectiveness. *Journal of Family Psychology, 10*, 35–44.

Schmidt, S. E., Liddle, H. A., & Dakof, G. A. (1996). Changes in parenting practices and adolescent drug abuse during multidimensional family therapy. *Journal of Family Psychology, 10*, 12–27.

Shoham, V., & Rohrbaugh, M. (1995). Aptitude × treatment interaction (ATI) research: Sharpening the focus, widening the lens. In M. Aveline & D. A. Shapiro (Eds.), *Research foundations for psychotherapy practice* (pp. 73–95). New York: Wiley.

Sommers, I., Fagan, J., & Baskin, D. (1993). Sociocultural influences on the explanation of delinquency for Puerto Rican youths. *Hispanic Journal of Behavioral Sciences, 15*, 36–62.

Szapocznik, J., & Hernandez R. (1988). The Cuban American family. In R. W. Habenstein, C. H. Mindel, & R. Wright (Eds.), *Ethnic families in America* (pp. 162–170). New York: Elsevier Press.

Szapocznik, J., Perez-Vidal, A., Brickman, A., Foote, F. H., Santisteban, D. A., Hervis, O., et al. (1988). Engaging adolescent drug abusers and their families into treatment: A strategic structural systems approach. *Journal of Consulting and Clinical Psychology, 56*, 552–557.

Szapocznik, J., Rio, A. T., Hervis, O. E., Mitrani, V. B., Kurtines, W. M., & Faraci, A. M. (1991). Assessing change in family functioning as a result of treatment: The Structural Family Systems Rating Scale (SFSR). *Journal of Marital and Family Therapy, 17*, 295–310.

Vega, W. A., Gil, A. G., Warheit, G. J., Zimmerman, R. S., & Apospori, E. (1993). Acculturation and delinquent behavior among Cuban American adolescents: Toward an empirical model. *American Journal of Community Psychology, 21*, 113–125.

Part III

Acculturation, Psychosocial Adjustment, and Health

7

The Relationship Between Acculturation and Ethnic Minority Mental Health

Pamela Balls Organista, Kurt C. Organista, and Karen Kurasaki

The purpose of this chapter is to provide an overview and analysis of research on the relationship between acculturation and mental health among African Americans, American Indians, Asian Americans, and Latinos. A review of the literature reveals that research in this area has been quite uneven across major ethnic groups in the United States. During the past 3 decades, there has been ample examination of this topic among Latinos including a review of 30 studies by Rogler, Cortés, and Malgady (1991). More modest attempts have been directed at Asian Americans (Gim, Atkinson, & Whiteley, 1990; Lee & Zane, 1998; Uba, 1994), but far less work has addressed this issue as it affects African Americans (Landrine & Klonoff, 1996; Snowden & Hines, 1999) and American Indians (Choney, Berryhill-Paapke, & Robbins, 1995). Therefore, this chapter includes an analysis of the research of these ethnic groups that begins with basic issues of conceptualization and measurement of distress and acculturation in African Americans and American Indians, as well as the insights gained from the more methodologically sophisticated studies of Asian Americans and large-scale prevalence studies of Latino populations.

Acculturative Stress

When individuals have contact with a new host society, they face many challenges, such as adjusting to a new language, different customs and norms for social interactions, unfamiliar rules and laws, and in some cases extreme lifestyle changes (e.g., rural to urban). *Acculturation* refers to the process of adjusting to these life changes. According to Berry and Kim (1988), the demands of adapting to these types of cultural differences can lead to increased stress, or *acculturative stress*. Accumulating evidence has suggested that acculturative stress may indeed have important implications for mental health. A number of researchers have found that greater acculturative stress increases the risk for developing psychological problems, particularly in the initial months of contact with the new host society (e.g., Yeung & Schwartz, 1986; Zheng & Berry, 1991).

According to contemporary theories of acculturation, the relationship between acculturation and mental health is likely to be mediated by a variety of variables, including the nature of the migration (e.g., forced vs. voluntary), the receptiveness of the host society, and the degree of similarity between the culture of origin and the new culture (Berry, 1997; Berry & Annis, 1974; Berry & Kim, 1988; Berry, Kim, Minde, & Mok, 1987). Therefore, it is important to consider a group's acculturation history to anticipate the likelihood of mental distress.

Another important consideration in studying the relationship between acculturation and mental health is the role of culture in the definition, experience, and expression of psychological distress. The growing awareness of this issue is exemplified by the inclusion of culture-bound syndromes (e.g., *ataque de nervious* among Latinos, *hwa-byung* among Koreans, and *spells* among African Americans) in the appendix of the fourth edition of the *Diagnostic and Statistical Manual of Mental Disorders* (*DSM–IV;* American Psychiatric Association, 1994) as well a growing body of literature on culture-specific disorders (Mezzich, Kleinman, Fabrega, & Parron, 1996; Ng, 1999; Simmons & Hughes, 1985; Tompar-Tiu & Sustento-Seneriches, 1995). Nevertheless, current Western nosology and health care professionals often overlook the link between symptoms and unique cultural or religious belief systems; mental health measures are often developed based on European-American norms. It is our hope that continued attention focused on the relationship between acculturative processes and adjustment will assist professionals in bridging the gap between traditional methodology and culture-based assessment and treatment protocols for diverse populations. For example, in chapter 10, Cortés uses a combined qualitative–quantitative research methodology to investigate acculturation and culture-specific idioms of distress in a group of Puerto Ricans.

American Indians

Although the number of studies that address the relationship between acculturation of American Indians and mental health are few, researchers have attempted to address the issues related to contact with mainstream society and consequent problems of mental distress. The lives of many American Indians continue to be characterized by disproportionately high levels of marginality, segregation, and socioeconomic problems. These forms of adaptation can be viewed as legacies of high acculturative stress that translate into higher risk for social, physical, and mental health problems.

In Choney and her colleagues' (1995) review of the literature on American Indian acculturation, they concluded that studies have been hampered by the inconsistent way in which researchers assessed acculturation. In most cases, acculturation is measured by a single question; the respondent is asked to endorse one of several statements regarding level of involvement with Indian and White cultures. For example, Johnson and Lashley (1989) asked Native American college students from 14 tribes to select from four different statements the one that best described their cultural commitment to Native American and Anglo American cultures. According to Choney et al. (1995), this type of inquiry represents a *deficit model* approach in which one assesses the unidirectional movement of an individual from traditional culture to majority culture. Implicit to the deficit model is the assumption that movement toward the White culture is healthy, whereas movement toward the other culture is more pathological. Such an approach fails to consider varying levels of acculturation, the fluidity of movement toward and away from one's culture, and the impact of the forced assimilation of American Indians during the early part of the 20th century. Because of this specific limitation, findings have varied in terms of the relationship between acculturation and mental health.

Hoffmann, Dana, and Bolton (1985) assessed the influence of acculturation on responses to an abbreviated form of the Minnesota Multiphasic Personality Inventory (MMPI–168; Overall & Gomez-Mont, 1974). The authors developed an acculturation instrument, the 32-item Rosebud Personal Opinion Survey (RPOS), based on an extensive literature review of previous instruments used to assess cultural issues of American Indians. Items from the RPOS assess several different components of acculturation, including language usage, value orientation, social behavior and customs, social interaction network, religious affiliation and practices, community of residence, occupational status, formal educational attainment, identification with traditional culture, and ancestry or blood quantum. Findings based on responses of 69 (37 men and 32 women) Rosebud Sioux indicated an association between lower acculturation (particularly the education/occupational component) and higher scores on several MMPI–168 scales, including depression, psychopathic deviate (significant for men), psychasthenia, schizophrenia, and social introversion.

Future efforts need to focus on development of an acculturation theory that incorporates values, behaviors, and other characteristics of American Indian culture. This is a formidable challenge because development of the theory would require a distillation of elements that are central to the Indian culture in general. Within the United States are hundreds of tribes and several languages that are spoken. Nonetheless, this challenge should not deter theorists from making some formulations about how cultural adaptation affects mental adjustment. For example, Choney et al. (1995) offered a "health model" of acculturation. A series of concentric circles are divided into four quadrants that represent four essential elements of the human condition—cognitive, behavioral, affective/spiritual, and social/environmental elements—domains that are similar to those of the traditional Indian medicine wheel. In addition, their model describes five different levels of acculturation: traditional, transitional, bicultural, assimilated, and marginal. Although the authors offer no empirical support for their model, their attempt to provide a multidimensional model that incorporates Indian culture and the possibility of several types of potential healthy outcomes is noteworthy. Clearly, additional development of measures of acculturation with large and diverse samples of American Indians and tests of this model are needed before its validity can be determined.

African Americans

Landrine and Klonoff (1994, 1996) noted that investigations of acculturation rarely include African Americans because research has primarily focused on the poorly defined concept of a "racial group" rather than on the ethnicity and culture of African Americans. Rather than exploring their traditional cultural beliefs, values, and practices, African Americans are often thought of as being American only, with their differences viewed solely as the result of regional and socioeconomic influences (Landrine & Klonoff, 1994).

It is important to be aware of basic methodological and conceptual issues that historically limit acculturation research with African Americans. Many popular measures devised to assess acculturation in other ethnic minority groups (e.g., Asian Americans, Latinos) include questions about English-language use or proficiency, length of U.S. residence, and compliance with traditional cultural beliefs and observance of cultural traditions. Some of these types of questions are particularly difficult to apply to African Americans (Snowden & Hines, 1999). Therefore, there are very few studies in the research literature that directly measure African American acculturation, and more specifically, assess its relationship to mental health.

The most popular measure of African American acculturation was developed less than 10 years ago. Landrine and Klonoff (1994) constructed an acculturation measure, the African American Acculturation Scale (AAAS), designed to assess various aspects of the group's culture. In the original version of the AAAS, eight dimensions were assessed: traditional African American family structures and practices, preference for African American things (e.g., African American newspapers, magazines, music, friends), preparation and consumption of traditional foods, interracial attitudes and cultural mistrust (e.g., mistrust of White people, belief that most White people are racists), traditional African American health beliefs and practices, traditional African American religious beliefs and practices, traditional African American childhood socialization, and superstitions. Basic to Landrine and Klonoff's concept of African American acculturation is the idea that acculturation may not be a process of going from traditional to acculturated, but may be more fluid; African Americans may begin their development as acculturated or bicultural individuals (especially if their parents are acculturated or bicultural).

A series of studies conducted by Landrine and Klonoff suggest that acculturation is indeed important to consider when predicting adjustment among African Americans. In one study the authors explored the nature of stress, coping, and symptomatology and their relationship to level of acculturation for African Americans (Landrine & Klonoff, 1996). They reasoned that acculturation should play a role in the type of coping that is used, the impact of stressful life events, and consequent stress-related symptoms. The AAAS was completed by 153 African Americans (83 women, 66 men, 4 unidentified) whose ages ranged from 15 to 70 years. They also completed several additional measures, including the Hopkins Symptom Checklist (HSCL–58; Derogatis, Lipman, Rickles, Uhlenhuth, & Covi, 1974) to assess a variety of psychiatric symptoms; the Psychiatric Epidemiology Research Interview (PERI)–Life Events Scale (Dohrenwend, Krasnoff, Askenasy, & Dohrenwend, 1978) to measure general life events; the Perceived Stress Scale (Cohen, Kamarck, & Mermelstein, 1983) to assess general stress; and the Ways of Coping Scale (Lazarus & Folkman, 1984) to measure different coping styles. Of all of the predictors (including social class) entered into a hierarchical regression, only acculturation accounted for a statistically significant amount of the variance in psychiatric symptoms among African Americans (Landrine & Klonoff, 1996). Further analyses suggested differences among acculturated African Americans compared with traditional African Americans in relation to predictors of psychiatric symptoms. Acculturated respondents tended to take responsibility or blame themselves for their problems, whereas traditional respondents tended to use denial as a coping strategy. Similarly, general stress seemed to play a more significant role in the symptoms of acculturated African Americans than of traditional African Americans.

A more recent scale of African American acculturation was designed and tested by Snowden and Hines (1999). Ten items were presented in a Likert-scale format. Items assessed race-related cultural and media preferences (e.g., music, radio, television), racial balance in primary group relationships (e.g., friends, church congregation, parties, neighborhoods), race-related attitudes (e.g., relying on relatives for help, desirability of interracial marriage), and degree of comfort in interactions with White individuals compared with African American individuals. Responses from 900 African Americans indicated good internal consistency reliability (coefficient alpha = .75). Analyses of the relationship between acculturation and several sociodemographic variables indicated gender differences. For men, high acculturation was associated with a lower level of belief in the importance of religion, a higher income, and a more urban residence. Among women, higher acculturation levels were associated with increased likelihood of being divorced or separated, a higher income, and urban residence. In contrast to men, highly acculturated African American women were more likely to report some degree of religious affiliation. Additional studies of this scale are needed to test its relationship to mental health and distress.

Essential to continuation of African American acculturation research is the need for better articulation of theory to guide the construction of measures. Landrine and Klonoff (1994, 1996) offered an exploration of domains that they believed to be central to African American culture, and they related these domains to specific outcome variables (e.g., coping and symptomatology). However, little attention is given to the formulation of a theory of African American acculturation in the United States that could serve as a basis for more systematic investigations of the link between acculturation and mental adjustment. That is, very little attention is given to the unique case of African American acculturation, which is less about native language and immigration issues and more about responses to overracialization. For example, current Afrocentric theorists (e.g., Nobles, 1985, 1986) have asserted the need to recognize and regenerate traditional African values (e.g., interconnectedness, spirituality, expressive communication and oral tradition, identity consciousness, appreciation of the fluidity of time) to better support and understand African Americans' psychosocial functioning from a cultural perspective. Similarly, Azibo (Atwell & Azibo, 1992; Azibo, 1989) stated that normalcy for people of African ancestry must be considered within a culture context in which personal identity as an African, social consciousness, values, and behaviors are balanced for a positive maintenance of the race. These issues must be resolved to advance the field toward larger scale, more sophisticated studies with theoretically grounded measures of African American acculturation that give insight into acculturation's role in psychological functioning and the expression of distress or adjustment.

Asian Americans

Researchers have responded to the continuous flow of immigration from Asian countries with great interest, which is evident from many recent studies that have attempted to assess the needs of this heterogeneous population. The studies reviewed in this section examine mental health outcomes of the acculturation process among Asian immigrants in Britain, Canada, New Zealand, and the United States. The majority of the studies focus on stress that accompanies tasks related to acculturation as the primary predictors of mental health. Difficulties learning a new language and problems seeking employment, for instance, are typical acculturation tasks that are associated with poorer mental health status. However, several studies also demonstrate that other mediating variables may be involved, including premigration trauma and acceptance from the dominant host society.

According to Zheng and Berry's (1991) longitudinal study of Chinese sojourners to Canada, physical and psychological symptoms related to acculturative stress increased until 4 months after migration. These physical and psychological symptoms related to acculturative stress began to gradually decline 5 months after migration. Similarly, recent Chinese immigrants who had lived in the United States for less than 1 year reported greater health problems (as measured by the General Health Questionnaire [GHQ]) and were more likely to qualify for a *DSM–III* diagnosis than immigrants who had lived in the United States longer (Yeung & Schwartz, 1986).

These findings support the premise that as acculturation increases, acculturative stress naturally decreases and consequently, mental health improves. Given the intensity and frequency of cultural differences we would expect newer immigrants to encounter in their daily living activities, other interesting questions arise. In which situations is this not the normal pattern? For some individuals, could problems adapting to the new host culture persist beyond the initial months or early few years? Do long-term mental health consequences accompany persistent problems in cultural adaptation? Furthermore, can researchers identify any characteristics that would predict when acculturative stress and related mental health problems might become chronic, long-term problems? Can anything be done during the early postmigration period to facilitate better cultural adaptation and thereby avert the negative mental health consequences of long-term acculturative stress?

Effects of Persistent Problems in Cultural Adaptation

Several studies have in fact documented that persistent problems in cultural adaptation are associated with a higher risk for long-term mental health problems. In a recent study of Southeast Asian refugees in the Northeastern United States, persistent acculturative stress was the strongest predictor of poorer mental health status more than 4 years after migration (Nicholson, 1997). Specifically, greater stress related to learning English and seeking employment were among the variables that predicted higher posttraumatic stress disorder (PTSD) and depression symptoms, as measured by the Harvard Trauma Questionnaire (HTQ; Mollica et al., 1992) and the 25-item Hopkins Symptom Checklist (HSCL–25), respectively. Nicholson's (1997) findings concur with findings reported by Westermeyer, Neider, and Vang (1984), who had conducted a similar study nearly 10 years earlier. Westermeyer et al. (1984) conducted a study of Hmong refugees in Minnesota at 1.5 and 3.5 years after their arrival in the United States. Using English language proficiency as an indicator of acculturation, they found a significant negative relationship between acculturation and psychological functioning. According to their findings, those at the 3.5-year follow-up who reported still having no English language proficiency scored significantly higher on the 90-item Symptom Checklist (SCL–90; Derogatis, 1977) depression subscale than those who reported at least some progress in learning English.

One of the problems with having limited English proficiency in the United States is that a lack of English language fluency affects functioning in other important daily domains such as employment (Westermeyer & Her, 1996); in turn, employment is related to well-being. The Hmong refugees in the Westermeyer et al. (1984) study who were still receiving welfare at the follow-up had higher scores on several SCL–90 subscales. In another study, Hmong who were still receiving welfare more than 8 years after migration to the United States showed more *DSM* Axis I disorders, more Axis IV psychosocial stressors, poorer occupational adaptation, and lower Global Assessment Scale (GAS) scores according to a clinical assessment (Westermeyer, Callies, & Neider, 1990). Individuals receiving welfare also had significantly higher symptom scores on the Brief Psychiatric Rating Scale (BPRS; Overall & Gorham, 1962) and Inpatient Multidimensional Psychiatric Scale (IMPS; Cairns, von Zerssen, Mombour, & Rackensperger, 1982) in this same 8-year Hmong follow-up study. Similarly, among members of a Southeast Asian sample, a group diagnosed with PTSD relied more on public assistance than those who did not have PTSD (Abe, Zane, & Chun, 1994).

Effects of Premigration Trauma

The studies presented so far indicate that when acculturative stress persists beyond the early postmigration period, there also can be long-term mental health consequences. Research findings have indicated that premigration factors, particularly traumatic experiences, are also strong predictors of poorer long-term mental health outcomes, regardless of the acculturation process. Refugees from Southeast Asia have reported experiencing bombing and fires during war, seeing or hearing people (often loved ones) being wounded or killed, experiencing torture, and experiencing rapes, robberies, shootings, and a lack of adequate food and water during their escape (Hauff & Vaglum, 1995; Kroll et al., 1989). According to the study conducted by Nicholson (1997), individuals who experienced the greatest number of traumatic premigration events had the most severe psychiatric symptoms more than 4 years postmigration. Hauff and Vaglum (1995) and Kroll et al. (1989) reported similar findings. In their investigation of Vietnamese refugees 3 years postmigration, Hauff and Vaglum (1995) found that premigration traumatic experiences, including combat experience, being wounded in the war, imprisonment, danger before migration, and separation from spouse during migration, correlated positively with level of symptomatology on the 90-item SCL–Revised (SCL–90–R; Derogatis, 1983). Kroll et al. (1989) reported that trauma experiences were significantly associated with higher depression and anxiety symptoms based on *DSM–III* criteria. Clarke, Sack, and Goff (1993) reported that war trauma significantly predicted PTSD and depression among a group of Cambodian adolescents at 6 years after migration.

Effects of Postmigration Factors

Several postmigration factors have also been identified by researchers as being related to poorer long-term mental health outcomes. Nicholson (1997) reported that poorer self-perceived health status had direct links to three psychiatric outcome measures: PTSD, depression, and anxiety. In addition, others have argued that important life changes that may occur as a result of migration, such as loss of one's previous social role or avocation, the need to rebuild one's social network, and separation from family supports, are related to poorer outcomes. Westermeyer et al. (1984) reported that the loss of one's previous social role or avocation was associated with greater symptoms on the SCL–90 at 3.5 years postmigration.

According to Hauff and Vaglum (1995), not having a close confidant and long-term separation from children or spouse were significantly associated with emotional distress, as measured by the SCL–90–R.

Postmigration factors related to refugee placement were found in one study (Westermeyer et al., 1984) to have a major influence on postmigration adjustment. Refugees who reported dissatisfaction in the frequency of sponsor visits (i.e., infrequent visits) had higher symptom levels on the SCL–90 3.5 years after migration. Similarly, Clarke et al. (1993) reported that resettlement stress accounted for approximately 12% of the variance in predicting PTSD in a 6-year postmigration follow-up of Cambodian adolescents. Finally, as expected, people's attitudes toward building a new life in the United States were associated with later outcomes. Those who believed their outlook in the United States was poor also showed higher levels of symptomatology at the follow-up (Westermeyer et al., 1984).

Sociodemographic Characteristics

Sociodemographic characteristics that have been found to be associated with poorer long-term mental health status are age, sex, whether one has been widowed, education, and socioeconomic status (SES). In a study of Cambodian refugees living in New Zealand, Cheung (1995) found that being older, widowed, less educated, and of a lower SES were significantly associated with a lower degree of acculturation, which was in turn significantly associated with higher levels of pathology, as measured by the 28-item GHQ (GHQ–28) scores. Similarly, Kroll et al. (1989) found that women who were widowed because of the war reported more severe depression and anxiety symptomatology based on *DSM–III* criteria. It is important to note that widowhood was not correlated with age; the majority of the women were widowed in their 40s and early 50s because of the war. However, we might speculate that the reason being older and widowed are associated with poorer outcomes is because these sociodemographic characteristics themselves are correlated with either more isolation or limited social supports. We might also speculate that lower education and SES are correlated with limited opportunities and more financial worries, which are in turn related to poorer mental health.

Effects of Cultural Orientation

According to Berry and Kim's (1988) model, there are four types of cultural orientations that can occur as an outcome of the acculturation process—assimilated, separatist, bicultural, and marginal. Individuals who are assimilated have completely adopted the behaviors and thinking of the dominant host culture to which they have migrated. In contrast, individuals who are separatists remain completely immersed in the language, activities, and beliefs of their culture of origin. Bicultural individuals are those who are more fluid between both their culture of origin and the new host culture. Finally, marginalists are isolated from their culture of origin and the dominant society. These different types of cultural orientations have been linked to different mental health outcomes.

Ying (1995) conducted a study of Chinese Americans to examine whether the four cultural orientations would predict greater or less depression, as measured by the Center for Epidemiological Studies Depression (CES–D) Scale (Radloff, 1977). According to her findings, bicultural activity orientation predicted lower depression (compared with all other cultural orientations), more positive and less negative affect (compared with the separatist orientation), and better life satisfaction (compared with separatist and marginal orientations). Although bicultural orientation predicted better mental health than the separatist orientation, a separatist activity orientation predicted lower negative affect and higher life satisfaction than the assimilated orientation in this study. Furthermore, assimilated activity orientation in this study mediated lower negative affect and higher life satisfaction than did marginality. Thus, according to Ying's findings, it seems that three cultural activity orientations (bicultural, assimilated, and separatist) are associated with better mental health outcomes than marginality, with biculturality being associated with the most favorable outcomes.

In a study of first-generation Chinese immigrants in Britain (Furnham & Li, 1993), participants' cultural orientations were assessed and their relationships to mental health status examined. The more traditional orientations were found to be associated with poorer mental health outcomes. Specifically, the belief that Chinese values are important and should be upheld was found to be correlated with psychological symptoms on the Langner–22. Similarly, a significant relationship was found between depression and the belief that Chinese should be spoken exclusively in the home, as measured by the Beck Depression Inventory (BDI; Beck, 1987). Finally, the attitude that Chinese children should date only other Chinese was found to be significantly associated with depression.

It is important to note that these investigations were conducted in isolation from other important social contexts such as the family. In fact, one might question whether the research findings regarding the acculturation and mental health relationship would still exist when considered within the context of the family. One study's findings at first glance seem to be counterintuitive because acculturation was associated with greater psychological problems. The study was conducted with Vietnamese American college students (Nguyen & Peterson, 1993). Among this sample, acculturation to the United States was positively associated with increased reports of depression symptoms. Because the sample comprised younger individuals, we might speculate that measuring acculturation of a college student may not tell the whole story. For example, if the students are acculturating more rapidly than their parents, then perhaps there are growing value differences, and thus tensions, between them and their less acculturated parents. Although such conclusions cannot be substantiated from Nguyen and Peterson's (1993) study, their findings underscore the importance of examining acculturation within the social context of the family.

Acceptance From Host Society

One question that has not been well examined is whether acculturation invariably leads to better mental health outcomes. On the one hand, greater acculturation might decrease the stress of daily living. On the other hand, if there is resistance among majority residents against newcomers, what might happen? According to Furnham and Li (1993), second-generation Chinese in Britain, who were more likely to report feeling that they were part of the host community, were significantly more likely than those who did not feel part of the host community to report greater psychological symptoms on the Langner–22. Why might they have found this? Could it be a function of discrimination in the host community? Furnham and Li did not test this specific question, so no answer exists for the individuals in their study. However, another study did examine discrimination specifically. In their study of Korean Americans in Los Angeles after the riots, Sasao and Chun (1994) reported that greater self-reported ethnic tension was significantly associated with being less happy. This finding was true regardless of whether the respondent was a direct victim of the riot violence, suggesting that psychologically, they all felt victimized.

Researchers have only begun to scratch the surface of what there is to know about acculturation and mental health among immigrants who originate from Asian countries. One problem that has slowed progress in the understanding of acculturation's impact on mental well-being has been conceptual. As mentioned in previous chapters, there has been a tendency to rely on a rather simple model of acculturative stress—as acculturation increases, stress from tasks related to daily living naturally decreases and results in better mental health. Current knowledge of how acculturation relates to mental health would be significantly enhanced by research designs that account for greater complexity in terms of how and under which conditions acculturation influences mental health outcomes. Research designs in the 1990s have gradually become more sophisticated. The findings from these recent studies reveal the importance of investigating potential mediating variables such as past trauma, health status, loss of one's previous social role and social support network, and resettlement experiences. Several findings also suggest the need to examine the acculturation and mental health relationship within the social contexts of family and society rather than in isolation.

Latinos

Rogler's Review of the Literature

For the past 30 years, the relationship between acculturation and mental health has been studied in Latinos more often than any other ethnic group. In fact, Rogler et al. (1991) published a seminal review of the literature on this topic, focusing on 30 empirical studies published between

1967 and 1989. Rogler et al. discovered that they could not integrate the literature because of a general lack of methodological uniformity. That is, the variance across studies in measures of acculturation (which ranged from scales to proxy variables), indexes of mental health (which ranged from *DSM* diagnoses to symptoms of stress), and Latino group studies, disallowed comparisons, let alone the prospect of meta-analyses. Indeed, 12 of the studies demonstrated positive relationships between acculturation and mental health, whereas 13 studies demonstrated negative relationships. Of the remaining five studies, three reported curvilinear relationships, and two reported mixed findings on different dependent variables.

Rogler et al. (1991) concluded that future research must be conducted with greater methodological uniformity. In addition, they noted that the conceptualization of acculturation as "exogenously stressful" (e.g., migration, loss of supports, adaptation to new country) must be expanded to consider simultaneous endogenous developmental changes that affect the way people perceive their experience. For example, although new immigrants and refugees experience significant stress related to migration and adaptation, they may also feel safe, hopeful, and better off than their compatriots in their countries of origin.

However, Rogler et al. (1991) also noted that, whereas new immigrants may make positive social comparisons to their country of origin counterparts, second-generation and later generation Latinos may make negative social comparisons to mainstream American society because of the different ways that prejudice, discrimination, and devalued ethnic minority status limit their once optimistic aspirations. Well-designed studies may help better address this intriguing idea of vulnerable minority status among Latinos and its mental health consequences.

Even in Rogler et al.'s (1991) otherwise equivocal review of the literature, five of six studies on alcohol and substance abuse consistently demonstrated a positive relationship between acculturation and problems in this important area. This pattern of alcohol and substance abuse is noteworthy for its compelling consistency in the more recent research described in the next section.

Prevalence Studies on Latinos

As research on Latino acculturation continues to either ignore or catch up with Rogler et al.'s (1991) recommendations, there is a small but growing number of epidemiological, population-based prevalence studies of Latino mental health that are helpful in informing the knowledge of the relationship between acculturation and mental health at the population level. Consistent with Rogler et al.'s recommendations, these surveys are more methodologically uniform in their epidemiological survey methods, *DSM*-based diagnoses, large representative samples of Latinos, careful translations and adaptations of instruments, and the inclusion of acculturation measures. Thus, they represent relatively more empirically sophisticated studies of acculturation and mental health.

The Hispanic Health and Nutrition Examination Survey. The Hispanic Health and Nutrition Examination Survey (HHANES) was the first major prevalence study of Latino health in the United States. The HHANES was conducted by the National Center for Health Statistics between 1982 and 1984 and included the following large samples of Latinos: 7,462 Mexican Americans in the five Southwestern states, 2,834 Puerto Ricans in the New York area, and 1,357 Cubans in Miami. Although the HHANES primarily consisted of a medical history examination, it also included a *DSM–III*-based measure of major depression from the Diagnostic Interview Schedule (DIS; Robins, Helzer, Croughan, & Ratcliff, 1981), a structured clinical interview that could be administered by nonclinician interviewers. The HHANES also included the CES–D Scale to measure recent symptoms of depression (Radloff, 1977). Assessment instruments were fully translated and administered in Spanish and English as needed.

Although the HHANES is limited in what it can teach about Latino mental health and acculturation, it provides a rare comparison of all three major Latino groups in America. As such, findings suggest that Puerto Ricans and Mexican Americans, with their acculturation histories of protracted conflict with mainstream society over issues such as colonization, land dispossession, and labor exploitation, should have higher rates of depression than other subgroups (e.g., early Cuban immigrants who obtained legal refugee status and government support).

Moscicki, Rae, Regier, and Locke (1987) did indeed find the highest rates of major depression in Puerto Ricans and the lowest in Cuban and Mexican Americans. Current, 6-month, and lifetime prevalence of major depression rates for Puerto Ricans are all more than double the rates of Mexicans and Cubans. The fact that Mexican and Cuban Americans did not differ in rates of major depressive disorder (MDD) seems inconsistent with acculturative stress theory but can be explained by acculturation differences in Mexican Americans that must be considered. For example, Moscicki, Locke, Rae, and Boyd (1989) conducted a follow-up study on the Mexican American individuals and found that "caseness" of depression, defined as a CES–D score of 16 or higher suggestive of major depression disorder, was predicted by an "Anglo orientation," which was assessed by whether the person was born in the United States, the preference for English vs. Spanish, and self-identification as Mexican American or Anglo vs. Chicano or Mexicano—even after controlling for SES.

Kaplan and Marks (1990) also examined the relationship between acculturation and depression in the Mexican American participants and found a positive relationship for younger Mexican American (ages 20 to 30 years) men and women, even after controlling for SES. For older Mexican Americans, no such relationship was found, and the study actually found a trend in the opposite direction. Kaplan and Marks concluded that younger Latinos may experience more social stress (e.g., workplace stress) and more distance from culture of origin than their older counterparts.

In a study of depression in Puerto Ricans, Vera et al. (1991) compared the HHANES U.S. Puerto Ricans to a probability group of island Puerto

Ricans and found comparable rates of CES–D caseness (28.1% and 28.6%). Although one would predict higher distress for more acculturated mainland Puerto Ricans, the distinction between mainland and island Puerto Ricans has been blurred by decades of unrestricted circular migration and because all Puerto Ricans are U.S. citizens. Furthermore, as a U.S. colony, the island of Puerto Rico has undergone dramatic Americanization during the 20th century, including transitioning from a rural, agrarian society to a more urban, industrial, and economic structure (Canino et al., 1987). In fact, the only Puerto Rico islandwide prevalence study, which was conducted in 1984, showed overall prevalence rates of mental disorders that were comparable to the U.S. general population (Canino et al., 1987). Still, it is worth noting that when Vera et al. (1991) compared U.S. and island Puerto Ricans at the lowest income level (i.e., less than $15,000 annual income), U.S. Puerto Ricans did indeed have higher levels of depression symptoms.

Angel and Guarnaccia (1989) investigated the relationship between depression and self-reported health in the HHANES. These researchers compared Puerto Ricans and Mexican Americans and found an inverse relationship in both samples. However, self-reported health and depression were worse in Puerto Ricans, and medical doctors similarly rated Puerto Ricans as less healthy than the Mexican Americans. Other reports comparing Mexican Americans to island Puerto Ricans show more somatic symptoms (Canino, Rubio-Stipec, Canino, & Escobar, 1992) and more instances of somatization disorder (Shrout et al., 1992) in Puerto Ricans. Even though the latter study also found higher rates of alcohol abuse and dependence and affective disorders in Mexican Americans, this was only true for U.S.-born Mexican Americans and not immigrant Mexican Americans. This finding again underscores the need to consider acculturation and suggests that more acculturated Mexican Americans may be at comparable risk to Puerto Ricans.

More recently, Lee, Markides, and Ray (1997) used the HHANES to compare patterns of heavy drinking (i.e., in excess of guidelines for safe alcohol consumption). Not surprisingly, they found a greater prevalence of previous heavy drinking in Mexican American (36%) and Puerto Rican men (35%) as compared to Cuban American men (17%), with the same albeit lower pattern for women (15%, 17%, and 5%, respectively). Puerto Rican men and women had the longest periods of previous heavy drinking (Ms = 6.2 and 4.4 years, respectively) as compared with Mexican American men and women (Ms = 4.6 and 2.8 years, respectively) and Cuban American men (M = 4.4 years [not enough Cuban women to calculate years]). Previous heavy drinking was related to current heavy drinking and various health risk factors and chronic medical conditions. For example, Mexican American women who were heavy drinkers in the past had higher rates of smoking, depression symptoms, and chronic medical conditions than Mexican American women with no history of heavy drinking. The same pattern was found for Puerto Rican men for smoking and chronic medical conditions and for Mexican American men for smoking. In sum, results of the HHANES survey reveal different levels of risk for mental health problems in Latino groups consistent with their histories of acculturative stress as discussed in this chapter.

Epidemiological Catchment Areas Study. Most of what is known about the prevalence of mental disorders in America has come from the huge epidemiological catchment areas (ECA) study sponsored by the National Institute of Mental Health during the 1980s (Robins & Regier, 1991). The ECA was conducted with population-based probability sampling, stratified by catchments in five major Americans cities, and used the DIS to make *DSM–III*-based diagnoses. As such, the ECA included large samples of Mexican Americans, African Americans, and non-Latino White individuals. Unfortunately, the ECA did not include Cuban Americans, and Puerto Ricans made up only 2% of the New Haven ECA catchment's area.

African Americans had higher rates of lifetime and 6-month prevalence of mental disorders (38% and 26%, respectively) as compared to White individuals (32% and 19%, respectively) and Mexican Americans (33% and 20%, respectively; Robins, Locke, & Regier, 1991). A closer examination of the higher rates of African Americans reveals that the rates were true primarily for men and women, ages 45 to 64, who were experiencing cognitive impairment and somatization disorder.

A closer examination of the seemingly comparable rates of Mexican Americans and non-Latino White individuals reveals important acculturation differences within the Mexican American sample (Burnam, Hough, Karno, Escobar, & Telles, 1987). That is, immigrant Mexican Americans have a lower overall lifetime prevalence than non-Latino White individuals (i.e., diagnoses of major depression, obsessive compulsive disorder [OCD], and drug abuse and dependence), whereas U.S.-born Mexican Americans have a higher lifetime prevalence (i.e., diagnoses of alcohol abuse and dependence, dysthymia, and phobia).

Reports comparing Mexican American and non-Latino White mental health are based on the Los Angeles ECA (LA–ECA; Robins & Regier, 1991), which was conducted in 1983 and 1984 and designed with a primary focus on Mexican Americans ($N = 1,244$). The LA–ECA reports reveal comparable lifetime (Karno et al., 1987) and 6-month (Burnam, Hough, Escobar, et al., 1987) prevalence of mental disorder in Mexican Americans and their White counterparts; a study by Burnam, Hough, Karno, et al. (1987) looked directly at the relationship between acculturation and lifetime prevalence in the Mexican American sample.

Burnam, Hough, Karno, et al. (1987) used a multidimensional scale of acculturation based on the pioneering scales of Cuellar, Harris, and Jasso (1980) and Szapocznik, Scopetta, Aranalde, and Kurtines (1978), which had excellent reliability (Cronbach's alpha = .97). Results revealed that acculturation was positively associated with a higher lifetime prevalence of several mental disorders (e.g., alcohol abuse and dependence, substance abuse and dependence, phobias), even after controlling for age, sex, and marital status. More specifically, U.S.-born Mexican Americans (who had higher acculturation scores) had higher rates of all of these disorders in addition to MDD and dysthymia.

The fact that immigrant Mexican Americans have far less prevalence of mental disorders than their U.S.-born counterparts is intriguing because the immigrants' SES is generally lower, and it is assumed they are experiencing stress from migration. One popular explanation for this finding is the *selective migration hypothesis*, which states that perhaps the Mexicans who immigrate to America are healthier than the Mexicans who do not immigrate. The other popular explanation is the *social stress hypothesis*, which suggests that the lower mental health of native-born Mexican Americans has to do with their especially stressful experience in America as a devalued and discriminated ethnic minority group. There seems to be more empirical support for a social stress model of Mexican American mental health. This model is based on survey research showing that U.S.-born Mexican Americans have poorer mental health than immigrant Mexican Americans. In turn, the immigrants have mental health that is comparable to their Mexico-based counterparts (Vega et al., 1998).

National Comorbidity Survey. The National Comorbidity Survey (NCS; Kessler et al., 1994) is the first mental health prevalence study based on national probability sample of adults ($N = 8,098$), including representative percentages of Latinos (9.7%) and African Americans (11.5%) in addition to non-Latino White individuals (75.3%, other = 3.5%). *DSM–III–R* diagnoses were assessed using a modified version of the Composite International Diagnostic Interview (CIDI), the current state-of-the-art structured diagnostic interview based on the DIS (World Health Organization, 1990).

Results published by Kessler et al. (1994) revealed generally comparable mental health profiles across ethnic groups, although Latinos had significantly higher levels of current affective disorders and comorbidity, which refers to simultaneous diagnoses of three more mental disorders. Unfortunately, the NCS represents a giant step backwards with regard to understanding Latino mental health and its relationship with acculturation because the NCS lumped together Latinos of various national origin backgrounds and only interviewed English-speaking Latinos. About half of Latinos participating in prevalence studies elect to do the interview in Spanish, which underscores the enormity of this omission (Robins & Regier, 1991). These methodological limitations were avoided in the following study.

Mexican American Prevalence and Services Survey. In the Mexican American Prevalence and Services Survey (MAPPS), Vega et al. (1998) surveyed a stratified random sample of 3,012 noninstitutionalized adults of Mexican background in Fresno, California. Like in the NCS, *DSM–III–R* diagnoses were made using the CIDI. To better understand the relationship between acculturation and mental health, Vega et al. compared U.S.-born Mexican Americans with short-term immigrants (those who had lived less than 13 years in the United States) and long-term immigrants (those who had lived 13 years or more in the United States). Furthermore, findings from this study were compared with those of the NCS and a Mexico City, Mexico, prevalence study. Thus, this study is extremely helpful in expanding on the prevalence studies reviewed in the previous sections.

Like the findings of the NCS, initial findings from the MAPSS revealed comparable prevalence rates in Mexican Americans and the general U.S. population (i.e., a lifetime prevalence rate of nearly 50% for any disorder assessed). However, further analyses of MAPSS data revealed comparable prevalence rates only for U.S.-born Mexican Americans. In contrast, immigrant Mexican Americans had only half of the general prevalence of U.S.-born Mexican Americans, a rate comparable to results of the Mexico City survey. Table 7.1 reveals the dramatic relationship between acculturation and mental disorders by comparing short- and long-term immigrants and U.S.-born Mexican Americans across virtually all major mental disorders assessed.

Regarding the relationship between acculturation and Mexican American mental health, Vega et al. (1998) concluded that their findings do not support the selective migration hypothesis, given the comparable prevalence rates for immigrants in the MAPSS and Mexicans in the Mexico City

Table 7.1. Lifetime Prevalence of Mental Disorders in MAPSS, Mexico City, and NCS Surveys

	MAPSS				NCS	
	Immigrants <13 years	Immigrants >13 years	U.S. born	Mexico City	Latinos	Total
Number of participants	884	851	1,145	1,733	305	5,384
Major depression	3.2%	7.9%	14.4%	7.8%	18.3%	17.2%
Manic depression	1.3%	1.6%	2.7%	1.3%	0.5%	0.4%
Dysthymia	1.6%	1.6%	5.2%	1.5%	8.6%	6.8%
Any affective disorder	5.9%	10.8%	18.5%	9%	20.4%	19.5%
Panic disorder	1%	2.6%	1.8%	0.4%	1.8%	3.5%
Agoraphobia without history of panic	3%	7.5%	11.8%	3.8%	6.8%	5%
Social phobia	3.8%	5.7%	11.8%	2.2%	19%	13.4%
Simple phobia	2.6%	7.9%	12%	3%	16.4%	11.1%
Generalized anxiety disorder	0%	0%	0%	1.1%	6.2%	5.4%
Any anxiety disorder	7.6%	17.1%	24.1%	8.3%	28%	25%
Alcohol abuse	0.5%	2.2%	5.2%	3.1%	6.6%	9.9%
Alcohol dependency	8.6%	10.4%	18.0%	8.2%	14.2%	15.1%
Substance abuse	0%	1.8%	3.4%	0.3%	3.3%	4.7%
Substance dependency	3%	5.3%	13.8%	0.8%	7%	7.9%
Any abuse or dependency	9.7%	14.3%	29.3%	11.8%	24.7%	28.2%
Any mental disorder	18.4%	32.3%	48.7%	23.4%	51.4%	48.6%

Note. MAPSS = Mexican American Prevalence and Services Survey; NCS = National Comorbidity Survey.
From "Lifetime Prevalence of DSM–III–R Psychiatric Disorders Among Urban and Rural Mexican Americans in California," by W. A. Vega et al., 1998, *Archives of General Psychiatry, 55*, 771–782. Copyright 1998, American Medical Association.

study. Instead the researchers concluded that "Mexican immigrants share the lower risk status of their national origin, but acculturation has deleterious effects on many aspects of their health at the population level" (p. 777).

Vega et al. (1998) ended their report with a series of questions, including the following: "Why does socialization into American culture and society increase susceptibility to psychiatric disorders so markedly? What are the risk factors? Is this process generalizable to other ethnic groups?" Obviously, these are complex questions requiring long and qualified answers based on new and improved research. However, a short answer can be ventured based on acculturation theory and the studies reviewed. That is, it would appear that the acculturation histories of different ethnic groups in America predispose the groups to varying degrees of acculturative stress and consequently, varying degrees of risk for mental disorders. This conclusion seems to be supported by the larger scale prevalence studies of Latinos reviewed in this chapter, which reveal the highest risk in Puerto Ricans and lowest risk in Cuban Americans for disorders such as major depression and significant symptoms, somatization disorder and significant symptoms, alcohol abuse and dependence, and related chronic medical conditions. Furthermore, the literature on Mexican Americans clearly shows a positive relationship between acculturation and mental disorders primarily because of the stress of being Mexican American in America as opposed to selectively migrating from Mexico.

Protective Factors and Risk Factors

Acculturation produces transitions that can be associated with a number of problems during the life span, including depression, anxiety, exposure to and use of alcohol and drugs, behavioral problems at home and in school, perceived discrimination, and negative expectations of the future (Vega & Alegria, 2001). It is important to consider which aspects of traditional culture protect individuals against mental health problems and ascertain how these aspects can be bolstered within different ethnic groups (Vega et al., 1998). For example, much has been written about healthy and protective aspects of traditional Mexican culture such as close and supportive extended family systems. As a core characteristic of Latino culture, familism is likely to buffer the family from acculturative stress and the effects of poverty but is probably simultaneously weakened by such challenging processes and situations. Sabogal, Marín, Otero-Sabogal, VanOss Marín, and Pérez-Stable (1987) studied the effects of acculturation on familism in a mixed sample of 452 Latino and 227 non-Latino White individuals. They found that perceptions of the family as highly supportive remained constant across Latinos of varying levels of acculturation. Even the most acculturated Latinos were more familistic than their non-Latino White counterparts. On the other hand, other dimensions of familism, such as sense of family obligation and use of family as behavioral and attitudinal referents, decreased with acculturation. This idea of slowly diminishing protective Latino cultural factors may help to explain why U.S.-born Mexican Americans and island Puerto Ricans do not have overall prevalence rates that greatly exceed the general U.S. population. That is, considering the considerably higher poverty rates of island Puerto Ricans (60%) and Mexican Americans (25%), as compared with the rates of non-Latino White individuals (7%), it is amazing that their mental health profiles are roughly comparable with regard to prevalence at the population level.

Many of the problems associated with acculturative stress are exacerbated by the considerable underutilization of mental health services because of many factors, including lack of affordable treatment and health insurance. Although underutilization has also been attributed to certain barriers within different cultures (e.g., stigma, overreliance on the family to cope with problems, culture-based disorders, use of folk healers and remedies), the empirical evidence is not compelling that these constitute obstacles—in comparison with the historical lack of mental health services that are available, accessible, culturally acceptable, and accountable to ethnic minority communities in need. For example, Vega and Alegria (2001) noted that although Latinos do use family and social networks to cope with emotional problems, they do not use them as a substitute for formal services. The same has been found in studies of folk healers and medicine use in Latinos (e.g., Higginbotham, Treviño, & Ray, 1990).

Conclusion

Much more research is needed to better understand the relationship of the acculturation process in various cultures and its relationship to mental health. A common theme among the reviewed studies is the need for a continued focus on conceptual issues involved in acculturation studies. Research devoted to the concept of acculturation for American Indians and African Americans is only in its infancy stage of development. Clearly, more attention must be placed on formulating a theory that describes the nature of acculturation for these groups and captures the intragroup heterogeneity and unique histories before researchers can venture into the exploration of acculturation's effects on adjustment.

Although there is a subtle trend toward developing more sophisticated studies with Asian Americans and Latinos, the research will continue to be limited unless consideration is given to investigating the role of mediating variables, such as trauma, physical health status, loss of social supports, and conflict experiences such as racism and discrimination. Furthermore, acculturation should be viewed as a process that must be assessed in individuals over time so that its dynamic quality can be studied. Thus, large-scale prospective studies will give us a better picture of the nature of acculturation and adaptation. Ultimately, as the understanding of the relationship between acculturation and mental health improves, clinicians will be able to design better interventions to promote the healthy adjustment in ethnic minority groups.

References

Abe, J., Zane, N., & Chun, K. (1994). Differential responses to trauma: Migration-related discriminants of post-traumatic stress disorder among Southeast Asian refugees. *Journal of Community Psychology, 22,* 121–135.

American Psychiatric Association. (1994). *Diagnostic and statistical manual of mental disorders.* (4th ed.). Washington, DC: Author.

Angel, R., & Guarnaccia, P. J. (1989). Mind, body, and culture: Somatization among Hispanics. *Social Science Medicine, 28,* 1229–1238.

Atwell, I., & Azibo, D. A. (1992). Diagnosing personality disorder in Africans (Blacks) using the Azibo nosology: Two case studies. In A. K. H. Burlew, W. C. Banks, H. P. McAdoo, & D. A. Azibo (Eds.), *African American psychology: Theory, research, and practice* (pp. 300–320). Newbury Park, CA: Sage.

Azibo, D. A. (1989). African-centered theses on mental health and a nosology of Black/African personality disorder. *Journal of Black Psychology, 15,* 173–214.

Beck, A. T. (1987). Cognitive therapy. In J. K. Zeig (Ed.), *The evolution of psychotherapy* (pp. 149–163). New York: Brunner/Mazel.

Berry, J. W. (1997). Immigration, acculturation, and adaptation. *Applied Psychology: An International Review, 46,* 5–34.

Berry, J. W., & Annis, R. C. (1974). Acculturation stress: The role of ecology, culture and differentiation. *Journal of Cross-Cultural Psychology, 5,* 382–406.

Berry, J. W., & Kim, U. (1988). Acculturation and mental health. In P. R. Dasen, J. W. Berry, & N. Sartorius (Eds.), *Health and cross-cultural psychology: Towards application* (pp. 207–236). Newbury Park, CA: Sage.

Berry, J. W., Kim, U., Minde, T., & Mok, D. (1987). Comparative studies of acculturative stress. *International Migration Review, 21,* 491–511.

Burnam, M. A., Hough, R. L., Escobar, J. I., Karno, M., Timbers, D. M., Telles, C. A., et al. (1987). Six-month prevalence of specific psychiatric disorders among Mexican Americans and non-Hispanic whites in Los Angeles. *Archives of General Psychiatry, 44,* 687–694.

Burnam, M. A., Hough, R. L., Karno, M., Escobar, J. I., & Telles, C. A. (1987). Acculturation and lifetime prevalence of psychiatric disorders among Mexican Americans in Los Angeles. *Journal of Health and Social Behavior, 28,* 89–102.

Cairns, V., von Zerssen, D., Mombour, W., & Rackensperger, W. (1982). Internal reliabilities of the scales from the Inpatient Multidimensional Psychiatric Scale. *Psychological Reports, 50*(3), 1223–1227.

Canino, G. J., Bird, H. R., Shrout, P. E., Rubio-Stipec, M., Bravo, M., Martinez, R., et al. (1987). Prevalence of specific psychiatric disorders in Puerto Rico. *Archives of General Psychiatry, 44,* 727–735.

Canino, I. A., Rubio-Stipec, M., Canino, G. J., & Escobar, J. I. (1992). Functional somatic symptoms: A cross-ethnic comparison. *American Journal of Orthopsychiatry, 629,* 605–612.

Cheung, P. (1995). Acculturation and psychiatric morbidity among Cambodian refugees in New Zealand. *International Journal of Social Psychiatry, 41,* 108–119.

Choney, S. K., Berryhill-Paapke, E., & Robbins, R. R. (1995). The acculturation of American Indians: Developing frameworks for research and practice. In J. G. Ponterotto, J. M. Casas, L. A. Suzuki, & C. M. Alexander (Eds.), *Handbook of multicultural counseling* (pp. 73–92). Thousand Oaks, CA: Sage.

Clarke, G., Sack, W. H., & Goff, B. (1993). Three forms of stress in Cambodian adolescent refugees. *Journal of Abnormal Child Psychology, 21,* 65–77.

Cohen, S., Kamarck, T., & Mermelstein, R. (1983). A global measure of perceived stress. *Journal of Health and Social Behavior, 24,* 385–395.

Cuellar, I., Harris, L. C., & Jasso, R. (1980). An acculturation scale for Mexican American normal and clinical populations. *Hispanic Journal of Behavioral Sciences, 2,* 199–217.

Derogatis, L. R. (1977). *The SCL-90: Administration, scoring and procedures manual—I.* Baltimore, MD: Johns Hopkins University Press.

Derogatis, L. R. (1983). *SCL-90-R: Administration, scoring and procedures manual.* Baltimore, MD: Clinical Psychometric Research.

Derogatis, L. R., Lipman, R. S., Rickles, K., Uhlenhuth, E. H., & Covi, L. (1974). The Hopkins Symptom Checklist (HSCL): A self-report symptom inventory. *Behavioral Science, 19,* 1–15.

Dohrenwend, B. S., Krasnoff, L., Askenasy, A. R., & Dohrenwend, B. P. (1978). Exemplification of a method for scaling life events: The PERI–Life Events Scale. *Journal of Health and Social Behavior, 19,* 205–229.

Furnham, A., & Li, Y. H. (1993). The psychological adjustment of the Chinese community in Britain: A study of two generations. *British Journal of Psychiatry, 162,* 109–113.

Gim, R. H., Atkinson, D. R., & Whiteley, S. (1990). Asian-American acculturation, severity of concerns, and willingness to see a counselor. *Journal of Counseling Psychology, 37,* 281–285.

Hauff, E., & Vaglum, P. (1995). Organized violence and the stress of exile: Predictors of mental health in a community cohort of Vietnamese refugees three years after resettlement. *British Journal of Psychiatry, 166,* 360–367.

Higginbotham, J. C., Treviño, F. M., & Ray, L. A. (1990). Utilization of curanderos by Mexican Americans: Prevalence and predictors: Findings from HHANES 1982–84. *American Journal of Public Health, 80*(Suppl.), 32–35.

Hoffman, T., Dana, R. H., & Bolton, B. (1985). Measured acculturation and MMPI–168 performance of Native American adults. *Journal of Cross-Cultural Psychology, 16,* 243–256.

Johnson, M. E., & Lashley, K. H. (1989). Influence of Native-American's cultural commitment on preferences for counselor ethnicity and expectations about counseling. *Journal of Multicultural Counseling and Development, 17,* 115–122.

Kaplan, M. S., & Marks, G. (1990). Adverse effects of acculturation: Psychological distress among Mexican American young adults. *Social Science Medicine, 31,* 1313–1319.

Karno, M., Hough, R. L., Burnam, M. A., Escobar, J. I., Timbers, D. M., Santana, F., et al. (1987). Lifetime prevalence of specific psychiatric disorders among Mexican Americans and non-Hispanic Whites in Los Angeles. *Archives of General Psychiatry, 44,* 695–701.

Kessler, R. C., McGonagle, K. A., Zhao, S., Nelson, C. B., Hughes, M., Eshleman, S., et al. (1994). Lifetime and 12-month prevalence of DSM–III–R psychiatric disorders in the United States. *Archives of General Psychiatry, 51,* 8–19.

Kroll, J., Habenicht, M., Mackenzie, T., Yang, M., Chan, S., Vang, T., et al. (1989). Depression and posttraumatic stress disorder in Southeast Asian refugees. *American Journal of Psychiatry, 146,* 1592–1597.

Landrine, H., & Klonoff, E. A. (1994). The African American Acculturation Scale: Development, reliability, and validity. *Journal of Black Psychology, 20,* 104–127.

Landrine, H., & Klonoff, E. A. (1996). *African American acculturation: Deconstructing race and reviving culture.* Thousand Oaks, CA: Sage.

Lazarus, R. S., & Folkman, S. (1984). *Stress, appraisal, and coping.* New York: Springer.

Lee, D. J., Markides, K. S., & Ray, L. A. (1997). Epidemiology of self-reported past heavy drinking in Hispanic adults. *Ethnicity and Health, 2*(1/2), 77–88.

Lee, L. C., & Zane, N. W. S. (Eds.). (1998). *Handbook of Asian American psychology.* Thousand Oaks, CA: Sage.

Mezzich, J. E., Kleinman, A., Fabrega, H., Jr., & Parron, D. L. (Eds.). (1996). *Culture and psychiatric diagnosis: A DSM–IV perspective.* Washington, DC: American Psychiatric Press.

Mollica, R. F., Caspi-Yavin, Y., Bollini, P., Truong, T., Tor, S., & Lavelle, J. (1992). The Harvard Trauma Questionnaire: Validating a cross-cultural instrument for measuring torture, trauma, and posttraumatic stress disorder in Indochinese refugees. *Journal of Nervous and Mental Disease, 180,* 111–116.

Moscicki, E. K., Locke, B. Z., Rae, D. S., & Boyd, J. H. (1989). Depressive symptoms among Mexican Americans: The Hispanic Health and Nutrition Survey. *American Journal of Epidemiology, 130,* 348.

Moscicki, E. K., Rae, D. S., Regier, D. A., & Locke, B. Z. (1987). The Hispanic Health and Nutrition Survey: Depression among Mexican Americans, Cuban Americans, and Puerto Ricans. In M. Garcia & J. Arana (Eds.), *Research agenda for Hispanics* (pp. 145–159). Chicago: University of Illinois Press.

Ng, A. T. (1999). Culture-bound syndromes. In E. J. Kramer, S. L. Ivey, & Y. Ying (Eds.), *Immigrant women's health* (pp. 249–256). San Francisco, CA: Jossey-Bass.

Nguyen, L., & Peterson, C. (1993). Depressive symptoms among Vietnamese-American college students. *Journal of Social Psychology, 133,* 65–71.

Nicholson, B. (1997). The influence of pre-emigration and postmigration stressors on mental health: A study of Southeast Asian refugees. *Social Work Research, 21*(1), 19–31.

Nobles, W. W. (1985). *Africanity and the Black family: The development of a theoretical model.* Berkeley, CA: Institute for the Advanced Study of Black Family Life and Culture.

Nobles, W. W. (1986). *African psychology: Towards its reclamation, reascension, and revitalization.* Oakland, CA: Black Family Institute.

Overall, J. E., & Gomez-Mont, F. (1974). The MMPI–168 for psychiatric screening. *Educational and Psychological Measurement, 34,* 315–319.

Overall, J. E., & Gorham, D. R. (1962). The Brief Psychiatric Rating Scale. *Psychological Reports, 10,* 799–812.

Radloff, L. S. (1977). The CES–D scale: A self-report depression scale for research in the general population. *Applied Psychological Measurement, 1,* 385–401.

Robins, L. N., Helzer, J. E., Croughan, J. L., & Ratcliff, K. S. (1981). The NIMH Diagnostic Interview Schedule: Its history, characteristics, and validity. *Archives of General Psychiatry, 38,* 381–389.

Robins, L. N., Locke, B. Z., & Regier, D. A. (1991). An overview of psychiatric disorders in America. In L. N. Robins & D. A. Regier (Eds.), *Psychiatric disorders in America: The epidemiologic Catchment Areas Study* (pp. 328–366). New York: Free Press.

Robins, L. N., & Regier, D. A. (Eds.). (1991). *Psychiatric disorders in America: The epidemiologic Catchment Areas Study.* New York: Free Press.

Rogler, L. H., Cortés, D. E., & Malgady, R. G. (1991). Acculturation and mental health status among Hispanics: Convergence and new directions for research. *American Psychologist, 46,* 585–597.

Sabogal, F., Marín, G., Otero-Sabogal, R., VanOss Marín, B., & Pérez-Stable, E. J. (1987). Hispanic familism and acculturation: What changes and what doesn't? *Hispanic Journal of Behavioral Sciences, 9,* 397–412.

Sasao, T., & Chun, C-A. (1994). After the *Sa-i-gu* (April 29) Los Angeles riots: Correlates of subjective well-being in the Korean-American community. *Journal of Community Psychology, 22,* 136–152.

Shrout, P. E., Canino, G. J., Bird, H. R., Rubio-Stipec, M., Bravo, M., & Burnam, M. A. (1992). Mental health status among Puerto Ricans, Mexican Americans, and non-Hispanic whites. *American Journal of Community Psychology, 20,* 729–752.

Simmons, R. C., & Hughes, C. C. (Eds.). (1985). *The culture-bound syndromes.* Boston: D. Reidel.

Snowden, L. R., & Hines, A. M. (1999). A scale to assess African American acculturation. *Journal of Black Psychology, 25,* 36–47.

Szapocznik, J., Scopetta, M. A., Aranalde, M. A., & Kurtines, W. (1978). Cuban value structure: Clinical implications. *Journal of Consulting and Clinical Psychology, 46,* 961–970.

Tompar-Tiu, A., & Sustento-Seneriches, J. (1995). *Depression and other mental health issues: The Filipino American experience.* San Francisco, CA: Jossey-Bass.

Uba, L. (1994). *Asian Americans: Personality patterns, identity, and mental health.* New York: Guilford Press.

Vega, W. A., & Alegria, M. (2001). Latino mental health and treatment in the United States. In M. Aguirre-Molina, C. W. Molina, & R. E. Zambrana (Eds.), *Health issues in the Latino community* (pp. 179–208). San Francisco, CA: Jossey-Bass.

Vega, W. A., Kolody, B., Aguilar-Gaxiola, S., Alderete, E., Catalano, R., & Caraveo-Anduaga, J. (1998). Lifetime prevalence of DSM–III–R psychiatric disorders among urban and rural Mexican Americans in California. *Archives of General Psychiatry, 55,* 771–782.

Vera, M., Alegria, M., Freeman, D., Robles, R. R., Rios, R., & Rios, C. (1991). Depressive symptoms among Puerto Ricans: Island poor compared with residents of the New York City area. *American Journal of Epidemiology, 134,* 502–510.

Westermeyer, J., Callies, A., & Neider, J. (1990). Welfare status and psychosocial adjustment among 100 Hmong refugees. *Journal of Nervous and Mental Disease, 178,* 300–306.

Westermeyer, J., & Her, C. (1996). English fluency and social adjustment among Hmong refugees in Minnesota. *Journal of Nervous and Mental Disease, 184*, 130–132.

Westermeyer, J., Neider, J., & Vang, T. F. (1984). Acculturation and mental health: A study of Hmong refugees at 1.5 and 3.5 years postmigration. *Social Science Medicine, 18*, 87–93.

World Health Organization. (1990). *Composite International Diagnostic Interview (CIDI), Version 1.0.* Geneva, Switzerland: Author.

Yeung, W. H., & Schwartz, M. A. (1986). Emotional disturbance in Chinese obstetrical patients: A pilot study. *General Hospital Psychiatry, 8*, 258–262.

Ying, Y-W. (1995). Cultural orientation and psychological well-being in Chinese Americans. *American Journal of Community Psychology, 23*, 893–911.

Zheng, X., & Berry, J. W. (1991). Psychological adaptation of Chinese sojourners in Canada. *International Journal of Psychology, 26*, 451–470.

8

Acculturation and Physical Health in Racial and Ethnic Minorities

Hector F. Myers and Norma Rodriguez

There is growing attention and concern over the persistent disparities in health status, morbidity, and mortality in racial and ethnic minority groups relative to Caucasian Americans in the United States (National Center for Health Statistics [NCHS], 2001). The public health significance of this problem is reflected in the priority given to this issue by the Surgeon General of the United States, by the publication of several special issues of major public health journals, and the establishment of the National Center on Minority Health and Health Disparities (NCMHD; January, 2001) at the National Institutes of Health. The top priority in this initiative is the identification of the factors that contribute to or maintain the persistent health disparities; identification of these factors would help improve the design of intervention and prevention strategies and decrease the disparities. The projected changes in the population demographics over the next 10 years make the need for better understanding and more effective action on this problem even more acute. Driven by the dual forces of immigration and a higher birth rate among ethnic minorities, it is projected that by 2010, the U.S. population will include a plurality of persons of color (i.e., 32.7% non-Caucasian Americans, 67.3% Caucasian Americans; U.S. Bureau of the Census, 2000). If the current health trends continue, the overall health status of the United States will decline and be accompanied by health care, social, and economic consequences.

The purpose of this chapter is to (a) provide a critical review of the role of acculturation and acculturative stresses as sociocultural factors in the persistent ethnic group differences in physical health status and (b) offer a conceptual framework for investigating these relationships. The chapter begins with a discussion of the major limitations of the current research on acculturation as a risk or protective factor in the health status differences among ethnic groups and Caucasian Americans. Next is a review of the extant evidence on the health status of the five major ethnic groups in the United States (i.e., African Americans, Asian Americans/Pacific Islanders, Hispanic Americans/Latinos, American Indians/Alaska

---

Preparation of this chapter was supported in part by Grant MH 54965 and Grant MH 47193 from the National Institute of Mental Health (NIMH).

Natives, and Caucasian Americans), with emphasis on seven specific health status indicators: life expectancy, causes of death, and prevalence of cardiovascular diseases (CVDs), cancer, diabetes, birth outcomes, and HIV/AIDS. The chapter then reviews and discusses the few studies that investigated whether recent ethnic minority immigrants or those who are acculturating to the United States have significant disease-specific differences in morbidity and mortality in comparison with Caucasian Americans or U.S.-born members of their own group. The chapter concludes with a summary of this evidence and suggests that the ability to understand health status changes as a function of stage of acculturation requires more complex and sophisticated models to test the concurrent and reciprocal effects of multiple contributors to health outcomes. Included in such a model are (a) health-relevant socioeconomic and sociocultural antecedents; (b) acculturative stage; (c) social mobility; and (d) changes in health knowledge, attitudes, beliefs, and health behaviors including health care utilization as important mediators of health status, morbidity, and mortality. Because each major ethnic minority group has a different social history in the United States, one must also consider the possibility that the pattern of relationships among the hypothesized variables in such a model could be different for each ethnic group. Therefore, the development and testing of group-specific models are as important as testing comparative models of acculturation and health.

The Role of Acculturation in Health

Recently, increased attention has been focused on the role of acculturation in the health status of immigrants and other ethnic groups residing in the United States. This increased attention is due in part to evidence pointing to the superior health status of recent immigrants over their nonimmigrant counterparts (e.g., Popkin & Udry, 1998); the attention is also partly a result of the use of acculturation in directly and indirectly predicting various other outcomes (e.g., mental health status, risk behaviors). However, as with research focusing on the relationship between acculturation and mental health (see Rogler, Cortés, & Malgady, 1991), the research on acculturation and chronic disease is plagued with a number of conceptual and methodological problems. As Palinkas and Pickwell (1995) pointed out, because of the inconsistencies in the ways that acculturation has been operationalized in epidemiological research, both the theoretical and clinical significance of the relationship between acculturation and disease remains unclear. Thus, this section of the chapter includes a discussion of how acculturation has been conceptualized and measured in the chronic disease literature and what is known about the relationship between acculturation and chronic disease.

A review of the existing literature reveals that the preponderance of research on acculturation examines mental health rather than chronic disease outcomes. The majority of the studies have focused on Latinos, particularly Mexican Americans, and a few studies highlighted Asian Americans/Pacific Islanders, especially Japanese, Koreans, and Southeast Asian Americans. Furthermore, many of the problems in definition and measurement that plagued early studies of acculturation and mental health are evident today in studies of acculturation and chronic disease. For instance, some studies have failed to discuss the role of acculturation in chronic disease and instead focus on disease outcomes as a function of racial and ethnic differences (Kingston & Smith, 1997; Lillie-Blanton, Parsons, Gayle, & Dievler, 1996; Pérez-Stable, Napoles-Springer, & Miramontes, 1997) or place of birth or geographical region (Acton, Preston, & Ruth-Najarian, 1996). Still other studies have relied on status variables (e.g., language, nativity, generation) to make inferences about the effect of acculturation on various physical health outcomes (e.g., English, Kharrazi, & Guendelman, 1997; Guendelman, Gould, Hudes, & Eskenazi, 1990; Ventura & Tappel, 1985). Unfortunately, studies that use these proxy variables assume that (a) members of the groups being compared (e.g., immigrants vs. nonimmigrants) are at the same stage of the acculturation process and consequently have similar acculturative experiences, and (b) the process of acculturation is linear and not interactive (Palinkas & Pickwell, 1995).

The majority of studies on chronic disease tend to focus on the contribution of acculturation to risk factors rather than actual health outcomes. This is not surprising from a preventative standpoint, particularly because there is substantial evidence demonstrating a link between risk factors and chronic disease (Myers, Kagawa-Singer, Kumanyika, Lex, & Markides, 1995). However, researchers need to develop models that can test the direct effects of acculturation on physical health outcomes in addition to the acculturative effects that are mediated or moderated by risk factors. For instance, research by Zambrana, Scrimshaw, Collins, and Dunkel-Schetter (1997) tested links between acculturation, risk factors, and birth outcomes and found that although higher acculturation was associated with prenatal risk factors, acculturation did not have a direct effect on infant gestational age or birthweight. Such models should also consider the possibility that acculturation does not necessarily precede the occurrence of a chronic disease (as illustrated in case studies of Cambodian refugees in the United States). The disease may precipitate or antedate the process of acculturation (Palinkas & Pickwell, 1995), or acculturation could be influenced by a third factor (e.g., socioeconomic changes). Despite these limitations, however, there is enough suggestive evidence to permit an initial synthesis and propose directions for new research.

The next section includes a review of the existing evidence of health status differences on life expectancy, causes of death, and five physical health issues: CVD and hypertension, diabetes, cancer, birth outcomes, and HIV/AIDS. Also reviewed are the available studies on each disorder that specifically investigated whether the group differences observed could be explained as a function of level of acculturation. However, as mentioned previously, the literature on acculturation and health is limited and has focused primarily on Mexican Americans and other Latinos.

Ethnic Group Differences in Health Status

Efforts to characterize the health status of U.S. populations of racial and ethnic backgrounds and to capture the full extent of the health status differences between these groups and Caucasian Americans are hampered by differences in the availability of relevant information for each group. Although the quality and amount of health data have improved significantly since this issue was formally raised in the *Secretary's Task Force Report on Black and Minority Health* (U.S. Department of Health and Human Services, 1985), available data continue to be uneven and fragmented. For example, inadequate differentiation of subgroups (e.g., by birthplace, tribal origin) of Hispanic Americans/Latinos, Asian Americans/Pacific Islanders, and American Indians/Alaska Natives continues to plague the field. Therefore, impressions of the health status of these groups as a whole (e.g., the relatively good health status of Asian Americans) fail to account for subgroups who have a significant health status disadvantage relative to other subgroups (e.g., Native Hawaiians and Southeast Asian Americans have a poorer health status than Japanese and Chinese Americans).

Despite these limitations, the available epidemiological evidence clearly indicates that the life expectancy and health status of the U.S. population has improved significantly since the turn of the century and is continuing to improve (NCHS, 2001). However, there continue to be significant differences in the burden of morbidity and mortality among ethnic minorities. For example, the overall life expectancy for Caucasian Americans is 77.2 years (74.3 and 79.9 years for men and women, respectively), compared with 71.1 years for African Americans (67.2 and 74.7 years for men and women, respectively). Compared with 1970 the improvement in life expectancy has been significant, especially for men overall (a 6.5% increase) and for African American men (a 7.2% increase) and women (a 6.4% increase; NCHS, 1999). Among those age 70 years and younger, African Americans, American Indians, and Hispanic Americans die at a significantly higher rate than Caucasian Americans. In addition, Asian Americans/Pacific Islanders as a whole have death rates comparable to Caucasian Americans, whereas Native Hawaiians and other South Pacific Islanders and Southeast Asian refugees have excess death rates comparable to those of Hispanic Americans. In all groups, women have a higher life expectancy than men (NCHS, 2001).

Leading Causes of Death

There are also noticeable differences in the leading causes of death in the various groups, which may reflect differences in biological vulnerabilities, as well as socioeconomic, sociocultural, and other lifestyle differences. Recent reports from the NCHS (1998) have indicated that CVDs and cancer are the leading causes of death for all major ethnic groups. After that, the groups then diverge in the relative ranking of diseases and their vulnerability for specific disorders. For example, HIV/AIDS has become the third and fourth leading cause of death for African American men and women and for Hispanic men but is not a major cause of death for the other groups. On the other hand, diabetes mellitus is one of the top five causes of death for women of color. Non-Hispanic Caucasian Americans and Asian Americans seem to be particularly susceptible to diseases of the lungs, including chronic obstructive pulmonary disease, pneumonia, and influenza. Native American men and women seem to be especially vulnerable to chronic liver disease. Finally, Native American men die from suicide at a higher rate than the other groups, and African American and Hispanic men are more likely to be victims of homicides than the other groups.

During investigations of the role of acculturation in health, these ethnic and gender group differences in the leading causes of death must be considered. Acculturative processes may make comparable contributions to risk for some outcomes across all groups (i.e., may serve as a general risk factor for CVD in all groups) but may also contribute to risk for different diseases in different groups (e.g., may be a specific risk factor for pneumonia in Asian Americans/Pacific Islanders but contribute to increased risk for diabetes in Hispanic Americans and American Indians).

CVD

In the past 20 years the coronary heart disease (CHD) death rate in the United States declined by 49%, and deaths from stroke decreased 58%. Despite these gains, heart disease continues to be the leading cause of death in the United States, and stroke is the third leading cause of death. In addition, although CVD is the leading cause of death for all ethnic groups, the prevalence rates for CHD, stroke, and hypertension vary significantly across groups (NCHS, 1995).

Caucasian Americans have the highest rate of CHD of all groups, and their rates of stroke are comparable to those of African Americans. However, African Americans have the highest rate of stroke-related mortality and the highest rates of hypertension and related sequelae of all groups. Thus, approximately 35% of African Americans are diagnosed with essential hypertension, and 23% of Hispanic Americans, 22% of Caucasian Americans, 12% of American Indians, and 9% of Asian Americans/Pacific Islanders have this disease. These differences in CVD rates are at least partially explained by differences in related biological and behavioral risk factors, including high normal cholesterol, hyperlipedemia, physical inactivity, excess weight, and smoking (American Heart Association, 1998).

There is substantial evidence indicating that the risk of CVD and hypertension increases with acculturation and that this phenomenon is evident across ethnic groups. There is also some evidence that groups who have a CVD advantage in their native country (e.g., Japanese who live in Japan) begin to lose that advantage with immigration and increasing acculturation to the United States (Kagan et al., 1974; Marmot et al., 1975; Reed et al., 1982). For example, studies by Marmot and colleagues (1975) of CHD among Japanese Americans in California and Hawaii and Japanese immigrants in Great Britain (Marmot, 1983) have shown that higher levels of acculturation (e.g., more Western education, more participation in Western institutions, more English-language use, adaptation of more Westernized lifestyles) are associated with higher rates of CVD.

The same pattern has been found in older adults. For instance, in a study of older Navajo adults, Kunitz and Levy (1986) found a greater prevalence of hypertension among more acculturated women than less acculturated women. Similarly, Espino and Maldonado (1990) found a positive relationship between level of acculturation and hypertension in Mexican Americans, ages 55 to 64, in the Hispanic Health and Nutrition Examination Survey (Hispanic HANES). Although the same pattern of association was not found for adults between the ages of 65 and 74, the authors speculated that the more acculturated older adults with hypertension may not have been adequately represented in their study because of attrition caused by the effects of hypertension or other medical disorders. Furthermore, this study found that acculturation exerted a more powerful influence on hypertension than socioeconomic status (SES).

It is also important to note, however, that although the majority of the evidence as of this writing has suggested that a positive association between acculturation and CVD and hypertension exists, some studies have failed to confirm this finding (Nanjundappa & Friis, 1988), and other studies have reported an inverse relationship (Hazuda, 1996). In the latter study, Hazuda (1996) examined the association between sociocultural status (assimilation, modernization, and SES) and hypertension among people of Mexican descent living in San Antonio, Texas, and Mexico City, Mexico. Her results showed that in San Antonio, the vulnerability for hypertension was greatest for Mexican Americans who were less assimilated and of a lower SES. In Mexico City, those with the greatest risk for hypertension were Mexicans with low levels of education. Thus, low SES was the most consistent risk factor for this disease, which is consistent with the preponderance of the evidence worldwide.

Reviews by Anderson and colleagues (Anderson & McNeilly, 1993; Anderson, McNeilly, & Myers, 1992) on a contextual model of hypertension underscore the role of ethnic differences in exposure to chronic sociocultural stressors (e.g., discrimination, racism, socioeconomic deprivation) mediated through differences in hostility and cardiovascular (CV) reactivity to account for Black–White differences in this disease and its sequelae.

Cancer

Incidence. Cancer incidence and mortality rates have declined in the United States in the 1990s, reversing a 20-year trend of increasing cancer rates and deaths (NCHS, 1998). However, cancer remains the second leading cause of death in the United States, and there are significant group differences in risk for cancer overall and mortality from specific types of cancer. For instance, although Asian Americans/Pacific Islanders as a group have the lowest cancer rates of any group, Korean men have the highest stomach cancer rates, Vietnamese men have the highest liver cancer rates, and Vietnamese women have the highest cervical cancer rates of all groups.

Furthermore, differences are evident as a function of gender. Among men, the highest incidence rates of all types of cancers are found in African Americans, followed by Caucasian Americans, Alaska Natives, Hawaiians, and Japanese. Among women, the highest overall rates are found in Alaska Natives, Caucasian Americans, and Asian Americans, followed by African Americans and Hawaiians.

However, these overall trends conceal important ethnic–gender group differences in relative risk for specific types of cancers. For example, African American men have the highest cancer incidence of prostate, lung, and oral cavity cancers, whereas non-Hispanic Caucasian men have the highest rates of bladder cancers of all groups. Breast cancer rates are highest in non-Hispanic Caucasian women, but African American women have the highest mortality rates from breast cancer. In addition, African American and Hispanic women have the highest mortality rates from cervical cancer, and Alaska Native and African American women have the highest incidence rates of lung and colorectal cancer of any group of women in the United States (American Cancer Society, 1997).

American Indians/Alaska Natives have lower overall cancer rates than non-Hispanic Caucasian Americans and African Americans, yet kidney cancer rates are highest among American Indian men, as are colorectal rates among Alaska Native men. In addition, American Indian women have the highest rates of ovarian and gallbladder cancers, and as noted previously, Alaska Native women have higher rates of colorectal and lung cancer than any other ethnic group in the United States (American Cancer Society, 1997).

These group differences in incidence and mortality from cancer overall and from specific types of cancer provide additional support for investigating differences in biological vulnerabilities and differences in lifestyle and other psychosocial variables. In their reports of ethnic differences in risk behaviors for chronic illnesses, Elder et al. (1991); Myers et al. (1995); and Carter, Pugh, and Monterrosa (1996) reported that ethnic groups differ in their patterns of cancer-related health risk behaviors, especially in smoking, obesity, alcohol consumption, total caloric intake, dietary intake of fats and fiber, and exercise. Furthermore, changes in these behaviors may reflect changes in level of acculturation. For example, as groups become more acculturated, they may increase their consumption of alcohol and calorie-dense and high-fat foods and reduce their consumption of fresh vegetables and grains.

Acculturation. Berry (1998) suggested that as acculturation increases, health status "migrates" to the national norm. An example of this phenomenon is illustrated in Lilienfeld's (1972) research on stomach and intestinal cancer rates of immigrants to the United States. Among the 14 groups studied, 11 had higher rates of stomach cancer in the countries of origin;

after migration, their rates dropped to levels comparable to those in the United States. Of the 14 groups studied, 11 also had lower rates of intestinal cancer in the countries of origin; after migration, the rates of all 14 groups increased. Although it is not clear why these shifts in cancer rates occur, several explanations have been offered, ranging from an increased exposure to shared risk factors in the physical environment, to exposure to culturally mediated risk factors from assimilation or integration (e.g., resistance to early cancer screening, increased consumption of red meat), to acculturative stress resulting from the process of acculturation. These explanations are not mutually exclusive and may contribute to enhanced risk concurrently or sequentially. Nevertheless, the majority of studies suggest that overall cancer rates increase as acculturation increases, and this increasing risk is mediated by changes in knowledge, attitudes, and behaviors (Balcazar, Castro, & Krull, 1995; Harmon, Castro, & Coe, 1996; Polednak, 1992; Suarez, 1994; Wolfgang, Semeiks, & Burnett, 1991).

Diabetes

Incidence. More Americans than ever have non-insulin-dependent diabetes mellitus (NIDDM), an increasing trend that has been occurring since 1980. Like hypertension, this disease is prevalent but often goes unrecognized and untreated, with an estimated 34% of those affected being undiagnosed and untreated (Centers for Disease Control [CDC], 1997). This disease is associated with various disabling conditions, including enhanced risk for end-stage renal disease, blindness, lower extremity amputations, periodontal disease, CHD, stroke, complications of pregnancy, functional limitations (e.g., mobility), and increased mortality. Epidemiological evidence reported by Carter et al. (1996) indicated that (a) minorities are disproportionately affected compared with Caucasian Americans, (b) women are more affected than men, and (c) American Indians have the highest prevalence of any group. However, there is substantial within-group variability in vulnerability to this disease among American Indians. For example, the Pima and Papago Indians have the highest prevalence of diabetes in the world, with rates around 50%. The rates in Hispanic Americans and African Americans are comparable (10.6% and 10.8%, respectively), although the rates among African Americans have increased dramatically (i.e., 33%) in the past decade (CDC, 1997). The rates for Hispanic Americans overall are somewhat deceptive because they also conceal subgroup differences among Hispanic Americans. For example, Puerto Rican men and Mexican American women have some of the highest rates, whereas Cuban women have the lowest rate. In addition, although Asian Americans typically have lower rates of many diseases, several studies reported prevalence rates of diabetes are higher in some Asian Americans/ Pacific Islanders than in other minority groups. For example, diabetes rates in Koreans, Filipinos, and Chinese in Hawaii are higher than those reported for Hispanic Americans, African Americans, and many American Indian tribes on the mainland (Carter et al., 1996).

Not only is this disease more prevalent among ethnic minorities, but minorities have proportionately more complications from diabetes. For example, compared with Caucasian Americans with diabetes, African Americans with diabetes are as much as 6.6 times more likely to develop end-stage renal disease. Mexican Americans with diabetes are 7 times more likely and American Indians with diabetes are 6.3 times more likely to develop end-stage renal disease than non-Hispanic Caucasians with diabetes. Ethnic minorities as a whole are twice as likely to become blind because of diabetes than are Caucasian Americans. In addition, African Americans are significantly more likely to have amputations because of diabetes than Caucasian Americans and Hispanic Americans. Except for Asian Americans/Pacific Islanders, ethnic minorities with diabetes are at higher risk for mortality from the disease than Caucasian Americans (Carter et al., 1996). The fact that Asian Americans/Pacific Islanders have a higher incidence of but lower mortality rate from NIDDM is intriguing but not yet well understood. The reason for this counterintuitive finding is an important question to be investigated in future research.

The observed differences in prevalence suggest that there are subgroups that differ in their genetic vulnerability to NIDDM (Bogardus & Lillioja, 1992; Knowler, Williams, Pettitt, & Steinberg, 1988; Neel, 1982; Wendorf & Goldfine, 1991). Also, the differences in functional outcomes of and mortality from this disease suggest that there are likely to be important group differences in lifestyle, early screening, treatment seeking, treatment adherence, disease duration and tolerance, as well as in health care access that result in disproportionate risk for the secondary consequences of diabetes to some groups (Carter et al., 1996).

Acculturation. Of particular relevance to the current review is the evidence of an elevated prevalence of diabetes in Westernized immigrants, with significantly higher rates among migrants than among native nonmigrants (Fujimoto, 1992; Kawate, Yamakido, & Nishimoto, 1979; Taylor & Zimmet, 1983). As with other chronic diseases, this pattern of increasing risk with increasing acculturation is likely mediated through changes in lifestyle, such as consuming a diet that includes higher total calories and fat, less fiber, along with reduced energy expenditure (Marshall et al., 1993).

Although the literature reported thus far has suggested that physical health status declines with increased acculturation, there are some exceptions. Among Mexican Americans, increased levels of acculturation, independent of SES, are associated with a reduced prevalence of diabetes (Hazuda, Haffner, Stern, & Eifler, 1988). An explanation that has been offered to account for this paradoxical finding involves "descending and ascending limbs" of the curve of modernization (Stern et al., 1991). According to this theory, as people become more affluent and stably acculturated, they attempt to live healthier lives by avoiding the unhealthy habits that are more prevalent during the initial stages, or ascending limb, of modernization. The initial stages of modernization include an increased intake of calories, fats, and refined sugars; a decreased consumption of fiber and complex carbohydrates; and a decrease in physical activity, all of which increase the risk for diabetes.

On the other hand, a study by Nanjundappa and Friis (1988) found no association between acculturation and diabetes. However, the authors cautioned that the least acculturated individuals may have been excluded from the study, thus limiting the authors' ability to detect any possible relationship between acculturation and diabetes. In addition, although not specific to acculturation, Carter et al. (1996) reported that there are a few studies that report an inverse relationship between SES and prevalence of diabetes among African Americans, Latinos, Japanese Americans, and Caucasian Americans. The latter studies suggested that the relationship between level of acculturation and prevalence of diabetes remains unclear, and higher SES, social mobility, or both may help decrease risk.

Birth Outcomes

Variations among groups. There is also ample evidence of persistent disparities in birth outcomes between African Americans and all other groups (NCHS, 2001). This discrepancy is evident regardless of the maternal or child outcome used. The one exception is mortality specifically related to birthweight; the mortality is lower for premature African American infants than for Caucasian American infants (Collins & David, 1990). For example, African American women are more likely to die from ectopic pregnancies and are 3 times more likely than Caucasian Americans to die in hospitals after hysterectomies. In addition, the rate of infants born with a low birthweight (i.e., <2,500 g) is 2 times higher for African Americans than for Caucasian Americans and other ethnic groups (14% vs. 6%; Schoendorf, Hogue, Kleinman, & Rowley, 1992), and African American mothers are 3 times more likely to have babies with a very low birthweight (i.e., <1,500 g). In addition, African American infants are 3 times more likely to die of causes attributable to perinatal events and 2 times more likely to die in the first month of life than Caucasian infants (Schoendorf et al., 1992).

This African American–Caucasian differential is more troubling when one considers the paradoxical finding that the infant mortality rate is lower among infants born to African American teens than to Caucasian Americans and older African American women (Geronimus, 1992). Also, although the low birthweight and infant mortality rates are higher in less educated and poorer women of all ethnic groups, the African American–Caucasian differences in rates for low birthweight and infant mortality are smaller among the less educated and larger among the most educated (Kleinman, Fingerhut, & Prager, 1991; Shiono, Rauh, Park, Lederman, & Suskar, 1997). This suggests that African American women gain less reproductive benefits from upward mobility than Caucasian American women.

The birth outcome picture is even more interesting when the data on the other ethnic groups are examined. For example, Hispanic women share many of the same socioeconomic disadvantages as many African American women, and in some cases, they may be more disadvantaged because of the added stress of immigrant status (e.g., no health insurance, poorer housing and work conditions, greater exposure to pollution). In addition, Hispanic women carry comparable burdens of morbidity and lifestyle risk factors. Regardless, Hispanic women as a whole have birth outcomes that are comparable to if not better than those of Caucasian non-Hispanic women. Thus, although Hispanic women have higher preterm birth rates, they have comparable rates of infants born with low and very low birthweights, despite being significantly poorer on average and having a poorer health behavior profile than non-Hispanic Caucasian women (Kleinman et al., 1991). A number of sociocultural explanations have been offered to account for these counterintuitive findings, including the protective effects of low acculturation and the availability of large and effective social networks of support that counteract other risk factors (Scribner & Dwyer, 1989).

Birth outcome data are more limited for the other ethnic groups, but the available evidence has suggested that controlling for SES, the birth outcomes for Native American women are only slightly worse than for non-Hispanic Caucasian women, and the outcomes for Asian Americans/Pacific Islanders are more favorable overall. However, there are important subgroup differences in each case, with Puerto Ricans, Hawaiians, and Filipino women having poorer outcomes on average than all other women except African Americans.

Acculturation. Previous studies have suggested that Mexican immigrant women have more favorable birth outcomes than their U.S.-born counterparts despite their higher social risk profile. For instance, Guendelman et al. (1990) found that second-generation Mexican American women were almost twice as likely to have low-birthweight infants in comparison to first-generation Mexican women. Similarly, research by Zambrana et al. (1997) on women of Mexican origin showed that a higher level of acculturation was associated with more prenatal stress, which in turn was associated with a preterm delivery and consequently a low-birthweight infant. Related research by Ventura and Tappel (1985) found that the rate of adolescent pregnancy was twice as high among U.S.-born Latinas than among Latinas born outside of the United States. Results of studies such as these suggest that the favorable reproductive outcomes of Mexican immigrant women may be due to their protective sociocultural orientation, which plays a crucial role in their adaptation to life in the United States.

Although there is substantial evidence to suggest that Mexican immigrant women experience more favorable reproductive outcomes than their nonimmigrant counterparts, it is not clear whether these benefits are sustained. To address this issue, Guendelman, English, and Chavez (1995) conducted a cross-sectional study of 708 infants of Mexican immigrants in San Diego County to determine whether health advantages were maintained at 8 and 16 months of age. Their results indicated that among infants born without serious medical conditions, 74% remained healthy. For the remaining 26%, however, their health status was compromised despite the use of preventive care because of social conditions such as large households; barriers to care; and maternal pregnancy complications, smoking, and employment. Furthermore, women born in Mexico who were newcomers to the United States and spoke Spanish exclusively were more likely than those who were not newcomers to have children with serious medical conditions. This suggests that other factors such as preexisting biological or social vulnerabilities may contribute to differences in risk among recent immigrants.

Still other studies have shown that the relationship between acculturation and reproductive outcomes is not so clear cut. For instance, English et al. (1997) conducted a population-based cross-sectional study of 4,404 births of immigrant and nonimmigrant women of Mexican origin in California to examine the effects of language use on reproductive outcomes. Six nativity/language subgroups were compared with respect to pregnancy risk factors, low-birthweight infants, and preterm deliveries. Controlling for relevant covariates, they found that U.S.-born Spanish speakers were at greatest risk for having low-birthweight infants, and Mexico-born English speakers were at the lowest risk for preterm delivery when compared with U.S.-born English speakers. The authors suggested that the process of acculturation for Mexican Americans is not a simple negative adaptation but rather is a complex process involving positive and negative adjustments that may depend on socioeconomic conditions or selection factors associated with migration (e.g., reasons for migration).

Overall, the majority of studies examining the relationship between acculturation and pregnancy outcomes have suggested that Mexican immigrant women have more favorable outcomes than Mexican American women. Nevertheless, there are studies that suggest a different pattern of results and suggest that the pattern of association is much more complex than past literature has considered. It is recommended that future studies in this area critically examine the contribution of acculturation, through its direct measurement rather than indirectly through the use of proxy variables, and assess its direct and indirect effects on reproductive outcomes.

HIV/AIDS

Incidence. During the past several years the incidence and mortality from HIV/AIDS in the United States has declined, although the rate of transmission from men to women has increased (CDC, 1998). HIV/AIDS continues to be a disease of men, especially Caucasian American men (46.2% of cases) and men who have sex with men (60% of cases). However, the greatest decline in HIV/AIDS incidence has been among Caucasian American men, whereas African Americans and Hispanic Americans are disproportionately overrepresented in the current wave of the disease. For example, in 1997, African Americans and Hispanic Americans accounted for 45% and 21% of the cases, respectively, compared with 33% for Caucasian Americans. Of even greater concern is the fact that, although the incidence rate among men is declining, the incidence rate of HIV in women and in teenagers has been increasing (CDC, 1998). HIV and AIDS in women disproportionately affects African Americans (62% of cases) and Hispanic Americans (23%). The same is true for children (75% of cases are either African American or Hispanic; CDC, 1998).

The rate of HIV infection and AIDS is infinitesimal among American Indians and Asian Americans/Pacific Islanders (CDC, 1998), but additional studies are needed to investigate subgroup differences in risk, especially among immigrant Asian Americans/Pacific Islanders and more urbanized American Indians.

Acculturation. In recent years, there has been increasing attention given to the role of acculturation in HIV/AIDS risk and prevention. As with other serious illnesses, most of the attention as of this writing has been focused on understanding how acculturation and other sociocultural variables, such as sexual attitudes, beliefs, and behaviors (e.g., VanOss Marín, Tschann, Gomez, & Kegeles, 1993; Hines & Caetano, 1998; Hines, Snowden & Graves, 1998) or knowledge about AIDS (e.g., Epstein, Dusenbury, Botwin, & Diaz, 1994; Klonoff & Landrine, 1997; Mikawa, Morones, Gomez, Case, et. al., 1992; VanOss Marín & Marín, 1990) affect risk factors. One study that examined risk behaviors among 112 Puerto Rican women (ages 14 to 49) found that a preference for English, which indicated higher acculturation, was significantly associated with increased AIDS risk (Peragallo, 1996). On the other hand, other studies reported a more complex and contradictory pattern of relationships among ethnicity, gender, acculturation, and risky sexual behaviors. For example, studies by Hines and colleagues on ethnic and gender differences in alcohol consumption and risky sexual behaviors indicated that among Hispanic Americans, less acculturated men drank more heavily and were more likely to engage in risky sexual behaviors than more acculturated men. However, among Hispanic women, the more acculturated drank more, whereas less acculturated women were more likely to have unprotected sex (Hines & Caetano, 1998).

Several studies suggested that sociocultural factors related to gender roles and attitudes toward condom use might account for the apparent greater sexual risk among less acculturated Latinas. As noted by VanOss Marín and colleagues, less acculturated Hispanic American women typically report having fewer sexual partners than more acculturated women because of more traditional gender role attitudes. They are also less likely to use condoms and tend to have poorer attitudes toward condoms, their partners are typically more resistant to condom use, and they often have more erroneous and pessimistic beliefs about HIV/AIDS risk (VanOss Marín, 1996; VanOss Marín, Gomez, Tschann, & Gregorich, 1997; VanOss Marín et al., 1993; VanOss Marín & Marín, 1990).

Studies of acculturation, alcohol use, and risky sexual behaviors in African American women have shown a different pattern of association between acculturation and risky sexual activity. For example, Hines and her colleagues (1998) in a national probability sample of 533 African American women found heaviest drinking among the least acculturated. However, it was the more acculturated African American women who were most likely to engage in risky sexual behavior, including having multiple partners, being nonmonogamous or in a nonmonogamous relationship, and not using condoms consistently.

These studies suggest that there is a complex association between level of acculturation and HIV/AIDS risk, and gender and ethnicity moderate this association. In addition, it will be important in future studies to investigate subgroup differences, especially among Hispanic Americans and Asian Americans/Pacific Islanders (e.g., there may be different associations between acculturation and risky sexual behaviors in Puerto Ricans, Cubans, and other Latin Americans in comparison with Mexican Americans, as well as between Chinese and Southeast Asian Americans).

Summary of Ethnic Differences in Health Status and Acculturation

Current epidemiological evidence documents the persistent health status differences in the U.S. population. Ethnic minorities, especially African Americans, American Indians, Native Hawaiians, and Southeast Asian Americans have a disproportionate burden of morbidity and mortality. However, these data demonstrate that there are substantial within-group differences in vulnerability to specific diseases and their sequelae and that factors such as lower SES, obstacles to accessing health care, and health behaviors contribute to the maintenance of these differences. In addition, there is growing evidence that acculturation to the United States is associated with negative changes in health status and that this apparent increase in disease risk is mediated through changes in lifestyle.

There is also the possibility that these apparent negative acculturative effects are an artifact of differences among countries in diagnostic accuracy and reliability of reporting of health statistics. This difference is likely to be greater between developed and underdeveloped countries.

Conceptual Model

As noted previously, data on the health status of ethnic minorities continue to be somewhat limited and uneven across disease conditions and ethnic groups. In addition, the research linking acculturation and chronic disease is even more limited, which makes it impossible to draw anything other than limited conclusions about the role acculturation plays in group differences in health status. This review of the extant literature indicates the need for more complex, multidimensional models that would allow investigation into whether acculturation increases or decreases health risk over time, taking into account other important health risk and protective factors. Studies to date have tested simplistic direct effects hypotheses of acculturation on the health outcomes of interest, often either failing to account for other relevant cofactors or treating them as covariates. To advance the field, however, future studies will require analytic models that include consideration of variables in multiple domains that should include (a) demographic characteristics, especially SES and related factors, (b) preexisting biological risks and resistances, (c) sociocultural risks and protective factors, (d) socioecological or social context factors, (e) acculturation processes, and more proximal contributors, such as (f) psychological factors, (g) health behaviors, and (h) health care access and availability as mediators of risk for disease and dysfunction. All of these factors may exert direct effects, indirect effects, or both on health status and changes in health status over time, and appropriate analytical procedures (e.g., structural equation modeling) will need to be used to test these possible effects. These variables may also exert different effects and have varying patterns of relationships depending on the stage of acculturation, ethnic group, gender, and the health outcome investigated.

Sociodemographic Influences

There is substantial empirical evidence of demographic differences (e.g., age, gender, race, ethnicity) in health status and disease risk. The most consistent and important of these factors is SES. There is a well-recognized SES–health gradient (Adler et al., 1994). People at the lower end of the SES distribution have disproportionately higher morbidity and mortality. This relationship is further complicated by ethnicity, with people of color being overrepresented among the poor population. More important, people of color are also more adversely affected by poverty than Caucasian Americans (Krieger, Rowley, Herman, Avery, & Phillips, 1993; Williams & Collins, 1995), probably because of the additional stress burden from racism and discrimination (Clark, Anderson, Clark, & Williams, 1999; Krieger et al., 1993; Williams, 1996; Williams, Yu, Jackson, & Anderson, 1997). Therefore, studies of acculturation must account for the possible independent effects of SES on health. In addition, changes in SES over time (i.e., social mobility), both positive and negative, have important health implications and may condition the effects of acculturation independently of other factors. For example, many immigrants, especially those who emigrated from their countries of origin to improve their life opportunities, had a relatively higher social status in their home countries (e.g., Filipino and Chinese health professionals). After immigrating to the United States, they encountered racism and anti-immigrant prejudices that resulted in a significant initial lowering of their social status. This negative social status change is likely to increase their burden of risk regardless of any acculturative changes that they might also make.

Thus, factors such as age, gender, SES, and social mobility (see Figure 8.1) can exert either direct effects on health (*path a*) or can mediate effects through several pathways, including by influencing the following:

- Acculturative processes (*path b*): The acculturative experience may be different for the poor population compared with the more affluent population.
- Sociocultural processes (*paths b* and *i*): Poor individuals may be more likely to rely more on folk cures to treat initial symptoms and delay professional intervention.
- Biological factors (*path d*): The poor population has a greater concentration of biologically less resilient people.
- Socioecological factors (*path c*): Poor individuals work in more hazardous settings, live in areas with greater residential density, and have poorer housing.
- Health behaviors (*paths b, i,* and *o*): The poor population may consume higher fat, higher salt diets.
- Health care access (*paths c* and *j*): Poor individuals have less access to and receive poorer quality health services.

Biological Risks and Resistance

There is also considerable evidence indicating that at least some of the differences among groups in prevalence of disease is attributable to differences in biologically mediated vulnerabilities. This is illustrated by the hypothesized sodium retention trait (Weinberger, 1993) and alpha-adrenergically mediated CV reactivity to stress (Anderson, Lane, Taguchi, & Williams, 1989; Anderson, Lane, Taguchi, Williams, Houseworth, et al., 1989) in African Americans that contribute to their greater risk for hypertension. These biological vulnerabilities are expressed over time in an earlier onset of symptoms, higher disease prevalence, faster disease progression, or all of these than in less vulnerable individuals or groups. However, few if any of the studies of differences in disease prevalence as a function of measured or inferred level of acculturation included careful assessment of premigration personal health histories, family health histories, or both. The proponents of the selectivity hypothesis have argued persuasively that the apparent health protective effects of low acculturation may be because immigrants are often the healthiest, most assertive, and resilient members of their native people and therefore are more resilient on average than their U.S.-born counterparts (Palinkas & Pickwell, 1995). By the same token, other studies that included more careful subgroups of the immigrant samples have reported that some subgroups of recent immigrants have a more disadvantaged health status than their U.S.-born counterparts (Guendelman et al., 1995). Thus, the health vulnerabilities of some immigrants were present before their migration and acculturation (e.g., refugees, rural poor), or the immigrants may have acquired additional health risks during the process of migration (e.g., Cambodian and Vietnamese refugees; illegal Hispanic immigrants crossing the U.S.–Mexico border who face a variety of physical and psychological risks during the crossing).

As shown in Figure 8.1, preexisting biological risks and resistances may exert direct effects on health or indirect effects through health behaviors

ACCULTURATION AND PHYSICAL HEALTH 179

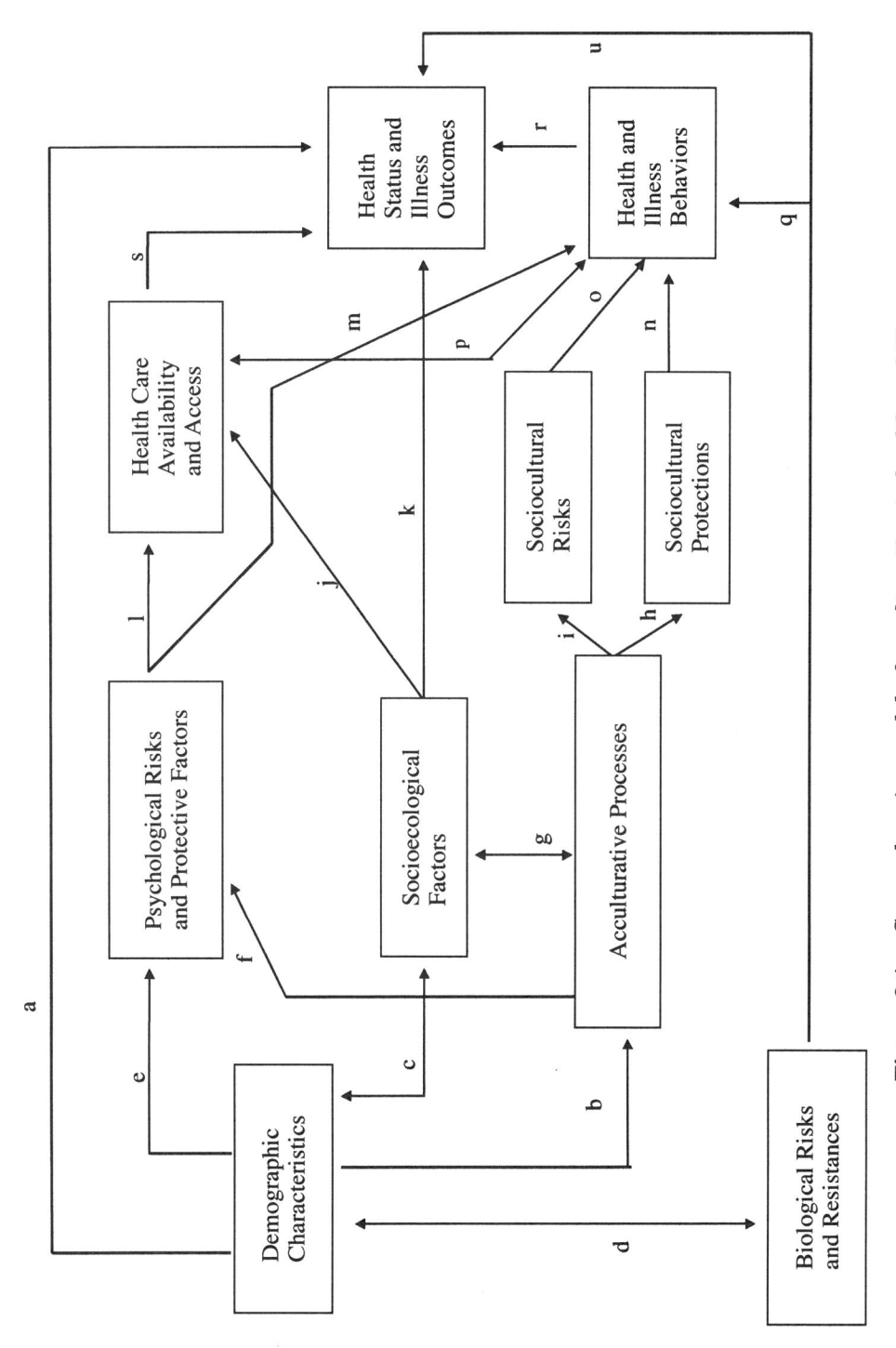

Figure 8.1. Comprehensive model of acculturation in health and illness.

(e.g., *paths q* and *u*—Biological risks are enhanced by smoking, consumption of alcohol or drugs, and obesity and can be reduced by healthy behaviors such as exercise, weight control, reduced salt, and fat intake).

Acculturative Processes

The biggest obstacles facing the field in advancing the understanding of effect of acculturation on health continue to be conceptual and methodological. Many studies reviewed continue to rely on proxy measures of acculturation (e.g., language, immigrant status), which reveal little about the process of acculturation. In addition, measures used need to reflect the multidimensional nature of acculturation (see chapter 2 for a review of acculturation measures) so that they do not simply tap language use and preference but instead incorporate other aspects of the process (e.g., changes in values, beliefs, and attitudes). In addition, there may be significant within- and between-group differences in the acculturative changes made, with some people or groups making some changes quickly (e.g., changing dietary habits and preferences), taking longer to make other changes (e.g., language), and resisting other changes (e.g., changes in attitudes and beliefs regarding the proper treatment of older adults or the relative importance of family obligations).

Psychosocial and Behavioral Mediators

As depicted in Figure 8.1, we hypothesize that acculturative processes are not likely to exert direct effects on health outcomes. Instead, we conceptualize those effects as ones that are mediated through various paths, including through sociocultural risks (e.g., *paths i, o,* and *r*—health and illness beliefs), protective factors (e.g., *paths h, n,* and *r*—social supports), and socioecological factors (e.g., *paths g* and *k*—exposure to noise, pollution, violence). Acculturation may also exert its effects indirectly through psychological processes (e.g., health locus of control), which in turn exert their effects through health and illness behaviors (e.g., *paths f, m,* and *r* —health care utilization) and health care access (e.g., *paths f, l,* and *s*— perceived obstacles to care). Thus, as the growing research evidence has suggested, as people and groups acculturate to the United States, they become more exposed to health-enhancing information (e.g., getting timely mammograms, reducing smoking) and may also change their perceived health locus of control (e.g., shift from passive to more active attitudes toward health, such as getting regular physicals and dental checkups).

Particularly noteworthy is the evidence indicating that negative health behavior changes are more likely to occur in second- and third-generation immigrants. These groups seem to lose whatever protections were afforded by their native country's lifestyle and begin incorporating various risky health behaviors, such as increasing their consumption of alcohol and recreational drugs; increasing their caloric intake and intake of fats, salts, and sugar; and reducing their energy expenditures by assuming a more sedentary lifestyle, all of which result in a higher prevalence of obesity. As a consequence, their risk for various diseases such as hypertension and heart disease, cancer, and diabetes seem to parallel increases in acculturation.

The pathways linking acculturation to the other factors in the proposed model are mainly theoretical because no studies have tested many of these hypothesized paths. Testing a comprehensive model such as the one that has been proposed requires a series of programmatically organized studies that include large samples that are diverse with respect to level of acculturation. Ideally, such studies would focus on one ethnic group at a time and be longitudinal, which would allow researchers to study the complex changes that occur over time in each ethnic group. In the mean time, however, initial studies could begin to validate the model by testing some of the hypothesized paths in specific groups. In any event, we believe that research guided by models such as the one proposed will help clarify whether acculturative processes play a significant role in changing health status of groups, how the acculturative effects are expressed, and whether the pattern of relationships observed will differ as a function of the groups studied, the stage of acculturation, and the disease outcome investigated.

Conclusion and Implications for Future Research

The evidence reviewed indicates that ethnic minorities have a disproportionate burden of morbidity and mortality compared with non-Hispanic Caucasian Americans. However, there are substantial group differences in the degree of the health differential and the types of disorders to which groups are more vulnerable. There is also some evidence that increasing acculturation to the United States is associated with an increased risk for disease and dysfunction (e.g., poorer birth outcomes in more acculturated Hispanic Americans) and that this increased risk is likely mediated by incorporating into their lifestyle more of the health-damaging behaviors that are integral to the lifestyle of Americans (e.g., eating more fast foods). However, we argue that the limited amount of research available, the reliance on proxy measures of acculturation, and the failure to account for many important cofactors that could account for the group differences observed limit the conclusions that can be drawn about the role acculturation plays in the health status of racial and ethnic minority groups in the United States. A more complex, multidimensional conceptual model, which should provide a more comprehensive test of the acculturation hypotheses, is offered as a guide to future research.

References

Acton, K. J., Preston, S., & Ruth-Najarian, S. (1996). Clinical hypertension in American Indians: A comparison of 1987 and 1992 rates from ambulatory care data. *Public Health Reports, 111*(Suppl. 2), 33–36.

Adler, N. E., Boyce, T., Chesney, M. A., Cohen, S., Folkman, S., Kahn, R. L., et al. (1994). Socioeconomic status and health: The challenge of the gradient. *American Psychologist, 49*, 15–24.

American Cancer Society. (1997). Cancer facts and figures. *Surveillance Research Report.*

American Heart Association. (1998). *Cardiovascular diseases biostatistical fact sheet.*

Anderson, N. B., Lane, J. D., Taguchi, F., & Williams, R. B., Jr. (1989). Patterns of cardiovascular responses to stress as a function of race and parental hypertension in men. *Health Psychology, 8,* 525–540.

Anderson, N. B., Lane, J. D., Taguchi, F., Williams, R. B., Jr., Houseworth, S. J., et al. (1989). Race, parental history of hypertension, and patterns of cardiovascular reactivity in women. *Psychophysiology, 26,* 39–47.

Anderson, N. B., & McNeilly, M. (1993). Autonomic reactivity and hypertension in Blacks: Toward a contextual model. In J. C. S. Fray & J. G. Douglas (Eds.), *Pathophysiology of hypertension in Blacks* (pp. 107–139). New York: Oxford University Press.

Anderson, N. B., McNeilly, M., & Myers, H. F. (1992). Toward understanding race difference in autonomic reactivity: A proposed conceptual model. In J. R. Turner, A. Sherwood, & K. C. Light (Eds.), *Individual differences in cardiovascular response to stress* (pp. 125–145). New York: Plenum.

Balcazar, H., Castro, F. G., & Krull, J. L. (1995). Cancer risk reduction in Mexican American women: The role of acculturation, education, and health risk factors. *Health Education Quarterly, 22,* 61–84.

Berry, J. W. (1998). Acculturation and health: Theory and practice. In S. S. Kazarian & D. R. Evans (Eds.), *Cultural clinical psychology: Theory, research and practice* (pp. 39–57). New York: Oxford University Press.

Bogardus, C., & Lillioja, S. (1992). Pima Indians as a model to study the genetics of NIDDM. *Journal of Cell Biochemistry, 48,* 337–343.

Carter, J. S., Pugh, J. A., & Monterrosa, A. (1996). Non-insulin-dependent diabetes mellitus in minorities in the United States. *Annals of Internal Medicine, 125,* 221–232.

Centers for Disease Control and Prevention. (1997). Diabetes at highest levels in the U.S.: Minority populations especially affected. *National diabetes fact sheet.*

Centers for Disease Control and Prevention. (1998). *HIV/AIDS surveillance report, 10*(2), 1–40.

Clark, R., Anderson, N. B., Clark, V., & Williams, D. R. (1999). Racism as a stressor for African Americans: A biopsychsocial model. *American Psychologist, 54,* 805–816.

Collins, J. W., & David, R. J. (1990). Effect of traditional risk factors on infant birthweight among Blacks and Whites in Chicago. *American Journal of Public Health, 80,* 679–681.

Elder, J. P., Castro, F. G., de Moor, C., Mayer, J., Candelaria, J., et al. (1991). Differences in cancer risk-related behaviors in Latino and Anglo adults. *Medicine, 20,* 751–63.

English, P. B., Kharrazi, M., & Guendelman, S. (1997). Pregnancy outcomes and risk factors in Mexican Americans: The effect of language use and mother's birthplace. *Ethnicity and Disease, 7,* 229–240.

Epstein, J. A., Dusenbury, L., Botwin, G. J., & Diaz, T. (1994). Acculturation, beliefs about AIDS, and AIDS education among New York City Hispanic parents. *Hispanic Journal of Behavioral Sciences, 16,* 342–354.

Espino, D. V., & Maldonado, D. (1990). Hypertension and acculturation in elderly Mexican Americans: Results from 1982–84 Hispanic HANES. *Journal of Gerontology, 45,* M209–M213.

Fujimoto, W. Y. (1992). The growing prevalence of non-insulin-dependent diabetes in migrant Asian populations and its implications for Asia. *Diabetes Research and Clinical Practice, 15,* 167–183.

Geronimus, A. T. (1992). The weathering hypothesis and the health of African-American women and infants: Evidence and speculations. *Ethnicity and Disease, 2,* 207–221.

Guendelman, S. S., English, P., & Chavez, G. (1995). Infants of Mexican immigrants. Health status of an emerging population. *Medical Care, 33,* 41–52.

Guendelman, S. S., Gould, J., Hudes, M., & Eskenazi, B. (1990). Generational difference in prenatal health among the Mexican American population: Findings from HHANES, 1982–84. *American Journal of Public Health, 80,* 61–65.

Harmon, M. P., Castro, F. G., & Coe, K. (1996). Acculturation and cervical cancer: Knowledge, beliefs, and behaviors of Hispanic women. *Women and Health, 24*(3), 37–57.

Hazuda, H. P. (1996). Hypertension in the San Antonio Heart Study and the Mexico City Diabetes Study: Sociocultural correlates. *Public Health Reports, 3*(Suppl. 2), 18–21.

Hazuda, H. P., Haffner, S. M., Stern, M. P., & Eifler, C. W. (1988). Effects of acculturation and socioeconomic status on obesity and diabetes in Mexican Americans. *American Journal of Epidemiology, 128*, 1289–1301.

Hines, A. M., & Caetano, R. (1998). Alcohol and AIDS-related sexual behavior among Hispanics: Acculturation and gender differences. *AIDS Education and Prevention, 10*, 533–547.

Hines, A. M., Snowden, L. R., & Graves, K. L. (1998). Acculturation, alcohol consumption and AIDS-related risky sexual behavior among African American women. *Women and Health, 27*(3), 17–35.

Kagan, A., Harris, B. R., Wilkelstein, W., Johnson, K. G., Kato, H., Syme, S. L., et al. (1974). Epidemiologic studies of coronary heart disease and stroke in Japanese men living in Japan, Hawaii, and California: Demographic, physical, dietary, and biochemical characteristics. *Journal of Chronic Diseases, 27*, 345–364.

Kawate, R., Yamakido, M., & Nishimoto, Y. (1979). Migrant studies among the Japanese in Hiroshima and Hawaii. In W. K. Waldhausl (Ed.), *Diabetes 1979: Proceedings of the 10th Congress of the International Diabetes Federation, Vienna, Austria, Sept., 9–14, 1979* (pp. 526–531). Princeton, NJ: Excerpta Medica.

Kingston, R. S., & Smith, J. P. (1997). Socioeconomic status and racial and ethnic differences in functional status associated with chronic diseases. *American Journal of Public Health, 87*, 805–810.

Kleinman, J. C., Fingerhut, L. A., & Prager, K. (1991). Differences in infant mortality by race, nativity status, and other maternal characteristics. *American Journal of Diseases of Childhood, 145*, 194–199.

Klonoff, E. A., & Landrine, H. (1997). Distrust of White Americans, acculturation, and AIDS knowledge among African Americans. *Journal of Black Psychology, 25*(3), 50–57.

Knowler, W. C., Williams, R. C., Pettitt, D. J., & Steinberg, A. G. (1988). Gm3,5,13,14 and Type 2 diabetes mellitus: An association in American Indians with genetic admixture. *American Journal of Human Genetics, 43*, 520–526.

Krieger, N., Rowley, D. L., Herman, A. A., Avery, B., & Phillips, M. T. (1993). Racism, sexism, and social class: Implications for studies of health, disease, and well-being. *American Journal of Preventive Medicine, 9*(Suppl. 6), 82–122.

Kunitz, S. J., & Levy, J. E. (1986). The prevalence of hypertension among elderly Navajos: A test of the acculturative stress hypothesis. *Cultural Medical Psychiatry, 10*, 97–121.

Lilienfeld, A. M. (1972). *Cancer in the United States*. Cambridge, MA: Harvard University Press.

Lillie-Blanton, M., Parsons, P. E., Gayle, H., & Dievler, A. (1996). Racial differences in health: Not just Black and White, but shades of gray. *Annual Review of Public Health, 17*, 411–448.

Marmot, M. G. (1983). Stress, social and cultural variations in heart disease. *Journal of Psychosomatic Research, 27*, 377–384.

Marmot, M. G., Syme, L., Kagan, A., Kato, H., Cohen, J. B., & Belsky, J. (1975). Epidemiologic studies of coronary heart disease and stroke in Japanese men living in Japan, Hawaii, and California: Prevalence of coronary and hypertensive heart disease and associated risk factors. *American Journal of Epidemiology, 102*, 514–525.

Marshall, J. A., Hamman, R. F., Baxter, J., Mayer, E. J., Fulton, D. L., Orleans, M., et al. (1993). Ethnic differences in risk factors associated with the prevalence of non-insulin-dependent diabetes mellitus. The San Luis Valley Diabetes Study. *American Journal of Epidemiology, 137*, 706–718.

Mikawa, J. K., Morones, R. A., Gomez, A., Case, H. L., Olson, D., & Gonzales-Huss, M. J. (1992). Cultural practices of Hispanics: Implications for the prevention of AIDS. *Hispanic Journal of Behavioral Sciences, 14*, 421–433.

Myers, H. F., Kagawa-Singer, M., Kumanyika, S. K., Lex, B. W., & Markides, K. S. (1995). Panel III: Behavioral risk factors related to chronic diseases in ethnic minorities. *Health Psychology, 14*, 613–621.

Nanjundappa, G., & Friis, R. (1988). Migration stress, acculturation, and chronic disease morbidity among Hispanic clinic patients. *Humboldt Journal of Social Relations, 15,* 93–104.

National Center for Health Statistics. (1995). *Healthy People 2000. Progress report for heart disease and stroke.* Hyattsville, MD: U.S. Department of Health and Human Services.

National Center for Health Statistics. (1996). Advance report of mortality statistics. *Monthly Vital Statistics Report, 45*(3S).

National Center for Health Statistics. (1998). *Healthy people 2000 review: Cancer, 1997.* Hyattsville, MD: Public Health Service.

National Center for Health Statistics. (1999). *National vital statistics report, 47*(28). Hyattsville, MD: Public Health Service.

National Center for Health Statistics. (2001). *Health, United States, 2001.* Hyattsville, MD: Public Health Service.

Neel, J. V. (1982). The thrifty genotype revisited. In J. Kobberling & R. Tattersall (Eds.), *The genetics of diabetes mellitus* (pp. 283–293). New York: Academic Press.

Palinkas, L. A., & Pickwell, S. M. (1995). Acculturation as a risk factor for chronic disease among Cambodian refugees in the United States. *Social Science and Medicine, 40,* 1643–1653.

Peragallo, N. (1996). Latino women and AIDS risk. *Public Health Nursing, 13,* 217–222.

Pérez-Stable, E. J., Napoles-Springer, A., & Miramontes, J. M. (1997). The effects of ethnicity and language on medical outcomes of patients with hypertension or diabetes. *Medical Care, 35,* 1212–1219.

Polednak, A. P. (1992). Cancer incidence in the Puerto-Rican-born population of Connecticut. *Cancer, 70,* 1172–1176.

Popkin, B. M., & Udry, J. R. (1998). Adolescent obesity increases significantly in second- and third-generation U.S. immigrants: The National Longitudinal Study of Adolescent Health. *Journal of Nutrition, 128,* 701–706.

Reed, D., McGee, D., Cohen, J., Yano, K., Syme, S. L., & Feinleib, M. (1982). Acculturation and coronary heart disease among Japanese men in Hawaii. *American Journal of Epidemiology, 115,* 894–905.

Rogler, L. H., Cortés, D. E., & Malgady, R. G. (1991). Acculturation and mental health status among Hispanics: Convergence and new directions for research. *American Psychologist, 46,* 585–597.

Schoendorf, K. C., Hogue, C. J. R., Kleinman, J. C., & Rowley, D. (1992). Mortality among infants of Black as compared with White college-educated parents. *New England Journal of Medicine, 326,* 1522–1526.

Scribner, R., & Dwyer, J. H. (1989). Acculturation and low birthweight among Latinos in the Hispanic HANES. *American Journal of Public Health, 79,* 1263–1267.

Shiono, P. H., Rauh, V. A., Park, M., Lederman, S. A., & Suskar, D. (1997). Ethnic differences in birthweight: Lifestyle and other factors. *American Journal of Public Health, 87,* 787–793.

Stern, M. P., Knapp, J. A., Hazuda, H. P., Haffner, S. M., Patterson, J. K., & Mitchell, B. D. (1991). Genetic and environmental determinants of type II diabetes in Mexican Americans: Is there a descending limb to the modernization/diabetes relationship? *Diabetes Care, 14,* 649–654.

Suarez, L. (1994). Pap smear and mammogram screening in Mexican-American women: The effects of acculturation. *American Journal of Public Health, 84,* 742–746.

Taylor, R., & Zimmet, P. (1983). Migrant studies in diabetes epidemiology. In J. I. Mann, K. Pyorala, & A. Teuscher (Eds.), *Diabetes in epidemiological perspective* (pp. 58–77). New York: Churchill Livingstone.

U.S. Bureau of the Census. (2000). Population Estimates Program, Population Division. *Projections of the resident population by race, Hispanic origin, and nativity: Middle series, 2001 to 2005; 2006 to 2010.* Washington, DC: U.S. Department of Commerce.

U.S. Department of Health and Human Services. (1985). *Report of the secretary's task force on Black and minority health.* Washington, DC.

VanOss Marín, B. (1996). Cultural issues in HIV prevention for Latinos: Should we try to change gender roles? In S. Oskamp & S. C. Thompson (Eds.), *Understanding and pre-*

venting HIV risk behavior: Safer sex and drug use (pp. 157–176). Thousand Oaks, CA: Sage.

VanOss Marín, B., Gomez, C. A., Tschann, J. M., & Gregorich, S. E. (1997). Condom use in unmarried Latino men: A test of cultural constructs. *Health Psychology, 16,* 458–467.

VanOss Marín, B., & Marín, G. (1990). Effects of acculturation on knowledge of AIDS and HIV among Hispanics. *Hispanic Journal of Behavioral Sciences, 12,* 110–121.

VanOss Marín, B., Tschann, J. M., Gomez, C. A., & Kegeles, S. M. (1993). Acculturation and gender differences in sexual attitudes and behaviors: Hispanic vs. non-Hispanic White unmarried adults. *American Journal of Public Health, 83,* 1759–1761.

Ventura, S. J., & Tappel, S. M. (1985). Child-bearing characteristics of the U.S.- and foreign-born Hispanic mothers. *Public Health Report, 100,* 647–652.

Weinberger, M. H. (1993). Salt sensitivity. In J. L. Izzo & H. R. Black (Eds.), *Hypertension primer* (pp. 89–90). Dallas, TX: American Heart Association.

Wendorf, M., & Goldfine, I. D. (1991). Archaeology of NIDDM. Excavation of the thrifty genotype. *Diabetes, 40,* 161–165.

Wolfgang, P. E., Semeiks, P. A., & Burnett, W. S. (1991). Cancer incidence in New York City Hispanics, 1982–1985. *Ethnicity and Disease, 1,* 263–272.

Williams, D. R. (1996). Racism and health: A research agenda. *Ethnicity and Disease, 6,* 1–6.

Williams, D. R., & Collins, C. (1995). Socioeconomic and racial differences in health. *Annual Review of Sociology, 21,* 349–386.

Williams, D. R., Yu, Y., Jackson, J. S., & Anderson, N. B. (1997). Racial differences in physical and mental health: Socio-economic status, stress and discrimination. *Journal of Health Psychology, 2,* 335–351.

Zambrana, R. E., Scrimshaw, S. C. M., Collins, N., & Dunkel-Schetter, C. (1997). Prenatal health behaviors and psychosocial risk factors in pregnant women of Mexican origin: The role of acculturation. *American Journal of Public Health, 87,* 1022–1026.

Part IV

Advances in Applied Research

9

Acculturation, Psychological Distress, and Alcohol Use: Investigating the Effects of Ethnic Identity and Religiosity

Fang Gong, David T. Takeuchi, Pauline Agbayani-Siewert, and Leo Tacata

As noted in the previous chapters, conclusive findings on the relationship between acculturation and mental health have remained somewhat elusive for many reasons. Namely, different types of outcome measures have been used, and specific social and cultural factors that may contribute to the association between acculturation and mental health are often overlooked. These are important research considerations given that specific elements of the acculturation process may be linked differentially to specific health outcomes. As immigrants adjust to a new society, their value orientations, attitudes, or behavior may change, which in turn affects their health status. Unfortunately, few studies have empirically examined these processes, especially as they relate to Asian American ethnic groups.

This chapter begins to fill some of the void in the acculturation literature by focusing on psychological distress and alcohol use. Psychological distress and alcohol consumption represent different types of measures, and we hypothesize that acculturation measures are uniquely associated with each outcome. Although psychological distress, especially in the form of depression, and alcohol use often occur simultaneously, they also have different associations with some social and cultural variables. For example, a consistent finding in the empirical literature is that women tend to have higher levels of psychological distress but lower levels of alcohol use than men (Rosenfield, 1999). In the same light, this chapter examines how acculturation may vary in its association with psychological distress and alcohol use. The chapter also contributes to the study of acculturation by concentrating on two overlooked factors that may be linked to health and may vary with acculturation: ethnic identity and religiosity.

Support for this chapter was provided in part by National Institute on Alcohol Abuse and Alcoholism (NIAAA) 09633, the Fetzer Institute, and National Institute of Mental Health (NIMH) 44331.

Acculturation is inconsistently associated with psychological distress among Asian Americans. The majority of the studies document that level of acculturation has an inverse association with psychological distress among various Asian American groups (Beiser, 1988; Padilla, Wagatsuma, & Lindholm, 1985; Shapiro et al., 1999; Sue, Sue, Sue, & Takeuchi, 1995; Westermeyer, Neider, & Vang, 1984). Others have presented different results. Findings from a study on Chinese Americans in Los Angeles demonstrate that those who only speak English are less likely to report lifetime depressive episodes and dysthymia. However, language use and length of residences in the United States were not associated with 12-month prevalence of depression and dysthymia (Takeuchi et al., 1998). Hurh and Kim (1988) reported a curvilinear relationship between acculturation and depression among Korean Americans, suggesting that bicultural strategies are negatively associated with psychological distress.

Fewer studies have been conducted to investigate the linkage between acculturation and alcohol use among Asian Americans. In Zane and Huh-Kim's (1998) comprehensive review of addictive behaviors of Asian Americans, they found that variations exist among different Asian ethnic groups. For example, in most estimates of alcohol dependence and alcohol use, the Chinese and Filipinos have the lowest rates among Asian Americans. In addition to intergroup variation, within-group variation also exists. Klatsky, Siegelaub, Landy, and Friedman's (1983) study showed immigrants are more likely to abstain from consuming alcohol than their American-born counterparts in each Asian ethnic group they examined. Based on such findings, Zane and Huh-Kim (1998) suggested that more attention be given to within-group variation on acculturation-based variables such as ethnic identity and cultural values. They also made a cautious note, maintaining that "it is unclear whether factors found to be related to one addictive problem ... also are, in general, factors that are related to any mental health problem" (p. 550).

To examine acculturation, psychological distress, and alcohol use in more detail, this chapter focuses on immigrants from one Asian American ethnic group, Filipino Americans. In the past, researchers have typically conceptualized Asian Americans as a homogeneous group, which has constrained analyses of interethnic differences in health behavior and status (Zane & Sasao, 1992). One consequence of this deficiency is that very little is known about one of the largest Asian American groups—Filipino Americans. The paucity of empirical studies extends beyond investigations of health. Despite the growth of Filipino American communities, less research has been conducted in these communities than in the two other large Asian American populations—Chinese and Japanese (Okamura & Agbayani, 1991). This trend is surprising because Filipino Americans are the second largest Asian American ethnic group (second to Chinese Americans), totaling 1.85 million people in 2000 and comprising 0.7% of the total population in the United States and 18% of Asian Americans (U.S. Bureau of the Census, 2000). The size of the Filipino American population should be considered within the context of the entire Asian American population. Asian Americans comprise approximately 3.6% of the population in the United States, or 10 million people (U.S. Bureau of the Census, 2000). In terms of percentage increase, Asian Americans are the fastest growing ethnic category in the United States, doubling its population from 1980 to 1990. It is estimated that by 2025, the Asian American population will triple.

Acculturation, Ethnic Identity, and Religiosity

Acculturation

As noted in other chapters in this book, acculturation has been conceptualized and measured in different ways. This chapter does not engage in that debate. Rather, our purpose is to empirically examine how a couple of acculturation indexes are linked to specific types of attitudes, values, and behaviors. In our analytical model, we consider the length of time immigrants have lived in the United States, age during immigration, and language abilities. The time variable has often been used as a measure for the amount of change and adjustment that immigrants undergo in the new country. It is hypothesized that the longer a person stays in the new country, the more acculturated that person is likely to be. Although this time variable assumes that people change or learn about a new culture at the same pace, it is a factor that is often included in analyses of acculturation. As another measure of acculturation, age during immigration is the developmental context of immigration. The age at which a person immigrates to the United States has the potential to be a powerful force in understanding social and cultural change. Consider the qualitatively unique challenges faced by a 5-year-old child who immigrates compared with the adjustments made by a 65-year-old woman who immigrates. The number of social groups and institutions (e.g., schools, clubs, friendship networks, family ties) geared toward teaching the child about the new society is far greater than those available for an elderly immigrant. A third acculturation measure is language ability. Speaking English is often the strongest acculturation measure associated with different health outcomes (Zane & Huh-Kim, 1998). English language abilities provide a measure about the ease with which immigrants can negotiate everyday transactions in the host society. In our analyses, we consider English language abilities as part of the cultural tools that allow immigrants to conduct transactions in different settings in the host society.

Ethnic Identity

Some factors overlap with acculturation measures but are often overlooked. Although a number of variables may be associated with acculturation and health (Zane & Sasao, 1992), this chapter considers the roles that ethnic identity and religiosity play. The chapter discusses whether ethnic identity is associated with less distress and alcohol use. We expand

Phinney's discussion of ethnic identity (see chapter 3) by conceptualizing it within the larger context of social networks. The construct of social networks is defined as a specific set of linkages among a defined set of people; the characteristics of the linkages as a whole may be used to interpret the social behavior of the people involved (Mitchell, 1969; see also Laumann, 1973; Laumann & Pappi, 1976). Social networks are the concrete intermediary structures through which macrostructural phenomena exert influence on individuals (Granovetter, 1973). When a person's social ties have greater access to societal resources and opportunities, the person has greater access to those resources and opportunities. Some sociologists thus refer to networks as "opportunity structures." In one sense, social networks provide people with social support, companionship, advice and information, and access to resources (Falloon & Pederson, 1985; Holmes-Eber & Riger, 1990). Social network composition and structure help to explain a wide range of social behavior, from the mobilization of social support to conjugal role behavior (Mueller, 1980). Accordingly, ethnic identity includes the social ties one has with one's ethnic community.

Ethnic identity and acculturation have often been conceptually indistinguishable in research on Asian Americans, which has made empirical research on Asian Americans difficult (Sue, Mak, & Sue, 1998). Mainly derived from the experiences of American-born individuals, ethnic identity tends to focus on people's relationships with their own ethnic group. In contrast, acculturation research seems more pertinent to immigrants and their relationship with the dominant culture. However, ethnic identity and acculturation are closely related, with the former being influenced by the latter. Researchers have developed a few Asian American ethnic identity models (e.g., orthogonal model and stage model) and acculturation models (e.g., linear model and independent model; Sue et al., 1998). Despite the conceptualization and theoretical models on ethnic identity and acculturation, extremely little is known about how ethnic identity is affected by acculturation and consequently how it contributes to mental health outcomes of Asian Americans. The new analyses presented in this chapter are intended to enhance the understanding about the associations between acculturation and ethnic identity.

Religiosity

Another factor relating to acculturation is religiosity. Religion is cited as a key social and cultural institution among many immigrants, especially Filipino Americans (Agbayani-Siewert & Revilla, 1995). Unfortunately, few studies have examined how acculturation is linked to religiosity and psychological health. The emerging epidemiological findings from the past 2 decades suggest that religious involvement is associated with lower alcohol use, greater well-being, lower rates of suicide and depression, and higher life satisfaction (Crawford, Handal, & Wiener, 1989; Idler, 1995). These general patterns may be especially salient for racial and ethnic minorities and people in low socioeconomic positions (Brown, Ndubuisi, &

Gary, 1990; Levin, Chatters, & Taylor, 1995). For example, religious activities are correlated with better health and higher life satisfaction among African Americans, even when socioeconomic status (SES) and other demographic variables are added as controls. The association between religious activities and health and life satisfaction is consistent for young and older African Americans (Levin et al., 1995).

Although research on religiosity and mental health generally documents a positive association between religious involvement and psychological well-being, few empirical studies have examined this relationship among Asian ethnic groups. It has been found that Korean Americans have lower rates of alcohol consumption than Koreans in their home country (Zane & Huh-Kim, 1998). Researchers have suggested that the difference is the influence of Korean American churches in the United States, which provides evidence of the negative associations between religiosity and alcoholism (Zane & Huh-Kim, 1998). Another study focusing on drinking behavior of Filipino American adults (Lubben, Chi, & Kitano, 1988) concluded that attendance at religious services was the only significant predictor of male and female drinking behavior. Their analyses suggested that for Filipino men, regular church attendance (compared with irregular church attendance) is tied to lower levels of heavy drinking. Among Filipino women, church attendance is associated with abstaining from drinking.

The analyses that follow test whether religiosity is associated with less distress and alcohol problems (i.e., whether religiosity provides a shared sense of values and beliefs that promotes cohesion and shared norms). As Durkheim (1951) postulated long ago, religion and religiosity promote social integration, which consequently leads to individual well-being. Having a high degree of religiosity may decrease the value of alcohol use as a means to enhance social skills or as a coping mechanism.

In summary, this chapter examines how acculturation is linked to psychological distress and alcohol dependence among Filipino American immigrants. We consider three primary issues: (a) How are common measures of acculturation linked to ethnic identity and religiosity? (b) What is the direction of the association between acculturation and psychological distress and alcohol dependence? (c) Do ethnic identity and religiosity have similar or different associations with psychological distress and alcohol dependence?

Analytical Model

Characteristics of Population Studied

In examining the interplay among acculturation, ethnic identity, and religiosity with psychological distress and alcohol use, we use recently collected data from the Filipino American Epidemiological Study (FACES). This survey was conducted from 1998 to 1999 in San Francisco and Honolulu. The survey's probability sample of Filipino American households generally represents the Filipino American population that lives in the area. The interviews were conducted in English, Tagalog, or Ilocano depending on the respondent's language preference. Interviews took an average of approximately 90 minutes to complete. Eligible persons included Filipino Americans, ages 18 to 65 years, who lived in San Francisco or Honolulu County. One eligible person within eligible households was randomly selected for the interview. A total of 2,285 interviews were completed, which resulted in an overall response rate of 78%. Among the 2,285 cases completed, 1,818 respondents were immigrants and 467 were American-born residents. In this chapter, we include only the immigrant sample in the analyses because we are focusing on the acculturation process. Our final analyses are based on 1,796 respondents after listwise deletion of missing values for all of the variables. Weights were applied to the sample data to adjust for demographic variables and the differential probabilities of selection within the household.

In this sample of Filipino Americans, 51% are female and 49% male (see Table 9.1). The mean age is 43. The majority of the respondents report being currently married (65%), 20% report being single, and the remainder

Table 9.1. Weighted Means, Standard Deviations, and Percentages of the Demographic, Acculturation, Mediator, and Distress Measures

Variables	Mean or percentage	(s.d.)
Demographics		
Age in years (18–65)	43.1	12.8
Education in years (0–23)	11.4	5.1
Gender		
Female	51.4%	
Male	48.6%	
Marital status		
Single	19.6%	
Separated/divorced/widowed	15.8%	
Married	64.6%	
Regions		
San Francisco	43.5%	
Honolulu	56.5%	
Acculturation measures		
Length of time in United States (0–55)	15.1	10.1
Age during immigration (0–65)	27.6	13.4
English proficiency (1–4)	3.6	.6
Ethnic identity (1–4)	3.6	.4
Religiosity (1–5)	3.1	1.1
Health outcomes		
Psychological distress (1–4)	1.3	.4
Probability of alcohol dependence (0–1)	0	.1

Note. $N = 1,796$.

have experienced some form of marital disruption such as separation, divorce, or widowhood (16%). Respondents report an average level of education of 11 years, or less than a high school degree. More than half of the respondents live in Honolulu County (57%), and the rest live in the San Francisco Bay area.

Acculturation Assessment

A critical feature of this chapter is to assess how different measures of acculturation relate to health outcomes. First, we assess acculturation by age of immigration: People who immigrate at younger ages tend to make transitions more quickly than immigrants who come at much older ages. The second measure is the length of residence in the United States (in years). It is often presumed that the longer the immigrants have lived in the United States, the more acculturated they are likely to be. Another measure of acculturation in our study is language proficiency. Because our sample consisted of immigrants, the vast majority had highly proficient Filipino language skills. Therefore, we only included English language abilities in the study. One item was used to assess English proficiency; it asks how well respondents understand English when it is spoken. The response categories had four scales, from *not at all* to *very well*. Higher scores mean higher language proficiency. We recognize that these are relatively limited measures of acculturation, and they might not fully capture the extent to which Filipino American immigrants embrace cultural values and practices of the host society. However, they provide a means to investigate how structural facets of acculturation such as age and language are tied to identity, values, attitudes, and behavior.

Ethnic Identity Assessment

Ethnic identity was measured with questions drawn from the Multigroup Ethnic Identity Measure (Phinney, 1992). Nine items were selected from a 14-item list according to the high factor loadings. (Items with factor loadings of less than 0.4 were excluded.) These questions tap into the degree of identification with Filipino ethnic identity, including identity search, affirmation, belonging, and commitment. Respondents were asked to rate the extent to which they agreed or disagreed with statements such as "I am happy that I am Filipino," "I feel a strong attachment toward the Filipino community," and "I feel good about the Filipino cultural and ethnic background." The response format was a 4-point Likert scale ranging from *strongly disagree* to *strongly agree,* with higher scores indicating higher ethnic identity. The alpha for the ethnic identity scale in this sample was .74.

Religiosity Assessment

Respondents were asked to rate three questions to gauge their religious behaviors, including attending religious services, participating in group activities of a spiritual or religious nature, and participating in private religious activities. The response items had five categories ranging from *never* to *once a week or more;* higher scores indicate higher religiosity. The reliability of the religiosity scale is .70.

Psychological Distress and Alcohol Dependence Assessment

We used the depression and subscale items from the Symptom Checklist–90–Revised (SCL–90–R; Derogatis, 1977) as our measure of psychological distress. Twenty items were chosen from the subscales to construct the distress index based on high reported factor loadings. Respondents were asked to assess the degree to which they had been bothered by these symptoms in the past 30 days, symptoms such as feeling blue, trembling, and crying easily. The items were rated on a 5-point scale, ranging from *not at all* to *extremely*. The Cronbach's alpha for this scale was .92, indicating high internal consistency of the items. A psychological distress scale consists of averaging item scores for each respondent. The score ranges from 1 to 5, with high scores representing a high level of distress symptoms.

The measure of alcohol dependence was derived from the short form of the University of Michigan's version of the Composite International Diagnostic Interview (UM–CIDI SF) (Kessler et al., 1994). The CIDI has demonstrated interrater reliability, test–retest reliability, and validity. Clinical diagnoses of cases derive from computerized scoring algorithm based on the third revised edition of the *Diagnostic and Statistical Manual of Mental Disorders* (*DSM–III–R*) criteria. First, we obtained a short-form score ranging from 0 to 7 (with a high score indicating high alcohol dependence), and then we assigned probability of caseness to respondents based on their short-form scores. The measure of alcohol problems indicates the probability of alcohol dependence, with scores ranging from 0 to 1 and low scores indicating low probability. Ideally, Tobit analysis technique would be the most appropriate for models predicting alcohol dependence because it is a limited dependent variable. We conducted both Tobit and ordinary least squares (OLS) regressions and found that the latter produced more conservative results. Consequently, only the results from the conventional OLS regression models are presented in this chapter.

Control Variables

A few demographic items were included as control variables in the analyses. Age was a continuous variable, with a range from 18 to 65 years. Gender was a dichotomous variable, with female coded as a *1*. Educational level is a common measure of SES and is a stable predictor of health. It was estimated by the number of years of schooling completed by respondents. Marital status was measured as two dummy-coded variables: (a) single and (b) widowed, separated, and divorced. Accordingly, married respondents were the marital status comparison group in subsequent analyses. Because the data were collected in two geographic areas, the San

Francisco Bay area and Honolulu County, we included the geographic region as one of the controls.

Analyses and Results

Although the average levels of psychological distress and alcohol in the group were relatively low, they are not entirely unexpected. As described previously in this chapter, the few existing studies have suggested that Filipino Americans generally report lower levels of these problems than other Asian ethnic groups (Sue et al., 1995; Zane & Huh-Kim, 1998). Moreover, Latino and Asian immigrants tend to report lower levels of psychological distress and alcohol problems, a phenomenon known as the *epidemiological paradox* (Landale, Oropesa, & Gorman, 2000; Rumbaut & Weeks, 1996). Accordingly, these low average levels are understandable given the composition of the sample.

Bivariate correlation analyses indicated that time in the United States and age during immigration are associated with ethnic identity, religiosity, psychological distress, and alcohol use (see Table 9.2). English language proficiency did not show a statistical significant correlation with ethnic identity and alcohol dependence. There was a positive association between ethnic identity and religiosity. In addition, psychological distress and alcohol use were also positively correlated, although the association was not high. The latter correlation reinforced the importance of considering discrete dependent variables to better understand how acculturation, ethnic identity, and religiosity operate in a group of Filipino immigrants.

The subsequent multivariate analyses followed several steps. First, we considered the multiple factors associated with ethnic identity and religiosity. Does acculturation have similar effects on ethnic identity and religiosity? Second, we investigated how acculturation measures, ethnic identity, and religiosity are associated with psychological distress and alcohol dependence. In all of the models, we controlled for demographic variables.

Table 9.3 displays the results from multiple linear regression models predicting ethnic identity and religiosity. *Model 1,* for ethnic identity and religiosity, focuses on the effects of age during immigration and English ability, controlling for demographic variables. *Model 2* replaces age during immigration with length of time in the United States. We conducted separate analyses for length of residence and age during immigration because there is high collinearity when all of the age variables, including the respondent's age, are included simultaneously in the statistical models.

In the regression results for ethnic identity, education, marital status, and geographic regions have consistent effects on ethnic identity across both models. Higher educational levels were negatively associated with ethnic identity. Respondents who were single or who had experienced marital disruption tended to have less ethnic identity than did married adults. Residents in San Francisco had, on average, less ethnic identity than did Honolulu residents. Age had a positive effect on identity only in the second

Table 9.2. Correlation Matrix

Variables	Time in United States	Age during immigration	English proficiency	Ethnic identity	Religiosity	Distress	Alcohol dependence
Time in United States	1						
Age during immigration	−.41***	1					
English proficiency	.28***	−.37***	1				
Ethnic identity	−.07**	.15***	.00	1			
Religiosity	.06***	.10***	.09***	.12***	1		
Distress	.06*	−.09***	.14***	−.11***	.05*	1	
Alcohol dependence	.07**	−.10***	.03	−.10***	−.08***	.20***	1

Note. *$p < .05$. **$p < .01$. ***$p < .001$.

Table 9.3. Ethnic Identity and Religiosity Regressed on Acculturation Measures and Demographic Variables

	Ethnic identity		Religiosity	
Variables	Model 1 b	Model 2 b	Model 1 b	Model 2 b
Intercept	3.393	3.396	1.735	1.727
Controls				
Female	.014 (.021)	.013 (.021)	.260*** (.050)	.259*** (.050)
Age	−.002 (.001)	.004*** (.001)	.010*** (.003)	.013*** (.002)
Education	−.014*** (.002)	−.014*** (.002)	.010 (.006)	.010 (.006)
Single	−.076* (.030)	−.076* (.030)	−.140 (.073)	−.141 (.073)
Separated/divorced/widowed	−.089** (.029)	−.088** (.029)	−.111 (.070)	−.109 (.071)
San Francisco	−.064** (.024)	−.065** (.024)	.013 (.058)	.014 (.058)
Acculturation				
Age during immigration	.006*** (.001)		.004 (.003)	
Time in United States		−.006*** (.001)		−.004 (.003)
English proficiency	.085*** (.019)	.084*** (.019)	.181*** (.045)	.183*** (.046)
R^2	.070	.069	.059	.059

Note. $N = 1,796$; b = unstandardized regression coefficient with standard error in parentheses.
*$p < .05$. **$p < .01$. ***$p < .001$, two-tailed.

model. The acculturation variables were associated with ethnic identity in the intuitive direction. Age during immigration was positively associated with ethnic identity. Filipino Americans who immigrated at an older age tended to have higher average levels of ethnic identity than did immigrants who came to the United States at a younger age. In *Model 2,* length of residence in the United States was also significantly associated with ethnic identity. The longer Filipino immigrants stayed in the United States, the lower their ethnic identity. In both models, English proficiency significantly affected ethnic identity in a positive direction.

Table 9.3 also provides the results of analyses examining religiosity. Across the models, age and gender showed significant statistical effects on religiosity. Older people reported higher religiosity levels than younger people, and women reported higher religiosity levels than men. Unlike the ethnic identity models, the effects of time in the United States and age during immigration on religiosity did not achieve statistical significance. Among various acculturation measures, only the language variable showed significant association with religiosity. English proficiency was positively correlated with religiosity.

The analyses presented in Table 9.3 show that common measures of acculturation have different associations with ethnic identity and religiosity. We continued with this line of inquiry by examining (a) how the different acculturation measures are linked to health and (b) whether ethnic identity and religiosity are associated with health independent of the acculturation measures. Table 9.4 includes multiple regression models using psychological distress and alcohol dependence as the two dependent variables. The analyses of each dependent variable include two statistical models. *Model 1* examines the effect of age during immigration and language proficiency controlling for demographic variables. *Model 2* adds ethnic identity and religiosity to the equation. In other analyses not shown, we conducted similar assessments, replacing age during immigration with length of residence. Because the results were quite similar, we present only the models for age during immigration.

Gender, marital status, and region of origin were associated with psychological distress in *Model 1.* Gender and marital status were associated with psychological distress in the expected direction: Women and respondents who experienced some marital disruption had higher levels of psychological distress. An intriguing finding was that respondents in San Francisco reported higher levels of psychological distress than did Honolulu residents. Among the acculturation variables, neither age during immigration nor English proficiency were associated with distress. In *Model 2,* only ethnic identity was associated with psychological distress; more identity was associated with less psychological distress.

When alcohol dependence was considered, the analyses showed slightly different patterns from the findings for psychological distress. In *Model 1,* gender, marital status, and geographical region were associated with alcohol dependence. Men reported higher average levels of alcohol dependence than women, and respondents who were experiencing marital disruption had higher levels of alcohol dependence than did married re-

Table 9.4. Distress and Alcohol Dependence Regressed on Time in United States, Language Proficiency, Mediators, and Demographic Variables

	Distress		Alcohol dependence	
	Model 1 b	Model 2 b	Model 1 b	Model 2 b
Intercept	1.101	1.268	.239	.541
Controls				
Female	.100*** (.019)	.098*** (.019)	−.137*** (.026)	−.128*** (.026)
Age	−.001 (.001)	−.001 (.001)	.000 (.002)	.000 (.002)
Education	−.003 (.002)	−.003 (.002)	−.002 (.003)	−.002 (.003)
Single	.037 (.028)	.034 (.028)	−.019 (.038)	−.029 (.038)
Separated/divorced/widowed	.081** (.027)	.077** (.027)	.072* (.037)	.062 (.037)
San Francisco	.315*** (.022)	.311*** (.022)	.154*** (.030)	.150*** (.030)
Acculturation				
Age during immigration	−.001 (.001)	−.001 (.001)	−.004** (.001)	−.004* (.001)
English proficiency	.021 (.017)	.024 (.017)	−.010 (.024)	.001 (.024)
Ethnic identity		−.056* (.022)		−.074** (.030)
Religiosity		.013 (.009)		−.030* (.012)
R^2	.160	.163	.043	.050

Note. $N = 1,796$; b = unstandardized regression coefficient with standard error in parentheses.
*$p < .05$. **$p < .01$. ***$p < .001$, two-tailed.

spondents. The geographical pattern was in the same direction as it is for psychological distress. Respondents in San Francisco reported higher levels of alcohol dependence than did Honolulu residents. Among the acculturation variables, only age of immigration was associated with alcohol dependence. Immigrants who came to the United States at younger ages were more likely to become dependent on alcohol than immigrants who arrived at older ages.

In *Model 2*, ethnic identity and religiosity had effects on alcohol dependence. High ethnic identity and religiosity levels lowered the risk for alcohol dependence. This was a slightly different pattern than the pattern found for psychological distress. Religiosity did not have a significant association with psychological distress. The cumulative influences of the models for the two health outcomes differ a great deal. When distress was regressed on demographics and acculturation measures, the model explained 16% of the variance in psychological distress. After the model introduced ethnic identity and religiosity, the total variance explained by the variables did not change much, indicating that these two variables do not seem to explain an additional variance in psychological distress. In contrast, the regression models only explained 4% to 5% of the variance in alcohol dependence. Ethnic identity and religiosity accounted for less than 1% of the variance in alcohol dependence.

Summary and Future Directions

This chapter has examined the effects of acculturation (including age during immigration, length of residence in the United States, and language abilities) on two different types of health outcomes among Filipino American immigrants. Our analyses addressed several research questions, the first of which is how acculturation links to other social and cultural factors, especially Filipino ethnic identity and religiosity. Findings suggest that acculturation is closely associated with these two measures but in slightly different ways.

We found that the developmental context of immigration and the time spent in the United States have strong implications for ethnic identity. Filipino Americans who immigrate to the United States at young ages or who have lived in the United States for a long time may gradually become less concerned with Filipino traditions and cultures, less likely to identify themselves as Filipinos, and less active in involving themselves in Filipino communities.

On the other hand, as measured by language abilities, results show that strong English proficiency enhances the sense of ethnic identity. In effect, because of the nature of this immigrant sample, those who are highly proficient in English are also very likely to be highly proficient in the Filipino language. It is therefore possible that immigrants who have significantly mastered both languages are more aware of their home culture and their host culture. The more they are informed of and sensitive to cultural nuances, the more they can appreciate and understand the differences between the Filipino and American cultures. As a result, they have a clearer sense of the meaning of Filipino traditions, cultures, and values, which reinforces their ethnic identity. In addition, if ethnic identity is considered within the larger context of social networks, it could be concluded that better language abilities may broaden immigrants' social networks, increase their social ties, and expand their social and psychological resources, all of which might be conducive to maintaining their Filipino ethnic identity.

Our models indicate that acculturation influences religiosity differently than it influences ethnic identity. Neither age during immigration nor length of residence is a significant predictor of religious behavior; only English language proficiency is a significant indicator. It confirms our speculation that higher language proficiency provides immigrants with cultural tools that assist their transactions and communications in various situations. In religious settings, immigrants whose English language abilities are very high may find themselves more willing and comfortable to attend religious services and activities.

Our second main research question addressed the association between acculturation and health outcomes, in particular psychological distress and alcohol dependence. Findings support our hypothesis that acculturation may be linked to various health outcomes in very different ways. Our analyses suggest that neither age during immigration nor English proficiency is linked to psychological distress. In contrast, alcohol dependence is affected by age during immigration but not language ability. Age during immigration has an inverse effect on alcohol dependence, implying that immigrants who arrive at younger ages may become accustomed to Western drinking behaviors. Such unique impacts of acculturation on various health measures suggest the significance of examining multiple mental health outcomes. If only a singular health outcome were considered, it would be impossible to detect the differential influences of various acculturation measures on different health consequences.

The last research question addressed was whether ethnic identity and religiosity have independent effects on distress and alcohol dependence when controlling for other demographic and acculturation factors. By answering this question, we attempted to explore the mechanisms by which acculturation is linked to health. Acculturation per se may not be adequate for investigating the association between immigrant status and health. More important, acculturation may play a very important role in shaping immigrants' attitudes and the behaviors that help them reject or adapt to cultural values and lifestyles of the host society. Among many factors that may be influenced by acculturation, the chapter focused on two variables: ethnic identity and religiosity. Our analyses showed that ethnic identity is an especially significant variable in predicting psychological distress. When immigrants face stress or other barriers in their daily lives, the ethnic bonds reduce psychological distress.

Ethnic identity and religiosity are significant factors in reducing the risk of alcohol dependence. Findings indicate that identity and religiosity partially mediate the effect of age during immigration on alcohol dependence. These results suggest that age during immigration has direct and indirect effects on alcohol dependence. Filipino Americans who immigrate to the United States at a more mature age are more likely to retain a higher level of ethnic identity. Consequently, identity and religiosity provide personal and social resources to aid individuals when they are confronted with daily difficulties or chronic strains.

This chapter sheds light on three important issues pertinent to research on acculturation and suggests some directions for future studies on the immigration process and health. First, it is important to identify a set of social and cultural factors that are linked to acculturation and consequently to health outcomes. In this study, only two factors were considered: ethnic identity and religiosity. Findings indicate they are closely related to acculturation, and they may be the mediating or independent links between acculturation and health outcomes. However, there are still many other factors worth further exploration in future research, such as value orientations, perceptions of discrimination, social support, social network, neighborhood composition, and SES. Examining these potential mediators or relevant factors will help researchers better understand the mechanism by which acculturation is linked to health and well-being of immigrants.

Second, the unique impacts of acculturation on psychological distress and alcohol dependence have lent support to the advantages of incorporating multiple health outcomes rather than a singular outcome. Different measures of acculturation are related to distress and alcohol dependence differently, and the intervening effects of ethnic identity and religiosity also present discrepant patterns when predicting different health outcomes. As a promising direction, future research on immigrant mental health could examine other health outcomes focusing on cultural expressions of distress that are unique in the countries of origins. It would be illuminating to study whether the expressions of distress change as immigrants become more settled in their new residences.

Finally, our study highlighted the importance of studying acculturation and psychological health in various geographical regions. Controlling for other demographic and acculturation variables, we found that Filipino immigrants living in San Francisco had lower levels of ethnic identity and higher levels of psychological distress and alcohol dependence than their Hawaiian counterparts. Such findings suggest that acculturation of Asian Americans may operate differentially in unique geographical regions. Different geographical areas vary in their receptivity to immigrant groups, the social and cultural resources available to immigrant and ethnic groups, and the level of SES inequality that exists. The differential impacts of geography call for more research to examine acculturation processes and psychological consequences in populations living in different geographical areas. Some of the important factors related to geography could be examined in future research, such as characteristics of immigrants in different regions, context of immigrants' entry into various geographical areas, objectives of immigration, and fulfillment of objectives.

References

Agbayani-Siewert, P., & Revilla, L. (1995). Filipino Americans. In P. G. Min (Ed.), *Asian Americans: Contemporary trends and issues* (pp. 134–168). Thousand Oaks, CA: Sage.

Beiser, M. R. (1988). Influence of time, ethnicity and attachment on depression in Southeast Asian refugees. *American Journal of Psychiatry, 145*, 46–51.

Brown, D., Ndubuisi, S. C., & Gary, L. (1990). Religiosity and psychological distress among Blacks. *Journal of Religion and Health, 29*, 55–68.

Crawford, M. E., Handal, P., & Wiener, R. L. (1989). The relationship between religion and mental health/distress. *Review of Religious Research, 31*, 16–22.

Derogatis, L. R. (1977). *SCL–90 administration, scoring and procedures manual-I for the (revised) version and other instruments of the psychopathology rating scale series*. Towson, MD: Clinical Psychometric Research.

Durkheim, E. (1951). *Suicide: A study in sociology*. Glencoe, IL: Free Press.

Falloon, L., & Pederson, J. (1985). Family management in the prevention of morbidity of schizophrenia: The adjustment of the family unit. *British Journal of Psychiatry, 147*, 156–163.

Granovetter, M. S. (1973). The strength of weak ties. *American Journal of Sociology, 78*, 1360–1380.

Holmes-Eber, P., & Riger, S. (1990). Hospitalization and the composition of mental patients' social networks. *Schizophrenia Bulletin, 16*, 157–164.

Hurh, W. M., & Kim, K. C. (1988). *Uprooting and adjustment: A sociological study of Korean immigrants' mental health*. Final report to National Institute of Mental Health. Department of Sociology and Anthropology, Western Illinois University, Macomb.

Idler, E. L. (1995). Religion, health, and nonphysical senses of self. *Social Forces, 74*, 683–704.

Kessler, R., McGonagle, K., Zhao, S., Nelson, C., Hughes, M., Ehsleman, S., et al. (1994). Lifetime and 12-month prevalence of DSM–III–R psychiatric disorders in the United States. *Archives of General Psychiatry, 51*, 8–19.

Klatsky, A. L., Siegelaub, A. V., Landy, C., & Friedman, G. D. (1983). Racial patterns of alcoholic beverage use. *Alcoholism: Clinical and Experimental Research, 7*, 372–377.

Landale, N., Oropesa, R. S., & Gorman, B. K. (2000). Migration and infant death: Assimilation or selective migration among Puerto Ricans? *American Sociological Review, 65*, 888–909.

Laumann, E. O. (1973). *Bonds of pluralism: The form and substance of urban social networks*. New York: Wiley.

Laumann, E. O., & Pappi, F. U. (1976). *Networks of collective action: A perspective on community influence systems*. New York: Academic Press.

Levin, J. S., Chatters, L., & Taylor, R. (1995). Religious effects on health status and life satisfaction among Black Americans. *Journal of Gerontology (Social Sciences), 50B*, S154–S163.

Lubben, J. E., Chi, I., & Kitano, H. (1988). Exploring Filipino American drinking behavior. *Journal of Studies on Alcohol, 49*, 26–29.

Mitchell, J. (1969). *Social networks in urban situations*. Manchester, England: Manchester University Press.

Mueller, D. P. (1980). Social networks: A promising direction for research on the relationship of the social environment to psychiatric disorder. *Social Science and Medicine, 144*, 147–161.

Okamura, J., & Agbayani, A. (1991). Filipino Americans. In N. Mokuau (Ed.), *Handbook of social services for Asian and Pacific Islanders* (pp. 97–115). Westport, CT: Greenwood Press.

Padilla, A. M., Wagatsuma, Y., & Lindholm, K. J. (1985). Acculturation and personality as predictors of stress in Japanese and Japanese-Americans. *Journal of Social Psychology, 125*, 295–305.

Phinney, J. (1992). The multigroup ethnic identity measure: A new scale for use with adolescents and young adults from diverse groups. *Journal of Adolescent Research, 7*, 156–176.

Rosenfield, S. (1999). Gender and mental health: Do women have more psychopathology, men more, or both the same (and why)? In A. V. Horwitz & T. L. Scheid (Eds.), *A handbook for the study of mental health: Social contexts, theories, and systems* (pp. 348–360). Cambridge, England: Cambridge University Press.

Rumbaut, R. G., & Weeks, J. R. (1996). Unraveling a public health enigma: Why do immigrants experience superior perinatal health outcomes? *Research in the Sociology of Health Care, 13B*, 337–391.

Shapiro, J., Douglas, K., Rocha, O., Radecki, S., Vu, C., & Dinh, T. (1999). Generational differences in psychosocial adaptation and predictors of psychological distress in a population of recent Vietnamese immigrants. *Journal of Community Health, 24*, 95–113.

Sue, D., Mak, W. S., & Sue, D. W. (1998). Ethnic identity. In L. C. Lee & N. W. S. Zane (Eds.), *Handbook of Asian American psychology* (pp. 289–323). Thousand Oaks, CA: Sage.

Sue, S., Sue, D. W., Sue, D., & Takeuchi, D. T. (1995). Psychopathology among Asian Americans: A model minority? *Cultural Diversity and Mental Health, 1*, 39–51.

Takeuchi, D. T., Chung, R. C., Lin, K. M., Shen, H., Kurasaki, K., Chun, C. A., et al. (1998). Lifetime and twelve-month prevalence rates of major depressive episodes and dysthymia among Chinese Americans in Los Angeles. *American Journal of Psychiatry, 155*, 1407–1414.

U.S. Bureau of the Census. (2000). *Census 2000 summary file 1*. Washington, DC: U.S. Government Printing Office.

Westermeyer, J., Neider, J., & Vang, T. F. (1984). Acculturation and mental health: A study of Hmong refugees at 1.5 and 3.5 years post-migration. *Social Science and Medicine, 18*, 87–93.

Zane, N. W. S., & Huh-Kim, J. (1998). Addictive behaviors. In L. C. Lee & N. W. S. Zane (Eds.), *Handbook of Asian American psychology* (pp. 527–554). Thousand Oaks, CA: Sage.

Zane, N. W. S., & Sasao, T. (1992). Research on drug abuse among Asian Pacific Americans. *Drugs and Society, 6*, 181–210.

10

Idioms of Distress, Acculturation, and Depression: The Puerto Rican Experience

Dharma E. Cortés

The study of the relationship between acculturation and mental health has presented multiple challenges to social science researchers (Berry, 1997; LaFromboise, Coleman, & Gerton, 1993; Rogler, Cortés, & Malgady, 1991; Rumbaut, 1997). Although findings from cross-cultural studies have established a relationship between acculturation and mental health, the direction and nature of this relationship have yet to be determined. Current models and studies conceptualize acculturation as a multidimensional process in which individuals' relationships with their culture of origin and the new culture are independent (Allen, Denner, Yoshikawa, Seidman, & Aber, 1996; Birman, 1994; Cuellar & Roberts, 1997; Dana, 1996; Phinney & Devich-Navarro, 1997). Additionally, current findings stress the importance of considering contextual factors when examining the relationship between acculturation and various constructs. This includes determining how these contextual factors influence individuals to endorse elements of one culture versus those from another culture (Trimble, 1996).

Assessing the relationship between acculturation and mental health problems poses important theoretical and empirical challenges. For example, mental health measures that are frequently used with ethnic minority groups are often normed with European-American samples. Such practices raise important questions about the validity of the mental health constructs being measured. This phenomenon, often referred to as the *category fallacy* (Good & Good, 1985; Kleinman, 1977), emerges when clinical categories of mental health problems are developed for one cultural group and then imposed on members of other cultural groups without consideration of their applicability. One way to resolve category fallacy issues is to use an inductive participatory approach in which members of a target population inform researchers about their experiences with acculturation

---

This research was supported by National Institute of Mental Health Grant MH30569 from the Services Research Branch of the Division of Applied and Services Research. The author acknowledges the influence of Lloyd H. Rogler's mentorship and work during her years as graduate student and during the implementation of the research study presented here.

and psychological distress (Rogler et al., 1991). The ultimate goal of such an approach is to uncover forms of acculturation and psychological distress that are indigenous to specific cultural groups.

Uncovering indigenous or collectively shared forms of acculturation and distress may provide insights into the influence of acculturation on the development and expression of mental health problems (Rogler et al., 1991). In this context, acculturation might play a role in shaping the content and expression of psychological distress in addition to affecting levels of distress. If that is the case, *modes* of expressing psychological distress may differ among individuals with different levels of acculturation (Rogler et al., 1991). For example, if it is assumed that highly acculturated individuals are culturally similar to members of the dominant society, then they may also be similar in the way they express psychological distress. However, psychological symptomatology among less acculturated individuals may not follow this pattern. By definition, less acculturated individuals are culturally different from the groups for whom conventional symptomatology scales have been developed. Thus, the question of whether standard measures of psychological symptomatology fit the realities of ethnic minority groups remains unanswered (Rogler et al., 1991). In fact, crucial life experiences contributing to mental health outcomes (e.g., migration experience, adjustment to a socioculturally different environment, discrimination, minority status) tend to be overlooked when using conventional measures of psychological symptomatology (Rogler, Cortés, & Malgady, 1994). In other words, conventional measures assess psychological distress without incorporating contextual factors related to the idiosyncratic life experiences of culturally diverse groups.

Assessing idioms of distress (i.e., in-group cultural constructions of psychological distress) provides an opportunity to examine how acculturation shapes the expression of psychological symptomatology. A previous study demonstrated that idioms of anger and perceptions of injustice underscore the cultural context in which Puerto Ricans experience mental health problems (Rogler et al., 1994). These two idioms shed light on help-seeking behaviors among Puerto Rican immigrants (Rogler et al., 1994) and demonstrate how their unique life experiences affect their mental health (Cortés, Rogler, & Procidano, 1995).

This chapter documents a research venture that was conducted at the Hispanic Research Center at Fordham University. The study methodology used a combined qualitative–quantitative research strategy to assess the relationship between acculturation and mental health in Puerto Ricans in New York. Thus, the methodology follows an experiential framework that considers fundamental processes related to migration, settlement experiences, and individuals' experiences as members of an ethnic minority group. Because researchers were cognizant of the influence of contextual factors on acculturation and psychological distress, the participants were exclusively Puerto Ricans from the New York metropolitan area. The study comprised three different stages: (a) a qualitative phase to develop measures of acculturation and idioms of distress, (b) a quantitative phase to assess the measures' psychometric properties, and (c) a model-testing phase that assessed the relationship between acculturation, idioms of distress, depressive symptoms, and sociodemographic indicators. As is discussed in this chapter, findings from the model testing illustrated how idiomatic expressions of distress are related to acculturation and depressive symptomatology. They also highlight the limitations of conventional mental health measures in capturing the nature of psychological distress for Puerto Ricans.

Qualitative Phase: Development of Acculturation and Idioms of Distress Measures

Rationale for Using Focus Groups

A majority of studies have examined the relationship between acculturation and mental health in isolation from relevant sociocultural and contextual variables (e.g., migratory and settlement experiences, minority status). This has primarily involved examining how sociocultural and sociodemographic factors mediate the relationship between acculturation and mental health. However, one main emphasis of the current study was to investigate how these contextual factors shape the process of acculturation and the experience and expression of psychological distress. This process included developing a conceptual model of acculturation and mental health anchored in the social and cultural experiences of Puerto Ricans. Focus groups were particularly well suited for this purpose because their open-discussion format allowed for examination of the participants' phenomenological conceptions of acculturation and psychological distress.

Focus Group Recruitment and Selection Criteria

Focus group participants were recruited from community-based organizations, colleges, churches, work places, and community multiservice agencies and through personal invitation by five different participant recruiters. To increase the likelihood for diverse group responses, an effort was made to recruit groups of individuals who did not know each other before the focus group sessions. Furthermore, participants were systematically selected to evaluate a wide range of experiences with acculturation and psychological distress; therefore, clinical and nonclinical participants (i.e., those receiving and those not receiving mental health and counseling services) were selected. The inclusion of individuals from the general population addressed the psychological distress experiences of those who did not seek help for their psychological problems or symptoms. Finally, participants were also selected according to their gender and generational status because these two variables significantly affect the experience of acculturation and psychological distress. For example, the impact of acculturation varies by gender and generational status, and psychological distress also differs according to gender and generation (Culberston,

1997; Koss-Chioino & Vargas, 1999). Men and younger immigrants tend to acculturate more rapidly than women and older immigrants (Koss-Chioino & Vargas, 1999). Women tend to report more depressive symptomatology than men (Giachello, 2001), and later generations of immigrants report more problem behaviors than their older counterparts (Vega & Alegría, 2001).

Focus Group Participants

A total of 69 individuals participated in the focus groups, and slightly more than half (55%) were women. The participants ranged from ages 18 to 66 years, with an average age of 39 years. Their years of education ranged from 0 to 17 years, with an average of 11 years. Almost two thirds (68%) of the participants were born in Puerto Rico, and their average stay in the United States was 24 years, with a range of 2 to 47 years.

The participants were distributed across six nonclinical and four clinical focus groups. The nonclinical focus groups were as follows: (a) first-generation males, (b) first-generation females, (c) second-generation males, (d) second-generation females, (e) first-generation males and females, and (f) second-generation males and females. The clinical sample was represented by the following focus groups: (a) first-generation females receiving mental health services, (b) first-generation males receiving counseling for alcohol abuse, (c) first-generation males and females receiving mental health services, and (d) second-generation males and females receiving counseling for substance abuse. Grouping individuals along these lines allowed us to document diverse viewpoints on acculturation and psychological distress.

Focus Group Format and Content

Each focus group met for two 2- to 2.5-hour sessions during a 1-week period, providing adequate time to discuss acculturation and psychological distress, deal with issues of trust and group dynamics, and process information between group members. The opening question for the first focus group session was, "How would you describe what is known as *'nuestra manera de ser'* [our way of being] among Puerto Ricans?" Throughout all ten focus groups, this query prompted responses addressing what it means to be Puerto Rican in Puerto Rico and in New York City. After this question, the discussion was steered toward the topic of Puerto Rican culture and how it changes in the United States over time. For example, focus group members were asked a series of questions: "What are the things that identify or characterize Puerto Ricans as a group?" "How does our way of being compare to the American culture?" "What are the things that change among Puerto Ricans when they come to live in this country?" and "What does it mean to become Americanized?"

The following quotations from three different focus group members illustrate some of their views about their own process of acculturation:

> When I came to this country, I came with the idea of accepting another culture and not with the idea of making mine disappear. I said to myself: "I am going to the United States and I am going to accept the North American culture." I did not picture myself saying: "Well, now I am going to acquire a new culture and mine will disappear." No, I came with the idea of continuing to practice my own culture and learn about a new one.
>
> We eventually adapt to the environment here, but there are things you cannot adapt to. Feelings, for example—that feeling about being Puerto Rican cannot be changed.
>
> I think it is obvious in the language, the *Spanglish*. You start your sentence in English and finish it in Spanish or vice versa. It is sort of like when you play with play dough. You have green and orange and you try to make a toy with both colors but then, at the end, you want to break it and you can't. So you just mash it together and you have a totally different color.

At the beginning of the second focus group session, the moderator, who conducted all 20 focus group sessions, reviewed the topics from the first session and invited group members to make additional comments. The moderator then asked the following question to initiate a discussion on psychological distress:

> When people move to another country that has a different culture, a different language, they often have to adjust to changes. These adjustments might or might not lead them to feel bad. How would you say a person could be affected by these changes?

After participants responded to this query, probes were used to explore their views on the problems that Puerto Ricans face in a new sociocultural environment, their reactions to such problems, and the expression and experience of psychological distress.

Content Analysis of Focus Group Discussions

The focus group contents were transcribed from audio tapes for analysis. The goal of the content analysis was to identify themes or domains from which questionnaire items could be developed to assess acculturation and idioms of distress. Domains that were identified in more than five groups were automatically selected for this process. The following domains related to acculturation were identified: importance of the family, food and cooking, collectivism, child-rearing practices, language, identity, music, holiday celebrations, sex roles, cultural and ethnic pride, religiosity, and feelings about being Puerto Rican. The identified domains related to idioms of distress were nostalgia, anger, and disillusionment; within these domains, the following were identified: injustice, frustration, suffering, bitterness, fear, racism, and hopelessness. Injustice, bitterness, and racism were related to the idiom of anger, whereas frustration and hopelessness were associated with the idiom of disillusionment. Hopelessness was connected to the idiom of nostalgia.

Development of Items

The development of items was guided by the domains and themes that were identified throughout the focus groups. In some instances, actual participant quotations were developed into items. Fifty items were developed to measure acculturation; 30 items were developed from the focus groups, and 20 items were used from an existing acculturation scale that was developed by Cortés, Rogler, and Malgady (1994). These acculturation items evaluated involvement in the Puerto Rican and American cultures. The items from the existing scale, which were also developed using focus groups with Puerto Ricans living in New York, addressed similar domains that were uncovered during the focus group sessions conducted in this study. Some of the questions in the acculturation scale included, "How much are Puerto Rican values a part of your life?" "How much are American values a part of your life?" "How proud are you of being Puerto Rican?" and "How proud are you of being American?"

Three sets of items were developed to assess the three identified idioms of distress (anger, nostalgia, and disillusionment). The idiom of anger stemmed from trials and tribulations that were encountered in the United States. Nostalgia related to yearning for what was left behind after moving to the United States. Finally, the idiom of disillusionment tapped into the disappointment they felt when their life circumstances did not meet their migratory expectations and goals. The anger measure consisted of 21 items (e.g., "I get angry when I see that Puerto Ricans are treated as second-class citizens in this country" "The longer I live in this country, the more hard-hearted I become"). The measures for nostalgia (e.g., "Many times when I think of how much I want to live in Puerto Rico, tears come out of my eyes" "When I think of Puerto Rico, I long for it like the first day I came to the United States") and disillusionment (e.g., "In this country I have not found what I came searching for" "Before coming to the United States, I had an image of this country that was completely different from what it is in reality") had 23 and 21 items, respectively.

The items for the acculturation and idioms of distress measures were first developed in Spanish and then translated into English by a bicultural and bilingual Latina psychology graduate student. Items were initially developed in Spanish because the majority of the participants preferred to speak this language in the focus groups, a step that reduced the probability of introducing language-related biases during the early stages of item development. To further address issues of translation and conceptual equivalence, the English-language versions of the measures were later back-translated into Spanish and cross-checked with the original Spanish-language items by a bilingual and bicultural Puerto Rican psychologist. Items were rated on a Likert-type scale (1 = *strongly disagree*, 2 = *disagree a little*, 3 = *agree a little*, and 4 = *strongly agree*). The final versions of the measures were reviewed by a Puerto Rican psychologist and a bilingual and bicultural professional editor who were knowledgeable about cultural issues in mental health.

Participants from the original focus groups were contacted and invited to participate in another focus group that was designed to gather their feedback on the newly developed items. Participants were divided into two focus groups based on their clinical and generational status: (a) first-generation males and females with clinical and nonclinical status, and (b) second-generation males and females with clinical and nonclinical status. All of the participants were asked to complete the acculturation and idioms of distress items and comment on whether the items were relevant to their experiences, comprehensible, and culturally appropriate. The participants preferred that the 4-point Likert scale be structured along a continuum of *strongly disagree* (1) to *strongly agree* (4) rather than use a 6-point anchored response format (i.e., 1 = *strongly disagree*, 6 = *strongly agree*). Taking this feedback into account, final versions of the measures were developed.

Quantitative Phase: Assessing Psychometric Properties of Measures

The acculturation and idioms of distress measures were administered to a convenience sample of 642 Puerto Ricans living in the New York City metropolitan area, Westchester County north of New York City, and New Jersey. Participants were recruited from churches, colleges, schools, and community centers. The participants were equally divided by gender and had a mean age of approximately 37 years. Participants possessed an average of 11.36 years of education and had lived in the United States for an average of 25 years (with a range of 1 to 66 years). Sixty-one percent were born in the United States. Similar to the scale development sample, participants in this sample included individuals who were receiving mental health services ($n = 65$) and counseling for alcohol abuse ($n = 115$). However, the participants in this phase of the study did not participate in the initial focus group sessions. In addition to completing the acculturation and idioms of distress measures, the participants were asked to answer questions about their sociodemographic backgrounds and to complete the Symptom Checklist–90–Revised (SCL–90–R; Derogatis, Rickels, & Rock, 1976), which is a multidimensional self-report symptom inventory that assesses nine clusters of psychopathology (somatization, obsessive–compulsive symptoms, interpersonal sensitivity, depression, anxiety, hostility, phobic anxiety, paranoid ideation, and psychoticism).

Factor Analysis of Acculturation Items

Maximum-likelihood factor analysis with varimax rotation was conducted for the 50 acculturation items (with 25 items that assessed involvement in Puerto Rican culture and 25 items that assessed involvement in American culture) using a two-factor solution in accordance with our bicultural conceptualization of this construct. Factor 1 (i.e., involvement in Puerto Rican culture) contributed to 12.5% of the variance, and Factor 2 (i.e., involvement in American culture) contributed to 7.4% of the variance.

Nineteen of the 25 items assessing involvement in Puerto Rican culture loaded .30 or higher on Factor 1 (Puerto Rican culture) and below .30 on Factor 2 (American culture). Fourteen items assessing involvement in American culture revealed a pattern that was similar to those in the Puerto Rican culture item stem. Results from this factor analysis thus resulted in a final set of 19 items for the involvement in Puerto Rican culture measure and 14 items for the involvement in American culture measure.

Reliability and Validity of Acculturation Measures

Alpha coefficients were computed to estimate the internal consistency of the two acculturation measures. Both exhibited high internal consistency; items measuring involvement in Puerto Rican culture yielded an alpha coefficient of .85, whereas the items assessing involvement in American culture yielded an alpha coefficient of .84.

Place of birth and number of years residing in the United States were used to estimate criterion validity. The premise behind these validity indicators is that individuals are more likely to adopt a new culture with prolonged and early exposure to the culture (Cortés et al., 1994). Zero-order correlations between acculturation subscale scores, place of birth, and number of years residing in the United States revealed significant relationships. Those born in the United States reported more involvement in American culture than those born in Puerto Rico. By the same token, individuals born in Puerto Rico reported more involvement in Puerto Rican culture. The same pattern was found for years of residence in the United States. Individuals who spent more years in the United States were more involved in American culture and less involved in Puerto Rican culture.

Factor Analysis of Idioms of Distress Measures

To determine whether the 64 idioms of distress items represented three distinct factors of anger, nostalgia and disillusionment, a maximum-likelihood factor analysis with varimax rotation was conducted using a three-factor solution. The items corresponding to anger grouped under one factor, whereas those corresponding to nostalgia and disillusionment grouped under the other two factors. Factor 1 (nostalgia) contributed 16.4% of the variance, Factor 2 (anger) contributed 13.7% of the variance, and Factor 3 (disillusionment) contributed 13.2% of the variance.

Following the same item reduction method that was used for the acculturation measures (i.e., discarding items that loaded lower than .30 for each factor), the final versions of the measures assessing nostalgia and disillusionment were reduced to 22 and 17 items, respectively. The anger measure still contained 21 items.

Reliability and Validity of Idioms of Distress Measures

The three idioms of distress measures had high internal consistency. The items assessing anger yielded an alpha coefficient of .94, whereas the items assessing nostalgia and disillusionment yielded alpha coefficients of .95 and .93, respectively. It was difficult to establish the criterion validity for these idioms of distress because they were not tied to specific diagnoses from the fourth edition of the *Diagnostic and Statistical Manual of Mental Disorders (DSM–IV)*. Still, the model testing stage of this study could be considered similar to validity testing because it examined the relationship of these idioms to depressive symptomatology.

Model Testing

Zero-order correlations were computed to examine the relationship among acculturation, idioms of distress, depression (as measured by the depressive cluster of the SCL–90–R), and sociodemographic variables. Involvement in Puerto Rican culture was positively related to depression, anger, nostalgia, and disillusionment. Involvement in American culture was inversely related to depression and the three idioms of distress. Depression was positively related to anger, nostalgia, and disillusionment. In terms of sociodemographic variables, individuals born in Puerto Rico reported low levels of involvement in American culture and high levels of involvement in Puerto Rican culture. The opposite was true for those born in the United States. More years of education was associated with involvement in American culture, whereas fewer years was related to involvement in Puerto Rican culture. Being born in Puerto Rico was associated with high levels of depression, anger, nostalgia, and disillusionment. Number of years residing in the United States was positively related to involvement in American culture and inversely related to nostalgia. Gender was only significantly related to number of years of education. Women had completed more years of education than men. Results from these analyses are presented in Table 10.1.

Three hierarchical regression analyses were computed to further examine the relationship among sociodemographic background, acculturation, idioms of distress, and depression. The first analysis examined sociodemographic variables (place of birth, gender, number of years in the United States, years of education) and acculturation variables (involvement in American and Puerto Rican cultures) as potential predictors of depression. Results indicated that place of birth was the only significant correlate of depression in the first step, explaining only 1.5% of the vari-

Table 10.1. Zero-Order Correlations: Acculturation, Idioms of Distress, Depression, and Sociodemographic Variables

	Place of birth[a]	Gender[b]	Years in United States	Years of education	Involvement in American culture	Involvement in Puerto Rican culture	Anger	Nostalgia	Disillusionment	Depression
Place of birth[a]		−.05	−.11**	−.30**	−.29**	.36**	.17**	.35**	.16**	.11**
Gender[b]			.01	.19**	−.06	.04	.04	−.04	−.07	.06
Years in United States				−.05	.24**	−.05	−.03	−.10**	−.05	−.04
Years of education					.16**	−.28**	−.19**	−.22**	−.31**	−.24**
Involvement in American culture						−.32**	−.23**	−.37**	−.33**	−.10*
Involvement in Puerto Rican culture							.23**	.64**	.28**	.10*
Anger								.41**	.56**	.35**
Nostalgia									.45**	.17**
Disillusionment										.32**

[a]Category values: 0 = born in United States; 1 = born in Puerto Rico.
[b]Category values: 0 = male; 1 = female.
*p < .05. **p < .01.

Table 10.2. Hierarchical Regression Analysis: Sociodemographic Variables and Acculturation as Predictors of Depression

Variables	Step 1	Step 2	Step 3	Step 4
Place of birth[a]	.107*	.105*	.029	.019
Gender[b]	.068	.068	.110*	.106*
Years in United States		−.023	−.044	−.035
Years of education			−.248**	−.243**
Involvement in American culture				−.041
Involvement in Puerto Rican culture				.002
R^2	.015*	.016*	.069**	.071**
Increment to R^2		.001	.54**	.002

Note. Standardized coefficients.
[a]Category values: 0 = born in United States; 1 = born in Puerto Rico.
[b]Category values: 0 = male; 1 = female.
*$p < .01$. **$p < .001$.

ance in depression. Results of this analysis are presented in Table 10.2. Gender was significantly related to depression only when number of years of education was considered in the third step of the equation. In this case, women and those with fewer years of education reported high levels of depression. Neither involvement in American culture nor involvement in Puerto Rican culture was significantly related to depression. This regression model explained 7% of the variance in depression.

The second hierarchical regression analysis was conducted to examine correlates of anger. Results from the analysis are presented in Table 10.3. Place of birth was significantly related to anger; individuals born in Puerto Rico had higher levels of anger than their U.S.-born counterparts. Gender was also positively related to anger only when number of years of education was considered. Women and those with fewer years of education reported higher levels of anger than men and individuals with more years of education. Finally, involvement in American and Puerto Rican cultures

Table 10.3. Hierarchical Regression Analysis: Sociodemographic Variables and Acculturation as Predictors of Anger

Variables	Step 1	Step 2	Step 3	Step 4
Place of birth[a]	.173***	.172***	.122**	.046
Gender[b]	.050	.050	.079*	.053
Years in United States		−.007	−.021	.015
Years of education			−.167***	−.122**
Involvement in American culture				−.151***
Involvement in Puerto Rican culture				.132**
R^2	.032***	.032***	.056***	.098***
Increment to R^2		.000	.24***	.042***

Note. Standardized coefficients.
[a]Category values: 0 = born in United States; 1 = born in Puerto Rico.
[b]Category values: 0 = male; 1 = female.
*$p < .05$. **$p < .01$. ***$p < .001$.

was significantly related to anger. Those who were more involved in American culture reported lower levels of anger. In contrast, those who reported greater involvement in Puerto Rican culture exhibited high levels of anger. This regression equation explained about 10% of the variance in anger.

The third and last regression analysis was conducted to examine how idioms of distress, in addition to involvement in American and Puerto Rican cultures, might better predict depression. To address the issue of multicollinearity among the measures of idioms of distress, two steps suggested by Pedhazur and Schmelkin (1991) were followed. The first step was to conduct a factor analysis to corroborate that the items loaded in three distinct factors. The second step was to enter the intercorrelated variables in one block. This regression analysis revealed that anger and disillusionment were positively and significantly related to depression in the fifth and last step of the regression equation (see Table 10.4). With regard to sociodemographic variables, women and those with less education were at significant risk for depression. Finally, gender, number of years of education, anger, and disillusionment explained about 17% of the variance in depression.

Discussion

Involvement in American and Puerto Rican cultures was unrelated to depression when sociodemographic factors and idioms of distress were considered. Involvement in both cultures, however, was related to anger. Puerto Ricans with high levels of involvement in American culture may have reported low levels of anger because they were thought of and ac-

Table 10.4. Hierarchical Regression Analysis: Sociodemographic Variables, Acculturation, and Idioms of Distress as Predictors of Depression

Variables	Step 1	Step 2	Step 3	Step 4	Step 5
Place of birth[a]	.107*	.105*	.029	.019	.014
Gender[b]	.068	.068	.110*	.106*	.102*
Years in United States		−.023	−.044	−.035	−.039
Years of education			−.248**	−.243**	−.180**
Involvement in American culture				−.041	.035
Involvement in Puerto Rican culture				.002	−.055
Anger					.229**
Nostalgia					.009
Disillusionment					.150*
R^2	.015*	.016*	.069**	.071**	.168**
Increment to R^2		.001	.54**	.002	.097**

Note. Standardized coefficients.
[a]Category values: 0 = born in United States; 1 = born in Puerto Rico.
[b]Category values: 0 = male; 1 = female.
*$p < .01$. **$p < .001$.

cepted as a member of the larger cultural group. The opposite could be true for Puerto Ricans who are highly involved in Puerto Rican culture and experience high levels of anger.

Being a woman and having little formal education are sociodemographic risk factors for depression. The general literature has suggested that gender differences in depression rates might be a result of women's proclivity to report depressive symptoms more readily than men (Culberston, 1997). If education is considered an indicator of socioeconomic status, this present study's finding corroborates past investigations that have consistently found an inverse relationship between depressive symptoms and socioeconomic status (Johnson, Cohen, Dohrenwend, Link, & Brook, 1999). Finally, the idioms of distress of anger and disillusionment were related to depressive symptoms as well. These two idioms of distress, unlike the idiom of nostalgia, seem to be more conducive to feelings of helplessness that may underlie depressive symptomatology. For example, individuals who feel nostalgic about life in Puerto Rico might cope with these feelings by daydreaming, traveling to the island, or having a romantic view of the past. However, the roots of their anger and disillusionment (i.e., discrimination, struggling with unfulfilled expectations and goals) may be embedded in their everyday environments. Thus, anger and disillusionment may be particularly salient risk factors for depression as witnessed for this New York Puerto Rican sample.

Conceptually, these findings emphasize the importance of considering the respondents' own views of acculturation and psychological distress when assessing the relationship between the two. Distinct relationships between cultural involvement and the expression of psychological distress were uncovered because acculturation was measured as independent involvement in both American and Puerto Rican cultures. However, this important finding would have been undetected if a unidimensional acculturation scale had been used.

The findings also shed light on the way acculturation shapes the expression of psychological distress. They suggest that involvement in Puerto Rican and American cultures does not predict depressive symptomatology. However, anger and disillusionment indeed predict depression. Thus, an assessment of the relationship between acculturation and mental health using a conventional measure of psychological distress (e.g., SCL–90–R's depression cluster) would have failed to establish a connection between the experiences of being Puerto Rican in New York and psychological distress. In other words, in-group experiences and expressions of psychological distress would have been completely overlooked if acculturation and depression were the only constructs under investigation. This research also highlights a fundamental shortcoming in the acculturation–mental health research field—the lack of specificity regarding the way acculturation and mental health components are related.

The field begs for models that move beyond testing unidirectional relationships between acculturation, sociodemographic factors, and mental health outcomes. To make strides in understanding *how* acculturation is related to psychological distress, it is important to contextualize the processes of acculturation and the experiences that lead to the emergence of psychological distress. The findings presented in this chapter illustrate how this may be accomplished when using a combined qualitative–quantitative approach to study and measure acculturation and psychological distress. As described previously, simply using a conventional scale to measure the existence of a direct relationship between acculturation and mental health did not detect any relationship. However, when nostalgia, anger, and disillusionment were added to the model, the latter anger and disillusionment were positively related to depressive symptomatology.

The most important finding in this study is that anger and disillusionment were better predictors of depression than cultural involvement. These idioms of distress may have been better predictors because they are anchored in the context of the participants' settlement and adjustment experiences rather than in abstract emotional experiences (e.g., feeling disinterested in things, feeling hopeless about the future, feeling worthless). In other words, anger and disillusionment more fully capture the unique and often stressful adjustment experiences that may lead to depressive symptomatology for Puerto Ricans in New York.

Conclusion

Idioms of distress are not being proposed as alternative measures of mental health problems among members of ethnic minority groups but rather as crucial factors that shape their psychological distress (Malgady, Cortés, & Rogler, 1996). Idioms of distress add another dimension to the understanding of psychological distress by underscoring salient immigration-related issues of displacement, loss, and unfulfilled expectations. Some quotes from focus group participants illustrate the linkage between their experiences as ethnic minorities and psychological distress. For instance, while talking about the connection among nostalgia, disillusionment, and depression, a participant observed: "They are tied to one another. When you feel nostalgic because you miss Puerto Rico, and when you are not able to satisfy that need, you can get depressed." Nostalgia was related to depression only at a univariate level during our preliminary data analyses, thus our findings partially support this proposition.

The data presented in this chapter also have important implications for the implementation of culturally competent treatment interventions. Providers of mental health services for immigrant and ethnic minority clients should consider the possible effects of migratory and resettlement experiences on psychological well-being. Assessment of an ethnic minority's experiences with loss and displacement may help to identify stressors associated with presenting problems and ultimately inform problem resolution strategies.

Finally, the findings corroborate the need to abandon simplistic models proposing a unidimensional and direct relationship between acculturation and mental health. If acculturation and mental health are affected by many different factors, it is counterintuitive to expect that acculturation, as an isolated concept, will significantly affect mental health outcomes (Rogler, 1994). Although progress has been made, the field awaits the development of a research program that systematically tests the process of acculturation and the relationship between acculturation and mental health. In particular, experientially driven conceptual models are needed. They should include other variables that influence the relationship between acculturation and mental health. Some of these variables are contextual factors such as settlement and adjustment experiences as well as social injustice and perceived discrimination.

As mentioned previously, research studies need to focus on addressing the level of specificity in which acculturation and mental health are related. So far, the use of conventional and "decontextualized" measures of acculturation and mental health outcomes has fallen short of yielding a better understanding of how acculturation is related to mental health problems. The findings presented in this chapter suggest that measures addressing the context of acculturation and mental health problems provide insight to their complex relationship. Thus, clinicians and researchers should ask themselves whether they are interested in simply determining whether a relationship between acculturation and mental health exists or in learning about the processes that lead to psychological distress among culturally distinct groups. The use of qualitative approaches in conjunction with traditional quantitative techniques will move the field closer to deciphering how specific aspects of acculturation affect mental health outcomes.

References

Allen, L., Denner, J., Yoshikawa, H., Seidman, E., & Aber, J. L. (1996). Acculturation and depression among Latina urban girls. In B. J. R. Leadbeater & N. Way (Eds.), *Urban girls: Resisting stereotypes, creating identities* (pp. 337–352). New York: New York University Press.

Berry, J. W. (1997). Immigration, acculturation, and adaptation. *Applied Psychology: An International Review, 46*(1), 5–68.

Birman, D. (1994). Acculturation and human diversity in a multicultural society. In E. J. Trickett, R. J. Watts, & D. Birman (Eds.), *Human diversity* (pp. 261–284). San Francisco, CA: Jossey Bass.

Cortés, D. E., Rogler, L. H., & Malgady, R. G. (1994). Assessing biculturality among Puerto Rican adults in the United States. *American Journal of Community Psychology, 22*, 707–721.

Cortés, D. E., Rogler, L. H., & Procidano, M. E. (1995, August). *Acculturation and appraisal mediate psychosocial risk for Puerto Rican immigrants.* Poster presented at the 103rd annual convention of the American Psychological Association, New York.

Cuellar, I., & Roberts, R. (1997). Relations of depression, acculturation, and socioeconomic status in a Latino sample. *Hispanic Journal of Behavioral Sciences, 19*, 230–238.

Culberston, F. M. (1997). Depression and gender: An international review. *American Psychologist, 52*, 25–31.

Dana, R. H. (1996). Assessment of acculturation in Hispanic populations. *Hispanic Journal of Behavioral Sciences, 18*, 317–328.

Derogatis, L. R., Rickels, K., & Rock, A. F. (1976). The SCL–90 and the MMPI: A step in the validation of a new self-report scale. *British Journal of Psychiatry, 128*, 280–289.

Giachello, A. L. (2001). The reproductive years: The health of Latinas. In M. Aguirre-Molina,

C. W. Molina, & R. E. Zambrana (Eds.), *Health issues in the Latino community* (pp. 179–208). San Francisco, CA: Jossey Bass.
Good, B., & Good, M. D. (1985). The cultural context of diagnosis and therapy: A view from medical anthropology. In M. Miranda & H. H. L. Kitano (Eds.), *Mental health research in minority communities: Development of culturally sensitive training programs* (pp. 1–27). Rockville, MD: National Institute of Mental Health.
Johnson, J. G., Cohen, P., Dohrenwend, B. P., Link, B. G., & Brook, J. S. (1999). A longitudinal investigation of social causation and social selection processes involved in the association between socioeconomic status and psychiatric disorders. *Journal of Abnormal Psychology, 108*, 490–499.
Kleinman, A. (1977). Depression, somatization and the "new cross-cultural psychiatry." *Social Science and Medicine, 11*, 3–10.
Koss-Chioino, J. D., & Vargas, L. A. (1999). *Working with Latino youth: Culture, development, and context*. San Francisco, CA: Jossey Bass.
LaFromboise, T., Coleman, H. L. K., & Gerton, J. (1993). Psychological impact of biculturalism: Evidence and theory. *Psychological Bulletin, 114*, 395–412.
Malgady, R. G., Cortés, D. E., & Rogler, L. H. (1996). Cultural expression of psychiatric symptoms: Idioms of anger among Puerto Ricans. *Psychological Assessment, 8*, 265–268.
Pedhazur, E. J., & Schmelkin, L. P. (1991). *Measurement, design, and analysis: An integrated approach*. Hillsdale, NJ: Erlbaum.
Phinney, J. S., & Devich-Navarro, M. (1997). Variations in bicultural identification among African American and Mexican American adolescents. *Journal of Research on Adolescence, 7*, 3–32.
Rogler, L. H. (1994). International migrations: A framework for directing research. *American Psychologist, 49*, 701–708.
Rogler, L. H., Cortés, D. E., & Malgady, R. G. (1991). Acculturation and mental health status among Hispanics: Convergence and new directions for research. *American Psychologist, 46*, 585–597.
Rogler, L. H., Cortés, D. E., & Malgady, R. G. (1994). The mental health relevance of idioms of distress: Anger and perceptions of injustice among New York Puerto Ricans. *Journal of Nervous and Mental Disease, 182*, 327–330.
Rumbaut, R. G. (1997). Assimilation and its discontents: Between rhetoric and reality. *International Migration Review, 31*, 923–938.
Trimble, J. (1996). Multilinearity of acculturation: Person–situation interactions. In International Association for Cross-Cultural Psychology (Ed.), *International congress* (pp. 173–186). Lisse, Netherlands: Swets & Zeitlinger.
Vega, W. A., & Alegría, M. (2001). Latino mental health and treatment in the United States. In M. Aguirre-Molina, C. W. Molina, & R. E. Zambrana (Eds.), *Health issues in the Latino community* (pp. 179–208). San Francisco, CA: Jossey Bass.

11

Acculturation, Alcohol Consumption, Smoking, and Drug Use Among Hispanics

Raul Caetano and Catherine L. Clark

As mentioned throughout this book, *acculturation*, broadly defined, is the extent to which ethnic group members participate in the cultural traditions, values, and practices of the dominant society (Snowden & Hines, 1998). As such, acculturation is often perceived as a powerful force shaping individuals' daily lives and quality of health. For instance, there seems to be a strong relationship between acculturation and medical care utilization. Less-acculturated Hispanics tend to face more barriers to utilizing medical care than other Hispanics because of social isolation and alienation, language constraints, and unfulfilled expectations about providers' relationships with clients (Chavez, Cornelius, & Jones, 1985; Chesney, Chavira, Hall, & Gary, 1982; Estrada, Treviño, & Ray, 1990; Vega & Amaro, 1994). Acculturation has also been associated with health-related risk behaviors such as alcohol use, smoking, and drug use (e.g., Carvajal, Photiades, Evans, & Nash, 1997; Deosaransingh et al., 1995; Graves, 1967; Padilla, Padilla, Ramirez, Morales, & Olmedo, 1977; Polednak, 1997). With this background in mind, the objective of this chapter is to discuss the influence of acculturation on drinking, drinking problems, smoking, and drug use among Hispanics. Also presented are new data regarding trends between 1984 and 1995 on the relationship between acculturation and alcohol consumption among Hispanics in the United States. This chapter focuses on Hispanics because a large proportion of research has studied this particular group, providing a more comprehensive database to analyze the relationship between acculturation and health-related behaviors.

The relationship between acculturation and drinking (alcohol) has been examined in nationwide and community samples of Hispanics in the United States. Across all of the studies, the most consistent findings sug-

---

Work on this chapter was supported by Grants AA-05595 and RO1-AA10013 from the National Institute on Alcohol Abuse and Alcoholism to the Alcohol Research Group, Public Health Institute, Berkeley, CA. The authors thank Kelly Raspberry for all of her assistance on this project.

gest that women who score higher on acculturation scales are more likely to consume alcohol, consume alcohol more frequently, and consume greater amounts of alcohol than those who are less acculturated (Black & Markides, 1993; Caetano, 1987a; Caetano & Medina Mora, 1988; Gilbert, 1987a; Lovato et al., 1994; Marín, Posner, & Kinyon, 1993; Markides, Ray, Stroup-Benham, & Treviño, 1990). Among men, the relationship is less clear. Some evidence shows a positive association between acculturation and alcohol consumption (Caetano, 1987a; Lovato et al., 1994; Marín et al., 1989), whereas other evidence suggests the opposite (Neff, Prihoda, & Hoppe, 1991). Still, another set of studies reveals a very complex association between acculturation and alcohol consumption. In a community sample of three generations of Mexican Americans in San Antonio, Texas, investigators discovered that drinking levels were highest among less-acculturated, second-generation Mexican American men (Neff, Hoppe, & Perea, 1987). Other analyses indicated that the relationship between acculturation and alcohol consumption depends on age, indicating that there was a positive relationship between acculturation and drinking for young women and a negative relationship between acculturation and drinking for middle-age men (Markides, Krause, & Mendes de Leon, 1988). Interestingly, the social context of drinking also varies by acculturation level. Those who are highly acculturated are more likely to frequent social settings where alcohol is consumed (e.g., restaurants, bars, parties) and to drink in these situations than those who are less acculturated (Caetano, 1987b).

Caetano and Medina Mora (1988) examined the alcohol consumption patterns of Mexican American immigrants to better understand the nature of the relationship between acculturation and drinking. Their results indicated that after living 1 to 5 years in the United States, immigrant men had already begun to drink more frequently, a pattern similar to the one shown by Mexican American men who were born in the United States. Among women, immigration from Mexico to the United States did not change their drinking patterns, suggesting that acculturation-related drinking patterns among women pertain primarily to those who were born in the United States.

Acculturation has also been linked to a variety of alcohol-related problems. Burnam, Hough, and Escobar (1987) found that lifetime prevalence of alcohol dependence among a sample of Mexican Americans in Los Angeles was highest among those in the high acculturation group. The study by Caetano and Medina Mora (1988) showed that highly acculturated Mexican American women were more likely to have experienced various social and legal problems related to their alcohol use than the respondents who were less acculturated. Slightly different results were attained by Neff and his colleagues (1987), who found that Mexican American men in San Antonio, Texas, who scored in the middle of the acculturation scale were the most likely to have experienced a range of alcohol-related problems.

In summary, this review suggests that the associations of acculturation with alcohol consumption and alcohol-related problems are complex and depend on gender, age, birthplace, generational status, national origin, and social setting. The existing evidence seems to most clearly indicate that acculturation is positively associated with alcohol consumption, especially among women. The results also suggest that acculturation-related analyses must control for the effects of various sociodemographic factors to protect against reporting spurious associations that may occur within sociodemographic categories across acculturation levels.

Acculturation and Beliefs About Drinking Alcohol

Scholars have examined beliefs about drinking to identify potential mechanisms by which acculturation may affect alcohol consumption patterns. Research conducted to date suggests that liberal drinking norms and liberal attitudes toward drinking and drunkenness are positively related to higher levels of acculturation, although these associations are modified by the amount of drinking in question, location of the consumption, and the respondent's age and gender (Caetano, 1987c; Caetano & Medina Mora, 1988). Marín and colleagues (1993) examined the relationship between acculturation and alcohol outcome expectancies and found that less acculturated individuals were more likely than highly acculturated individuals to endorse various positive and negative outcomes and believe that alcohol use results in emotional and behavioral impairment (e.g., loss of coordination, lack of self-control, carelessness, becoming argumentative and emotional). Previously, Caetano and Medina Mora (1990) found that reasons for drinking also vary by acculturation status. Those with high levels of acculturation tend to use alcohol for social reasons (e.g., drinking to celebrate), whereas those with low levels of acculturation tend to use alcohol to reduce tension (e.g., drinking to forget their worries).

In general and contrary to the incongruous findings on the relationship between acculturation and drinking, there is consistent evidence supporting the positive association between acculturation and liberal beliefs about alcohol consumption. Additionally, this link between acculturation and liberal beliefs appears to hold across both immigrant groups and U.S.-born Mexican Americans (Cervantes, Gilbert, Salgado de Snyder, & Padilla, 1991; Gilbert, 1987a).

Trends in Acculturation, Drinking, and Alcohol-Related Problems and Beliefs

We conducted a series of trend analyses of data collected in 1984 and 1995 from cross-sectional, nationally representative samples of Hispanics in the United States. Details of these two surveys can be found in Caetano and Clark (1998a, 1998b). The surveys are probably the most comprehensive data set available to date that allows an exploration of the relationship between acculturation and alcohol and tobacco consumption. Both surveys used multistage random probability samples of U.S. Hispanics 18 years of age and older. Response rates were 72% for the 1984 survey and 77% for the 1995 survey. Because of the clustered sampling designs, all standard errors were corrected with the Software for Survey Data Analysis (SUDAAN) statistical package. Analyses were also conducted with data weighted to correct for probability of selection into the sample and nonresponse rates.

The measure used to assess acculturation in this project was originally developed for data analysis of the Hispanic population in 1984. Exploratory principal-components analysis of data collected using the 26 original questions included in the 1984 National Alcohol Survey yielded one major factor responsible for 30% of the variance. All items with factor loadings higher than .54 were selected to form the acculturation scale. With the exception of the items that assess language use, all other items are scaled with a Likert-type format, with endpoints ranging from *strongly agree* to *strongly disagree*. The final 12 items in the scale include issues such as ability to speak English and use of English with family, neighbors, and coworkers; relationship patterns with Hispanics and non-Hispanics; and preference for Hispanic media (e.g., books, television, radio).

The scale provides a unidimensional measure of acculturation. This type of measurement assumes acculturation is a continuum that reflects increasing adaptation to and adoption of an Anglo American culture in various areas of daily life. In this style of measurement, those at the bottom of the scale are considered low in acculturation (i.e., they maintain a strong connection with the culture of their original country). Those scoring in the middle of the scale are thought to have moderate ties to both cultures. For instance, they may state that about half of the people they meet socially are other Latinos, whereas individuals in the low part of the scale would state that all or nearly all of the people they meet socially are Latinos. Those in the middle may say that they watch Spanish television or listen to Latino music "about half the time," whereas those at the bottom of the scale may say that they do so "most or all the time."

In contrast to the unidimensional approach are the orthogonal measures, which assess adoption of Anglo American culture separately from maintenance of Latino culture. Unfortunately, there have been no assessments of the correlation between these two measures. In addition, researchers have yet to conduct studies comparing analysis of the association between acculturation and drinking with acculturation that is assessed alternatively by unidimensional and orthogonal measures in the same sample. It is therefore difficult to speculate about the impact of these different approaches on assessments of the relationship between acculturation and drinking.

For the analyses presented here, scores on the scale are divided into three groups representing low, medium, and high levels of acculturation. The cut-off points for these groups are based on data collected in the 1984 survey, forcing roughly one third of the respondents to fall into each group.

To measure alcohol consumption, we used a modified version of Cahalan, Roizen, and Room's (1976) Quantity Frequency Index. The questions concerning respondents' alcohol consumption that were used to create this index were identical in 1984 and 1995 and assessed drinking in the 12 months before the survey interview. Questions about the consumption of wine, beer, and liquor were asked separately. The respondent's frequency of drinking was coded into 11 categories ranging from *never* to *three or more times a day*. Quantity of consumption was assessed by asking for the number of drinking occasions in which the respondent drank five or six, three or four, and one or two glasses each of wine, beer, and liquor. This information on quantity and frequency of drinking wine, beer, and liquor was combined and used to classify respondents according to whether they drink five or more drinks of any beverage per occasion at least once a week, at least once a year, or never. Combining these categories with the frequency of drinking any alcoholic beverage provides the following categories:

- *Frequent heavy drinker:* Drinks once a week or more often and has five or more drinks at a sitting at least once a week or more often. (A drink is a 1-oz glass of liquor, a 4-oz glass of wine, or a 12-oz can of beer.)
- *Frequent drinker:* Drinks once a week or more often and may or may not drink five or more drinks at a sitting less than once a week but at least once a year.
- *Less frequent drinker:* Drinks 1 to 3 times a month and may or may not drink five or more drinks at least once a year.
- *Infrequent:* Drinks less than once a month but at least once a year and does not drink five or more drinks at a sitting.
- *Abstainer:* Drinks less than once a year or has never drunk.

In both surveys, respondents were presented with a comprehensive list of 29 social and dependence alcohol-related problems and asked to report whether they had experienced each of these problems in the 12 months before the interview. The items address 14 specific problem areas such as impaired control, withdrawal, binge drinking, belligerence, accidents, and work-, financial-, and health-related problems (Hilton, 1991). In addition, respondents were asked questions measuring situational norms and attitudes toward drinking and sociodemographic variables.

Trends in Drinking Patterns Among Hispanics Between 1984 and 1995

As shown in Table 11.1, the only common trend between 1984 and 1995 for both genders and almost all acculturation levels was an increase in rates of abstention. Other drinking patterns showed different trends across different acculturation levels. For example, among men, frequent heavy drinking decreased in the low acculturation group, increased in the medium acculturation group, and remained stable in the high group. Among women, rates of frequent heavy drinking were low, which is typical of women regardless of ethnicity (Caetano & Clark, 1998b).

Table 11.1. Trends in Alcohol Consumption Patterns by Acculturation: 1984 and 1995

| | Acculturation level (%): Men ||||||
| | Low || Medium || High ||
	1984 (188)	1995 (265)	1984 (219)	1995 (302)	1984 (198)	1995 (198)
Abstinence from drinking	27	42*	20	30*	21	34*
Infrequent drinking	10	11	19	11*	5	13*
Less frequent drinking	28	22	14	23*	23	17*
Frequent drinking	15	12	36	15*	32	18*
Frequent heavy drinking	20	13	11	22*	19	18

| | Acculturation level (%): Women ||||||
| | Low || Medium || High ||
	1984 (300)	1995 (307)	1984 (299)	1995 (327)	1984 (246)	1995 (183)
Abstinence from drinking	70	77	47	55*	32	31
Infrequent drinking	8	8	28	18*	32	18*
Less frequent drinking	18	8*	14	21*	15	25*
Frequent drinking	2	6	7	4	20	20
Frequent heavy drinking	1	1	5	2	2	6

Note. Ns shown in italic in parentheses.
*Tests of proportions comparing 1984 with 1995 within acculturation group were statistically significant at $p < .05$. All columns do not add up to 100 because of rounding.
Abstinence from drinking = drinks less than once a year or has never drunk; Infrequent drinking = drinks less than once a month but at least once a year and does not drink five or more drinks at a sitting; Less frequent drinking: drinks 1 to 3 times a month and may or may not drink five or more drinks at least once a year; Frequent drinking = drinks once a week or more often and may or may not drink five or more drinks at a sitting less than once a week but at least once a year; Frequent heavy drinking: drinks once a week or more often and has five or more drinks at a sitting at least once a week or more often.

A logistic regression analysis was conducted to examine the sociodemographic predictors of abstention vs. drinking at least one drink within the 12-month period before the interview. Results indicated that men were more likely than women to drink, college graduates were more likely to drink than those who had not graduated from high school, and Cubans and Cuban Americans were more likely to drink than Mexicans and Mexican Americans. Likewise, those who were interviewed in 1984 were more likely to drink than those who were interviewed in 1995. On the other hand, those who were age 60 years or older were less likely to drink than those who were ages 18 to 29 years, and homemakers were less likely to drink than those who were employed outside the home.

Another logistic regression analysis was conducted to assess the sociodemographic predictors of frequent heavy drinking. The results of this analysis indicated that being unemployed, male, and U.S. born were risk factors for frequent heavy drinking. In contrast, older age, being classified in the "other" employment category (a category consisting mostly of students and people with disabilities), and having a Puerto Rican or Cuban heritage decreased the risk of frequent heavy drinking.

Trends in Alcohol-Related Problems Among Hispanics Between 1984 and 1995

Problem prevalence has remained mostly stable for men in the low and high acculturation groups, but rates for several problem areas have increased for men in the medium acculturation group between 1984 and 1995 (see Table 11.2). Among women, problem prevalence has remained stable across all acculturation groups (see Table 11.2). A logistic regression analysis was conducted to examine the sociodemographic predictors of having one or more alcohol-related problems in the year before the survey. The results showed that being male, having been born in the United States, being classified in the medium acculturation group, and a weekly alcohol consumption of 10 drinks or more were factors of risk for problem development. Protective factors were older age, higher levels of education, being a homemaker, having been interviewed in 1984, and being Puerto Rican.

Trends in Situational Norms Regulating Drinking Among Hispanics Between 1984 and 1995

Most remarkably in the data shown in Table 11.3, men and women in the medium acculturation group became more liberal in their assessments of drinking norms in the 11-year time span. Greater proportions of medium-acculturation respondents in 1995 agreed that drinking was acceptable for a parent spending time with small children, for a woman out at a bar with friends, and for a couple of coworkers having lunch. Trends for norms among the highly acculturated individuals indicated signs of increased liberalism and increased conservatism. Trends among less acculturated men remained stable, whereas trends among less acculturated women were mixed, with increases in liberal and conservative norms.

A multiple regression analysis testing the associations between sociodemographic predictors and situational norms indicated that higher levels of income, being separated or divorced, being male, and having been born in the United States were positively related to more liberal situational norms in the drinking of alcoholic beverages. Older age, having been interviewed in 1984, being Puerto Rican, and being low or medium in acculturation were negatively related to liberal situational norms.

Trends in Attitudes Toward Drinking and Drunkenness Among Hispanics

Trends in attitudes toward drinking and drunkenness between 1984 and 1995 are shown in Table 11.4. During the 11-year time span, attitudes

Table 11.2. Trends in Alcohol-Related Problems by Acculturation Among Those With at Least One Problem: 1984 and 1995

| | Acculturation level (%): Men ||||||
| | Low || Medium || High ||
	1984 (188)	1995 (264)	1984 (194)	1995 (303)	1984 (198)	1995 (198)
Salience of drinking	9	7	4	17*	8	6
Impaired control	15	14	5	17*	7	9
Withdrawal symptoms	9	7	3	9	6	5
Relief drinking	1	0	1	3	2	1
Tolerance	2	1	2	2	3	3
Binge drinking	2	1	1	2	2	0
Belligerence	11	5*	3	16*	4	11*
Accidents	0	1	1	1	1	1
Health-related problems	8	8	5	7	5	3
Work-related problems	5	3	1	4	3	2
Financial problems	3	4	1	6	1	2
Problems with police	3	5	2	8*	3	3
Problems with spouse	7	11	9	21*	6	7
Problems with people other than spouse	8	9	4	10*	6	5

| | Acculturation level (%): Women ||||||
| | Low || Medium || High ||
	1984 (300)	1995 (307)	1984 (299)	1995 (327)	1984 (246)	1995 (183)
Salience of drinking	1	2	4	5	4	6
Impaired control	1	1	4	5	4	7
Withdrawal symptoms	1	2	2	3	1	6
Relief drinking	1	1	0	1	0	4
Tolerance	1	1	1	2	0	4
Binge drinking	0	0	0	0	0	0
Belligerence	1	0	5	4	4	6
Accidents	0	0	0	0	0	0
Health-related problems	2	2	3	4	4	5
Work-related problems	0	0	0	1	0	3
Financial problems	0	0	0	1	0	4
Problems with police	1	0	2	0	0	1
Problems with spouse	1	1	3	5	0	5
Problems with people other than spouse	1	3	3	4	5	4

Note. Ns shown in italic in parentheses.
*Tests of proportions comparing 1984 with 1995 within acculturation group were statistically significant at $p < .05$.

generally remained the same for all acculturation by gender groups except for males with medium acculturation. This group of men seemed to have become more polarized in their beliefs, conservatively and liberally. Of the 11 attitude items, the men with medium acculturation responded more

Table 11.3. Proportion Endorsing "Any Drinking" in Different Social Settings: 1984 and 1995

| | Acculturation level (%): Men ||||||
| | Low || Medium || High ||
	1984 (188)	1995 (265)	1984 (219)	1995 (302)	1984 (198)	1995 (198)
A parent spending time with small children	23	23	12	22*	25	13*
A husband having dinner out with his wife	58	61	66	74*	80	85
A man out at a bar with friends	74	81	81	87	85	91
A woman out at a bar with friends	46	55	56	65*	68	83*
At a party at someone else's home	81	79	80	87*	92	94
With a couple of coworkers out for lunch	11	22*	13	37*	26	26
With friends at home	74	66	79	80	87	84
With friends after work	43	41	56	60	75	65*
When driving a car	4	5	6	15*	16	14

| | Acculturation level (%): Women ||||||
| | Low || Medium || High ||
	1984 (300)	1995 (307)	1984 (299)	1995 (327)	1984 (246)	1995 (183)
A parent spending time with small children	19	12*	6	13*	7	7
A husband having dinner out with his wife	56	66*	68	68	83	84
A man out at a bar with friends	66	72	71	79*	94	90
A woman out at a bar with friends	34	44*	54	66*	81	83
At a party at someone else's home	69	74	75	77	91	88
With a couple of coworkers out for lunch	7	15*	11	24*	8	28*
With friends at home	54	57	65	70	84	78
With friends after work	30	27	47	42	70	48*
When driving a car	1	2	5	3	3	13*

Note. Ns shown in italic in parentheses.
*Tests of proportions comparing 1984 with 1995 within acculturation group were statistically significant at $p < .05$.

conservatively to the following three statements: "Having a drink is one of the pleasures of life," "Drinking brings out the worst in people," and "Having a drink is a way of being friendly." The men with medium acculturation also responded more liberally to the following three statements: "Getting drunk is an innocent way of having fun," "People would lose respect for a woman who spends any time in bars," and "People would lose respect for a man who spends any time in bars." Some other changes in

Table 11.4. Proportion Endorsing Attitudes Toward Drinking: 1984 and 1995

| | Acculturation level (%): Men ||||||
| | Low || Medium || High ||
	1984 (188)	1995 (265)	1984 (219)	1995 (302)	1984 (198)	1995 (198)
Nothing is good about drinking.	74	80	59	66	41	54*
Getting drunk is fun.	23	28	16	25*	45	24*
People would lose respect for a woman who spends any time in bars.	84	94*	85	75*	66	50*
People would lose respect for a man who spends any time in bars.	71	82*	71	58*	26	39
Drinkers have more fun.	21	23	17	17	7	7
Drinkers have more friends.	28	30	23	17	10	9
A party isn't really a party unless alcoholic beverages are served.	27	35	25	20	26	16*
Having a drink is one of the pleasures of life.	52	62*	51	39*	40	37
Drinking brings out the worst in people.	85	78	67	85*	73	66
Having a drink is a way of being friendly.	56	52	62	48*	50	49
It does some people good to get drunk once in a while.	24	27	19	25	18	24

| | Acculturation level (%): Women ||||||
| | Low || Medium || High ||
	1984 (300)	1995 (307)	1984 (299)	1995 (327)	1984 (246)	1995 (183)
Nothing is good about drinking.	88	87	81	80	53	68*
Getting drunk is fun.	14	14	9	14	6	16*
People would lose respect for a woman who spends any time in bars.	92	91	81	83	65	57
People would lose respect for a man who spends any time in bars.	88	83	64	58	41	36
Drinkers have more fun.	17	19	8	7	3	10
Drinkers have more friends.	25	25	15	11	12	14
A party isn't really a party unless alcoholic beverages are served.	19	16	13	8	11	14
Having a drink is one of the pleasures of life.	39	48*	22	19	26	32
Drinking brings out the worst in people.	82	86	88	91	94	77*
Having a drink is a way of being friendly.	39	38	35	23*	42	29*
It does some people good to get drunk once in a while.	12	17	9	15	12	16

Note. Ns shown in italic in parentheses.
*Tests of proportions comparing 1984 with 1995 within acculturation group were statistically significant at $p < .05$.

attitude trends were noted within the other acculturation-by-gender groups, but they were few and inconsistent.

In a multivariate regression analysis of sociodemographic predictors of attitudes toward drinking, being separated or divorced, never having been married, being male, and having been born in the United States were factors positively related to more liberal attitudes. Variables negatively related to liberal attitudes were ages 30 to 39 and 60 and older, being in the "other" employment category, and having a Puerto Rican heritage. Interestingly, there was a statistically significant level of acculturation by year of survey. This finding indicates that medium acculturation in 1984 was positively related to liberal attitudes as compared with high acculturation in 1995.

Acculturation, Alcohol Use, and Alcohol-Related Problems: Conclusions

Most of the extant research examines the relationship between acculturation and drinking, whereas fewer investigations address the association between acculturation and alcohol-related problems. Across the literature on acculturation and drinking, the most consistent findings show more liberal norms and attitudes and an increase in women's drinking. The consistency of findings regarding women's drinking can perhaps be explained by examining differences in drinking norms between those women living in the United States and those living in Latin America. As suggested by Caetano and Medina Mora (1988), norms regulating alcohol consumption by women in Latin American countries are strict, resulting in high rates of abstention among women. In contrast, norms regulating alcohol consumption in the United States are more liberal, likely leading to higher rates of drinking than in Latin America. The relationship between acculturation and drinking is not as dramatic for men because the norms regulating men's alcohol consumption are liberal, both in the United States and in Latin American countries. Thus, the acculturation of Hispanic men to United States drinking norms does not necessarily result in substantial changes in drinking behavior.

The pattern of results from our trends analyses are stronger for problems, norms, and attitudes than for drinking patterns. Overall, the most robust findings from the multivariate analyses show only a slight influence of acculturation on trends in drinking and frequent heavy drinking. The analysis of problems shows that members of the medium acculturation group are 2 times more likely than those in the high acculturation group to report an alcohol problem, regardless of year of survey and of other sociodemographic factors. Neff et al. (1987) reported similar results, and other data have shown individuals with medium acculturation to be most at risk for intimate partner violence (Caetano, Schafer, Clark, Cunradi, & Raspberry, 1998). It may be the case that men in the medium acculturation group (as measured in this study) have no strong ties to any one culture, which may result in more alcohol-related problems.

Acculturation and Cigarette Smoking

The findings on the relationship between acculturation and cigarette smoking are inconsistent. Some studies have suggested that higher levels of acculturation are linked to a greater likelihood of smoking, daily cigarette use, and smoking more cigarettes per day, particularly for women (Casas et al., 1998; Landrine, Richardson, Klonoff, & Flay, 1994; Lee & Markides, 1991; Marín, Marín, Otero-Sabogal, Sabogal, & Pérez-Stable, 1989; Moreno, Laniado-Laborin, & Sallis, 1994; Palinkas et al., 1993; Ramirez & Gallion, 1993; Smith & McGraw, 1993; Vega, Gil, & Zimmerman, 1993; Williams, Binkin, & Clingman, 1986). Other results have shown no relationship between acculturation and smoking, especially when the effects of education and income are controlled (Haynes, Harvey, & Montes, 1990; Lovato et al., 1994; Markides, Coreil, & Ray, 1987). Research on the association between acculturation and attitudes toward cigarette smoking has shown that those who are less acculturated are less likely to see the difficulties associated with quitting smoking (Campbell & Kaplan, 1997; Carvajal et al., 1997; Marín, Pérez-Stable, Marín, Sabogal, & Otero-Sabogal, 1990). The inconsistency in findings in this literature comes from comparisons of results that do and do not control important confounding variables (e.g., education, income). When studies control potentially confounding variables, the results reveal no relationship between acculturation and smoking.

Acculturation and Drug Use

In terms of drugs other than alcohol and tobacco, the number of studies assessing the direct relationship between acculturation and substance use is quite sparse. In one study, acculturation was positively associated with inhalant and PCP [1-(phencyclohexyl)piperidine HCl] use among a sample of children and adolescents in Los Angeles (Peréz, Padilla, Ramirez, Ramirez, & Rodriguez, 1980). Using data collected from the Hispanic Health and Nutrition Examination Survey (HHANES), a large-scale survey of Hispanics residing in the Southwestern United States, the Northeastern United States, and Dade County, Florida, researchers found that acculturation was positively related to marijuana and cocaine use in the previous year, even when the effects of sociodemographic variables were controlled (Amaro, Whitaker, Coffman, & Heeren, 1990). On the other hand, in a clinical sample of Mexican American youth who were referred by the courts to a drug abuse prevention program in Austin, Texas, there was no relationship between acculturation and substance use (Barrett, Joe, & Simpson, 1991).

Recently, Felix-Ortiz and Newcomb (1995) have analyzed, in a fairly sophisticated study, the influence of acculturation on drug use. The study incorporated multiple indexes of acculturation and cultural identity (e.g., language proficiency and preference, familiarity with Latino and U.S. culture) and a newly developed construct, defensive Latino activism. *Defen-*

sive Latino activism was defined as a multifaceted construct assessing activism emerging principally out of feelings of hostility or a need for revenge. Felix-Ortiz and Newcomb proposed that this type of activism is found among some Latinos who perceive discrimination, withdraw from mainstream European American and Latino cultures, and adopt anti-White attitudes. Using structural equation modeling techniques, they found that for males, use of multiple drugs was predicted by greater English proficiency, less familiarity with Latino culture, and more defensive Latino activism. Among females, alcohol use was related to low Spanish proficiency, high English proficiency, and lack of Spanish language preference, whereas inhalant use was predicted by greater defensive Latino activism for females.

It seems, therefore, that some evidence has suggested that highly acculturated Hispanics living in the United States, particularly females, are at risk for various forms of substance use. In general, this pattern of consumption may be a result of women having to struggle with the acculturation process more than men, particularly when women have the opportunity to take on new roles that may conflict with their traditional heritage (Berry, 1997). In addition, because drug use is relatively uncommon among women in Latin American countries, as women acculturate and adapt to the United States, increased opportunities for and more relaxed attitudes toward drug use develop.

A View of the Future

The inconsistency in acculturation effects among consumption of alcohol, cigarette smoking, and drug use examined in this chapter reflects the real-life complexity of the effect of acculturation on human behavior. For instance, acculturation would not be expected to have a constant and linear effect throughout immigrants' lifetimes in the host country. Individuals go through different developmental stages during their lives, each of which is subject to different psychological and societal expectations. Younger men in the United States typically drink more than older men, thus the effect of acculturation on drinking is likely to differ depending on immigrants' developmental stage on arrival in the host country. Younger immigrant men are more likely to acculturate to norms that are more permissive than older immigrant men. Additionally, younger immigrants may also acculturate more easily and rapidly than older immigrants, who may be more attached to the attitudes and norms of their native country.

Geographical inconsistencies in acculturation should also be expected. In a large country such as the United States, immigrants settle in different locations that have different drinking norms and cultural values, providing different pathways to acculturation. For instance, comparisons of drinking patterns and attitudes toward drinking of Mexican Americans in Texas and Mexican Americans in California showed differences that are consistent with the general cultural and traditional views of drinking in these two states (Caetano, 1989). This finding suggests that Mexican immigrants in Texas are acculturating to a different host culture than the Mexican immigrants in California.

Other sociodemographic characteristics of immigrants may also trigger a different acculturation pattern. For instance, there are many differences across income and education groups in alcohol use and norms regulating alcohol consumption. Hispanics in the higher educational strata and those with "professional" occupations (particularly women) have more social opportunities to drink than other Hispanics (Gilbert, 1987b). Thus, immigrants who are in these upper strata of education and income are bound to find Hispanic and Anglo reference social groups that are different from those found by immigrants in lower income and education categories. Different reference social groups probably also leads to different acculturation patterns.

Changes in the country of origin over time also affects the process of acculturation of immigrant groups. Kitano, Chi, Law, Lubben, and Rhee (1988) suggested that acculturation research is somewhat flawed because it has traditionally assumed that behaviors in the immigrant's country of origin remain static over time and that the process of acculturation has a fixed base and always follows the same direction. For instance, acculturation researchers have assumed that young immigrant women of Hispanic or Asian origin always begin to drink more as they acculturate to U.S. norms. However, anecdotal information shows that norms and attitudes regulating alcohol and cigarette smoking by women in Latin American and Asian countries are becoming more liberal. If these norms and attitudes are shifting, one would expect the effect of acculturation on immigrant women's drinking and smoking to disappear over time as U.S. norms and attitudes become more similar to norms in other countries.

Overall, the literature on the relationship between acculturation and substance use, including our most recent findings described in this chapter, suggests that acculturation is a complex, multidimensional process. The acculturation process contains behavioral and cognitive components and depends not only on generational status and the amount of time spent in the United States but also on culture of origin, education, occupation, age, gender, marital status, knowledge of English, reasons for immigration, and culture of the host country. Clearly, the process of acculturation is not identical for all immigrants and does not affect all areas of life equally and within the same time frame. Such findings force researchers and clinicians to consider curvilinear relationships between acculturation level and any outcome variables they choose to examine. Additionally, future research must be directed toward understanding those individuals who could be classified as being in the middle of acculturative dimensions and to developing appropriate prevention interventions for them.

References

Amaro, H., Whitaker, R., Coffman, G., & Heeren, T. (1990). Acculturation and marijuana and cocaine use: Findings from HHANES, 1982–1984. *American Journal of Public Health, 80*(Suppl.), 54–60.

Barrett, M. E., Joe, G. W., & Simpson, D. D. (1991). Acculturation influences on inhalant use. *Hispanic Journal of Behavioral Sciences, 13*, 276–296.

Berry, J. W. (1997). Immigration, acculturation, and adaptation. *Applied Psychology, 46*, 5–68.

Black, S., & Markides, K. S. (1993). Acculturation and alcohol consumption in Puerto Rican, Cuban-American, and Mexican-American women in the United States. *American Journal of Public Health, 83*, 890–893.

Burnam, M. A., Hough, R. L., & Escobar, J. (1987). Six-month prevalence of specific psychiatric disorders among Mexican Americans and non-Hispanic Whites in Los Angeles. *Archives of General Psychiatry, 44*, 687–694.

Caetano, R. (1987a). Acculturation and drinking patterns among U.S. Hispanics. *British Journal of Addiction, 82*, 789–799.

Caetano, R. (1987b). Acculturation, drinking and social settings among U.S. Hispanics. *Drug and Alcohol Dependence, 19*, 215–226.

Caetano, R. (1987c). Drinking and family drinking, attitudes and problems among U.S. Hispanic women. *Alcohol, Health and Research World, 11*(2), 26–55.

Caetano, R. (1989). Differences in alcohol use between Mexican Americans in Texas and California. *Hispanic Journal of Behavioral Sciences, 11*, 58–69.

Caetano, R., & Clark, C. L. (1998a). Trends in alcohol-related problems among Whites, Blacks, and Hispanics: 1984–1995. *Alcoholism, Clinical and Experimental Research, 22*, 534–538.

Caetano, R., & Clark, C. L. (1998b). Trends in drinking patterns among Whites, Blacks and Hispanics: 1984–1995. *Journal of Studies on Alcohol, 59*, 659–668.

Caetano, R., & Medina Mora, M. E. (1988). Acculturation and drinking among people of Mexican descent in Mexico and the United States. *Journal of Studies on Alcohol, 49*, 462–471.

Caetano, R., & Medina Mora, M. E. (1990). Reasons and attitudes toward drinking and abstaining: A comparison of Mexicans and Mexican-Americans. *Epidemiologic trends in drug abuse: Community epidemiology work group proceedings* (pp. 173–191). Rockville, MD: National Institute of Drug Abuse.

Caetano, R., Schafer, J., Clark, C. L., Cunradi, C., & Raspberry, K. (1998). *Intimate Partner Violence, Acculturation, and Alcohol Consumption among Hispanic Couples in the U.S.* Unpublished paper, Public Health Institute, Berkeley, CA.

Cahalan, D., Roizen, R., & Room, R. (1976). Alcohol problems and their prevention: Public attitudes in California. In R. Room & S. Sheffield (Eds.), *The prevention of alcohol problems: Report of a conference* (pp. 354–403). Sacramento: California State Office of Alcoholism.

Campbell, K. M., & Kaplan, C. P. (1997). Relationship between language orientation and cigarette-smoking beliefs of Latinas. *American Journal of Health Behavior, 21*, 12–20.

Carvajal, S. C., Photiades, J. R., Evans, R. I., & Nash, S. G. (1997). Relating a social influence model to the role of acculturation in substance use among Latino adolescents. *Journal of Applied Social Psychology, 27*, 1617–1628.

Casas, J. M., Bimbela, A., Corral, C. V., Yanez, I., Swaim, R. C., Wayman, J. C., & Bates, S. (1998). Cigarette and smokeless tobacco use among migrant and nonmigrant Mexican American youth. *Hispanic Journal of Behavioral Sciences, 20*, 102–121.

Cervantes, R. C., Gilbert, M. J., Salgado de Snyder, N., & Padilla, A. M. (1991). Psychosocial and cognitive correlates of alcohol use in younger adult immigrant and U.S.-born Hispanics. *International Journal of the Addictions, 25*(5A & 6A), 687–708.

Chavez, L. R., Cornelius, W. A., & Jones, O. W. (1985). Mexican immigrants and the utilization of US health services: The case of San Diego. *Social Science and Medicine, 21*, 93–102.

Chesney, A. P., Chavira, J. A., Hall, R. P., & Gary, H. E. (1982). Barriers to medical care of Mexican Americans: The role of social class, acculturation, and social isolation. *Medical Care, 20*, 883–891.

Deosaransingh, K., Moreno, C., Woodruff, S. I., Sallis, J. F., Vargas, R., & Elder, J. P. (1995). Acculturation and smoking in Latino youth. *Health Values, 19*, 49–52.

Estrada, A. L., Treviño, F. M., & Ray, L. A. (1990). Health care utilization barriers among

Mexican Americans: Evidence from HHANES 1982–1984. *American Journal of Public Health, 80*(Suppl.), 27–31.

Felix-Ortiz, M., & Newcomb, M. D. (1995). Cultural identity and drug use among Latino and Latina adolescents. In G. J. Botvin, S. Schinke, & M. A. Orlandi (Eds.), *Drug abuse prevention with multiethnic youth* (pp. 147–165). Thousand Oaks, CA: Sage.

Gilbert, M. J. (1987a). Alcohol consumption patterns in immigrant and later generation Mexican American women. *Hispanic Journal of Behavioral Sciences, 9*, 299–313.

Gilbert, M. J. (1987b). *Lifestyle integration of alcohol consumption: Mexican American and Anglo American couples in a southern California community.* Paper presented at the 1987 annual meeting of the American Psychological Association, New York.

Graves, D. T. (1967). Acculturation, access, and alcohol in a tri-ethnic community. *American Anthropologist, 69*, 306–321.

Haynes, S., Harvey, C., & Montes, H. (1990). Patterns of smoking among Hispanics. *American Journal of Public Health, 80*, 47–53.

Hilton, M. E. (1991). A note on measuring drinking problems in the 1984 national alcohol survey. In W. B. Clark & M. Hilton (Eds.), *Alcohol in America: Drinking practices and problems* (pp. 51–70). Albany: State University of New York Press.

Kitano, H. H. L., Chi, I., Law, C. K., Lubben, L., & Rhee, S. (1988). Alcohol consumption of Japanese in Japan, Hawaii and California. In L. H. Towle & T. C. Harford (Eds.), *Cultural influences and drinking patterns: A focus on Hispanic and Japanese populations* (NIAAA, USDHHS, ADAMHA, Research Monograph No. 19, DHHS Pub. No. ADM 88-1563; pp. 99–133). Washington, DC: U.S. Government Printing Office.

Landrine, H., Richardson, J. L., Klonoff, E. A., & Flay, B. (1994). Cultural diversity in the predictors of adolescent smoking: The relative influence of peers. *Journal of Behavioral Medicine, 17*, 331–345.

Lee, D. J., & Markides, K. S. (1991). Health behaviors, risk factors, and health indicators associated with cigarette use in Mexican Americans: Results from HHANES. *American Journal of Public Health, 81*, 859–864.

Lovato, C. Y., Litrownik, A. J., Elder, J., Nunez-Liriano, A., Suarez, D., & Talavera, G. A. (1994). Cigarette and alcohol use among migrant Hispanic adolescents. *Family and Community Health, 16*, 18–31.

Marín, B. V., Pérez-Stable, E. J., Marín, G., Sabogal, F., & Otero-Sabogal, R. (1990). Attitudes and behaviors of Hispanic smokers: Implications for cessation interventions. *Health Education Quarterly, 17*, 287–297.

Marín, G., Marín, B., Otero-Sabogal, R., Sabogal, F., & Pérez-Stable, E. (1989). The role of acculturation in the attitudes, norms, and expectancies of Hispanic smokers. *Journal of Cross-Cultural Psychology, 20*, 399–415.

Marín, G., Posner, S. F., & Kinyon, J. B. (1993). Alcohol expectancies among Hispanics and nonhispanic whites: Role of drinking status and acculturation. *Hispanic Journal of Behavioral Sciences, 15*, 373–381.

Markides, K., Coreil, J., & Ray, L. A. (1987). Smoking among Mexican-Americans: A three-generation study. *American Journal of Public Health, 77*, 708–711.

Markides, K., Krause, N., & Mendes de Leon, C. F. (1988). Acculturation and alcohol consumption among Mexican Americans. *American Journal of Public Health, 78*, 1178–1181.

Markides, K., Ray, L. A., Stroup-Benham, C. A., & Treviño, F. (1990). Acculturation and alcohol consumption in the Mexican American population of the southwestern United States: Findings from HHANES, 1982–1984. *American Journal of Public Health, 80*(Suppl.), 42–46.

Moreno, C., Laniado-Laborin, R., & Sallis, J. F. (1994). Parental influences to smoke in Latino youth. *Preventive Medicine, 23*, 48–53.

Neff, J. A., Hoppe, S. K., & Perea, P. (1987). Acculturation and alcohol use: Drinking patterns and problems among Anglo and Mexican American male drinkers. *Hispanic Journal of Behavioral Science, 9*, 151–181.

Neff, R. K., Prihoda, T. J., & Hoppe, S. K. (1991). "Machismo," self-esteem, education and high maximum drinking among Anglo, Black and Mexican-American male drinkers. *Journal of Studies on Alcohol, 52*, 458–463.

Padilla, E. R., Padilla, A. M., Ramirez, R., Morales, A., & Olmedo, S. (1977). Inhalant, *marijuana and alcohol use among barrio children and adolescents.* Unpublished paper, University of California, Los Angeles.

Palinkas, L. A., Pierce, J., Rosbrook, B. P., Pickwell, S., Johnson, M., & Bal, D. G. (1993). Cigarette smoking behavior and beliefs of Hispanics in California. *American Journal of Preventive Medicine, 9,* 331–337.

Peréz, R., Padilla, A. M., Ramirez, A., Ramirez, R., & Rodriguez, M. (1980). Correlates and changes over time in drug and alcohol use with a Barrio population. *American Journal of Community Psychology, 8,* 621–636.

Polednak, A. P. (1997). Gender and acculturation in relation to alcohol use among Hispanic (Latino) adults in two areas of the Northeastern United States. *Substance Use and Misuse, 32,* 1513–1524.

Ramirez, A. G., & Gallion, K. J. (1993). Nicotine dependence among Blacks and Hispanics. In C. Orleans & J. Slade (Eds.), *Nicotine addiction: Principles and management* (pp. 350–364). New York: Oxford University Press.

Smith, K. W., & McGraw, S. A. (1993). Smoking behavior of Puerto Rican women: Evidence from caretakers of adolescents in two urban areas. *Hispanic Journal of Behavioral Sciences, 15,* 140–149.

Snowden, L. R., & Hines, A. M. (1998). *A scale to assess African American acculturation.* Unpublished manuscript, University of California, Berkeley.

Vega, W. A., & Amaro, H. (1994). Latino outlook: Good health, uncertain prognosis. *Annual Review of Public Health, 15,* 39–67.

Vega, W. A., Gil, A. G., & Zimmerman, R. S. (1993). Patterns of drug use among Cuban American, African American, and White non-Hispanic boys. *American Journal of Public Health, 83,* 257–259.

Williams, R. L., Binkin, N. J., & Clingman, E. J. (1986). Pregnancy outcomes among Spanish-surname women in California. *American Journal of Public Health, 76,* 387–391.

Author Index

Numbers in italics refer to listings in the reference sections.

Abe, J., 146, *158*
Aber, J. L., 207, *221*
Abramson, I., *119*
Acton, K. J., 165, *181*
Adler, N. E., 177, *182*
Agbayani, A., 190, *205*
Agbayani-Siewert, P., 192, *205*
Aguilar-Gaxiola, S., *160*
Ahmeduzzaman, M., 109, *117*
Ahuna, C., 47, *59,* 65, *81*
Akutsu, P. D., 104, *114*
Alden, L., 22, 29, *37*
Alderete, E., *160*
Alegría, M., 156, 157, *160,* 210, *222*
Alexander, J. F., 121, 123, *133*
Alipuria, L., 66, 67, *80*
Allen, L., 207, *221*
Allen, R., 88, *92*
Allen, W. R., 98, *118*
Alvirez, D., 86, *91,* 104, *113*
Amaro, H., 109, *114, 119,* 223, 234, *236, 239*
American Cancer Society, 169, *182*
American Heart Association, 167, *182*
American Psychiatric Association, 140, *158*
Amero, H., 107
Anderson, J., 48, *57*
Anderson, N. B., 168, 177, 178, *182, 185*
Angel, R., 152, *158*
Angold, A., 99, *114*
Annis, R. C., 7, 12, 140, *158*
Apospori, E., 122, *135*
Arakaki, M., 49, *59*
Aranalde, M., 85, *93,* 153, *160*
Arbona, C., 69, 73, *78,* 107, *119*
Arce, C., 105, *117*
Arnold, B., 22, *36,* 42, *58,* 65, *79,* 83, 85, *91*
Askenasy, A. R., 143, *159*
Atkins, C., *119*
Atkinson, D., 39, 43, 47, 51, 56, *57, 58,* 73, 77, *78,* 139, *159*
Attneave, C., 77, *78*
Atwell, I., 144, *158*
Avery, B., 177, *183*
Aycan, Z., 33, *34*
Azelton, L. S., xviii, *xxi*
Azibo, D. A., 144, *158*

Bal, D. G., *239*
Balcazar, H., 170, *182*
Balka, E. B., 107, *114*

Balls Organista, P., xxvi, *xxvi*
Bankston, C., 71, *78*
Barnouw, V., 84, *91*
Barrett, M. E., 104, 107, *114,* 234, *237*
Baskin, D., 106, *118,* 122, *135*
Bates, S., *237*
Baxter, J., *183*
Beals, J., 99, *115*
Bean, F. D., 86, *91,* 104, *113*
Beauvais, F., 63, *80,* 99, *117, 118*
Beck, A. T., 148, *158*
Beiser, M., 17, 33, *35,* 190, *205*
Bell, R., 89, *92*
Bellow, S., 8, *12*
Belsky, J., 101, 111, *116, 183*
Bernal, M. E., 105, *116*
Berry, J., xxiii, xxiv, xxv, *xxvi,* 7, *11, 12,* 17, 21, 22, 24, 25, 26, 27, 28, 29, 30, 31, 33, 34, *34, 35, 36, 37,* 39, 40, 42, 49, *58,* 63, 64, 66, 74, 75, 79, 90, *91,* 123, *133,* 139, 140, 144, 147, *158, 161,* 169, *182,* 207, *221,* 235, *237*
Berryhill-Paapke, E., 139, *158*
Betancourt, H., 54, *58,* 86, *93,* 104, *118*
Bhavnagri, N., 101, *117*
Bimbela, A., *237*
Binkin, N. J., 234, *239*
Birba, L., *92*
Bird, H. R., *158, 160*
Birman, D., 21, *35,* 85, 91, *91,* 105, 108, *114,* 207, *221*
Birz, S., 7, *12*
Black, L., 96, *114*
Black, S., 224, *237*
Boehnlein, J., 102, *114*
Bogardus, C., 171, *182*
Bollini, P., *159*
Bolton, B., 141, *159*
Botwin, G. J., 175, *182*
Bourhis, R., 25, 26, 27, 30, *35, 36*
Bova, C. A., 50, *59*
Boyce, T., *182*
Boyd, J. H., 151, *159*
Boyd-Franklin, N., 96, 97, *115,* 124, 125, *134*
Bravo, M., 121, *134, 158, 160*
Bray, J. H., *134*
Brickman, A., *135*
Bronfenbrenner, U., 70, *79,* 111, *114*
Brook, J. S., 107, 108, *114,* 129, *134,* 219, *222*

Brooks, A. J., 104, 107, *114*
Brown, D., 192, *205*
Bujaki, M., 21, *35,* 75, *79*
Bulcroft, K., 98, *114*
Bulcroft, R., 98, *114*
Buriel, R., 66, 67, 68, *79,* 87, *92,* 105, 106, 107, 108, *114, 118*
Burlew, A. K., 8, *12*
Burnam, M. A., 153, *158, 159, 160,* 224, *237*
Burnett, W. S., 170, *185*
Burns, B. J., 99, *114*
Burzette, R. G., xviii, *xxi*
Busch-Rossnagel, N. A., 107, 108, *115, 117*

Caetano, R., 175, *183,* 224, 225, 227, 233, 235, *237*
Cahalan, D., 226, *237*
Cairns, V., 146, *158*
Callies, A., 145, *160*
Cameron, J., 25, *36,* 69, *79*
Camilleri, C., 27, 28, *36*
Campbell, K. M., 234, *237*
Candelaria, J., *182*
Canino, G. J., 121, *134,* 152, *158, 160*
Canino, I. A., 152, *158*
Caraveo-Anduaga, J., *160*
Cardoza, D., 67, *79*
Carlos, M. L., 104, *116*
Carmody, D., 98, *114*
Carter, J. S., 169, 170, 171, 172, *182*
Carvajal, S. C., 223, 234, *237*
Casas, J. M., 234, *237*
Case, H. L., 175, *183*
Caspi-Yavin, Y., *159*
Castaneda, A., 106, *117*
Castro, F. G., 170, *182, 183*
Catalano, R., *160*
Centers for Disease Control and Prevention, 170, 174, 175, *182*
Cervantes, R. C., 225, *237*
Champion, J. D., 109, *114*
Chan, S., *159*
Chance, N. A., 7, *12*
Chang, B., 86, *93,* 104, *118*
Chatters, L., 98, *118,* 193, *205*
Chavez, G., 173, *182*
Chavez, J. M., 106, 107, *114*
Chavez, L. R., 223, *237*
Chavez, N., *12*
Chavira, J. A., 223, *237*
Chavira, V., 31, *37*
Chen, M. S., Jr., *57*
Chesney, A. P., 223, *237*
Chesney, M. A., *182*
Cheung, P., 147, *158*
Chi, I., 193, *205,* 236, *238*

Chiarella, M., 63, *80*
Chiu, L. H., 101, *114*
Choney, S. K., 139, 140, 141, *158*
Chou, E., 63, 74, *80*
Chun, C., 56, *59, 160, 206*
Chun, K., xxvi, *xxvi,* 104, *114,* 146, 149, *158*
Chung, R. C., *206*
Clark, C. L., 225, 227, 233, *237*
Clark, M., 22, *36*
Clark, R., 177, *182*
Clark, V., 177, *182*
Clarke, G., 146, 147, *158*
Clifford, E., 97, *114*
Clingman, E. J., 234, *239*
Coatsworth, J. D., *135*
Coe, K., 170, *183*
Coffman, G., 107, *114,* 234, *236*
Cohen, J., *183, 184*
Cohen, P., 129, *134,* 219, *222*
Cohen, R., 104, *114*
Cohen, S., 143, *158, 182*
Coleman, H., 74, *80*
Coleman, H. L. K., 10, *12,* 207, *222*
Collins, C., 177, *185*
Collins, J. W., 172, *182*
Collins, L. M., *92*
Collins, N., 165, *185*
Connell, J. P., 97, *114*
Contreras, J. M., 105, *114*
Cooney, R., 65, *81,* 104, *117,* 124, *134*
Coreil, J., 234, *238*
Corin, E., 102, *117*
Cornelius, W. A., 223, *237*
Corral, C. V., *237*
Cortés, D. E., 104, 105, *114,* 139, *160,* 164, *184,* 207, 208, 212, 214, 220, *221, 222*
Costello, E. J., 99, *114*
Cota, M. K., 105, *116*
Cousins, J. H., 46, *59,* 106, *114*
Covi, L., 143, *159*
Cowen, E. L., 97, *116*
Crawford, M. E., 192, *205*
Crichlow, W., 97, *114*
Cromwell, S. L., *116*
Cronbach, L., 111, *114,* 122, *134*
Cross, W., 73, 74, 75, 77, *79*
Croughan, J. L., 151, *160*
Crouter, A., 70, *79*
Cuellar, I., 22, *36,* 42, 45, 49, 50, 52, *58,* 65, 70, 71, 72, *79,* 83, 85, *91,* 153, *158,* 207, *221*
Culberston, F. M., 209, 219, *221*
Cunradi, C., 233, *237*

Dakof, G. A., 121, *135*
Damon, W., 75, *79*

AUTHOR INDEX

Dana, R. H., 141, *159*, 207, *221*
Dasen, P. R., 17, *35, 37,* 64, *79*
David, R. J., 172, *182*
de Ardon, E. T., *116*
Delaney, H. D., 41, 46, *58*
De Leon, B., 109, *114–115*
de los Angeles, 41, *59*
Del Valle, M., 109, *115*
Demetriou, A., 89, *92*
de Moor, C., *182*
Denner, J., 207, *221*
Deosaransingh, K., 223, *237*
Derogatis, L. R., 143, 145, 146, *158, 159,* 196, *205,* 213, *221*
Devich-Navarro, M., 67, 74, *80,* 207, *222*
Deyo, R. A., 99, *115*
Diaz, T., 175, *182*
Diaz-Guerrero, R., 32, *36*
Dick, R. W., 99, *115*
Dievler, A., 165, *183*
Dimas, J. M., 107, *115*
Dinh, T., *206*
Dion, K., 88, *93*
Dishion, T. J., 121, *134*
Dohrenwend, B. P., 143, *159,* 219, *222*
Dohrenwend, B. S., 143, *159*
Dona, G., 27, 29, *36*
Douglas, K., *206*
Drapeau, A., 102, *117*
Dumka, L. E., 106, *115*
Dunkel-Schetter, C., 165, *185*
Durkheim, E., 193, *205*
Dusenbury, L., 175, *182*
Dwyer, J. H., 173, *184*
Dyer, S., 100, *119*

Edgerton, R., 87, 88, *91,* 104, *115, 116*
Edwards, R. W., 99, *117, 118*
Efklides, A., 89, *92*
Ehsleman, S., *205*
Eifler, C. W., 171, *183*
Eitzen, D., 4, *12*
Elder, J. P., 169, *182, 237, 238*
Endler, N., 32, *36*
English, P., 165, 173, 174, *182*
Enomoto, K., 56, *59*
Epstein, J. A., 175, *182*
Erikson, E., 73, 74, *79*
Erkanli, A., 99, *114*
Escobar, J., 5, *12,* 152, 153, *158, 159,* 224, *237*
Eshleman, S., *159*
Eskenazi, B., 165, *182*
Espin, O. M., 109, *115*
Espino, D. V., 168, *182*
Estrada, A. L., 223, *237*
Evans, R. I., 223, *237*

Fabrega, H., Jr., 140, *159*
Fagan, J., 106, *118,* 122, *135*
Fairchild, D. G., 99, *115*
Fairchild, M. W., 99, *115*
Falloon, L., 192, *205*
Faraci, A. M., *135*
Farmer, E. M., 99, *114*
Feagin, J. R., 8, *12*
Feinleib, M., *184*
Feldman, S., 69, *81,* 89, *91,* 102, 103, *117*
Felix-Ortiz, M., 65, 76, 77, *79,* 234, *238*
Ferdman, B., 74, *79*
Ferguson, D., 75, *80*
Fernandez, D., 22, *37*
Fernandez, T., 22, *37,* 41, *59*
Fhagen-Smith, P., 73, 74, *79*
Fingerhut, L. A., 172, *183*
Fisher, C. B., 108, *115*
Fisher, R., 4, *12*
Flaherty, J., 7, *12*
Flannery, D. J., 106, *115*
Flay, B., 234, *238*
Florack, A., 27, *37*
Flores, C., 69, *78*
Flores, J., 64, 70, *80*
Florsheim, P., 97, *115*
Folkman, S., 31, *36,* 143, *159, 182*
Follette, W. C., 127, *134*
Foote, F. H., *135*
Ford, K., 50, *59*
Fracasso, M. P., 108, *115*
Franco, J. N., 46, *58*
Freeman, D., *160*
Fridrich, A. H., 106, *115*
Friedman, G. D., 190, *205*
Friis, R., 168, 172, *184*
Fu, V., 100, 101, *116*
Fujimoto, W. Y., 171, *182*
Fuligni, A. J., 105, 108, *115*
Fulton, D. L., *183*
Furnham, A., 148, 149, *159*

Gaines, S., Jr., 76, *79*
Gallegos, P., 74, *79*
Gallion, K. J., 234, *239*
Gamba, R. J., 41, 42, 50, 52, *58*
Garcia, M., 22, *36*
Gary, H. E., 223, *237*
Gary, L., 193, *205*
Garza, C. A., 105, *116*
Gaviria, M., 7, *12*
Gayle, H., 165, *183*
Geronimus, A. T., 172, *182*
Gerton, J., 10, *12,* 74, *80,* 207, *222*
Ghuman, P. A. S., 22, *36*
Giachello, A. L., 210, *221*
Gil, A. G., 107, 108, *115,* 122, *135,* 234, *239*

Gilbert, M. J., 224, 225, 236, *237, 238*
Gim, R., 39, 47, *57, 58,* 139, *159*
Ginorio, A. B., 109, *115*
Giordano, T., 121, *134*
Glazer, N., 104, *115*
Goff, B., 146, *158*
Goffman, E., 55, 56, *58*
Goldfine, I. D., 171, *185*
Gollan, J., 127, *134*
Gomez, A., 175, *183*
Gomez, C. A., 175, *185*
Gomez-Mont, F., 141, *160*
Gonzales, N. A., 104, 106, 108, *118*
Gonzales-Huss, M. J., 175, *183*
Gonzalez, G., 83, 85, *91*
Good, B., 207, *222*
Good, M. D., 207, *222*
Gordon, M., 6, *12,* 76, *79*
Gorham, D. R., 146, *160*
Gorman, B. K., 197, *205*
Gorman-Smith, D., 97, *115*
Gould, J., 165, *182*
Gowan, M., 109, *115*
Granovetter, M. S., 192, *205*
Grant, D., 103, *116*
Graves, D. T., 223, *238*
Graves, K. L., 175, *183*
Graves, T., 19, *36*
Grebler, L., 88, *91,* 109, *115*
Green, V., 109, *116*
Gregorich, S. E., 175, *185*
Griffith, J., 87, *91,* 105, *115*
Grossman, D. C., 99, *115*
Guarnaccia, P. J., 121, *134,* 152, *158*
Guendelman, S., 165, *182*
Guendelman, S. S., 165, 173, 178, *182*
Gurin, P., 76, *79*
Gursen, M. D., 107, *114*
Gurung, R., 75, *79*
Guthrie, R., 57
Guzman, R. C., 88, *91,* 109, *115*

Habenicht, M., *159*
Habenstein, R. W., 86, *92*
Hacker, A., 77, *79*
Haffner, S. M., 171, *183, 184*
Hall, R. P., 223, *237*
Hallowell, A. I., 17, *36*
Halpern-Felsher, B. L., 97, *114*
Hamman, R. F., *183*
Handal, P., 192, *205*
Hanson, M. J., 57, *58*
Harjo, S. S., 99, *115*
Harmon, M. P., 170, *183*
Harris, B. R., *183*
Harris, L. C., 45, *58,* 153, *158*
Hart, D., 75, *79*

Harvey, C., 234, *238*
Hauff, E., 146, 147, *159*
Haynes, S., 234, *238*
Hazuda, H. P., 168, 171, *183, 184*
Hecht, M., 66, *80*
Heeren, T., 107, *114,* 234, *236*
Helms, J., 8, 9, *12,* 73, *79*
Helzer, J. E., 151, *160*
Her, C., 145, *161*
Heras, P., 102, *115*
Herman, A. A., 177, *183*
Hernandez, R., 108, *118,* 131, *135*
Herskovits, M., xxiii, *xxvi*i, 6, *12,* 18, *37,* 84, *92*
Hervis, O., *118, 135*
Hervis, O. E., *135*
Higginbotham, J. C., 157, *159*
Hilton, M. E., 227, *238*
Hines, A. M., 51, *59,* 139, 142, 143, *160,* 175, 176, *183,* 223, *239*
Hines, P. M., 96, 97, *115,* 124, *134*
Hisserich, J. C., *92*
Ho, C., 103, *115*
Ho, D. Y., 55, *58*
Ho, E., 30, *36*
Hoelker, P., 27, *37*
Hoffman, T., 141, *159*
Hofstede, G., 83, *91,* 128, *134*
Hogue, C. J. R., 172, *184*
Holmes-Eber, P., 192, *205*
Holtzworth-Munroe, A., 121, *133*
Hoppe, S. K., 224, *238*
Horenczyk, G., 74, *81*
Horvath, A. O., 57, *58*
Hough, R. L., 153, *158, 159,* 224, *237*
Houseworth, S. J., 178, *182*
Hovey, J. D., 123, *134*
Hrynevich, C., 76, *81*
Hsu, F. L. K., xix, *xxi*
Hu, H. C., 55, *58*
Huang, D., 71, *81*
Hudes, M., 165, *182*
Hughes, C. C., 140, *160*
Hughes, M., *159, 205*
Huh-Kim, J., 43, *58,* 190, 191, 193, 197, *206*
Hui, M., 63, 71, *80*
Hurh, W. M., 190, *205*
Hurtado, A., 76, *79*
Hutnik, N., 67, *79*
Hwang, K. K., 56, *58*

Idler, E. L., 192, *205*
Imperia, G., 109, *117*
Ito, J., xvii, *xxi*

Ja, D., 100, *118*

Jackson, J. S., 177, *185*
Jackson, K. M., 106, *115*
Jacobson, N., 127, *134*
Jain, A., 101, 111, *116*
Jameson, P. B., 121, *133*
Jaramillo, P. T., 106, *119*
Jasinski, J. L., 110, *116*
Jasso, R., 45, *58*, 153, *158*
Jean-Gilles, M., *135*
Jobe, J., *12*
Joe, G. W., 104, 107, *114*, 234, *237*
Johnson, J., 109, *114*
Johnson, J. G., 219, *222*
Johnson, K. G., *183*
Johnson, M., *239*
Johnson, M. E., 141, *159*
Johnson, T., 10, *12*
Jones, O. W., 223, *237*
Joy, A., 63, *80*
Juang, L., 77, *79*

Kagan, A., 167, *183*
Kagan, S., 106, *116*
Kagawa-Singer, M., 165, *183*
Kahn, R. L., *182*
Kalin, R., 24, 26, 27, 34, *35*, *36*
Kamarck, T., 143, *158*
Kaplan, C. P., 234, *237*
Kaplan, M. S., 151, *159*
Karno, M., 87, 88, *91*, 104, *115*, *116*, 153, *158*, *159*
Katims, D. S., 106, *119*
Kato, H., *183*
Katz, D., 4, *12*
Kaufman, S., 22, *36*
Kauh, T. O., 101, *116*
Kawate, R., 171, *183*
Keefe, S., 64, 68, 69, 73, 76, *80*, 105
Keefe, S. E., 104, *116*
Keefe, S. M., 86, 87, *91*
Kegeles, S. M., 175, *185*
Kelly, J. G., xviii, *xxi*
Kennedy, A., 31, 32, 33, *37*
Kessler, R., 196, 154, *159*, *205*
Kharrazi, M., 165, *182*
Khoo, G., 47, *59*, 65, *81*
Kilmer, R. P., 97, *116*
Kim, B. S. K., 51, *58*
Kim, C., 63, 71, *80*
Kim, J., 74, *80*
Kim, K. C., 190, *205*
Kim, S. J., 39, *58*
Kim, U., 21, 30, 31, *35*, *36*, 75, *79*, 139, 140, 147, *158*
Kim, Y., 103, *116*
King, C. A., 123, *134*
Kingston, R. S., 165, *183*

Kinyon, J., 83, *92*, 224, *238*
Kirk, B., 39, *59*
Kitano, H., 193, *205*, 236, *238*
Klatsky, A. L., 190, *205*
Kleinman, A., 140, *159*, 207, *222*
Kleinman, J. C., 172, 173, *183*, *184*
Klimdis, S., 88, *92*
Klonoff, E. A., 22, *36*, 42, 49, *58*, 86, 88, *92*, 96, 113, *116*, 139, 142, 143, *159*, 175, *183*, 234, *238*
Kluckhohn, C., 84, *91*
Kluckhohn, F. R., 83, *91*
Knapp, J. A., *184*
Knight, G. P., 105, 106, *116*
Knowler, W. C., 171, *183*
Kohatsu, E., 77, *81*, 88, *92*
Kolody, B., 109, *119*, *160*
Kosloski, K., 105, *117*
Koss-Chioino, J. D., 210, *222*
Kranau, E. J., 109, *116*
Krasnoff, L., 143, *159*
Krause, N., 224, *238*
Krieger, N., 177, *183*
Kroll, J., 146, 147, *159*
Krull, J. L., 170, *182*
Kumanyika, S. K., 165, *183*
Kunitz, S. J., 168, *183*
Kunn, P., *57*
Kurasaki, K. S., xix, *xxi*, 206
Kurtines, W., 22, *37*, 41, *59*, 85, *93*, 104, 107, *118*, 122, *135*, 153, *160*

LaDue, R. A., 99, *116*
LaFromboise, T., 10, *12*, 74, 78, *80*, 98, 113, *116*, 207, *222*
Lai, E., 7, *12*
Lalonde, R., 25, *36*, 69, 76, *79*, *80*
Lambert, M. J., 57, *58*
Lambert, W. E., 26, *37*
Landale, N., 197, *205*
Landrine, H., 22, *36*, 42, 49, *58*, 86, 88, *92*, 96, 113, *116*, 139, 142, 143, *159*, 175, *183*, 234, *238*
Landy, C., 190, *205*
Landy, D., 88, *92*
Lane, J. D., 178, *182*
Laniado-Laborin, R., 234, *238*
LaPerriere, A., *135*
Larkey, L., 66, *80*
Laroche, M., 63, 71, 73, *80*
Lashley, K. H., 141, *159*
Laumann, E. O., 192, *205*
Lavelle, J., *159*
Law, C. K., 236, *238*
Lay, C., 102, *116*
Lazarus, R. S., 31, *36*, 143, *159*
Leaper, C., 88, *92*, 109, *116*

Lecroy, C. W., 104, 107, *114*
Lederman, S. A., 172, *184*
Lee, D. J., 152, *159,* 234, *238*
Lee, E., 124, *134*
Lee, L. C., 139, *159*
Lega, L., 22, *36*
Leong, F., 63, 74, *80*
Leung, P., *114*
Levant, R. F., *134*
Levenson, R. W., 50, *58*
Levin, J. S., 193, *205*
Levy, J. E., 168, *183*
Lew, A. S., 88, *92*
Lew, S., 42, 47, *59*
Lex, B. W., 165, *183*
Li, Y. H., 148, 149, *159*
Liddle, H. A., 121, *134, 135*
Liebkind, K., 17, *36,* 74, *81*
Lilienfeld, A. M., 169, *183*
Lillie-Blanton, M., 165, *183*
Lillioja, S., 171, *182*
Lim, Y. M., *116*
Lin, C. Y., 100, 101, *116*
Lin, K. M., *206*
Lindholm, K. J., 190, *205*
Link, B. G., 219, *222*
Linton, R., xxiii, *xxvi*i, 6, *12,* 18, *37,* 84, *92*
Lipman, R. S., 143, *159*
Lisansky, J., 86, *93,* 104, *118*
Litrownik, A. J., *238*
Locke, B. Z., 151, 153, *159, 160*
Lopez, I. R., 105, *114*
Lopez, S. R., 54, *58*
Lovato, C. Y., 224, 234, *238*
Lovell, M., 103, *116*
Lovett, M., 8, *12*
Lubben, J. E., 193, *205*
Lubben, L., 236, *238*
Luborsky, L., 57, *58*
Luna, I., 105, *116*
Lynch, E. W., 57, *58*

MacAdams, E. A., 109, *117*
Mackenzie, T., *159*
Madsen, M. C., 106, *116*
Magnus, K. B., 97, *116*
Mak, W. S., 192, *206*
Maldonado, D., 168, *182*
Maldonado, R., 22, *36,* 42, *58,* 65, 70, *79,* 85, *91*
Malewska-Peyre, H., 28, *36*
Malgady, R. G., 139, *160,* 164, *184,* 207, 208, 212, 220, *221, 222*
Manson, S. M., 99, *115*
Marger, M. N., 97, *116*
Marín, B., xxvi, *xxvi,* 71, *80,* 104, *118,* 234, *238*

Marín, B. V., 83, *92,* 124, 132, *134,* 234, *238*
Marín, G., 41, 42, 47, 50, 52, *58,* 71, *80,* 83, 84, 86, 87, 90, *92, 93,* 104, 105, *116, 118,* 124, 132, *134,* 156, *160,* 175, *185,* 224, 234, *238*
Markides, K. S., 152, *159,* 165, *183,* 224, 234, *237, 238*
Marks, G., 83, *92,* 151, *159*
Marmot, M. G., 167, 168, *183*
Marshall, J. A., 171, *183*
Martin, J., 66, *80*
Martinez, J. L., Jr., 47, *60*
Martinez, R., 41, 46, *58, 158*
Maruyama, M., 56, *57*
Matsui, S., 56, *57*
Matsumoto, D., 84, *92*
Matsushita, Y., 39, 43, *58*
Matute-Bianchi, M., 77, *80*
Mayer, E. J., *183*
Mayer, J., *182*
McGee, D., *184*
McGoldrick, M., 121, *134*
McGonagle, K., *159,* 205
McGraw, S. A., 234, *239*
McLoyd, V. C., 97, *116*
McNeilly, M., 168, *182*
Mead, M., 11, *12*
Medina Mora, M. E., 224, 225, 233, *237*
Meehl, P., 111, *114*
Mehta, V., 75, *79*
Mendes de Leon, C. F., 224, *238*
Mendoza, R., 7, 8, *12,* 41, 42, 47, 48, *58, 59*
Mercado, R., 106, *114*
Mermelstein, R., 143, *158*
Messé, L., 29, *37,* 102, *117*
Mezzich, J. E., 140, *159*
Mikawa, J. K., 175, *183*
Milligan, C., 99, *115*
Minde, T., 31, *35,* 140, *158*
Mindel, C. H., 86, 88, *92,* 104, *117*
Miramontes, J. M., 165, *184*
Mishra, R. C., 28, *36*
Mitchell, B. D., *184*
Mitchell, J., 192, *205*
Mitrani, V., 121, *135*
Mock, L. O., xviii, *xxi*
Moeschberger, M., *57*
Moghaddam, F., 25, *36,* 76, *80*
Mohatt, G., 98, *116*
Moise, C., 25, 30, *35, 36*
Mok, D., 31, *35,* 140, *158*
Mollica, R. F., 145, *159*
Mombour, W., 146, *158*
Montenegro, R., 109, *117*
Monterrosa, A., 169, *182*
Montes, H., 234, *238*
Montgomery, G. T., 45, *59*

AUTHOR INDEX

Montiel, M., 109, *117*
Montreuil, A., 26, *36*
Mont-Reynaud, R., 89, *91*
Moore, J. W., 86, 88, *91, 92*, 109, *115*
Morales, A., 223, *238*
Moreno, C., 234, *237, 238*
Morones, R. A., 175, *183*
Morten, G., 73, *78*
Moscicki, E. K., 151, *159*
Mosley, G., 109, *118*
Moynihan, D. P., 104, *115*
Mueller, D. P., 192, *205*
Muir-Malcolm, J. A., 121, *135*
Munroe, R. H., 28, *36*
Munroe, R. L., 28, *36*
Myers, H. F., 165, 168, 169, *182, 183*

Nader, P., *119*
Nanjundappa, G., 168, 172, *184*
Napoles-Springer, A., 165, *184*
Nash, S. G., 223, *237*
National Center for Health Statistics, 163, 166, 167, 168, 172, *184*
Nava, M., 71, *81*
Ndubuisi, S. C., 192, *205*
Neel, J. V., 171, *184*
Neff, J. A., 224, 233, *238*
Neff, R. K., 224, *238*
Negy, C., 87, *92*, 109, *117*
Neider, J., 145, *160, 161*, 190, *206*
Nelson, B., 22, *37*
Nelson, C., *159, 205*
Newcomb, M. D., 234, *238*
Ng, A. T., 140, *160*
Nguyen, C., 103, *116*
Nguyen, H., 77, *79*, 102, *117*
Nguyen, H. H., 29, *37*
Nguyen, L., 148, *160*
Nguyen, N. A., 100, *117*
Nguyen, T., 102, *116*
Nicholson, B., 145, 146, *160*
Nishimoto, Y., 171, *183*
Nobles, W. W., 144, *160*
Nomura, C., 129, *134*
Norman, R. D., 41, 46, *58*
Norris, A. E., 50, *59*
Novy, D., 69, *78*
Nunez-Liriano, A., *238*
Nyberg, B., 70, *79*

Ocampo, K. A., 105, *116*
Oetting, E., 63, *80*, 99, *117, 118*
O'Guinn, T. C., 109, *117*
Okamura, J., 190, *205*
Olmedo, E., xxiv, *xxvi*, 7, *12*, 17, *35*, 39, *58*
Olmedo, S., 223, *238*
Olson, D., 175, *183*

Olvera-Ezzell, N., 107, *114*
Onwughalu, M., 77, *81*
Orleans, M., *183*
Oropesa, R. S., 197, *205*
O'Rourke, D., *12*
Orozco, S., 45, *59*
Ortiz, V., 65, *81*
Otero-Sabogal, R., 47, *58*, 83, 87, *92*, 104, *118*, 124, *134*, 156, *160*, 234, *238*
Overall, J. E., 141, 146, *160*

Padilla, A. M., xxiv, *xxvi*, 17, 22, 27, 28, *37*, 39, *59*, 64, 68, 69, 73, *80*, 86, *92*, 104, 105, *116*, 190, *205*, 223, 225, 234, *237, 238, 239*
Padilla, E. R., 223, *238*
Pagel, M., 127, *134*
Palinkas, L. A., 164, 165, 178, *184*, 234, *239*
Papouchis, N., 88, *92*
Pappi, F. U., 192, *205*
Park, M., 172, *184*
Park, S., 56, *59*
Parker, J., 32, *36*
Parron, D. L., 140, *159*
Parsons, P. E., 165, *183*
Patel, N., 101, *117*
Patterson, G. R., 106, *117*, 121, *134*
Patterson, J. K., *184*
Patterson, T., *119*
Paulhus, D., 22, 29, *37*
Pederson, J., 192, *205*
Pedhazur, E. J., 218, *222*
Peng, T., 76, *79*
Peragallo, N., 175, *184*
Perea, P., 224, *238*
Peréz, R., 234, *239*
Pérez-Stable, E. J., 47, *58*, 83, 87, *92*, 104, *118*, 124, *134*, 156, *160*, 165, *184*
Perez-Vidal, A., *118*, 122, *135*, 234, *238*
Perreault, S., 25, *35*
Peterson, C., 148, *160*
Pettengill, S., 103, *117*
Pettigrew, T., 77, *80*
Pettitt, D. J., 171, *183*
Phillips, L. R., *116*
Phillips, M. T., 177, *183*
Phinney, J., 31, *37*, 63, 64, 65, 66, 67, 68, 70, 71, 73, 74, 75, 76, 77, *80, 81*, 195, *205*, 207, *222*
Photiades, J. R., 223, *237*
Pickwell, S., 164, 165, 178, *184, 239*
Pierce, J., *239*
Pierce, R., 22, *36*
Piontkowski, U., 27, 30, *37*
Plake, B., 7, *12*
Planos, R., 107, *117*

Polednak, A. P., 170, *184,* 223, *239*
Poortinga, Y., 17, *35, 37,* 64, *79*
Popkin, B. M., 164, *184*
Portes, A., 72, *81*
Posner, S., 83, *92,* 224, *238*
Power, S., 21, *35,* 75, *79*
Power, T., 101, *117*
Power, T. G., 106, 107, *114, 119*
Prager, K., 172, *183*
Preston, S., 165, *181*
Prihoda, T. J., 224, *238*
Procidano, M. E., 208, *221*
Pugh, J. A., 169, *182*

Quintana, S. M., 105, *117*

Rackensperger, W., 146, *158*
Radecki, S., *206*
Radloff, L. S., 148, 151, *160*
Rae, D. S., 151, *159*
Rainieri, N., 88, *92*
Ramirez, A. G., 46, 47, *59,* 234, *239*
Ramirez, M., 106, *117*
Ramirez, M., III, 41, 42, 45, 46, *59*
Ramirez, O., 105, *117*
Ramirez, R., 223, 234, *238, 239*
Ramirez-Valles, J., 99, *119*
Ramos-Grenier, J., 121, *134*
Ramos-McKay, J. M., 109, *117*
Raspberry, K., 233, *237*
Ratcliff, K. S., 151, *160*
Rauh, V. A., 172, *184*
Ray, L. A., 152, 157, *159,* 223, 224, 234, *237, 238*
Raymond-Smith, L., 105, *114*
Redfield, R., xxiii, *xxvii,* 6, *12,* 18, *37,* 84, *92*
Reed, D., 167, *184*
Reed, E., 76, *79*
Regier, D. A., 151, 153, 154, *159, 160*
Reid, J. B., 121, *134*
Revilla, L., 102, *115,* 192, *205*
Rezentes, W. C., III, 48, 49, *59*
Rhee, S., 103, *117,* 236, *238*
Richardson, J. L., *92,* 234, *238*
Richman, J., 7, *12*
Rickard-Figueroa, K., 42, 47, *59*
Rickels, K., 143, *159,* 213, *221*
Riger, S., 192, *205*
Riley, C., *114*
Rio, A., *118, 135*
Rios, C., *160*
Rios, R., *160*
Ritzler, B., 88, *92*
Rivera-Arzola, M., 121, *134*
Rivera-Mosquera, E. T., 105, *114*
Robbins, R. R., 139, *158*

Roberts, R., 76, 77, *79, 81,* 207, *221*
Robins, L. N., 151, 153, 154, *160*
Robles, R. R., *160*
Rocha, O., *206*
Rock, A. F., 213, *221*
Rodriguez, J. M., 105, *117*
Rodriguez, M., 234, *239*
Rodriguez, O., 124, *134*
Rodriguez, R., 106, *114*
Rogler, L., 65, 67, *81,* 104, *117,* 124, *134,* 139, 149, 150, *160,* 164, *184,* 207, 208, 212, 220, 221, *221,* 222
Rohner, R., 103, *117*
Rohrbaugh, M., 122, 127, *134, 135*
Roizen, R., 226, *237*
Romero, A., 76, 77, *81*
Romero, I., 71, *81*
Room, R., 226, *237*
Roopnarine, J. L., 109, *117*
Roosa, M. W., 106, *115*
Roosens, E., 76, *81*
Root, M., 10, *12,* 63, *81*
Rosario, L., 109, *117*
Rosbrook, B. P., *239*
Rosenfield, S., 189, *206*
Rosenthal, D., 69, 76, *81,* 88, 89, *91, 92,* 102, 103, *117*
Rothstein, K., 105, *114*
Rousseau, C., 102, *117*
Rowley, D., 172, 177, *183, 184*
Rubio-Stipec, M., 121, *134,* 152, *158, 160*
Rueschenberg, E., 87, *92,* 105, 107, 108, *118*
Rumbaut, R., 66, 76, *81,* 197, *206,* 207, *222*
Russell, C. K., *116*
Russo, N., 109, *114*
Ruth-Najarian, S., 165, *181*
Ryder, A., 22, 29, *37*

Sabatier, C., 27, 29, 30, *35*
Sabogal, F., 47, *58,* 83, 87, 90, *92,* 104, 105, 108, *118,* 124, *134,* 156, *160,* 234, *238*
Sack, W. H., 146, *158*
Salgado de Snyder, N., 225, *237*
Sallis, J., *119,* 234, *237, 238*
Sam, D., xxiv, *xxvi,* 17, 21, 28, 31, *35,* 63, 66, 74, *79*
Samaniego, R. Y., 104, 106, 108, *118*
Sanchez, J., 22, *37*
Santana, F., *159*
Santisteban, D., *118,* 121, 122, *134, 135*
Santos, Y., 46, *59*
Sasao, T., 149, *160,* 190, 191, *206*
Schafer, J., 233, *237*
Schauffler, R., 72, *81*
Schmelkin, L. P., 218, *222*
Schmidt, S. E., 121, *135*

Schmitz, P., 31, 32, *37*
Schoendorf, K. C., 172, *184*
Schonpflug, U., 73, *81*
Schwartz, M. A., 140, 144, *161*
Scopetta, M. A., 41, *59,* 85, *93,* 153, *160*
Scribner, R., 173, *184*
Scrimshaw, S. C. M., 165, *185*
Searle, W., 21, 32, *37*
Segal, U., 101, *118*
Segall, M., 17, *35, 37,* 64, *79*
Seidman, E., 207, *221*
Semeiks, P. A., 170, *185*
Sénécal, S., 25, *35*
Senour, M., 109, *118*
Shapiro, J., 190, *206*
Shaver, P., 109, *118*
Shen, H., *206*
Shiono, P. H., 172, *184*
Shoham, V., 122, 127, *134, 135*
Shon, S., 100, *118*
Shrout, P. E., 152, *158, 160*
Siegelaub, A. V., 190, *205*
Simmons, R. C., 140, *160*
Simpson, D. D., 104, 107, *114,* 234, *237*
Sinha, D., 28, *36*
Smetana, J., 101, 103, *119*
Smith, J. P., 165, *183*
Smith, K. W., 234, *239*
Snow, R. E., 122, *134*
Snowden, L. R., 51, *59,* 139, 142, 143, *160,* 175, *183,* 223, *239*
Snyder, D. K., 109, *117*
Social Science Research Council, xxiii, *xxvii,* 6, *12,* 18, *37*
Sodowsky, G., 7, *12*
Solis, J., *92*
Sommerlad, E., 22, 28, *37*
Sommers, I., 106, 108, *118,* 122, *135*
Soto, E., 109, *118*
Spindler, G., 6, *12*
Spindler, L., 6, *12*
Srinivasan, S., xx, *xxi*
Steele, C. M., xx, *xxi*
Steinberg, A. G., 171, *183*
Stephenson, M., 51, *59*
Stern, M. P., 171, *183, 184*
Stollak, G., 29, *37,* 102, *117*
Stoner, S., 99, *115*
Stouthamer-Loeber, M., 106, *117*
Streltzer, J., 49, *59*
Strodbeck, F. L., 83, *91*
Stroup-Benham, C. A., 224, *238*
Stuewig, J., 104, 107, *114*
Suarez, D., *238*
Suarez, L., 170, *184*
Suarez-Orozco, C., 76, *81*
Suarez-Orozco, M., 6, 7, *12,* 76, *81*
Sudman, S., *12*

Sue, D., 39, *59,* 68, 73, *78, 81,* 190, 192, 197, *206*
Sue, S., xvii, xix, *xxi,* 55, *59,* 68, *81,* 190, 197, *206*
Suinn, R., 42, 47, *59,* 65, 71, *81*
Sung, B., 100, *118*
Supik, J. D., 46, *59*
Suskar, D., 172, *184*
Sustento-Seneriches, J., 140, *160*
Swaim, R., 63, *80,* 99, *118,* 237
Syme, L., *183*
Syme, S. L., *183, 184*
Szapocznik, J., 22, *37,* 41, 42, 44, 45, 50, *59,* 85, *93,* 104, 107, 108, *118,* 121, 122, 129, 131, *135,* 153, *160*

Taguchi, F., 178, *182*
Tajfel, H., 68, 70, 76, *81*
Takeuchi, D. T., 190, 197, *206*
Talavera, G. A., *238*
Tan, S., *114*
Tang, T., 88, *93*
Tappel, S. M., 165, 173, *185*
Tate, J., 75, *80*
Tatum, B., 77, *81*
Taylor, D., 26, *35,* 76, *80*
Taylor, R., 98, *118,* 171, *184,* 193, *205*
Telles, C. A., 153, *158*
Teske, R., 22, *37*
Thompson, R. H., 8, *12*
Thompson, V. L. S., 98, *118*
Thorton, M. C., 98, *118*
Thurman, P. J., 99, *118*
Timbers, D. M., *158, 159*
Ting-Toomey, S., 69, 73, *81*
Tolan, P. H., 97, *115*
Tomiuk, M., 71, *80*
Tompar-Tiu, A., 140, *160*
Tonks, R., 75, *81*
Tor, S., *159*
Torres-Matrullo, C. M., 109, *118*
Tran, H., *114*
Tran, T., 103, *116*
Treviño, F., 157, *159,* 223, 224, *237, 238*
Trevino, M., 109, *115*
Triandis, H. C., 51, *59,* 86, *93,* 104, *118*
Trickett, E. J., 85, 91, *91*
Trimble, J., xxiv, *xxvi,* 7, 8, 9, *12, 13,* 17, *35,* 39, *58,* 77, *81,* 98, *116,* 207, *222*
Truong, T., *159*
Tsai, J., 42, 43, *59*
Tschann, J. M., 175, *185*
Turner, J., 68, 70, 76, *81*

Uba, L., 67, *81,* 100, *118,* 139, *160*
Udry, J. R., 164, *184*
Uhlenhuth, E. H., 143, *159*

AUTHOR INDEX

Umemoto, D., 56, *59*
U.S. Bureau of the Census, 97, *118,* 163, *184,* 190, 191, *206*
U.S. Department of Health and Human Services, 166, *184*
Usinger, P., 97, *114*

Vaglum, P., 146, 147, *159*
Valencia-Weber, G., 109, *116*
Valentine, S., 109, *118*
Valin, D., 88, *92,* 109, *116*
Valle, J. R., 109, *119*
Vang, T., 145, *159, 161,* 190, *206*
VanOss Marín, B., 47, *58,* 87, *92,* 124, *134,* 156, *160,* 175, *184, 185*
Vargas, L. A., 210, *222*
Vargas, R., *237*
Vasquez, A., xxv, *xxvii*
Vedder, P., 74, *81*
Vega, W., 5, *12,* 104, 107, 108, 109, *115, 118–119,* 122, *135,* 154, 155, 156, 157, *160,* 210, *222,* 223, 234, *239*
Ventura, S. J., 165, 173, *185*
Vera, E. M., 105, *117*
Vera, M., 151, 152, *160*
Vigil, P., 42, 47, *59*
Villavicencio, S., 87, *91,* 105, *115*
von Zerssen, D., 146, *158*
Vu, C., *206*
Vu, K. C., *114*

Wagatsuma, Y., 190, *205*
Wall, J. A., 107, 108, *119*
Walter, B., 100, *119*
Ward, C., xxiv, *xxvii,* 17, 21, 31, 32, 33, *37*
Warheit, G. J., 122, *135*
Warnecke, R., *12*
Washienko, K. M., 100, *119*
Waters, M., 67, 78, *81*
Wayman, J. C., *237*
Weeks, J. R., 197, *206*
Weinberger, M. H., 178, *185*
Weisburd, D., 124, *134*
Wendorf, M., 171, *185*
Westermeyer, J., 145, 146, 147, *160, 161,* 190, *206*
Wewers, M. E., *57*

Whitaker, R., 107, *114,* 234, *236*
Whiteley, S., 39, *58,* 139, *159*
Whiteman, M., 107, *114*
Wiener, R. L., 192, *205*
Wilkelstein, W., *183*
Williams, C., 30, *37*
Williams, D. R., 177, *182, 185*
Williams, H. L., 100, *117*
Williams, R. B., Jr., 178, *182*
Williams, R. C., 171, *183*
Williams, R. L., 234, *239*
Williamson, L., 31, *37*
Win, P. E., 107, *114*
Wintrob, R., 7, *12*
Wolfgang, P. E., 170, *185*
Woodruff, S. I., *237*
Work, W. C., 97, *116*
World Health Organization, 154, *161*
Wyman, P. A., 97, *116*

Yamakido, M., 171, *183*
Yanez, I., *237*
Yang, M., *159*
Yang, P. H., 51, *58*
Yano, K., *184*
Yau, J., 101, 103, *119*
Yeh, M., 55, *59*
Yeung, W. H., 140, 144, *161*
Yin, Z., 106, *119*
Ying, Y. W., 103, *119,* 148, *161*
Yoshikawa, H., 207, *221*
Young, K., 55, *59*
Young, M., 21, *35,* 75, *79*
Yu, Y., 177, *185*

Zack, N., 10, *13*
Zak, I., 22, *37*
Zambrana, R. E., 165, 173, *185*
Zane, N., xvii, *xxi,* 43, 55, 56, *58, 59,* 139, 146, *158, 159,* 190, 191, 193, 197, *206*
Zapata, J. T., 106, *119*
Zayas, L. H., 107, *117,* 124, *134*
Zhao, S., *159, 205*
Zheng, X., 140, 144, *161*
Zhou, M., 71, *78*
Zimmerman, M. A., 99, *119*
Zimmerman, R. S., 122, *135,* 234, *239*
Zimmet, P., 171, *184*

Subject Index

Access to care, 223
Acculturation, generally
  change parameters in patterns of, 6–7, 40–41, 42–43
  current conceptualization in psychology research, xxiii–xxiv, 5, 7–9, 18–19
  definition and scope, xxiii, xxv, 5–6, 223
  dimensionality of concepts, 7–8, 18, 22–25, 27, 29
  forced, 24, 25
  relationship to mental health, xvii, xviii, xxv, 39, 139–140, 144–145, 157, 189, 190, 203, 207, 219–221
  research challenges, xvii–xviii, xix–xx, 5, 110
  research topics in, 17
  social change and, 4–5, 9–10
Acculturation expectations, 25
Acculturation Rating Scale for Mexican Americans, 45
Acculturation Rating Scale for Mexican Americans–Revised, 49
Acculturation Scale for Southeast Asians, 48
Acculturation strategies, 18
  assessment, 28–29
  behavioral change process, 30–32
  collectivistic, 25
  components, 21
  cultural-level processes, 21
  family processes, 123
  individualistic, 25
  individual-level processes, 21–22
  levels, 25–26
  locus of views in, 25–27
  national policymaking and, 34
  outcomes, 21, 29–33
  preferences, 21, 22–24
  types of, 24, 123. See also *specific strategy*
Acculturative disorganization, 7
Acculturative stress, 26
  clinical significance, 139–140
  coping responses, 31–32
  family factors in, 123
  formation, 31
Achievement orientation, 88
Adaptation, 21
  as acculturation outcome, 32
  among second-generation (U.S.-born) ethnic minorities, 42–43
  bipolar and orthogonal models, 42–43, 54
  definition, 32
  economic, 33
  goals, 113
  psychological, 32
  sociocultural, 32–33
Adaptive executive systems, 125, 127
Adjustment, 31
Adolescents
  acculturation effects on parental relations, 102–103, 107–108
  delinquency, 113, 122–123
  family factors in development of, 97, 101–102, 122–125, 129
  parental leadership and decision-making behaviors, 100–101, 102, 103, 106–107, 126–127
Affective functioning
  emotional expressivity, 130
  in families, 132
  research needs, 10
African American Acculturation Scale, 49, 51, 142
African Americans, 67
  acculturation research, 96–98, 142, 143–144, 157
  assessment of acculturation, 49, 51, 88
  ethnic identity, 74, 77
  family systems and functioning, 125
  mental health, acculturation and, 142–144, 153, 154
  morbidity and mortality, 166, 167, 169, 170, 171, 172, 174–175, 178
  religiosity, 193
Age during immigration, 191, 195, 197–200
Alcohol use
  acculturation experience of Asian Americans and, 190, 193, 197–204
  acculturation experience of Hispanics and, 223–233, 235–236
  age during immigration and, 197, 202
  assessment, 196
  attitudes toward, 225, 236
  ethnic identity and, 191–192, 202, 203–204
  psychological distress and, 189
  religiosity and, 192, 193, 202, 203–204
  sociodemographic correlates, 228–229, 233, 236
Allopatricity, 96–97

SUBJECT INDEX

American Indians
  acculturation research, 98–100, 141
  ethnic identity, 77
  mental health, acculturation and, 140–142
  morbidity and mortality, 166, 167, 168, 169, 170, 173, 175
Anger, 211–212, 215, 217–219, 220
Anthropological research, xxiii
  acculturation concepts in, 5–6
  concept of social change, 4, 5
  dimensionality of acculturation concepts, 22
Aptitude by Treatment Interaction, 122
Asian Americans
  alcohol use among, acculturation and, 190
  assessment of acculturation, 47, 48, 51, 100
  ethnic identity, 75
  family structure and functioning, 100–103, 127, 131
  implications of cultural concept of face, 55–58
  mental health, acculturation and, 144–149, 190
  morbidity and mortality, 166, 167–169, 175
  population trends, 190–191
  regional differences in immigration experience, 204
  See also specific ethnic group
Asian Values Scale, 51
Assimilation, 22, 98
  acculturation and, xxv, 6, 123
  as acculturation strategy, 24, 26
  behavioral change for, 31
  definition, 123
  mental health and, 147–148
Attitudes, 21
  acculturation effects on cultural values, 85–86
  in acculturation level, 39–40, 52
  in acculturation strategies, 24, 28–29
  measurement of, 26–27, 39–40, 52
  of second-generation ethnic minorities, 42–43
  toward alcohol consumption, 225, 236
Avoidance, as acculturation coping mechanism, 32

Behavioral Acculturation Scale, 44
Bicultural Involvement Questionnaire, 44–45
Biculturalism, 63–64
  American Indian acculturation experiences, 98
  assessment, xix
  compound labeling in self-identification, 66–67, 69
  family functioning and, 102, 110
  forms of bicultural identity, 74
  mental health and, 147–148
  research needs, 10
  transnational identity, 113
Biculturalism/Multiculturalism Experience Inventory, 45–46
Bidimensional Acculturation Scale, 50
Brief Acculturation Scale, 50

Cancer, 168–170
Census, 67–68
Children's Acculturation Scale, 46
Children's Hispanic Background Scale for Mexican Americans, 46–47
Chinese immigrants
  acculturation attitudes, 42–43
  alcohol use among, acculturation and, 190
  cultural values, 89
  ethnic identity, 69
  mental health, acculturation and, 144, 148, 190
  morbidity and mortality, 170
Cigarette smoking, 234
Collectivism, 106, 132
  in acculturation strategies, 25
  in Asian American family values, 100, 101
  as cultural value, 89
Community context, 76
Competitive behavior, 106
Conflict avoidance/resolution, 129–130
Content validity of acculturation measures, 40, 43–54, 111
Coping mechanisms, 31–32
  among African Americans, 142–143
  religiosity, 193
Coronary heart disease, 167–168
Cubans/Cuban Americans
  acculturation effects on family functioning, 104, 105, 108
  assessment, 44, 85
  mental health, 151
  morbidity and mortality, 170
Cultural Life Styles Inventory, 47–48
Culturally-sensitive practice, 132–133
Cultural vitality, 30
Culture conflict, 31
  in parent–child acculturation experience, 123–124
Culture learning, 31
Culture shedding, 31

SUBJECT INDEX 253

Daily living habits. *See* Lifestyle preferences
Defensive Latino activism, 234–235
Delinquency
   family factors, 122–123
   research needs, 113
Depression, 145, 146, 148
   acculturation and, 190, 215–217, 219
   alcohol use and, 189
   among Hispanic immigrants, 151, 152, 153
   culture-specific expressions of, 219, 220
   gender differences, 210, 219
   religiosity and, 192
   sociodemographic risk factors, 217, 218, 219
Development, family systems, 130–132
Development, individual
   age during immigration as factor in acculturation, 191, 202
   ethnic identity change in, 63, 73–76
   family factors, 122–125, 129
   family system development and, 130–132
   parent–child relations, 97
Diabetes, 170–172
Dimensionality of acculturation constructs, 7–8, 18, 22–25, 27, 29, 52–54
Discrimination, 98, 111–112
   ethnic identity and, 76–77
   mental health and, 154
Disillusionment, 211, 212, 214–215, 219, 220
Diversity, 25, 26, 34
Dominant culture
   acceptance of minorities in, as mental health factor, 149
   acculturation effects in, 7, 18
   attitude assessment, 26–27
   determinants of acculturation outcomes in, 30
   forced acculturation, 24, 25
   influences of immigrants on, 112–113
Dominican population, 107, 108

Ecological–cultural–behavioral model of acculturation, 7
Economic adaptation, 33
   acculturation experiences of African American families, 97–98
   gender role and, 126
   physical health status and, 177–178
Educational attainment, 197, 215, 218, 228
Emotional expressivity, 130
Environmental factors in acculturation, xviii–xix, 207
   family processes, 111–112

research needs, xxi, 10
retention of ethic identity, 76–77
situational acculturation, 7–8, 10
Ethnic identity, 8–9
   acculturation and, 64–65, 78, 192, 203
   age during immigration and, 197–200
   alcohol use and, 203–204
   assessment, 195
   challenges in assessing, 65
   components of, 65
   compound labeling, 66
   contextual factors in retention of, 76–77
   definition, 63
   development, 63, 73–76
   discrimination and, 76–77
   educational attainment and, 197
   generational differences, 64–65, 78
   mental health and, 191–192, 200
   models of change in acculturation, 63–64
   self-identification/self-label, 66–68
   social networks and, 191–192
   strength and valence, 68–73
   transnational, 113
Ethnic loyalty, 69
Ethnocide, 25
Exclusion, 25
Expectations, acculturation, 25

Face, as cultural value, 55–58
Family systems and functioning, xxiv–xxv
   acculturation effects on cultural values regarding, 85, 86–88, 90
   acculturation research topics, 95–96, 121
   acculturative stress mediation, 123
   adaptation goals, 113
   adaptive executive systems, 125, 127
   African American acculturation experiences, 96–98
   American Indian acculturation experiences, 98–100
   Aptitude by Treatment Interaction research, 122
   Asian American acculturation experiences, 100–103
   assessment and measurement of acculturation experiences, 110–111
   biculturalism in, 102, 110
   bonding, 129
   boundary relations, 132
   in child development, 122–125
   children of mixed cultural background, 10
   conflict resolution, 129–130
   contextual factors in acculturation experience, 111–112
   development of, 130–132

Family systems and functioning (*continued*)
differing acculturation strategies in, 123
extended families, 127–128
familialism construct, 104–105, 124–125, 156–157
Latino acculturation experiences, 103–110
leadership and decision-making in, 125–129
mental health and, 148, 156–157
parent–child relations, 97, 100–103, 106–108, 123–124, 126–127, 129, 130–131
patterns of acculturation, 110
peer relations and, 107–108, 124
research inadequacies, 110–113
therapeutic intervention, 122, 123–124, 125, 127, 132–133
traumatic life events, 131–132
Fatalism, 85–86
Filipinos/Filipino Americans
alcohol use among, acculturation and, 190, 193, 197–204
ethnic identity assessment, 195
morbidity and mortality, 170
religiosity, 193, 195–196, 197–204
U.S. population, 190–191
Focus group research, 209–212
Folk beliefs, 85, 157
Forced acculturation, 24, 99
Fractionization, 96–97

Gender roles
acculturation effects on cultural values regarding, 88
clinical implications, 127
HIV risk, 175
Latino acculturation experience, 109
parental decision-making behaviors, 125–126
substance use among Hispanics and, 233, 235
General Ethnicity Questionnaire, 50
Generational status
cohort differences, 112
ethnic identity change, 64, 70, 78
as marker of acculturation, 64–65, 69–70
Goal setting, 113
Greek immigrants, 89
Group processes
change in ethnic identity, 64
cultural vitality, 30
determinants of acculturation outcomes, 30
ethic identity, 68
research needs, 33

Help-seeking behavior, 39, 104, 157, 223

implications of face as cultural value, 55, 56–58
Hispanic Health and Nutrition Examination Survey, 151–153
Hispanics
alcohol use patterns, 223–233, 235–236
assessment of acculturation, 44–45, 46, 47, 50, 85–88
cigarette smoking patterns, 234
defensive Latino activism, 234–235
emotional expressivity, 130
familialism, 104–105, 124–125
family structure and functioning, 126, 131, 132
morbidity and mortality, 166, 167, 169, 170, 172–173, 174–175
regional variation in immigration experience, 235–236
substance use patterns, 234–235
See also Latino population; *specific ethnic group*
HIV/AIDS, 167, 174–176
Hmong refugees, 145–146
Hypertension, 167, 168, 178

Identity achievement, 73
Immigration
changes in host country as result of, 112–113
pre-migration acculturation, 112
Individual differences
in help-seeking behavior, 39
person–environment fit as factor in acculturation, xviii–xix
in selecting acculturation strategies, 18
subgroups of ethnic minorities, 43
Individualism
as acculturation strategies, 25
in Asian American family values, 100, 101
as cultural value, 89
Individual-level change
acculturation effects, xxiv
acculturation orientation and, 26
acculturation strategies and, 21–22
adaptation process, 32–33
cultural/group level acculturation and, 4, 19–21
determinants of acculturation outcomes, 30
dimensionality of acculturation concepts, 22–25
ethnic identity, 64
research needs, 9–10, 33–34
research variables, 21
response to acculturation problems, 31

Institutional functioning
　cultural values and, 128–129
　family leadership for, 128
　locus of acculturation orientation, 25–26
Integration, 22
　as acculturation strategy, 24
　behavioral change for, 31
　definition, 123
　dominant–nondominant group relations for, 24
　individual–group relations for, 24–25
Interpersonal/social relations
　in acculturation process, xix
　alcohol use patterns, 224
　concept of face, 55
　ethnic identity change, 71–72
　measures of acculturation in, 41
　peer *vs.* family influence, 107–108, 124
　social networks and ethnic identity, 191–192

Japanese/Japanese Americans, 67, 167–168

Koreans/Korean Americans, 149, 193
　morbidity and mortality, 169, 170

Language
　acculturative stress and, 145
　ethnic identity change, 71–73, 202–203
　as measure of acculturation, 41, 52, 58, 191, 195
　parent–child relations in immigrant families, 103, 128, 129
　religiosity and, 200
Latino population
　acculturation effects on family functioning, 90, 103–110
　mental health, acculturation and, 149–157
　See also Hispanics
Leadership, in families, 125–129
Life expectancy, 166
Lifestyle preferences
　as measure of acculturation, 41–42
　physical health and acculturation, 170, 171–172, 180–181
Longitudinal study designs, 111

Machismo, 85, 109–110
Marginalization, 22, 97
　as acculturation strategy, 24
　behavioral change for, 31
　definition, 123
　mental health and, 147–148
Marital relations, 103, 109–110
　ethnic identity and, 197
　extended family systems, 127–128
　family leadership and decision-making, 125–127
　mental health and, 200
Measurement
　acculturation and mental health, 208–215
　acculturation and physical health, 164–165, 177
　acculturation attitudes, 26–27
　African American acculturation experience, 142, 143–144
　assessment of acculturation strategies, 28–29
　assessment of face as cultural value, 55–58
　assumptions about acculturation change parameters, 40–41, 42–43, 54, 141
　category fallacy, 207
　challenges in acculturation research, xvii–xviii, xix–xx, 5, 17–18, 40, 54, 180
　change in ethnic identity, 64–65, 78
　construct validation, 111
　content validity of current methods, 40, 43–54
　cultural identification, 27–28
　culture-specific expressions of distress, 204–205, 219–220
　deficit model of acculturation, 140–141
　dimensionality of acculturation constructs, 7–8, 22, 52–54, 110
　equivalence between studies, 9, 149–150
　ethnic identity development, 75, 195
　ethnic self-identification, 66–68
　ethnographic interviews, 111
　family acculturation strategies, 110–111
　longitudinal studies, 111
　mental health outcomes, 204
　proxy variables, xvii–xviii, xx–xxi, 39–40, 52, 180, 191, 195
　psychosocial domains, 41–42, 54
　social change studies, 9, 10–11
Melting pot, 25
Mental health
　acceptance into host society and, 149
　acculturation and, xvii, xviii, xxv, 39, 139–140, 144–145, 157, 189, 190, 203, 207, 219–221
　African American acculturation experience and, 142–144
　age during immigration and, 197
　alcohol use and, 189
　American Indian acculturation experience and, 140–142
　Asian American acculturation experience and, 144–149

Mental health (*continued*)
  culture-specific disorders, 140
  culture-specific expressions of distress, 204–205, 219
  ethnic identity and, 191–192
  family factors in, 122–123, 156–157
  Latino acculturation experience and, 149–156
  physical health and, 180–181
  premigration trauma and, 146
  protective factors, 156–157
  religiosity and, 192–193, 203–204
  research needs, 139, 149, 157
  selective migration hypothesis, 154, 155–156
  service utilization, 157
  social stress hypothesis, 154
  sociodemographic factors, 147, 209–210
  See also Help-seeking behavior
Mexican American Prevalence and Services Survey, 154–156
Mexicans/Mexican Americans
  acculturation effects on family functioning, 104–106, 107, 108
  assessment of acculturation, 45, 46–47, 49, 86–87
  gender roles, 88
  marital relations in acculturation, 109–110
  mental health, 151, 152, 153–157
  morbidity and mortality, 168, 170, 171, 173–174
  second-generation immigrants, 67, 69, 70, 71
  substance use patterns, 224, 235–236
Minority status, significance of, xix–xx
Multiculturalism, 25, 34

Na Mea Hawai'i Scale, 48–49
National Comorbidity Survey, 154
National identity, 30
  in bicultural identity, 74
Negative effects of acculturation, xix, 7
  acculturative stress, 26, 31
  individual-level research, 21
  personality differences, 9–10
Nicaraguan population, 108
Nostalgia, 211, 212, 214–215, 219, 220

Obstacles to acculturation, 6

Physical appearance, differences in
  acculturation preferences and, 30
  ethnic identity change and, 76–77
Physical health
  access to medical services, 223
  acculturation and, xxv, 164–165, 169–170, 171–172, 173–174, 175–176, 181

biological vulnerability, 178–180
birth outcomes, 165, 172–174
cancer, 168–170
causes of death, 166–167
coronary heart disease, 167–168
diabetes, 170–172
Hispanic Health and Nutrition Examination Survey, 151–153
HIV/AIDS, 174–176
psychosocial mediators, 180–181
research base, 164–165, 166, 181
research needs, 176–177
risk factors, 165, 177–181
selective migration hypothesis, 178
sociodemographic factors, 177–178
trends, 166
Posttraumatic stress disorder, 145, 146, 147
Pre-migration acculturation, 112
Pre-migration trauma, 146
Pressure cooker, 25
Psychological acculturation, 7, 19
Puerto Ricans, 67
  acculturation and mental health, 208, 209–210, 215–221
  culture-specific expressions of depression, 219–220
  family functioning, 104, 105, 107–108, 124
  gender role acculturation, 109
  mental health, 151–152
  morbidity and mortality, 170, 173, 175

Race/ethnicity
  definitions, 8–9
  mixed race children, 10
Reframing, 123–124
Regional variation in immigration experience, xviii–xix, 204, 235–236
Religiosity
  acculturation and, 203
  age during immigration and, 197, 198
  alcohol use and, 203–204
  assessment, 195–196
  demographic characteristics of immigrants, 200
  Filipino acculturation experience and, 193, 195–196, 197–204
  language proficiency and, 200
  mental health and, 192–193, 203–204
Research needs, xx–xxi
  acculturation and mental health, 149, 157, 219–221
  acculturation effects on cultural values, 83, 90–91
  African American acculturation experience, 142, 143–144

family acculturation experience, 110–113
group processes, 33
individual outcomes in acculturation, 33–34
mental health outcome measures, 204
physical health status and acculturation, 165, 176–177, 181
psychosocial domains for assessment, 58
regional variation in immigration experience, 204
social change processes, 9–11
substance use, 113
Rosebud Personal Opinion Survey, 141

Salvadorans, 105
School experience, xviii
Second-generation ethnic minorities, 42–43
ethnic identity, 64, 68–69, 77, 78
ethnic self-identification, 66–67
health behaviors, 180–181
parent–child relations in Asian American families, 100–103
Selective migration hypothesis, 154, 155–156, 178
Self-concept
assessment of cultural orientation, 27–28, 42
changes in acculturation process, 8
in choice of acculturation strategy, 30
face as cultural value, 55
minority–majority relations and, xx
national identity, 30
racial self-hatred, xx
See also Ethnic identity
Separation, 22
behavioral change for, 31
definition, 123
mental health and, 147–148
Sexual behavior, HIV transmission and, 174–176
Short Acculturation Scale for Hispanics, 47
Situational acculturation, 7–8, 10
Social functioning. *See* Interpersonal/social relations
Social identity theory, 68
Sociocultural change
acculturation and, 4–5, 9–10
adaptation process, 32–33
dimensionality of acculturation concepts, 22
individual-level change and, 19–21
integration strategy, 24
pressures for and resistance to, 4
research needs, 9–11

theoretical conceptualization of, 3–4
Spousal abuse, 109–110
Stephenson Multigroup Acculturation Scale, 51–52
Stereotyping, xix–xx, 9
Stroke, 167
Substance use, xxv, 85
acculturation and, 223, 234–235, 236
among American Indian youth, 99–100
among Hispanic immigrants, 152
cigarette smoking, 234
research needs, 113
sexual behavior and, 175–176
See also Alcohol use
Suicidal behavior, 192
Suinn–Lew Asian Self-Identity Acculturation Scale, 47

Therapeutic relationship, 55, 56–58
Third-generation ethnic minorities, 67, 78
Trauma experience
family functioning and, 131–132
premigration, 146

Value Acculturation Scale, 44
Values, cultural
acculturation effects, 83, 85–91
acculturation patterns in American Indian families, 98–99
in acculturation process, xxiii
achievement orientation, 88
assessment of, as measure of acculturation, 40, 52, 54
attitudes toward institutions, 128
collectivism and individualism, 89, 132
definition, 84
as expressed in problem-solving strategies, 85
extended family systems and, 127–128
familialism, 86–88, 90
family relations and, 130–131
gender role beliefs, 88
implications for service delivery, 91
implications of concept of face, 55–58
personal values and, 84
principle of return, 96–97
research needs, 90–91
Values, personal, 84
Vietnamese/Vietnamese Americans
ethnic identity, 71
gender roles, 88
mental health, acculturation and, 148
morbidity and mortality, 169
premigration trauma among, 146

About the Editors

Kevin M. Chun, PhD, is Associate Professor of Psychology and Asian American Studies at the University of San Francisco, Senior Investigator at the University of California–San Francisco, and Alumni Scholar at the National Research Center on Asian American Mental Health, University of California–Davis. He completed his BS in psychology at Santa Clara University, his PhD in clinical psychology at UCLA, and a psychology internship at the Palo Alto Health Care System of the Department of Veterans Affairs. His research focuses on processes of adaptation and their relation to health and psychosocial adjustment for Asian American immigrants and refugees. Publications include *Readings in Ethnic Psychology: African Americans, American Indians, Asian Americans, and Hispanics/Latinos*, which he coedited with Pamela Balls Organista and Gerardo Marín. He is also a contributing author to a number of scholarly works, including *Handbook of Asian American Psychology* and *Ethnocultural Approaches to Understanding Posttraumatic Stress Disorder: Issues, Research, and Clinical Applications*.

Pamela Balls Organista, PhD, is Associate Professor of Psychology at the University of San Francisco. She completed her bachelor's degree in psychology and Black studies at Washington University, her PhD in clinical psychology at Arizona State University, and a clinical psychology postdoctorate in the Department of Psychiatry at the University of California–San Francisco. Her research interests include prevention interventions and ethnic minority health issues. Publications include *Readings in Ethnic Psychology: African Americans, American Indians, Asian Americans, and Hispanics/Latinos,* which she coedited with Kevin M. Chun and Gerardo Marín, and several articles on migrant laborers and AIDS and on stress and coping in primary care patients. She was the founding Faculty Coordinator of the Ethnic Studies Certificate Program at the University of San Francisco and in 1998 was appointed the Director of Academic Advising in the College of Arts and Sciences at the University of San Francisco.

Gerardo Marín, PhD, is Professor of Psychology and Associate Dean in the College of Arts and Sciences at the University of San Francisco and an APA Fellow. He received his PhD in social psychology from De Paul University. He has written more than 135 publications on topics that are relevant to Hispanics, including cultural norms and attitudes, risk behaviors, culturally appropriate methodology, and acculturation. He is the author of two widely used acculturation scales for Hispanics and was the editor of the recent *Surgeon General's Report on Smoking* regarding the four ethnic minority groups. In 1991, he coauthored the book *Research*

With Hispanic Populations with Barbara VanOss Marín and is also the author of the forthcoming book *Culturally Appropriate Research*. He has been a reviewer for various publications, including *American Psychologist, Journal of Personality and Social Psychology, Hispanic Journal of Behavioral Sciences, American Journal of Community Psychology, Journal of Cross-Cultural Psychology*, and *Journal of Community Psychology*.